The Structure and
Dynamics of The Human Mind

The Structure and
Dynamics of THE HUMAN MIND

Edoardo Weiss, M.D.

Grune & Stratton   1960
New York   London

Contents

ACKNOWLEDGMENTS viii
INTRODUCTION ix

Section One: Preliminary Survey of the Mental Structure

I First Approach to the Ego Phenomenon 2
II The Formulation of the Ego and Its Functions . 5
III The Integrative Function of the Ego 8
IV Allo- and Autoplasticity 11
V The Dynamic Aspect of the Ego 15
VI Interpersonal Relationships 19
VII Interpersonal Communications. The Phenomenon
of Identification 25
VIII Superego Formation 30
IX The Phenomenon of Repression 36
X The Concept of the Id 42
XI Interaction of the Three Mental-Substructures . 50
XII Divergent Ego Concepts of Psychoanalysis . . 59

Section Two: The Ego and the External World

XIII Pleasure-Pain and Reality Principles 72
XIV Reality Testing and Sense of Reality 83
XV The Dynamic Survival of the Ego 95
XVI Thinking and Acting 105
XVII Ego Economy in Thinking and Behavior . . . 114
XVIII Span Disturbances and Spastic Ego Paresis . . 122
XIX Ego States and Ego Stages 134

Section Three: The Id and the Instincts

XX First Approach to the Study of the Id 146
XXI Instincts and Drives 154
XXII The Libido Theory 163

XXIII   Infantile Sexuality 172
XXIV   The Genital Phase 182
XXV   Narcissism and Object Love 195
XXVI   Object Libido and Interpersonal Relationships . 205
XXVII   The Cathexes 215
XXVIII   Instinct Dichotomy 225
XXIX   Diverging Concepts of Drives 236

Section Four: Superego and Related Drive Controlling Factors

XXX   More About the Reality Principle 252
XXXI   Resonance Identification 261
XXXII   The Psychic Presence 271
XXXIII   More About the Superego 282
XXXIV   The Phenomenon of Ego Passage 293
XXXV   Structural Split 305

Section Five: Ego Defenses

XXXVI   The Concept of Ego Defenses 320
XXXVII   Unsuccessful Repression 328
XXXVIII Defense Failure in Phobias 339
XXXIX   Denial 358
XL   Reaction Formations, Undoing and Isolation . 370
XLI   Subject-Object Shift 379

Section Six: The Dream Phenomenon and the Dreaming Ego

XLII   Psychology Approach to the Dream Phenomenon 388
XLIII   The Manifest and the Latent Dream Content . 396
XLIV   The Dream Work and Aspects of Wish Fulfillment 406
XLV   Sleep-Disturbing Dreams 416
XLVI   Clarifying Dream Examples 424
XLVII   Bodily and Mental Pain in Dreams 432
XLVIII   Dreaming Egos and Schizophrenic Egos . . 444
XLIX   Dreams in General Anesthesia 450

NAME INDEX 459

SUBJECT INDEX 463

To the Memory of My Teachers
Sigmund Freud and Paul Federn

Acknowledgments

I wish to express my gratitude to Mr. Ernst Federn, son of Paul Federn, who demonstrated his great interest by reading the manuscript in progress and by giving me very helpful suggestions. I am also indebted to Mrs. Mary R. Gardner, for her careful attention and excellent work in editing the manuscript. My thanks are also due to Mr. Jeremiah A. O'Mara, librarian of the Chicago Institute for Psychoanalysis, for further editorial assistance and for compiling the bibliographic quotations and the index.

The author is grateful to those publishers who have kindly granted permission to use certain passages, as specifically acknowledged elsewhere in the book, from the publications indicated:

Basic Books, Inc., New York, for Federn's *Ego Psychology and the Psychoses.*

W. W. Norton Co., New York, for Freud's *New Introductory Lectures on Psycho-Analysis.*

The Hogarth Press Ltd., London, for Freud's *Beyond the Pleasure Principle,* his *Collected Papers,* and his *The Ego and the Id,* as well as for *The Standard Edition of the Complete Psychological Works of Sigmund Freud.*

For the use of dreams and other clinical material originally published in certain of his own papers the author gratefully acknowledges permissions received from the editors of the following journals:

Bulletin of the Menninger Clinic
International Journal of Psycho-Analysis
Journal of the American Psychoanalytic Association
Psychoanalytic Quarterly
Samiksa: Journal of the Indian Psycho-Analytical Society.

Introduction

SOME writers, having published various papers in their lifetime, reach an age when they experience a narcissistic wish to collect their "productions" into a single volume. I now find myself a member of this group. I am not satisfied, however, merely to collect my papers as they were written originally and published in Italian, German and English. Over the years I have made a continuing study of the work of other psychoanalysts, especially that which appeared following publication of my own papers. As a result of this study, together with my progress in experience and understanding, I have modified some earlier concepts and would now express myself in different ways. Therefore, I take satisfaction in presenting my ideas here in a new and revised form, integrated with all that I have learned about psychoanalysis itself.

It is hoped that this motivation may lead to a treatise of psychoanalysis which will be a guide, helpful to students of this science and to others interested in this discipline.

The present plan is to start with one volume, a general presentation of the structure and dynamics of the human mind. I also hope to publish a second volume which will include a systematic presentation of the psychological approach to mental disturbances, both neuroses and psychoses, and a discussion of psychological techniques which can be used for the treatment of different personalities and different forms of mental illness. The subject of this latter discussion will be not only the classic psychoanalytic technique for the treatment of psychoneuroses, but also many modifications in psychotherapy applicable to mental pathological conditions—both neuroses and psychoses—which do not respond to classical psychoanalysis.

In this volume I have elaborated extensively on Paul Federn's ego psychology with which I became thoroughly familiar through a continuing exchange of ideas with Federn over a period of many years. In compiling and organizing this volume many memories related to my earliest approach to psychoanalysis presented themselves to my mind, outlining, as it were, the history of my progress in psychodynamic understanding of the human mind, especially through my acquaintance and relationship with Freud and Federn. In the following account some details of the relationship between these two men will be revealed.

While in my last year of Gymnasium (secondary school) I became fascinated by Freud's *Interpretation of Dreams* and his analysis of Wilhelm Jensen's novelette *Gradiva*. Since it had been my intention to study medicine at the University of Vienna, where I was to spend six years, I decided to visit Professor Freud to ask him how I could become better acquainted with his psychological theories and also understand myself better. I saw him for the first time in October 1908. He was then fifty-two years old; his face was beardless,[1] and he wore a trimmed moustache. His penetrating and sympathetic eyes and very friendly facial expression made me feel greatly at ease and gave me the feeling of being immediately understood. He caught my thoughts even before I finished my sentences. This first impression of him remains indelible in my mind. I remember in particular his gesture of farewell as I left—his arm upraised in a warm salute before he shook hands with me. And I shall never forget how pleased he was that I was interested in psychoanalysis. I soon learned why he was so grateful to anyone who showed serious interest in his theories. He still felt isolated. At that time all the leading professors in the Vienna medical faculty not only rejected as absurd his great and original findings (without taking pains to become acquainted with them) but on every occasion made the most vicious and derogatory remarks about his teachings. Two years later when I was working as a medical student in a neurological department, the chief of the department, a highly recognized authority, presented the case of a severely hysterical woman. Afterwards he approached me and whispered: "Freud would say that she became hysterical because as a child she saw her grandmother urinating."

Through my own experiences I became aware that Freud's isolation, though no longer as complete as it had been, was still a factor which must have aroused great bitterness in him. Only a slowly increasing group of academically educated people recognized

Freud's analytical genius, his extremely scrupulous investigating attitude, his unshakable courage, his great moral strength, and his indefatigable endurance in dealing with the difficulties arising from the resistances and transference reactions of his patients. Besides, he had already begun to experience disappointments from some of his close adherents. It was at this time that Freud became disillusioned with Alfred Adler who parted from him shortly thereafter. The meetings of Freud with his adherents resembled, in a way, the sessions of a secret society where topics were seriously discussed which encountered the derision of the official clinicians—infantile sexuality, the essential role of sexuality in neurotic afflictions, the unconscious, the interpretation of dreams. Out of a desire to protect the seriousness of his university lectures, which were held at the psychiatric clinic headed by Professor Wagner von Jauregg, Freud justifiably decided to limit attendance to only those students, psychologists, and physicians who obtained his permission individually. In the Freudian group, which soon became organized into the Vienna Psychoanalytic Society, the issue of "loyalty" to Freud's teachings inevitably crept in, although it was not so verbalized. This was due to the experience that resistance against the unconscious could deprive one of already acquired knowledge about unconscious mental activity, and also to the temptation to avoid ostracism by the official representatives of the medical faculty. To follow the scientific revelations of Freud required great courage and a strong interest in the new psychological achievements, far exceeding any opportunistic inclination.

This was the situation in the "psychoanalytic movement" at the time I approached Freud as a young student. Among the few analysts of that time Paul Federn was, in Freud's judgment, the appropriate one for me. And so in February, 1909, when Federn was thirty-seven years old and still practicing internal medicine in addition to psychoanalysis, I started my personal analysis with him. Slender, bald-headed, with a full black beard, gray eyes, and a gentle facial expression, he soon gave me a feeling of closeness which persisted later in friendship with him until his death. On the wall to the right of the analytic couch, as I remember, hung the above-mentioned oil painting of the beardless Freud as I had seen him four months before. But since it drew too much of my attention during analytic sessions, it was soon removed and replaced by another less interesting picture. In the course of my analysis, and much more in my later friendship with him, I became well acquainted with Federn's personality, of which I can describe only a few traits here.

My association with Federn had tremendous effects on my future scientific development, and before going further, I should like to point out that this book will be a presentation of both the ideas of the great Freud and those of his faithful adherent Paul Federn. Indeed, I should add that in the realm of ego psychology, Federn should be looked upon less as a pupil of Freud than as an original thinker, and that their concepts in this field cannot be reconciled.

It was long after I had terminated my analysis with Federn and had myself become a member of the Vienna Psychoanalytic Society before Federn came to his important and revolutionary findings in the field of ego psychology and the psychoses, which, without his immediate realization, were at variance with Freud's concepts of the ego and the psychotic afflictions. Federn's place in the history of psychoanalysis is many sided and may be seen to have four distinct phases.

Federn read Freud's *Interpretation of Dreams* when he was thirty and remained forever fascinated by it. His teacher in internal medicine, Hermann Nothnagel, who was also family physician to the woman who was to become his wife, gave him an introduction to Freud in 1902. Afterwards as a wedding gift Nothnagel promised to refer all his future English patients to Federn. It is a curious parallel that nineteen years later Freud, when struck by cancer, made Federn his personal substitute, which meant that all who called upon Freud were automatically referred to Federn.

Federn became a member of Freud's inner circle as the fourth of the adherents to psychoanalysis; Adler, Stekel and Reitler had preceded him. Although Federn was less conspicuous in the society meetings than his predecessors, the records show that many times Freud referred to Federn as the one who best understood the core of a particularly difficult problem. Federn's first office was that of comptroller. Of the many hundred sessions which are recorded, he missed only one or two. In a note which Freud wrote to him at this time we read: "Unerhörterweise kamen Sie gestern nicht zur Sitzung." (It is outrageous that you missed the meeting yesterday!) After Federn emigrated to the United States in 1938 Freud wrote the following statement (in English) for the purpose of helping him to establish himself there without having to take the medical board examinations: "Ever since feeling hampered by the effects of my operation in 1923 I have established Dr. Paul Federn as my substitute in leading the Vienna Psychoanalytic Group, acknowledging him hereby as the most prominent member, equally distinguished by his scientific work, his experience as a teacher, and his success in therapeutics. I consider it an absurdity that he should have to pass an examination in general medicine before being permitted to teach and practice psychoanalysis in any country." [2] Freud considered Federn much more as an equal than as a pupil, but Federn himself took on the role of apostle; he considered himself the "Apostle Paul" to the master Freud.

I return now to the first phase of Federn's activity as a psychoanalyst. From 1902 to 1914 Federn's support of Freud was unwavering. In his papers on masochism and sadism (1913 and 1914) and in his contributions to dream analysis (1914) Federn was already approaching these problems for the first time with the addition of an ego-psychological point of view. His strong positive father transference to Freud was an important factor in all his attitudes toward psychoanalysis, both in regard to his adherence to Freud's views and his own diverging ideas, which he was very late in recognizing as such.

Federn's father, Salomon Federn (1832-1920), was a very prominent physician in Vienna and his family was one of the leading names in liberal circles there. Politically, Federn was a Social Democrat and was elected to a local government post in the city of Vienna. He was also very active in the Social Democratic physicians' society, served on the board of the Settlement House in Vienna, and often took stands on social issues. Freud, on the other hand, always abstained from such activities. In their personal character as well, the two men were very different. Federn was a dreamer and a romantic, at times subject to great discouragement and at times overoptimistic; Freud was very realistic.

Federn was a man of unshakable loyalty to groups in whose ideas he believed and to their leading exponents. This trait was not only an expression of his honest, open, and reliable character but also an expression of his admiring attachment and devotion to his prominent father, which became transferred on to other father figures. It is hardly surprising that he was a convinced Austrian patriot. Jones's report that he believed in England's victory as early as 1914 is not correct.[3] I remember vividly a discussion with Federn when I—at that time strongly identified with the Italian character of my native Trieste—disagreed essentially with his Austrian patriotic feelings. Federn's combination of devotion to democratic socialism and his strong patriotism is evidence of how much he lacked Freud's realism and scepticism.

Neither Freud nor Federn originally wished to be a physician. Freud was interested in basic research; Federn wanted to become a biologist. As therapists, however, Federn was more a physician and would fight harder against great odds to help the patient than Freud in whom the scientist was always stronger than the healer. Federn combined both qualities. In a number of cases over the years when I encountered difficulties in some psychoanalytic treatment, I consulted Freud, usually in writing. And in this way I became acquainted with his negative reaction to patients who had weak, unreliable, dishonest, or criminal character traits. In his opinion only a minority of patients deserved our therapeutic efforts and time. He believed that "where there is no ego, analysis has lost its rights." Many such patients I dismissed from treatment on his advice. And Freud had no inclination, either, to deal therapeutically with psychotic patients who, in his opinion, could not establish a workable transference to the analyst, because of their "narcissistic withdrawal" and because their egos were not approachable as were those of patients who were merely neurotic. Federn, on the other hand, accepted many such patients who would have been rejected by Freud. In his opinion psychopathic and psychotic egos were weak egos which could be helped by psychotherapy. Later August Aichhorn excelled in this attitude in his therapeutic successes with the *verwahrloste Jugend* ("juvenile delinquents") of Vienna during the troubled years following the First World War.[4]

Federn's trip to the United States in 1914 marked the end of the first phase of his psychoanalytic activities. C. P. Oberndorf, Smith Ely Jelliffe, Dorian Feigenbaum, and many others were deeply impressed with him here. Some account of his impact on the New York psychoanalysts is recorded in Oberndorf's *History of Psychoanalysis in America*.[5]

Paul Federn returned to Austria in July 1914 just after the outbreak of World War I. On his way back the Italian liner on which he was traveling was stopped by the British at Gibraltar. Federn, however, escaped detention as an enemy subject, for at that time the nations of the world scrupulously adhered to the principles of the Geneva Convention which specifically forbade internment of physicians as enemy aliens.

The period from 1914 to 1923 may be considered as the second phase of Federn's psychoanalytic activity. In this period of his life much of Federn's time was spent in didactic analyses, for not only was he one of the leading training analysts in Vienna but Chairman of the Education Committee of the Vienna Society. Many of his students of these years later attained great fame either for contributing new and original ideas to psychoanalytic theory and practice or in bringing psychoanalysis to many European countries and to the United States. I myself belong historically to the earlier phase. Federn also developed ideas on social psychology closely parallel to those of Freud, and it is interesting to note that his major work in this field "Zur Psychologie der Revolution: Die vaterlose Gesellschaft" [6] was published in 1919, nearly three years before the appearance of Freud's *Group Psychology and the Analysis of the Ego*.[7] At this time too, Federn became interested in the phenomenon of delinquency.

In 1923 Federn became Freud's personal deputy and two years later co-editor of the *Internationale Zeitschrift für Psychoanalyse*. He also developed his earliest phenomenological concepts of the ego and of psychoanalytic approach to the treatment of psychoses. Gradually his ego concept departed from that of Freud. This third phase extends to 1938, when Federn departed for the United States. His achievements from 1938 to 1950, a fourth phase, are documented in his book *Ego Psychology and the Psychoses*.

After 1923 Federn became increasingly interested in ego psychology from the phenomenological point of view. In his strict scientific approach to the ego phenomenon he started with an accurate description of the ways in which the individual experiences his own existence and the functions inherent in such experiences. He equated "ego" with "ego feeling." (This latter term was often used by my friend Viktor Tausk, and I do not know who first used the term, Federn or Tausk.) On the basis of his objective findings Federn constructed theories, but unfortunately in some of his earlier publications he did not express himself clearly regarding his new concepts. I myself could not always follow his expositions in every minute detail, and it was only through lengthy discussions in many letters and some few personal meetings that I succeeded in recognizing the great scientific and therapeutic value of his findings and the theories derived from them.

Federn's concept of the *medial*, that is, intransitive, ego experience, together with his assumption that the ego does not develop from the id but exists from the very beginning of life in the mother's womb long before it can discover a non-ego territory, found support in the belief of many biologists that a germ of consciousness (which Federn called "rudimentary ego feeling") pertains to every protoplasmic organism, even the lowest ones. His description of many ego states and ego stages, his concept of the ego as a coherent unity with multiform, flexible dynamic boundaries, his assigning to these boundaries the function of "sensing reality" (which is not "testing reality"), all have led to greater understanding of various ego phenomena, such as the feeling of estrangement (now called "derealization") and the feeling of depersonalization. These pathological sensations, Federn showed us, are not due to a withdrawal of object cathexis but to a deficiency of ego cathexis either at the boundaries or at some portion of the mental or bodily ego. In Federn's concept the psychotic process is not a regression of the libido to a primary narcissistic position but a direct consequence of deficient ego cathexis. In his teachings psychotic hallucinations and delusions are not unsuccessful attempts at restitution of the lost external reality, but the result of a dynamic lesion at the ego boundaries.

Among the reasons for Federn's lack of clarity in communicating his own difficult and original findings was his unshakable loyalty to Freud, in whose statements he believed without any mental reservation, at least as long as Freud was alive. Federn could never have become a "secessionist" like Adler, Jung and Stekel. His unwavering devotion to Freud hampered him in expressing his divergencies from Freud in any but an ambiguous way. Even in the field of ego psychology and psychotic afflictions he presented his findings not as original ones but as confirmation of Freud's basic psychoanalytic concepts and their applications to new phenomena. On occasion I commented to Federn that his concepts were often at variance with some of Freud's but he did not accept my remarks. He kept insisting that I was wrong and tried to explain how all of his expositions had already been implied in one or another statement of Freud's.

After 1930 some psychoanalysts close to Freud, who had attended Federn's seminars, published a series of books and articles on ego psychology without mentioning any of Federn's contributions. This greatly disappointed and embittered Federn.

After Freud's death Federn felt freer in expressing his own ideas and even spoke of the "few errors" of Freud. But it was not until a few days before his own death (in 1950) that he recognized how very much his ego psychology was in disagreement with Freud's ego concepts.[7a] In his will Federn expressed the desire that I collect his papers on ego psychology and the psychoses, in one volume, and I complied wholeheartedly.

Freud's reaction to Federn's ego psychology is of interest. Freud's mind was strongly and consistently directed toward the exploration of the unconscious, in antithesis to all previous psychologists who had equated the mental phenomena with the content of consciousness. In his strenuous work over a period of forty years Freud had succeeded in unearthing the mental activity of the id, which alone could help us to understand the most puzzling conscious phenomena. His mind became so strongly committed to the train of thought developed from his original discoveries that it was difficult for him to follow diverging trains of thought, such as those of Federn when he ventured into a phenomenological study of the ego. Freud was open-minded, yet he could not give his attention to Federn's findings or grasp their importance. As mentioned, Freud was responsive to Federn's loyalty and appreciated all his achievements in psychoanalysis prior to his presentations on ego psychology. But in Freud's opinion (expressed to some of his close adherents) Federn's introduction of new terms in ego psychology revealed nothing new, and he doubted whether it would be of value for better understanding of the ego and its functions. In brief, Freud was not very positively impressed by Federn's original findings.

Paul Federn's son Ernst, who provided me with some of the details of his father's life mentioned above, suggested the following hypothesis for this lack of appreciation of Federn's work on the part of Freud.[8]

(1) Federn's supportive attitude opened a way for him to help the ego-disturbed patient which was blocked to Freud because of his realistic and searching approach. Freud was therefore not in a position to observe the same patients as Federn.

(2) Federn was convinced that psychoanalysis is a tool for the betterment of society, and he saw the insanity of the individual as a parallel to the insanity of the world.[9] Freud recognized the latter and regretted it but he considered any endeavor for social change to be futile. As mentioned earlier, Federn was a romanticist and reformer, Freud a realist and searcher.

NOTES

(1) As seen in the oil portrait of Freud by M. Oppenheimer (also known as Max Mopp) which is erroneously dated "October 1909" (instead of 1908). Catalogue of the Freud Cententary Exhibit of the American Psychoanalytic Association, held at the Morrison Hotel, Chicago, and the New York Academy of Medicine, April and May, 1956. New York, The Association, 1956, p. 75.

(2) This letter in Freud's handwriting is in the possession of Federn's son, Mr. Ernst Federn of New York.

(3) Jones, Ernest. The Life and Work of Sigmund Freud. 3 vols. New York, Basic Books, 1953-1957, Vol. 2, p. 173.

(4) Aichhorn, August. Verwahrloste Jugend. Leipzig, Internationaler psychoanalytischer Verlag, 1925. (English: Wayward Youth. New York, Viking Press, 1935. A new edition in English is in preparation.) The term *verwahrloste* (literally, "neglected," "spoiled by neglect") has no exact English equivalent; however, the syndrome described by Aichhorn is roughly equivalent to what we know as juvenile delinquency.

(5) Oberndorf, Clarence P. A History of Psychoanalysis in America. New York, Grune & Stratton, 1953, p. 118.

(6) Federn, Paul. Zur Psychologie der Revolution: Die vaterlose Gesellschaft. Der österreichische Volkswirt, 11:571-574, 595-598. This appeared in late May 1919. An enlarged version (29 pages) was later published as Nos.

12-13 of the pamphlet series "Der Aufstieg: Neue Zeit- und Streitschriften" (Vienna, Anzengruber, 1919).

(7) Freud, Sigmund. Group Psychology and the Analysis of the Ego (1921). London, Hogarth, 1922.

(7a) Letter from Paul Federn to Edoardo Weiss, dated April 12, 1950.

(8) See Federn, Ernst. On the Therapeutic Personality as Illustrated by Paul Federn and August Aichhorn. *In press.*

(9) *Cf.* Federn, Paul. Mental factors in the world depression. J. Nerv. & Ment. Dis., 79:43-58, 1934.

Section I

Preliminary Survey
of the Mental Structure

I

First Approach to the Ego Phenomenon

THE ego is considered by some psychoanalysts as the core of the personality and by others as a substructure of the mind. In order to present what is known about the ego, unfolding its specific nature and functional position within the "mental apparatus," it is also necessary to provide a short summary of our knowledge of the other two substructures of the mind, the id and the superego, with which the ego is inseparably interlocked. In the first section of this book, however, we shall merely indicate some mental processes related to the other two substructures. For the moment this may be sufficient for our approach to the ego phenomenon. Later we shall discuss in detail all the mental processes in order to deepen our insight into them.

The psychological term "the ego" should first of all be considered from the most natural point of view. "Ego" is the Latin word for "I," the pronoun of the first person singular, which is used by everyone to denote himself. The use of this pronoun as a noun would be "the I," but the Latin "the ego" has been substituted in English.

If we are to grasp the conceptual implication of the use of this pronoun as a noun, we must consider the essential difference between a person's immediate experience of his own existence and what he can possibly know and understand about the inner experience of others. We can gain some knowledge and comprehension of the inner experiences of other persons only indirectly, i.e., from their expressions and reactions to various events in various situations. They behave and express themselves in a manner identical or similar to that in which we ourselves behave when moved by specific feelings and emotions or by specific impulses and thoughts. Everyone is directly aware only of his own inner existence and its characteristics, to which he refers by using the pronoun "I." The noun "the ego" is used, in psychology and philosophy, as a synonym

2

for a person's own experienced bodily and mental existence. It is, however, not synonymous with the mind nor with consciousness.

Before Freud ego phenomena were equated with mental phenomena, and only the contents of consciousness were regarded as mental processes. But since his pioneering discoveries, this view can no longer be maintained. Freud revealed that the field of mental phenomena extends far beyond the range of consciousness, and that the mind has a specific structure, i.e., that it is composed of functionally differentiated parts. Psychology became a "depth psychology." Thus, the ego, as conceived by Freud, is but one of the substructures of the mind.

It is indeed difficult to acknowledge that what a person experiences of himself constitutes only a functionally distinct portion of the mind. But we have to face still another conceptual difficulty. During the course of his psychoanalytic work Freud came to realize that not even all psychic activities which must be regarded as ego manifestations are conscious. If this is so, then the criterion for distinguishing between the ego and other mental substructures cannot be the state of consciousness but rather the specific way in which each substructure functions within the total mental activity. This statement may seem confusing. For if the concept of the ego is related to everyone's immediate experience of his bodily and mental existence, then how can the ego include unconscious phenomena and functions? The noun "the ego" is indisputably synonymous with the experience of one's existence, and no special agreement among the psychoanalysts is necessary to use this term in precisely this sense. Indeed, it should not be used otherwise, since we all indicate by this pronoun only what is encompassed in our self-experience. But no one ever includes unconscious phenomena and functions in what he calls "I"; such an extended use of the term "the ego" would be inconsistent with its actual meaning.

It is indeed bewildering to learn that the ego, being synonymous with self-experience, extends over unconscious contents and is responsible for unconscious processes. Our bewilderment will cease, however, when we realize that not everything is conscious in the very phenomenon which everyone actually senses as "I." What everyone feels of himself goes far beyond the contents which are conscious to him at any given moment. We must realize that what everybody denotes by the pronoun "I" is the subjective sensation of the feeling of his own bodily and mental existence. "I" is not synonymous with one's consciousness, but with the feeling of one's existence in its whole extension. It is this feeling, the "ego feeling," which extends over unconscious phenomena.

Among psychoanalysts it was Paul Federn who approached the ego problem from a phenomenological point of view. In his opinion the term "ego" is synonymous with "ego feeling." He declared: "Although Freud's theory of the ego and the id is well formulated, it is not this theory but the familiar phenomenon of ego feeling that proves the existence of the ego." [1] To equate ego with ego feeling is certainly consistent with what we all mean when we use the pronoun "I." It is a continuous and, after every interruption, a re-established coherent experience unity. This feeling extends also over some unconscious mental phenomena, and in waking life only the feeling of "I-ness" is permanently conscious in its whole extension.

The field of unconscious mental phenomena over which the conscious ego feeling extends is that which Freud termed the "preconscious." The confidence of every healthy person in his knowledge and past experiences, in his ability to behave and to express himself in a coherent way, rests precisely on the extension of the ego feeling over the preconscious, which is the domain of the ego. We shall pay due attention to this in a later chapter.

NOTES

(1) Federn, Paul. Ego Psychology and the Psychoses. Edited with an introduction by Edoardo Weiss. New York, Basic Books, 1952, p. 212.

II

The Formulation of the Ego and Its Functions

ONLY among Federn's followers is ego synonymous with ego feeling. Most psychoanalysts consider ego feeling as but one of the ego's functions, although they do give credit to Federn for his accurate and penetrating descriptions of many ego-pathological phenomena.

In Freud's formulation the ego is that functionally differentiated part of the mind which enters into communication with the external world and acts as an intermediary between biological needs —the instincts and the drives—and the external world. It is a special organization which develops from an original cortical layer, provided with organs for receiving stimuli and with an apparatus for protection against excessive stimulation. In its struggle for survival it develops many functions which enable it to deal with the internal demands of the instinctive drives and with the conditions of the external world.[1] In fact, Freud initially called the self-preservative drives "ego drives." Of the countless functions of the ego we shall now consider but a few in order to become better acquainted with its position within the mind.

First of all, let us consider the perceptive function. The perception of internal stimuli is called introspection, that of external stimuli can be called extraspection.

We have good evidence for assuming that in earliest infancy the child hallucinates, as every healthy person does later on only in his dreams. As the child develops, his ego learns to discriminate between the internal (mental) and external origins of the perceived stimuli. In other words, he has begun to distinguish between "real" and "unreal." (We should note in passing that in psychoanalytic terminology "real" means existing in the external world and "unreal" existing only in the mind.) This discriminatory capacity puts an end to the hallucinatory perceptions, and the products of the mind

5

are henceforth recognized as memories and thoughts. In Freud's interpretation this capacity develops initially from the ego's mastery of the motor apparatus. Motility enables the ego to change its position in relation to the external world as well as to produce changes in the world of objects. Thinking is essentially a trial acting with minimal or no employment of muscular activity. This complex function is also based on memory and is enhanced by the acquisition of language. In point of fact, thinking ensues from anticipation of action. Through bodily movements the external objects change their spatial position in relation to one's person, while the position of internal, mental stimuli is not altered by movements. The memory and thinking functions also participate successively in this complicated learning process, which Freud called "reality testing."

We shall soon learn that the ego's capacity to discriminate between internal and external data is not based exclusively on a "testing" of reality. In his phenomenological studies of the ego Federn came to the conclusion that the ego's capacity to discriminate between ego and non-ego, or between what he calls "inner mentality" and "external reality," is due to the immediate perception of "real" and "unreal," independent of any reality testing, by a particular sense which he calls "sense of reality."

From this and many other findings of Federn we can easily understand that equating ego with ego feeling aids us substantially in solving many ego-psychological problems which could not be comprehended otherwise. Discrimination between ego and non-ego, real and unreal, is related to the ego feeling which has a bodily and mental extension. Every phenomenon which appears within the flexible limits of the ego feeling is felt as mental, i.e., as unreal; and every stimulus which impinges on the bodily and mental ego feeling boundaries from without is felt as existing in the external world, i.e., as real. The ego's inner boundaries limit its extension toward the non-ego mental territory. Hallucinations are perceived mental processes over which ego feeling does not extend. In the healthy personality such mental processes are kept from the ego's perception except in the state of sleep when the partially awakened ego dreams. Then they are felt as real, precisely because they break through the weakened inner ego boundaries from without. We shall deal with the dynamic character of the ego feeling and its inner and outer boundaries in the course of our presentation of the general psychodynamics of the mind.

In his definition of the ego Freud himself implied that it is that part of the mind which deals with and handles reality.

NOTES

(1) Waelder, Robert. The principle of multiple function. Psychoanal. Quart., 5:45-62, 1936. The author elaborates on the multiple, simultaneous motivations of every ego function.

III

The Integrative Function of the Ego

AN integer is a number which is not a fraction, something which is entire. Integrating means completing, to make entire. Any object which has entireness can be mutilated, that is to say, damaged or made less than whole, be it a living being or one of its productions which serves a purpose. The concept of entireness has not only a spatial but also a temporal connotation. When we speak of someone's whole life we mean his life in its entire temporal extension. In order to complete a deed we must perform subsidiary acts in a proper succession in time. The entireness or mutilation of a musical composition, for example, can be conceived of only in its temporal extension.

In all psychoanalytic concepts of the ego, integration has been recognized as its most important function. Its very task of acting as an intermediary between the instinctive drives and the external world implies integration. In its broadest sense integration is understood as a "meaningful," that is, goal-directed, succession of acts or processes. It is characteristic of life in general. We find highly integrated processes in the vegetable and animal kingdoms. W. B. Cannon gave due recognition to the "purposefulness" of the interrelated physiological processes by calling his well-known work in physiology, *The Wisdom of the Body*.[1] To what startling "meaningful" combinations of processes the animal body can resort under conditions of disease or stress is now common knowledge to every student of biology. Life is engaged in a continuous "problem-solving" struggle, a struggle which is often doomed to failure.

The biological organization of living beings, with its stupendous performances and chemical productions which man cannot duplicate, reveals the need and the capacity of a living being to unify conflicting forces, to remove destructive ones, and to modify unfavorable conditions in order to preserve its integrity and to assure its future development.

What is the difference between biological integration and the integration performed by the ego? Is the difference perhaps that the ego is consciously guiding its integrative behavior, while biological integration occurs quite automatically? This is not so since the ego performs many integrative acts quite unconsciously, although in our opinion it has the conscious feeling of its unconsciously accomplished integration.

Certainly consciousness plays an essential role in the ego's integrative behavior. Perceiving pleasant and painful, internal and external stimuli, remembering past experiences from which one learned what to expect in the future, and thinking occur mostly in the light of consciousness. But the ego also reacts with feelings of confidence to unconsciously achieved successes, and with uncertainty or discouragement to unconsciously suffered failures in its integrative efforts. This is further proof that the coherent conscious ego feeling unity extends over the preconscious, which is actually felt as the "I."

We may now ask, in which cases does integration become an ego function which requires consciousness or, at least, the participation of the coherent ego unity? To answer this question we have only to remember that the ego acts as an intermediary between the internal and the external world and that it develops functions in compliance with this role. All mental activities which are preparatory to the purposeful handling of external reality are subservient to the integrative function of the ego. In order to act as a coherent unity the ego must unify or settle conflicting impulses within itself and plan their gratification in accordance with understood conditions in the external world. It must also be able to time properly not only the satisfactions of single instinctive drives and wishes but also the single subsidiary acts which eventually lead to gratification of each drive. The integrative task often requires postponement or renunciation of some drive satisfaction. We also recall that thinking, a kind of trial acting, develops from the anticipation of acting. The importance of this mental activity for the ego's integrative behavior cannot be overestimated. Some may remark that animals also act upon the external world, that they have to do so in order to survive and to satisfy their needs, and we shall answer that they too have egos and consciousness. But an animal's ego is more poorly organized and much less endowed than the human one. Those who are interested in its study must approach its investigation only from a behavioristic point of view, not necessarily with reference to the human ego.

The physiological organism responds to stimuli by internal changes. However complicated and appropriate they may be, they occur according to fixed patterns. Physiological adaptation to changed environmental conditions or to unusual activities and stress of the individual does not consist in alterations of external reality but in inner alterations within the organism. These occur in all individuals of the same species in exactly the same way, so much so that physiological experiments can be better compared to experiments in physics or in chemistry than to experiments in psychology.

It is very important to note that the inner physiological integrative processes occur only according to fixed, reflex-like patterns. In the ego's integrative behavior, however, this is not always the case. It is true that the way the ego handles reality or arranges mental phenomena, in preparation for action, does sometimes show rigid patterns. This is the case in instinctive acts. Many integrative processes of the ego are common to all or to most individuals, as, for instance, when a compromise of conflicting wishes is reached. Some fixed patterns of the so-called ego-defenses belong to the best-studied integrative mental processes. This is a very broad field of investigation with which we shall deal in due time.

NOTES

(1) Cannon, Walter B. The Wisdom of the Body. New York, Norton, 1932. A revised and enlarged edition was published in 1939.

IV

Allo- and Autoplasticity

SANDOR FERENCZI gave the name "autoplastic" to those processes which enable an organism to acquire and modify its shape and functional parts; similarly, he called "alloplastic" the meaningful transformation by an organism of its environment. Thus the fur of animals can be considered an autoplastic production, while a bird's nest is essentially alloplastic. The marvelous autoplastic organizations of plants and animals required millions of years to develop. On the other hand, the wonderful alloplastic technical achievements of man which permit him to become master of the external world at an ever increasing pace have taken only a few thousand years, and in recent decades technological progress has surpassed anything hitherto imaginable.

While alloplastic productivity per se is not peculiar to the human race, those alloplastic objects formed by animals show a rigid uniformity and are built quite instinctively. They cannot be compared with the tools, buildings and machines created by man, which enable him to reach continuously new goals. Man's integrative capacity developed from the ego's ability to manage reality and from its struggle to master new situations. Indeed, we are quite justified in calling "creations" the new integrative achievements which have arisen from man's efforts to solve new problems.

When we are confronted with a new integrative task, our consciousness is focused on our mental and physical activity. The perception of an unexpected situation which must be dealt with promptly and actively draws our attention to it and to our integrative procedure. Conversely, consciousness withdraws from responses which become automatic and occur according to fixed learned patterns. These no longer need the guide of awareness. In the "creative genius," however, the mental ego extends over a much broader preconscious territory than in ordinary people. The ego feeling itself is conscious in its entire extension, but this is not

11

true of the single contents and productions of the operating preconscious. Creative processes, which are highly integrative phenomena, can unfold unconsciously only when they are invested by
the ego-feeling unity. This is another way of saying that they unfold in the preconscious. The genius does not necessarily feel that
it was he himself (his "I") who produced the creation which appeared in his mind. Often the solution of a problem or some creative
thought enters his mind without any conscious elaboration on his
part, like an inspiration from without. But as soon as the desired
mental production enters the preconscious, in other words, as soon
as it is egotized, the individual experiences a feeling of confidence
and relief even before he tries to express this production consciously.

A passage from Federn's paper "Ego Psychological Aspect of
Schizophrenia" [1] may be quoted here: "Some people have a
narrow mental ego. The productive genius [on the other hand] has
the greatest scope of mental contents. Convincing examples have
been presented to me by writers, scientists, and musicians, but none
were comparable with the story of Mozart in Prague. Two days before the première of his *Don Giovanni* he had not yet started to
compose the overture. His friends, the opera director, and orches-
tra were in excited suspense, while the genius himself uncon-
cernedly enjoyed a gay party. Late in the evening he wrote the
music without any later correction; he said that the whole musical
score suddenly and simultaneously presented itself clearly to his
mind. This is the outstanding and almost unbelievable example of
the enlargement of a mental ego, and also proof that the greatest
and most complicated production is done unconsciously. Probably some parts of the work had previously become conscious and
had returned to preconsciousness."

The superior intellect of man—this formidable integrative tool—
is not the only factor responsible for his superb achievements in
understanding and mastering reality: The transmission of acquired
knowledge and technical devices from generation to generation
through thousands of years plays a much greater role in this progress. Each new generation continues to develop and perfect that
treasure of knowledge which it inherited from its ancestors. We
have borrowed the term "inherited" from the vocabulary of biology

in order to show the combination of acquired achievements from parents to children.

Biological heredity is autoplastic, inherent in the genes, while that of acquired knowledge and technical achievement is based on alloplastic media, such as oral and written communication. The phenomenon of interpersonal communication and relationships, of interpersonal and social integration, is another vast field for exploration. The ego cannot be understood in its development and structuralization without an accurate study of the manifold relationships between various egos, and the ways by which one ego can understand and influence another. Interpersonal communication, by means of which various data are transmitted from one ego to another, produces also autoplastic changes within the affected egos.

For a better understanding of what is to follow let us digress for a moment into the terminology introduced by Sigmund Freud which makes comprehension of the dynamic process clearer. The application of physical concepts for the explanation of psychical phenomena was termed by Freud "metapsychology." Metapsychology comprises the dynamic, the economic, and the topographical points of view. The term "dynamic" refers to the forces involved (no doubt an allusion to the dynamics in classical physics); "economic" is concerned with the forces' proportional strength in the interaction; while "topographical" is used to designate the division into "mental localities," or the specific psychic substructures in which mental phenomena take place. But these topographically conceived structures should not be looked upon as anatomical parts of the brain; they refer only to the mental substructures which are imagined figuratively as special entities.

The concepts of allo- and autoplasticity must also be considered in connection with the two ways in which mental tension can be relieved. A drive, a wish or a thought can have varying degrees of intensity. The "charge of energy" which determines this degree of intensity of mental contents is called *cathexis*. Cathexis is correlated to some nervous excitation, and we distinguish between a fixed form of cathexis and a movable one, just as in physics we distinguish potential energy from kinetic energy. The nervous tension which is correlative to the cathexis finds release in two forms of outlet: (1) By discharge into muscular activity which leads to action whereby the individual changes his spatial position in respect to the environment and in this way deals with reality. Here the release constitutes the means for alloplastic production. (2) By discharge into internal, vasomotor, vasosecretory, and visceral processes which is sensed by the ego in its end effects. Thus blushing, blanching, or accelerated heart beat are experienced as various feelings, affects, and emotions. This latter kind of discharge is merely autoplastic. It does not bring about any change in the individual's position in relation to his environment. Emotional factors, however, constitute motivations for the individual to act, that is, to make use of his muscular apparatus. Among the emotions, fear and anxiety play a special role in the integrative behavior of the ego by inducing it to develop various defense mechanisms.

The cathexes of mental contents normally find an outlet in feelings, emotions and motor activities only when they are invested by the ego, in other words, only when they belong topographically to the ego. The ego does not have the same capacity of mastery over experienced emotions as it has over its muscular actions. Nevertheless, the feelings, affects, and emotions which develop in the ego contribute to its continuously changing states.

NOTES

(1) Federn, Paul. Ego psychological aspect of schizophrenia. In Ego Psychology and the Psychoses, p. 223.

V

The Dynamic Aspect of the Ego

IN Glover's definition cathexis is "the investment of an idea with instinctual energy giving rise ordinarily to interest and to affect appropriate to the aim of the instinct: an unconscious process fully experienced in consciousness only when there is no unconscious obstacle to the emergence of the impulse." [1] In fact the German words used by Freud, which have been translated in English as "cathexis," are *Besetzung* and *Besetzungsenergie* [2]; the first is the mental content invested with the energy, and the second the investing energy itself. Let us now consider cathexis as the energy itself. In this sense cathexis is not merely a result of an energetic tension which seeks discharge after it has surpassed a certain degree of intensity. It is a biological process derived from somatogenic drives, which mobilizes the mental activities. In some respects it is synonymous with "interest." Thus, it differs from an aimless charge of energy because it is goal-directed. The wind, a flowing river, the force of gravity, a bent metal spring or the potential energy stored in coal may perhaps be compared with the nervous energy to which cathexis is correlated, but only when an integrative mechanism constructed by man is applied to these forces.

From the very beginning of his psychological investigations Freud had the goal-directed nature of cathexis in mind. In formulating his theory of the "dualism of instincts" Freud went beyond the field of psychology into the field of general biology. He assumed that life pursues two basic goals, from which all the many drives of living beings derive.

At first he thought that the two basic instincts tended toward self-preservation and preservation of the species, which he called "ego instincts" and "sexual instincts," respectively. The dynamic expression of the sexual instincts, that is the sexual cathexis, was called "libido." Later (1920) he revised his theory and assumed that living matter struggles between the urge to preserve life, both the self and the race, and the silent urge to disintegrate and die. He called the first basic instinct "Eros," and included in it the urge to bind an increasing number of biological units and groups of units to larger and larger organizations. The second he called the "death instinct." He kept the term libido to designate the dynamic expression, cathexis, of Eros. The "synthetic function" of the ego, described by Nunberg,[3] is an expression of Eros. Such function does lead, in fact, to preservation of life and development through binding and synthetic processes. Furthermore, through synthesis or union, new combinations are also achieved, as a new living being is created through the union in love of male and female. In the third section we shall examine Freud's dualism of instincts and theories advanced by other psychoanalysts who reject Freud's instinct dualism or his assumption of a death instinct.

In any case, the cathexis unfolds its activity in the frame of an integrative organization. Freud gave a clear expression to this character of cathexis by calling it *Besetzungsenergie*. *Besetzung* is derived from the verb *besetzen*, meaning "to occupy, to hold or fill up (a place)" and also "to garrison." By the figurative use of this term Freud thus compared a charge of mental energy to a military occupation. And just as an army unit can be shifted from one area to another, a charge of mental energy can be put to different uses. In the *Glossary for the Use of Translators of Psycho-Analytical Works*,[4] which renders *Besetzungsenergie* as "cathectic energy," this connotation is lost, although the meaning of "holding" or "retaining" is inherent in the Greek word *kathexis*. The dynamic nature of ego feeling, in other words of the ego itself, is of greatest importance for an understanding of the ego's functions, its changing states, and its pathology. The ego can be felt with varying degrees of intensity. It is, therefore, obvious that its metapsychological basis must be a state of cathexis which is experienced in the ego feeling. Federn's metapsychological definition of the ego is as follows: "The basis of the ego is a state of psychical cathexis of certain interdependent bodily and mental functions and contents, the cathexes in question being simultaneous and interconnected, and also continuous. The nature of these functions, and the center around which they are grouped, are familiar."[5] We can say briefly that from the phenomenological point of view the ego is a coherent and continuous experience unity. From the metapsychological point of view it is a coherent and continuous cathexis unity. This cathexis is called "ego cathexis."

When a person loves or hates himself, and when he thinks of himself, his ego becomes the object of his love, his hate, or his thoughts. As Federn pointed out, the ego is subject and object simultaneously. As subject it is known by the pronoun "I," and as object it is called "the self." Heinz Hartmann and his school use the term "self" with a different meaning which we shall discuss after we have presented the other two psychic substructures.

The ego as subject is experienced in various ways which can be indicated in terms made familiar by grammar. The active ego cathexis is experienced in the ego's planning, thinking, acting, and, in its most elementary form, in the phenomenon of attention. The passive ego cathexis is experienced in the need to be stimulated. The reflexive cathexis is manifested in self-love or self-hate. The twofold role of the ego, as subject and object, is here very evident. In its original and most primitive form, however, the ego cathexis, or rather the corresponding ego feeling, can be classified, not according to these three categories, but by the middle voice as it is used in classical Greek. Federn termed this neutral objectless form of ego cathexis "medial" cathexis. In English grammar the middle voice is expressed by certain intransitive phrases, such as, "I grow," "I thrive," "I live," "I exist," "I prosper," "I develop," and, in the case of a predominant destructive component, by "I perish," "I age," "I die."

The perpetual manifestation of the ego cathexis is the medial one. Federn, who fully accepted Freud's dualism of instincts, distinguished, accordingly, between libido and the cathexis derived from the death instinct, which he called *mortido,* derived from the Latin *mors,* meaning death. The ego feeling is derived from a fusion of libido and mortido, in different proportions. In his opinion it is the medial libido component of the ego cathexis which is responsible for the feeling that everyday life, with its sensations and its motor and intellectual functions, is not an empty, dull or disagreeable experience but a pleasantly familiar one. Body and mind combine to procure for the ego this enigmatic enjoyment of life itself.

All bodily and mental functions and contents which are invested with ego cathexis and thus are felt as belonging to one's ego can be called "egotized." The importance of the phenomena of egotization and de-egotization may be illustrated by the following example:

A man dreamed of someone suffering from a severe headache and felt great sympathy for the sufferer. Then as he woke up he realized that it was he himself who had a headache. The ego cathexis, the corresponding ego feeling, was withdrawn from a mental content, the headache, which was attributed in the dream to another person. We can say that a part of an ego state became a representation of an object through de-egotization of this part. Upon awakening this part became egotized, thus united with the individual's ego feeling. In other words, an object representation then became a part of an ego state.

We shall soon learn that parts of other real persons also can be egotized. This phenomenon is called "identification" and plays a paramount role in interpersonal relationships.

NOTES

(1) Glover, Edward. Psycho-Analysis. A Handbook for Medical Practitioners and Students of Comparative Psychology. 2d ed. London, Staples, 1949, p. 342.

(2) Cf. the verb besetzen, "to cathect." In an effort to overcome the lack of uniformity in English words chosen to render the German psychoanalytic terminology, Ernest Jones (aided by Barbara Low, John Rickman, and others) compiled A Glossary for the Use of Translators of Psycho-Analytical Works (London, Baillière, Tindall & Cox, 1924) (International Journal of Psycho-Analysis, Supplement 1). This glossary has established "cathexis" as the correct translation for Besetzung, and "cathectic energy" for Besetzungsenergie, etc. (p. 6). A second edition (1946), compiled by a group headed by Alix Strachey, retains these translations (p. 12). The glossary has served as a quasi-official guide for psychoanalytic translators.

(3) Nunberg, Herman. The synthetic function of the ego (1930). Int. J. Psychoanal., 12:123-140, 1931.

(4) See note 2 above.

(5) Federn, Paul. Ego Psychology and the Psychoses. Edited with an introduction by Edoardo Weiss. New York, Basic Books, 1952, p. 94. For two other definitions of the ego by Federn, see Chapter XII.

VI

Interpersonal Relationships

AS we said earlier we can gain knowledge of the inner experiences of our fellow-beings only indirectly, that is, through their expressions and reactions. But this knowledge is not based on conclusions drawn from their perceived expressions and reactions. We became aware of other egos by attributing automatically to other persons the same kind of inner life that we ourselves have. Because their physical structure, their expressions and behavior are like ours, we simply equate their egos with ours. This equation is so prompt and so spontaneous that we have the impression of actually "perceiving" the egos of other persons.[1]

Even while we equate other egos with our own, we are still quite aware that other persons are in many respects different from ourselves. The inner life of a mother is different from that of her children. A child's ego is different from that of an adult. A woman does not feel the same in every respect as a man. Then too, persons of the same age and sex show tremendous differences in their feelings, wishes, needs, and behavior. Therefore, we realize that the equation of our own ego with those of other persons is not with reference to the great variety of contents of the many egos, but only to the essential features which all egos have in common.

Two questions now come to the fore: (1) How can we understand the contents and dispositions of other egos which are different from those which we experience? (2) What are the factors that determine our attraction or repulsion from other persons?

In the first place we know that some differences in the contents of two egos are only differences in intensity of single contents. From his expressions and behavior we may realize that another person is more or less interested than we in one achievement or another, that his emotional reactions in a given situation are stronger or weaker than ours. Furthermore, we can sometimes understand in others the expressions of urges, desires, or emotions which we ourselves experienced in the past. In this way an adult can understand many expressions and behavior patterns of children and younger people. More than this, we are sometimes able to understand emotional contents and thoughts in other persons that we apparently never have experienced. The reciprocal understanding of normal men and women of some feelings and desires of the opposite sex, for instance, belongs to this category. The psychological mechanism of this kind of comprehension derives from particular ego functions which will be thoroughly discussed in a later chapter.

However much we seem to know about the inner experiences of other people, we are forced to realize that in many cases we are totally incapable of grasping even important contents in the egos of others. Interpersonal communication between two or more people does not often lead to adequate reciprocal understanding of their respective emotional contents and tendencies. We conclude that we do not know all the concrete feelings, inclinations and desires which they encompass. Sometimes we attribute to another ego some of our own mental contents which it does not encompass. This is called "projection," a misleading term since it has sometimes been used with different meaning.

To what extent is our attraction to other persons and our repulsion from them determined by our understanding of their egos? We know that two or more persons can enter into many different kinds of relationships. We depend on certain persons for obtaining satisfaction of some of our needs. In a way we make use of them, as we make use of some inanimate objects. Other persons we avoid or may even wish to get rid of, when they harm us or interfere with our sought-after goals. Because the respective behavior of the persons who benefit or harm us is motivated by their emotional trends toward us, we try to recognize their feelings toward us, but we do not need to understand their whole inner life. Our "relation" to such people has a utilitarian motive. It may, however, lead to a real relationship. The love of a child for his parents has such an origin, since they provide him with satisfaction of vital needs.

A small child is unable to understand much of his mother's inner life. Her emotional needs, her thoughts and problems are beyond his capacity. Nevertheless, he becomes extremely alert to her feelings toward him. He is profoundly affected by her smile, her voice, and her touch as well as by her stern face and rude manners. How can he discern from his mother's expressions whether her feelings are good or bad? To say that he has learned to interpret his mother's expressions by associating her behavior with her expressions is not quite satisfactory. The child himself experiences and expresses pain, anger, anxiety, satisfaction and pleasure, and his mother's expressions awaken in him their true psychological significance. After all, we inherit a disposition for different feelings and emotions, which we all express in similar manner. We smile, we laugh, we cry. As the child grows older he reveals unmistakably that he does increasingly understand his mother's love, anxiety and anger, and also that he participates in her joy and pain. This love of a child for his parents, which develops out of gratification of his vital needs, Freud called "object love of the anaclitic type." According to Freud one has this kind of love for the nursing woman and the protecting man, and also for all persons who substitute for them.

On the other hand, some persons may be the objects of our emotional needs or instinctive drives without having been our instruments for procuring gratification of vital needs. Emotional needs may derive from many sources as we shall see. A drive has an object and a goal and is powered by a cathexis of varying intensity. Freud called the dynamic strength of the drive "impetus." Through satisfaction of the drive its cathexis is discharged. Our interest in objects is called object love or object libido, as opposed to ego libido. Freud introduced the term "narcissism," derived from the Greek Narcissus myth, to designate the ego libido. This term has often been used in a somewhat loose way, since not every form of ego libido corresponds to the self-love of the mythical Narcissus. In the objectless medial ego libido—I exist, I live—the self does not appear as object of love at all. In order to love an object one must have this medial libido. But one can easily see that an increase of object love means a decrease in self-love. This is a metapsychological, or more precisely, an economic consideration. In general the libido-economic point of view plays an important role in our psychodynamic orientation.

Let us now ask why do adults long for and love children? Does an adult understand a child? We know that we do not remember our earliest ego stages from the time of our birth. Our functions and orientation develop slowly. We acquire new knowledge, and with it new desires come into being. Our integrative capacity and our sense of responsibility increase with our emancipation from our dependent needs. Earlier ego stages become more and more incompatible with the mature ego. Indeed, by the time we are adults, so many essential features, needs and reactions of our former ego structures have been forgotten that parents sometimes have to be taught by child psychologists how to understand and treat their children. This difficulty will be better understood when we discuss the phenomenon of repression.

Still, everyone has passed through childhood and thus has experienced successively within himself the developmental stages of the "child ego." An adult can usually understand a child's way of having fun. He realizes that the child is unable to feel responsible for his actions as an adult does. The adult perceives the child's egocentric "narcissistic" orientation, his attachment to the persons who care for him, etc., all of which are appropriate to the child's physical appearance and abilities. On the other hand, adults do not understand and even ignore some important tendencies and reactions of children.

A growing individual is forced gradually into adult attitudes, and with them the feeling of responsibility so difficult to endure. As life forces adaptation to reality upon him he is compelled sooner or later to relinquish childhood. Maturing experiences, the development of intelligence and a growing sense of reality enable him to do this. It would be a mistake, however, to think that earlier developmental ego stages disappear completely in the adult personality, or that they are entirely forgotten. Rather, they become incompatible with the ways an adult must feel and act, and therefore they are excluded from the way an adult ego feels itself to be.

In various situations, however, the features of some "child ego" reappear in the adult. Almost everyone feels the need to "play the child" once in a while, but in each case only according to his memory of an early ego state. Psychotic persons, and sometimes those who are senile, may regress much more completely to ego stages of childhood, thus demonstrating that former ego stages are stored somewhere in our minds, outside of the current ego. We shall understand where later on. The pleasure which some well-adjusted persons derive from certain kinds of social entertainment and from sports and games is obviously due to the feeling of being a child again. This serves as a temporary refuge from the strains and stresses of reality. It is also a well-known fact that people frequently regress to child-like expressions in love play and flirtation, especially when they are under the influence of alcohol.

But no one is spared the difficult task of growing up. Reality does not allow an adult to keep on feeling like a child except on rare occasions. Life itself, with its exigencies and obligations, compels us to feel adult, to have an adult sense of responsibility for our behavior and actions, and to give up immature attitudes and childish ways of thinking.

Even when we have excluded them from the current ego state, former ego stages may, however, maintain a strong cathexis. Sometimes they reappear in the consciousness of the adult ego, not as a part of an ego state but as an object representation. We illustrated the process of de-egotization above in the incident of the dreamer whose headache seemed in the dream to belong to another person. We said that through the withdrawal of ego cathexis from a certain content, a phenomenon which we called de-egotization, a part of an ego state was turned into an object representation. This phenomenon is called "externalization," meaning appearing outside of one's own ego.

In dreams externalized parts of ego states appear as dream persons, because every dream consists of hallucinations. In the waking life of a normal ego externalized portions of ego states are perceived as object representations. Many of our former ego states undergo precisely this process of externalization. No longer feeling ourselves to be children, we surrender childish attitudes to *actual* children. Our desire to satisfy wishes and tendencies of childhood, and to enjoy former dependent gratifications, is then turned into a longing for appropriate persons with whom we can obtain such satisfactions vicariously. The actual finding of such objects in the external world is designated as "object finding." Ego stages of childhood remain in us, more or less cathected, but arouse very little subjective feeling beyond occasional nostalgia for childhood. A normally developed individual accepts his own adulthood and succeeds in giving up his childish traits and needs because he is able in some degree to de-egotize, that is, externalize, his own infantile ego stages and to find vicarious gratification with those who still are children.

Freud called this kind of love "object love according to the narcissistic type." [2] One has this kind of love for those who seem to be what one's self is, what one's self was, what one's self would like to be, or the person who once was a part of one's self. We may add that such a love object is chosen according to the externalized image of one's own present, past or desired ego. The love of parents for children is only one example. We shall learn that in heterosexual love also the process of externalization is important. In normal development feminine urges of males and masculine urges of females are not egotized but appear externalized in the representation of persons of the opposite sex. The ego then craves vicarious gratification of such urges.

A description of interpersonal relationships only in terms of anaclitic and narcissistic object choice cannot of course account for all the characteristics of all kinds of relationships, nor for the inner motivations for them. It cannot explain completely the phenomenon of loneliness. The ego's need for associating with other egos which are similar and also very different in content and capacity from itself, and also the need for integration into a social community, deserves special consideration.

NOTES

(1) It is possible that deeper investigation at some future time might reveal the existence of a further source of knowledge and understanding of other people's egos, besides the instinctive equation of their egos with our own.

(2) Freud, Sigmund. On narcissism: An introduction (1914). Standard Edition, 14:67-102. London, Hogarth, 1957. See especially pp. 87-91.

VII

Interpersonal Communications
The Phenomenon of Identification

ESTABLISHMENT of dynamic boundaries, with clear separation between an egotized body ego and the external world, is a slow process. In the initial ego phase the ego extends over the whole of its perception. This initial extension of ego feeling over objects of the external world or parts of them is called by some psychoanalysts "primary identification." However, this term is also used in a different meaning, as we shall soon see. Federn called the first ego phase, which includes the whole perceived universe, the "ego-cosmic" phase. Gradually a part of the external world is sensed by the infant as non-ego, i.e., object world, but for a time his mother, and later only her breast, is still encompassed within his bodily ego. Eventually the ego-cathected boundaries withdraw also from the breast, and these boundaries then constitute a sense organ which discriminates between ego and non-ego. But the ego tends to "recapture" the lost portion of itself which has become the world of objects. It distinguishes then bad objects and qualities from good ones and tries to hold for itself the good and reject the bad.

After the child has learned to recognize the face and movements of his mother and other persons of his environment, his perception of them is followed by innate responses, as every physiological stimulus is followed by a reaction. In a reflexlike manner the infant tries to catch with his mouth everything which he likes, with the same attitude he has toward the nipple. In other words, he tries instinctively to "incorporate orally," like the mother's milk, everything he likes. This is the only way he can relate to an object.

Another automatic response accompanies his urge for oral incorporation of love objects. He copies the movements and expressions of the mother and other people, for which he shows an increasing understanding. This phenomenon is also called by some psycho-analysts "primary identification," which means that he tries instinctively to make himself identical with the perceived persons. The urge to take oral possession of a love object actually leads to an autoplastic reproduction of it. The importance of this phenomenon for the ego's development and establishment of relationships with other egos cannot be overestimated. The first expression of the child's relationship to another person is his identification with him.

Touch, visible facial expressions, gestures and movements are the earliest means of interpersonal communication. To these vocal sounds of the mother and of other persons are added. Progressively the infant succeeds in grasping the meaning of single words, of sentences, and of speech in general. He tries to reproduce these sounds, and by the end of his first year of life, or a little later, he succeeds. Thus the growing child becomes able to communicate in more and more ways as well as to participate in varying degrees in the emotional experiences of the persons with whom he comes in contact.

At the same time, through his various identifications with other persons, his ego acquires its own characteristics. In order to gain the correct concept of the increasing structuralization of the child's ego one must consider the phenomenon of egotization. Identification is not a mere imitation of other people's expressions and behavior. Their autoplastic reproductions become real features of one's own ego and are felt as such. For example, in our speech we do not sense that we are just repeating verbal expressions which we heard in our childhood. We feel our verbal function, rather, as an inseparable part of ourselves. We may know that in our infancy we learned from our mothers and other people to reproduce the verbal sounds, but we know this only intellectually. We cannot possibly trace the acquisition of our language to its actual origin. The same is true for many of our behavior traits and of our way of thinking. Most of our egotized concepts about human society and the world in general have resulted from our earliest identifications. But to describe the phenomenon of identification merely as an act of imitation is to ignore the most important feature of the phenomenon, that the autoplastic reproduction is egotized and no longer felt as related to an object.

A child learns who he is by being recognized and named by his mother and other persons. *They* know who he is. The human ego is a social ego. Each acquires its identity by virtue of being one among other egos. Initially, the child does not use the pronoun "I" to designate himself but speaks of himself in the third person, using his given name. His name distinguishes him from "equivalent" egos of his environment.

The ego's surrender of the external world, i.e., its abandoning of the egocosmic stage, is followed by, and almost coincides with, its awareness of other egos. The "I" feels surrounded by many "Thous" and feels itself to be a member of the "We." Other bodily and mental egos inhabit the discovered external world and constitute a special category of "objects." In these objects the ego will find externalized states of itself—present, past or prospective states. Conversely, some autoplastic duplications of these objects or parts of them will become egotized and therefore included within one's own ego. This is the phenomenon we have just designated as "identification."

Many forms of identification can be distinguished, and each of them plays a special role in our interpersonal relationships. We learned that primary identification, in the second meaning mentioned, shapes the ego's structure, and it is evident that the environment and culture in which the child grows up contribute substantially to this structuralization. Emotional understanding of our fellow-beings is based upon a kind of identification which we may call "resonance identification."

The phenomenon of emotional or mental resonance can well be compared with a musical chord struck on a piano and echoed on another instrument. We speak of resonance identification when that emotional state which the ego duplicates within itself continues to be acknowledged by it in the other ego. As in the second instrument, emotional states of other people are only echoed and not permanently established in one's own ego. All our vicarious gratifications from the inner experiences of other individuals are based on emotional resonance. We also participate emotionally in other persons' sufferings. The phenomena of sympathy, empathy, pity, and compassion are all based on resonance identification, although they differ from one another. But the distress which we may feel in perceiving other people's disastrous experiences is not necessarily or solely due to our participation by resonance in their painful states.

Often it is due to our realization that the same misfortune can happen to us. For instance, to see a severely psychotic person, senselessly screaming, gesticulating, soiling and gibbering, automatically evokes in us the feelings, "There but for the grace of God go I." The fear and horror that untrained persons have of the insane, as they imagine them, are generally known and understood. The possibility of ego disintegration and loss of the sense of reality is a truly frightening thought. This author has also encountered psychotic patients who, in better contact with their environment, recognized the fear which they aroused in others.

Feelings of sympathy and compassion, especially for persons we love and/or identify with emotionally, function as "moral" factors in our behavior with our fellow-beings. Sometimes we refrain from our pursuit of pleasure because we may hurt others. The restraining factors of resonance identification, however, do not constitute the phenomenon of "conscience." Conscience is a function of the mental substructure called the "superego," which we shall discuss in the next pages.

In order to maintain the feeling of its own individual existence, the ego is very dependent on contacts with other egos. This is well illustrated by the terrifying experiences of solitary mountain climbers, of shipwrecked seamen, or of persons who venture alone into the desert. Such a person—alone on a glacier, or drifting on a raft in the open sea, or wandering in the desert vastness, without sight of another human being for an extended length of time—is sometimes caught in a panic which compels him to run or speed-up his raft (as the case may be) in an uncontrollable urge to contact another creature—any living soul.

The most essential factor operative in interpersonal relationships is the ego's need for survival and self-assertion. The ego as a member of a group is motivated in its behavior by two sets of urges, which are manifested in different persons in different proportions. On the one hand, the self-preservation drive, expressing itself in a new form, induces the ego to assert itself. The ego feels its own existence more strongly when it is noted and acknowledged by the group. We call narcissistic its urge to assert itself and to gain status within the group, the community and society. To feel useless and unimportant causes deep depression. Each person develops in his mind an idea of an ideal figure, the "ego ideal." The more closely he approaches this ideal, the more he feels gratified in his narcissism; and the more he differs from it, the more he feels injured.

On the other hand, the "ego feeling" extends to a "we feeling," and the self-preservative drive acquires another aspect. It grows to include a drive for preservation of the group, society and mankind. In extreme cases an individual may sacrifice himself to save the group. In such cases the "we feeling" of the self-preservative drive has become more important than the "ego feeling." The "we feeling" can be called the "social ego."

Besides strengthening the ego, the "we" may be felt also as the ego's continuation. When we speak of events which occurred in times prior to our birth and also of prospective future events, we equate our predecessors and successors with ourselves. Although the "I" cannot be thought of as existing prior to one's birth or after one's death, the enlarged "we" feeling can be extended in time in both directions, into the past and into the future: "There was a time when *we* had no railroads or telephones," one may say. And, "Sometime *we* will conquer space."

Aging persons care about the persons they will leave behind and are interested in making provision for those who will live after their death. In the phenomenon of extension of the self-preservative drive to other persons the process of externalization plays the most important role. There are many ways in which we find portions of ourselves in other persons. One illustration was given above in our explanation of parental love.

So far we have discussed the ego's social behavior in terms of identification and externalization, with reference to anaclitic and narcissistic love and with reference to the self-preservation and self-assertive drives. Still we have not fully explained what factors determine our feelings of closeness and attraction or enmity and antagonism to other individuals, or what factors, besides resonance identification, serve as controls and restraints upon us in our interpersonal relationships. To this end, and in order to understand more clearly the various states and emotional attitudes of the ego, we must now consider the two other mental substructures with which the ego is inseparably related, the superego and the id.

VIII

Superego Formation

WE have in our mental apparatus an internalized and egotized authority which directs and censures our behavior and our thoughts. In fact, this internal authority monopolizes the ego's function of self-observation. We do some things, without the motivation of pleasure, because we have the feeling that they are "right," and we reject certain temptations because we feel that they are "wrong." This feeling of "conscience," or moral responsibility for our behavior, is the main function of the superego and the most commonly recognized. But the concept of conscience is in itself ambiguous, and furthermore, the superego formation cannot be described merely as an internalized and egotized policeman. In order to comprehend the complexities of the superego and the ego's relation to it, we must understand its origin. We must also have some knowledge of the instinctive drives which arise from the id, since the ego struggles continually to integrate opposing demands of these two substructures.

The various instinctive drives and their development will be considered in detail in the third section. For the purpose of this discussion, however, we may accept the fact that sexual drives are present in the individual from the beginning of life and pass through several developmental stages before they lead to their biological function. These discoveries of Freud, although cause for great shock at the time, are now becoming increasingly better accepted among educated people.

The superego arises from the process of identification of the incorporative type.[1] The importance of primary identification for the ego's structuralization has been illustrated above. In later life, too, the processes of identification, partial and total, are constantly taking place. Identification in later life, however, is not called "primary identification," despite the fact that such identification does bring about lasting autoplastic changes in the ego.

30

One of the many functions of identification is the replacement of a love object. This function is especially clear in the ego's reaction to the death of a person whom it cannot renounce. In an attempt to overcome its grief reaction the ego makes itself similar to the dead person, thus substituting him by autoplastic duplication. We may call this type of identification a "substitutive" one. The object becomes incorporated in the ego. Substitutive identification occurs also when the internalized person is still alive. It plays an important role in the child's relationship with his parents. Moreover, psychoanalytic investigation has revealed that such identifications express not only positive, loving feelings toward the internalized person but also feelings of hostility.

We have already discussed the connection between the innate tendency toward oral incorporation, or "eating up" the object, and the process of identification. But we should likewise note that whenever an object is eaten up, it is by the same token destroyed. In the beliefs of primitive peoples and in folklore a person acquires the features and properties of the beings—human and otherwise—that he devoured. The very act of "substitution" contains the implication of removing the substituted object, and substitutive identification is often the result of both positive and negative feelings toward the person who has been internalized. To have feelings of both love and hate for an object is called "ambivalence."

To understand the development of the superego formation we must make use of further knowledge regarding interpersonal relationships within the family, not only relationships between parents and children, but also between siblings. This knowledge, and the conclusions we draw from it, can also be applied to some aspects of group psychology, although it is not our purpose to enter here into this broad field of investigation.

The child has an ambivalent emotional attitude toward his parents, as we shall see, and also toward his siblings. Siblings compete with each other. A newborn child is felt by his siblings as an intruder with whom they must share parental love. Yet the parents' condemning attitude toward manifest hostility eventually induces them to accept the newcomer and share the parents with him. The anaclitic love for his parents, which develops from the child's dependence on them for satisfaction of his vital needs, enhances his identification with them, both resonance identification and permanent structural identification. Therefore, when he realizes that his parents love his siblings also, he has two opposing responses. On one hand, he is jealous and desires his siblings' disappearance; on the other, he feels that he must love them as his parents do and as they expect him to do. As a rule common interests, the sharing of the parents and mutual identification with them lead to a strong "we feeling" which includes siblings and parents. Protective attitudes of brothers and motherly feelings of sisters toward younger siblings are common and well-understood occurrences.

These positive feelings, however, are to some degree the effect of a struggle. In its effort to integrate or ward off hostile feelings the ego mobilizes various affects and emotions. Feelings of love for another person, for example, can be enhanced by successful repression by the ego of hostile impulses toward him. Thus, feelings of hatred, which are encompassed in an ambivalent attitude toward another person, may remain eclipsed, but they are not necessarily deprived of their drive cathexis. Feelings of love may increase as a defense against repressed hostility. Such an increased love is called "reaction formation," and its dynamic expression is a "counter-cathexis or anti-cathexis" to the cathexis of the repressed drives. Without such a counter-balancing force the ego could not ward off successfully the objectionable drives. For the time being, let us keep in mind that the positive feelings of siblings to each other and to the parents may have various components.

Boys and girls alike develop anaclitic love for their mothers. But under normal conditions boys remain more affectionate toward their mothers, and girls turn their tender attachment to their fathers. This preference of the child for the parent of the opposite sex is a normal manifestation of the sexual drive. It becomes more apparent between the ages of two and five. Sexual attraction and curiosity is a common observation among siblings and toward the parent of the opposite sex.

How much a boy needs his father emotionally is clear to everyone. He longs for his father's protection and teaching, for his praise and recognition. Father represents for him an image of virility and power, which serves as a model for his own development, as an "identification pattern." On the other hand, the child resents his father's control, prohibitions and punishments. We shall soon learn that many of the child's emotional attitudes, and the most important ones, are not preserved in adult memory, but are eclipsed by the phenomenon of repression. This is so in the complications of a boy's relation to his father. These complications derive from his tender attachment to his mother, which shows clearly a sexual character. From his longing for his mother strong feelings of rivalry toward his father develop. These feelings of the child toward his parents were designated by Freud as the "oedipus complex," a term taken from the Greek myth of King Oedipus who killed his father and unwittingly married his own mother. Likewise, a girl feels in her mother a rival in her love for her father.

These psychological events in the child's development might be considered as a mild ontogenetic repetition of the most decisive phase of development of human society, though many anthropologists would disagree. From anthropological studies of primitive societies as well as from research in comparative religion, Freud reached the conclusion that in a certain phase of social development brothers allied themselves with one another to kill their father so as to have access to the women who, previously, were in the father's exclusive possession. Without further elaboration on this subject, it is sufficient to say that a boy's feelings toward his father are constitutionally very ambivalent. The child's identification with the parent of the same sex is a substitutive one. The boy himself wishes to become the father. From such an identification, which is most apparent between the ages of five and twelve, the superego develops. The libidinal as well as the aggressive cathexes, which adhered to the oedipus complex, then give strength to the superego. Other later authority figures also become integrated in this powerful substructure.

In order to grasp fully the nature of the superego one has to realize that identifications with powerful and perfect images, to which the ego cannot possibly measure up, must effect the ego in a particular way. How can the child's ego integrate its feelings of smallness, weakness, ignorance, and utter dependency on parental figures, with its feelings of being powerful and omniscient itself? Identification with these figures, whom the child loves and fears and without whom he could not survive and develop, must lead to a special structural differentiation within the ego. It is this structural development which gives rise to an ego state which cannot be fused with one's authentic ego nor with those internalized images which it could assimilate. This ego state lives an essentially autonomous existence and develops its own boundaries which separate it from the ego, but it is nevertheless related to the rest of the unified ego. Therefore, in agreement with Federn's concept of the ego as a mental state, the present author considers the superego not only as a substructure of the mind, but as an ego state as well.

Fear of being punished and losing parental love undergoes a transformation through identification with parental figures, and the fear of those external dangers is replaced by one's own conscience with its feelings of guilt and need for self-punishment. The fear of a specific punishment for sexual desires is the innate fear of being deprived of the penis. Freud called this fear "castration fear," although this term does not correspond to the actual meaning of the feared punishment.

One must not forget that the superego is encompassed in the ego feeling, although it forms a separate structure within the ego. Freud gave expression to this state of affairs by characterizing the superego as "a step within the ego." This expression conveys clearly the idea of the unevenness existing between the ego and the supergo. It would be consistent with this concept to call the superego the "above me," which is externalized in the concept of God, the heavenly father.

Although there are forerunners of the superego, Freud considered it as the heir of the oedipus complex. It would, however, be a mistake to consider every kind of early or later identification as pertaining to the superego. In the developmental process of becoming a man, exercising all mature masculine functions, the masculine ego has to free itself from the domination and restrictions of the (archaic) father by internalizing him, or to use the common psychoanalytic term, by "introjecting" him within itself. An analogous process occurs in the female. As a matter of fact, the superego contains both parents.

Normally the individual is unaware of the moral demands of the superego which influence his thoughts and behavior. The superego may take a threatening and aggressive role or a loving and protecting role, depending on the quantity and quality of its cathexis. In conditions of misfortune one may experience feelings of self-consolation, without, however, attributing these feelings to any separate portion of his mind. In this case he himself assumes autoplastically the attitude, toward himself, of a benevolent father who pats his head with the words, "Don't worry; everything will turn out all right." But not everyone possesses such a supporting and encouraging superego.

Let us repeat that the superego, which shows in different individuals different degrees of severity and loving support and also different demands and exigencies, is an egotized portion of the mind. Therefore, the ego feels the requests of the superego as its own. The ego simply does not feel like committing criminal acts and does perform its duties, out of an inner disposition to do so. It feels morally comfortable when it behaves in one way, and feels guilty, ready to accept or impose punishment upon itself, when it behaves in another. Briefly, the function of a well-developed superego is no longer related to the thought of a parental figure or any other external authority. Only in the case of forbidden temptations, and even more of forbidden deeds which have been committed, does the ego feel within itself a split between its drives and actions and the superego.

Later we shall become acquainted with another mental phenomenon which is also responsible for our moral behavior and is strongly related to the thought of persons with whom one is in emotional contact. This author called this phenomenon, which is related to the superego, "psychic presence."

NOTES

(1) In psychoanalytic literature this phenomenon is called "introjection," an expression for the ego's acquisition of the qualities of the object by its oral incorporation. We must realize, however, that the metapsychological phenomenon of the extension of ego cathexis over the autoplastic duplication of the object has nothing to do with an act of throwing (of "jecting") something within one's self. Therefore, we prefer to avoid the term "introjection."

IX

The Phenomenon of Repression

THE ego struggles continuously to achieve the best possible integration, although it seldom succeeds completely. Its instinctive drives and various wishes urge it to seek gratification. But the conditions of the external world, its regard for the rights of others, and its understanding of the consequences of its actions limit this search for gratification. In addition, it must conform to its conscience, a function, as we have just seen, which is exercised by the superego. If as Freud says, it is difficult to serve two masters, then it must be even more difficult to serve three: the instinctive drives arising from the id, the external world, and the superego.

Sometimes the integrative task which the ego has to face is too difficult. This situation can be better grasped if we compare an inner danger with an external one.

Self-preservation requires the restraining of the afflux of stimuli and excitation from the periphery of our body to the central nervous system. Our body possesses an anatomical barrier—the skin with its corneous layer—against stimuli from the external world. The very vulnerable brain is also protected by the skull. In normal conditions external stimuli enter the mental apparatus only in small quantities through the peripheral sense organs. Stimuli are perceived according to their nature as visual, auditory, olfactory, tactile sensations, etc. If, however, the protective barrier is broken through in some place, an unchecked stream of excitation enters the central mental apparatus from the point of lesion. This condition is called "trauma" or "a traumatic condition," meaning "injury."

In Freud's description, an immense "counter-charge" is called upon in order to create all around the breach a *dynamic* barrier against the penetrating excessive stimulation. The ego experiences pain. As an economic consequence of such a defensive effort a widespread paralysis or diminution of other mental activities follows, since a great amount of cathexis, which powers these functions, is employed for the conversion of the invading new excitation from a free-floating into a "quiescent" charge of energy. In other words, the "erupting stream" must be stopped. It must be "bound."

The ego, however, is provided with no such protective anatomical barrier (*Reizschutz*) against *internal* stimuli. If such stimuli are excessive, it must deal with them dynamically, as it does in case of a lesion of the anatomical barrier against external stimuli. Among the internal stimuli we must first consider those which power the instinctive drives. The ego, as a unity, must meet and deal with these stimuli in a way appropriate to its integrative task. If drives which interfere with this task reach an uncontrollable strength, the ego may feel traumatized in a manner analogous to breaking through the anatomical barrier against external stimuli. The ego's reaction to a threat of a traumatic condition is the feeling of anxiety. If the threat is mild and the ego can cope with it, the anxiety experience has the character of a "danger signal." If, however, the threat is a trauma of unmasterable nature, the ego enters into a state of panic which paralyzes it. It becomes impoverished of available cathexis quantities.

Psychoanalysis describes many ways in which the ego resorts to defensive measures. In the ego's defensive efforts the shifting and displacement of the egotizing cathexis plays a great role. For example a drive may be externalized and ascribed to another person. In psychoanalytic literature we call this phenomenon "projection," a term which is used for different processes.[1] On the other hand a feared object may become incorporated into the ego.

When he conceived the most important defense mechanism—repression—Freud made his most original discovery. This and the other pioneering discoveries of Freud dwarfed all previous psychological knowledge and unfolded a completely new field of mental phenomena. Freud asserted that mental phenomena per se are unconscious, and from the time of his earliest researches he conceived the phenomenon of consciousness only as a sense organ for the perception of mental qualities. In his view, mental phenomena come into being independently, whether or not they are perceived by the ego, just as objects and phenomena of the external world exist independently, whether or not they are perceived by an individual.

The relation of consciousness to the ego and ego feeling will require special consideration later.

Freud discovered that objectionable drives condemned by the superego, as well as the memories of shocking experiences, can remain altogether excluded from the ego's field of operation. They remain excluded even from the preconscious. In Federn's concept the ego feeling does not extend over the repressed drives and memories. The implication of the process of repression is that the ego does not become conscious of these repressed drives and memories, nor does the ego feeling extend over them, even when they reach a high degree of intensity. Thus, whether or not they become included within the ego depends not only on the degree of intensity of a drive or memory, but also on the ego's readiness and integrative capacity to include them in its field of operation.

The act of repression is rightly considered by Freud as a performance of the ego. Yet, in his opinion, the repressive process itself, as well as the repressed contents, are completely unconscious to the ego. It is quite understandable that the act of repression implies a strong dynamic exertion on the part of the ego, proportional to the strength of the repressed content. The ego has to resist the impact of the repressed drives and the related representations and memories, which tend to force their way into the ego's territory. The conditions and specific mental material of repression will be dealt with later.

The phenomenon of repression should not be confused with *conscious* efforts on the part of the ego to keep some mental content out of its consciousness. The recognition of this phenomenon required a special act of discovery by Freud. Its description from a phenomenological point of view is not "I am repressing" but "repression occurs and I do not know anything about it."

Repression seems similar to the involuntary physiological phenomena, such as the reflexes. We do not perform them; they take place in us. But although we become aware of some reflexes, we remain unaware of the phenomenon of repression. One important question forces itself now upon our minds: If we equate ego with conscious ego feeling, and consider repression as an act of the ego, must the ego not feel that it is repressing something?

The phenomenon of repression is not well suited to demonstrating that the ego feeling actually extends over all the ego's performances. Repression takes place just at the inner border of the ego, which separates it from the inner non-ego territory. All phenomena and contents within the non-ego mental territory are of course devoid of any ego feeling. Accordingly, it does not extend over the repressed contents. The ego is not conscious of, nor has any feeling of, the repressed drives and memories. But the ego has a conscious feeling of its resistances against the repressed material, although it cannot possibly sense what this material is. Freud believed, however, that the ego's resistance against the repressed contents was also unconscious to it. At any rate, according to Freud, the ego acquires certain conscious features and behavior patterns which reveal to the psychoanalyst the nature of the repressed drives. This is the case, for instance, in reaction formations mentioned above.

We now return to our analogy between the phenomenon of repression and the physiological reflex mechanism. In the process of repression the ego withdraws from objectionable mental contents actually in a reflexlike manner. In fact, the withdrawal can be considered as an intermediate act between a physiological reflex and a voluntary act. In a similar way a person withdraws his hand in a "reflexlike" manner from a hot object with which it accidentally comes in contact. If we ask the person who withdrew his hand, "Who made this movement?", he will certainly answer, "I." In fact, in the act of withdrawal he used his voluntary muscular apparatus, the control of which is felt as a function of the ego. In many other reflexlike actions, likewise, functions which are ordinarily used by the ego may participate. But, whereas in the reflexlike withdrawal of the hand the ego knows very well wherefrom it withdraws the hand, in the case of repression the ego ignores completely which mental content it has left behind in the non-ego mental field. Therefore, it is difficult to understand how the ego's resistance, which maintains the repression dynamically, can be encompassed in the ego feeling while the contents against which the resistance is directed are not encompassed.

In cases in which no ego function participates in the reflex act, one does not indicate that the "I" was the author of the act. If we ask of someone whose pupils contract under stimulation from light or whose heart pounds under some physical or emotional stress,

"Who are the authors of these acts?", he will never say, "I," but rather "My pupils contract, not I." "My heart is pounding, not I."

For a full understanding of the "id" it is necessary to realize that the feeling of "I-ness" does not extend over *all* mental processes which take place in our own mind.

Mental representatives of the most important instinctive drives, and memories of emotional events which had decisive influence in the development of a child's personality, undergo repression. We mentioned some of these in the last chapter, namely, the oedipus complex, castration fear, and ambivalent feelings toward parents and siblings. Because of this repression in his own experience the unprepared reader has difficulties in accepting these findings. His resistance against them arouses in him the sensation that the human mind, especially his own, could not have harbored such contents. Here we have an example of the way in which the superego participates also in the formation of our judgments as well as in the function of reality testing.

Before concluding this preliminary presentation of the process of repression we should mention that Freud postulated a first phase of this phenomenon, which he called primal repression (*Urverdrängung*). It consists of the refusal by the ego to admit into consciousness the mental representatives of a given instinctive drive. The correct description of this process is that such representatives do not obtain preconscious cathexis, that is, ego cathexis. This blockage determines what Freud calls a "fixation" of a drive in the unconscious. This means that from then on the drive and its mental representatives remain unchanged in the unconscious id, constituting a center of attraction for other mental contents. Later in life the derivatives of the mental contents which underwent primal repression, as well as emotional contents of other origin which entered into an associative connection with the repressed ones, undergo repression proper. The dynamic description of repression proper must consider both the pulling force and the pushing force. The ego rejects a given mental content; it pushes it away. Simultaneously this content is pulled into the unconscious id by the center of attraction just mentioned. Unpleasant or objectionable mental contents and urges of the adult ego which are *not* derivatives of the repressed ones or have *not* entered into an associative connection with them, cannot be repressed. The ego must deal with them in other ways.

NOTES

(1) The author prefers to avoid this term, used in the sense of externalization, as he does the term "introjection" for incorporation. See Note (1) to Chapter VIII.

X

The Concept of the Id

ALL prepsychoanalytic psychology (which was merely ego psychology) contributed very little to the understanding of the ego phenomenon itself. However, through psychoanalytic investigation, which extends its studies over the ego's relation to that extraterritorial mental field called "the id," many functions of the ego as well as its normal and pathological manifestations have been brought nearer to our comprehension.

In order to understand the meaning of the term "the id," let us continue briefly with our consideration of the phenomenon of repression. What happens to the repressed mental contents? We learned that they cannot become conscious, that they are excluded from the field covered by ego feeling, and are accordingly unavailable to the ego. But repression does not extinguish them altogether as mental phenomena. It is true that repressed mental contents are not subjected to the countless ego functions. They do not have access to the voluntary muscular apparatus, which is monopolized by the ego. They are not included in the ego's thinking process. They are not subjected to reality testing and have no relation to the sense of reality. But they do have a kind of existence quite different from that familiar to us from conscious experiences. In the id there is no discrimination between real and unreal, that is, between material existing in the object (or external) world and material only thought of. The psychological processes to which id phenomena are subjected would seem extremely strange to the ego. And yet their existence as mental phenomena is unmistakably revealed by their indirect effects on the ego, namely, by some of the ego's behavior patterns and conscious mental contents, feelings and emotions. They are revealed in many character traits of both well-adjusted and neurotic persons. They may appear as distant derivatives of, or reaction formations to, repressed mental phenom-

ena. They are revealed in dreams, in the hallucinations of psychotics, in the symptoms of neurotics, in mistakes and failures in the
ego's functioning, and in many other observable manifestations. All
these phenomena become comprehensible only through the inter-
polation of the derived id phenomena and the understanding of the
specific psychological laws to which they are subjected.

To clarify the meaning of the designation "the id" we return once
more to the comparison of the id phenomena with physiological
phenomena. We understand that the extraterritorial mental phenomena, that is, the id, are beyond the ego's control just as are the
physiological processes. When the ego becomes aware of some
effect of phenomena in either of these two fields, it does not indicate
"I" as the source of such effects but uses instead a pronoun indicat-
ing someone or something else. Prepsychoanalytic psychology did
not distinguish, among the internal non-ego phenomena, the physiological from the mental. Dreams and the hallucinations of psychotics were thought to be produced by undetectable, minute,
accidental brain stimulations, and no psychological significance was
sought behind them.

Freud, who discovered the psychological field of the non-ego
mental phenomena, designated it by the neutral impersonal pronoun of the third person, using it as a noun. In German this term is
"*das Es*," which was borrowed from Nietzsche by Georg Groddek
who introduced it to psychoanalysis with a slightly different meaning. The English translation of this noun would be "the it," but again
as with the ego it was replaced by the Latin "the id." The ego-alien
mental field is called "the id" because it is not felt by anyone as belonging to what he calls "I." This strengthens our opinion that the
ego and ego feeling are equivalent.

We said that in the process of repression drives and memories are
not absorbed by the ego but are left behind in the id. This implies that instinctive drives and memories arise in general from the
id, whether they are included by the ego within its field of operation
or not. We must consider them in their dynamic aspect as expression
of forces exerting a pressure on the ego in order to be encompassed
into its unity. Normally only through the ego's intervention can their
tension find an outlet into feelings, affects and emotions, as well as
into muscular actions. On the other hand, we know that the ego *can-*

not choose the wishes and drives which it would like to possess but can only deal in various ways, according to its integrative organization and capacity, with the instinctive drives which it experiences. When the ego absorbs mental contents arising from the id, it feels them as belonging to itself. They then determine the ego's emotional motivations for its behavior and its states. We can say that such contents, having been absorbed, are invested by the ego, or ego feeling. The expression "they are egotized" means that they are taken into the field of operation of the ego and thus are no longer subjected to the processes of the id.

If we ask of a person who is angry, or who hates or loves something or somebody, or who experiences various urges and desires, "Who has these experiences?", he will answer naturally, "I am angry," "I hate or love," and so on. Sometimes an ego may feel desires and emotions which it does not like to have. In other cases it fails to experience certain wishes and longings which it would like to experience. Such situations of inner disappointments and conflicts make the ego realize clearly that it has not the power to choose its own instinctive drives and emotions. It lacks the capacity to produce or prevent the emergence of wishes and urges according to its likes or dislikes.

We are well aware that our needs and instinctive drives are products of specific physiological stimulations. Hunger, thirst, the need for oxygen, etc., are derived from well-studied physiological conditions. Love and the sexual drives are responses to specific hormonal functions. We know too that emotional states may in turn have an effect on the functioning of the endocrine glands, for there exists a complex interaction between emotional and physiological phenomena. This has become particularly clear from studies in psychosomatic medicine. Physicians who underestimate the inhibiting and stimulating power of psychological factors over the instinctive drives, and the endocrine system responsible for them, often resort to a hormonal therapy in cases of drive deficiencies or for disturbances whose effects may be due to psychological factors.

In order to summarize and simplify the issue we shall say that excitations within the organism, due to various biological processes, power the instinctive drives with their pertinent cathexes. The specific directions of such driving forces are due not only to constitutional predispositions but also to the environmental experiences of the individual, particularly in the most decisive phases of his development. All mental representatives of the various instinctive drives, conscious as well as repressed ones, come into being in the id before they obtain ego cathexis. They are rooted in the id where they are provided with drive cathexis. The accepted ones, which cause specific emotional and driving ego states, obtain, in addition to the drive cathexis, the preconscious ego cathexis. We shall now try to elucidate the decisive dynamic consequences of the drives' inclusion within the ego unity.

It is evident that the vital needs strongly resist the repressive attempts of the ego, whereas drives which are not essential for physical survival can yield to repression and renunciation of satisfaction of such drives can be endured. The process to which the unegotized mental phenomena are subjected can best be investigated through the perceived results of their action. The most accessible source for such an investigation is the dream experience.

In every dream we can distinguish the non-ego from the ego mental field. Upon awakening the dreamer realizes that it was the "I" which had the dream. But the ego states and the manner of the ego's operation during a dream are quite different from those of waking life. This illustrates the ego's continuity in spite of its continuously changing states. It is the ego itself, the same ego of waking life, which perceives the dream scenes and images and which reacts to them. Again, if we ask a person who had a dream whose production the dream was, he would certainly not say, "I." *It* just happened that a dream world, that is, an hallucinated one, appeared to his perception but in a manner similar to that in which the real external world presents itself to him in waking life. In a state of sleep some inner phenomena are perceived by him as external realities, though upon awakening they may seem illogical and strange. Since we see no sense in most of our dreams—some dreams could not even be fancied by the dreamer—we can easily understand the belief of the prepsychoanalytic psychologists that dreams were the effect of brain stimulations. But as we discovered, every dream scene has a psychological meaning, emerging from a special mental activity whose "id character" now appears very clear to us. We also realize that the unrevealed meaningful content of the dream must have undergone a distortion in the id, so that our comprehension of it became obscured.

The specific techniques used in dream interpretation will be discussed in a later section. Here we shall report a short dream merely
to illustrate some of the psychological processes to which mental representations are subjected in the id. A woman dreamed that she was
leafing through a book and noticed that the pages were sticky and
stained. She was horrified to find that the stains were those of blood
and could not think how such marks came to be on the book. She
became more and more troubled and finally awoke with sensations
of pain. Actually, this pain was caused by contractions of the uterus,
for during sleep menstruation had set in, some days after it was due.

In the state of sleep this woman's dreaming ego was quite unaware
that menstruation had taken place. Yet the bloodstains in her dream
were undoubtedly related to the onset of this process. Her genitalia
do not actually appear in the dream but are symbolically represented
(or "substituted") by pages of a book. While an analysis of this
dream disclosed nearly all of the woman's sexual history, we shall
concentrate at this point on the substitution of the pages of the book
for her genitalia. What actually happened was that one representation became substituted by another while a part of her body was
externalized. Here we see a general process which takes place in the
id.

Single representations or images are easily substituted by others
through paths of what may seem the most superficial associations.
But accurate analysis of concrete cases often shows a deeper, more
significant connection between original and substituted images.
At any rate, substitution of one representation by another reveals
that in the id the stimulating charge of energy, the cathexis, is not
"bound" to single representations but finds itself in a "free-floating"
state, arousing the representations on which it becomes displaced.
This differentiation between "free" and "bound" energy, which explains a great number of psychodynamic processes, was made very
early by Freud and his collaborator Josef Breuer.[1]

Freud called the process of free-floating cathexis the "primary
mental process." This primary process is characteristic of the operation of mental activity in the id. Cathexis, blocked from emotional
and motoric discharge, flows from one mental content to another,

causing a state which seems extremely chaotic. Substitution of one representation by another is not the only effect of the primary mental process. The cathexes of two or more representations may condense themselves on one representation, thus arousing this representation to a high degree of intensity. Or two or more representations may be evoked simultaneously, giving rise to a single representation which is a combination of two or more representations. One idea may even be substituted by its opposite. A crowd, for instance, may stand for the idea of secrecy.

It is evident that in a mental system in which the primary mental process rules no thinking comparable to the known process of the ego can take place. According to Freud, the concept of time is not contained in the mental operation of the id. In the id mental contents are not arranged in a time sequence. An event which should follow another may precede it in the dream.

The ways in which mental contents are affected by the primary mental process can be inferred from the products which eventually do come to the ego's awareness. All representatives of the drives and all memory traces of past experiences are located in the id. Those contents which do not become ego-cathected, that is, do not obtain preconscious cathexis, are subjected to the primary mental process. In other words, the drive cathexis does not adhere, in the id, to the single mental contents, but migrates from one to another along associative and inherited (archaic unconscious) paths. Such a shift of cathexis may result in a displacement of feelings, affects and emotions from an original mental content to one which then does come to the ego's consciousness.

In the dream the woman's preoccupation about her menstruation appeared displaced and thus substituted by her worries about the bloodstained pages of a book. This cathexis could not be discharged into an affect as long as it adhered to a representation which lacked the binding preconscious cathexis, but as soon as the displaced cathexis aroused a representation which did come to her consciousness, then the cathexis found an emotional outlet. Such affect displacements are very frequent and particularly evident in the symptomatology of phobias and obsessional neuroses.

This dream also illustrates many other effects of the primary mental process. In the id opposite tendencies do not annul each other but lead to a compromise formation. In the course of this woman's analysis we learned that she wanted to be sure that she could conceive, but for practical reasons she had decided to take the necessary precautions against pregnancy. She would have been surprised if menstruation had not occurred. As a child she had not been told about sexual functions, and when at the age of eleven she experienced her first menstruation, she was frightened by the bleeding. She feared she might have injured herself through masturbation, for which she felt very guilty. Playing with female genitalia is frequently displaced in dreams to the representation of handling or turning the pages of a book. The condensation of thoughts which appears in this dream is quite clear.

More data from this woman's history show further effects of the mobile state of the cathexis. The delay in her menstruation had worried her. But this worry aroused in the id, through associative paths, the repressed feeling of guilt which she had experienced when she indulged in masturbation, namely, that her bleeding was the result of self-inflicted injury. In the id time and causality relationships do not exist; we must add them in our interpretation by proper words. In the dream the idea that "she was turning the pages of a book and noticed that they were sticky and stained" has the following meaning : *Because* (this word has to be added) she had masturbated her genitalia were bleeding. The ego's feeling in the dream that "she was mortified to observe that the marks were bloodstains" has two meanings when we reverse the effect of the primary mental process. It means that at the time of her first menstruation she was mortified when she noticed the bleeding, but also that she was unhappy at not having obtained proof that she could conceive as normal women can. As mentioned before, "she was surprised at this and could not think how such stains came to be on the book." This expresses surprise at the opposite fact, namely, that she would have been surprised if she had failed to menstruate in view of the precautions taken. The image of being "soiled" or "stained," as well as of being "infected," is a frequent substitution for having been impregnated. We also notice that bodily pain, caused by contractions of the uterus, does not appear as such in the dream but is replaced by mental distress.

We have not concluded our analysis of this dream, and the data presented here were chosen solely to illustrate some effects of the primary mental process. The goal of the dreaming activity will be dealt with in a later section when the dream theory is presented.

Many more traits characterize the primary mental process. Since the id has no integrating unity which can evaluate mental content, no denial of a fact or rejection of an impulse can occur. In our thinking during waking life we can affirm or deny a content or accept or reject a wish. But concepts of "yes" and "no" do not exist in the id. Either a mental content is aroused there or it does not appear. Besides, in the id mental contents are not expressed in words.

When mental contents arising from the id are taken into the sphere of operation of the ego, i.e., when they also become cathected by the unifying ego cathexis, the primary mental process comes to an end. The preconscious cathexis fixes the cathexis derived from the id on the single mental contents, binds it, so that it can then no longer be displaced to other contents. The egotized mental contents are no longer substituted by others. Verbal expressions are added to the representations of sensorial qualities. This fixing or binding process by the preconscious cathexis was called by Freud the "secondary mental process." This fixation of the cathexis to the pertinent contents is an understandable prerequisite for the ego's functions: logical thinking; determining relationships of time, space and causality; distinguishing between real and unreal; making judgments, affirmations and denials, etc. It is only through the operation of the secondary mental process that the unity becomes properly dynamically equipped to deal with external reality in seeking gratification of egotized needs and instinctive drives arising from the id.

NOTES

(1) Breuer, Josef, and Freud, Sigmund. Studies on Hysteria (1893-1895). Standard Edition, 2. London, Hogarth, 1955. See especially the footnote on p. 194.

XI

Interaction of the Three Mental Substructures

WE learned in the preceding chapters that mental contents which became absorbed by the ego have emerged from the id. If their access to the ego is blocked, mental data are subjected to the primary mental process. But when mental material is included within the ego unity, it is bound by its cathexis to the pertinent contents. This is the secondary mental process. In this process representations of things (objects) obtain verbal expressions, and words express also relations of time, space and causality. Even though non-verbal thinking acts do occur, the acquisition of verbal expressions is essential for the thinking process.

Inclusion of all mental material within the ego would amount to a unification of the id and the ego. There would be no separation between these two substructures but only two *phases* of mental activity. Some psychoanalysts assume that this state of affairs must prevail in the first year of life. However that may be, the secondary mental process unifies the accepted mental data of the id with the ego.

Inherent in the phenomenon of life itself is the existence of a unifying or binding tendency. The concepts of "synthesis" and "integration" are expressions of this tendency, without which life could not be imagined. Freud called this tendency Eros, and to its dynamic expression he gave the name, libido. Nunberg sees Eros as "the tendency to join other objects, with the aim of creating a new unit." [1] In the integrative and synthetic activity of the ego the libido is devoid of sexual meaning; in other words, it is desexualized. In his concept of the synthetic function, Nunberg considers not only the unifying process but also the new creation resulting from it. In fact, this is consistent with the meaning of the term "synthesis": putting together different things from which a new form comes into being. The term "integration" means bringing together the parts into a whole, irrespective of a new derivative formation. Whether in the living substance there is a basic tendency to create new forms of existence, or whether life in itself is basically conservative and any new creation is only the result of a successful effort to preserve life against newly arising obstacles, is a question which cannot be answered at this point. In any case, Nunberg's concept of the synthetic function includes integrating activities and encompasses, in addition, the idea of bringing forth a new form. The synthetic capacity of living matter constitutes *the* puzzle of life. In its most basic manifestation it is revealed in the creation of the most complex chemical compositions of organic substance, wherein different chemical elements are synthetized into new combinations with properties quite different from those of the original elements.

Nunberg describes in detail the synthetic processes, on the psychological level, performed by the ego, which does not tolerate contradictions. He examines the ways in which the ego tries to bring the various instinctual trends into harmony with the requirements of the external world and the superego. The search for causal connections between events which succeed each other is also an expression of the need to bind one event with the other. It is generally known that children ask more "whys" about observed and learned phenomena than adults can answer. Lack of causal understanding is often compensated by fictitious explanations, a mental attitude which is called "rationalization."

We have learned that much psychological material does not emerge into the ego's awareness in its original aspect but that only distant unrecognizable derivatives of them may be captured by the ego. We speak in this case of distortions of the latent id contents due to the primary mental process. Thus, we must distinguish the latent from the manifest content of mental experiences of the ego. The manifest content of instinctual trends, desires and memories is experienced by the healthy ego in waking life as inner phenomena, that is, as mental. But in dreams and in the hallucinations and delusions of psychotics, the manifest content is sensed as external reality. This difference in experience is due to the degree of functional (dynamic) capacity of the above-mentioned sense of reality. It is useful to repeat that sensing reality is the main function of the ego boundaries. In the psychotic and dreaming ego state mental contents from outside the ego strike the weakened inner ego boundaries without being included by the ego within itself. Therefore they are experienced as external realities. Conversely, in the waking state of the healthy ego its inner boundaries are cathected strongly enough to prevent the ego's perception of repressed wishes and memories. In order to reach the ego's awareness mental contents must first be included within the ego. Then, however, they are perceived as mental phenomena, that is, with "thought qualities." Freud explained that dreams, hallucinations and delusions are due to a deficiency in the testing of reality. Federn in his exploration of the psychotic process has come to different conclusions.

When mental contents undergo distortions as a result of the primary mental process, they may appear confusing to the ego. It is evident that through substitutions and fusions such contents, which are also unrelated to each other in terms of time, space and causality, may seem senseless to the rational ego. This is so whether the manifest content is perceived by the ego as external reality—as in dreams, hallucinations and delusions—or as inner mentality—as in the mental symptoms of phobic or obsessional patients.

Analysis of concrete cases shows that the ego's rational capacity has a selective influence over the substitute representations which eventually reach the ego's awareness. As we shall learn when we discuss phobias and obsessional neuroses, the source of the ego's fears in these conditions is always some internal danger arising out of unconcious conflicts.

Drives and temptations which are strongly cathected but repressed exercise a pressure toward the ego in order to be included by it. In the projective type of phobias the threat of the repressed urges, and of the dreaded consequences of their satisfaction, is projected onto external objects or situations. The representation of an aggressive or punitive father, or of one's own aggressive urges which may be absorbed by the superego in form of aggression against one's self, can be displaced on the representation of a wild animal or some destructive force of nature. The child's misinterpretation of adult sexual activity, which he may have witnessed, is that of a man aggressively overpowering a woman. This misconception of sexuality may be displaced also on the idea of aggression or any kind of frightening collision. Accordingly, affects and emotions inherent in the representatives of all sorts of repressed urges may be experienced in their displacement on substitutive representations. Not only are the objects and situations which the patient fears phobically chosen according to their relation to the specific repressed urges and the consequences of their satisfaction, but they must also be suitable for a rationalization of the phobic anxiety. Thus, one patient fears dogs because he can meet them in reality and they can bite him. Another is afraid to ride in a train because there may be an actual danger of collision, and so forth. In the phobia of the projective type the patient behaves like a person who is afraid of a possible real danger, but his fear is very exaggerated.

We understand that the rational need and capacity of an efficient ego revises the effects of the primary mental process, so that the perceived mental contents with their affective coloration make sense. This sense, however, is unrelated to the actual repressed material. In a dynamically defective ego such a secondary revision is more or less lacking. In fact, fears of quite absurd and impossible content are indicative of a schizophrenic affliction, latent or manifest, which is a disease of the ego. On the other hand, the most evident secondary revision of manifest contents is found in the delusional systems of intelligent paranoid patients. These patients often display such an ability to combine the most minute observable data, by simultaneous neglect of all the facts to the contrary, into such a logical structure, that often they are able to convince people in their environment that their persecutory fears are justified. From these and other clinical pictures we learn that a diseased ego may be deficient in one function and very efficient in another. In such patients a defective sense of reality is the result of weakly cathected inner boundaries, even while their thinking function is very efficient. Therefore, their capacity for testing reality would be quite adequate if only they felt the need to use it. But, as Federn has demonstrated, these patients do not make any attempt to scrutinize the feeling of certainty inherent in their delusional thoughts. Since their thoughts are felt to correspond to reality, the patients cannot possibly discover any error in their delusional conclusions.

Without embarking here on the concrete psychological mechanisms of paranoid delusions, we want only to mention that Federn elaborated a therapeutic approach to newly manifested delusions.

If the therapist can establish a proper rapport of confidence with the patient, he can direct the patient's attention and thoughts in a logical manner toward the facts which are in contradiction with the delusional content. When the patient is then induced to use his intellect for a proper testing of reality, he can no longer believe in the content of his delusion. His feeling of certainty about it dissolves, and he comes to recognize its mental origin. In other words, intelligent paranoid patients can maintain their delusions as long as they succeed in performing an effective secondary revision of the manifest content, so that it becomes compatible with their rational needs. The operation of the synthetic function of the ego appears here very evident. And the secondary revision of manifest contents illustrates also Waelder's concept of the "principle of multiple function." Any act and function of the ego must take care of various needs simultaneously. The ego's functions synthesize the gratification of various demands.

Substitutions of repressed representations are revealed not only in neurotic symptoms and dreams, but also in our conscious thinking of waking life. Such substitutions can be detected most easily in wishful fantasies, in that mental activity which we call daydreaming. Some people indulge in fantasies which are not always or exclusively directed by their conscious intentions. Sometimes thoughts appear in their minds without being consciously chosen. In the daydreamer's imagination the idea of an event or image usually appears interpolated. This phenomenon is quite similar to the appearance of dreams during sleep. The main difference between the two, however, is that the latter are experienced as hallucinations, with the character of "external reality," while thoughts which force themselves into a person's waking fantasy are sensed as "internal mentality," as unreal. In any case, in conscious fantasies as in dreams we can distinguish a latent from a manifest content.

Freud gave the name "introversion" to excessive indulgence in fantasies at the expense of satisfaction derived from external reality. In his opinion introversion is the precursor of neurosis.

An adult female patient reported a daydream which she had frequently in her teens while in high school. She was very fond of her English teacher, a handsome young man. But unfortunately she was poor in English composition. Her daydream was this:

She had written the most beautiful composition, and the teacher was reading it to the class. She thought particularly of two of her schoolmates who would be very envious of her success and her praise from the teacher. When the teacher was through with the reading, he handed her his fountain pen as a present. With it from now on she could write her compositions. Often in the midst of this fantasy the thought intruded itself upon her mind that the teacher's wife had died. This idea was not consciously chosen by her; nevertheless she felt she must integrate it into the framework of her daydream. In one version when the teacher arrived home after school he learned that his wife had been struck by a car and had died in the hospital. But for some reason the girl could not stick to this version. According to a more acceptable version, his wife had died from influenza, a disease which had actually taken many lives at the time of her fantasy. Since she was unable to disregard the idea of the death of the teacher's wife, her imagination was faced with the task of integrating the intruded idea with the rest of her fantasy. Even in her daydreaming she could not tolerate inconsistencies, and so she asked herself this question: If the teacher's wife had been so sick or had died right at the time of her own scholastic performance, how could the teacher have shown such enthusiasm about her composition? For the sake of coherence, therefore, the daydreaming girl had to make additions or alterations in the content of her fantasy. One solution might have been that the teacher's wife had been stricken by influenza long before the girl's performance. But, she thought, in previous years there was no lethal epidemic of influenza, so she must have died from another disease. This example illustrates a conscious secondary revision in operation.

There are two points which we want to make here. First, that this fantasy had a latent content. The patient had two sisters with whom as a child she could not compete in her father's love. The two envious schoolmates of her daydream were substitutes for her sisters. It is clear that the oedipus complex appears in a displacement on the teacher and his wife. Such a duplication, a new addition as it were of an old fantasy concerning the parents or siblings in a displacement on other people, is a very frequent occurrence. When it occurs during a psychoanalytic treatment, projected on the person of the therapist, we speak of transference. Feelings, emotions and expectancies appear repeated in a new edition, that is, transferred to the person of the psychoanalyst. Secondly, we notice that the ego, which does not tolerate contradictions and inconsistencies, performs a secondary revision of the raw material emerging from the id. Some additions, changes and alterations cannot be interpreted as pertaining to the latent content but take place only to smooth the facade of the manifest content.

In the first edition of his *Interpretation of Dreams* (1900), Freud showed that secondary revision occurs also in the ultimate formation of dreams during sleep. Thus, we realize that the ego's synthetic function also plays a part in shaping the manifest content of dreams. Alterations and distortions of the latent content are due, as we have seen, to the primary mental process. But then a secondary revision by the ego takes place in order to offset the confusion derived from substitutions and condensations to which the representations were subjected in the id. Some selecting action among the possible substitutive images, interpolations and additions are the work of the synthetic function of the ego, which operates by virtue of the secondary mental process. We conclude, therefore, that the ego has some activity even in the state of sleep while dreaming. It is true that the ego perceives its dreams passively. Nevertheless, as Freud has shown in his immortal work, the ego's censorship is never completely asleep.

This censoring agency, as Freud called it, is responsible for two effects: (1) It tries—and not always with success—to ward off expressions of representatives of repressed drives and wishes, unless through distortions these are no longer recognized in their true nature. (2) It performs the secondary revision of the manifest content as mentioned. But as everyone can experience from his own dreams, the secondary revision of dreams is often deficient, and it may even be entirely missing. Everybody can recall some very confusing and senseless dreams, or rather, confusing manifest content in their dreams. Lack of logical connections between single dream scenes and quite absurd sequences of events characterize these dreams if they are remembered at all upon awakening. This aspect of some dreams is an evident proof that the ego in dreaming state is not awakened to its full mnemonic and rational capacity. The most important events of one's own life may be completely ignored.

A person might dream that he is still living in an apartment or in a city which he had left many years ago. Another might dream of attending college without remembering that he had already received a master's or doctor's degree many years before. People dream of making boat trips on land without being aware that boats navigate only on water. Prepsychoanalytic psychologists who became interested in the dream phenomenon described only these deficiencies of the ego in its functioning during dreams, without the vaguest idea that all dreams have a latent meaning.

In the first chapter of the *Interpretation of Dreams,* where he reviews the scientific literature on dreams, Freud mentioned such observations by various authors. For example, there is Strümpell who said (1877), "In dreams our memory of the ordered contents of waking consciousness and of its normal behavior is as good as completely lost." A similar idea is expressed by Jodl (1896): "Every kind of conscious activity occurs in dreams, but only in an incomplete, inhibited, and isolated fashion." This author also said that "there is no critical faculty in dreams, no power of correcting one set of perceptions by reference to the general content of consciousness." But Freud did not follow up the conditions of the ego in the state of dreaming. His studies were directed elsewhere. The exploration of the ego at that time would have handicapped his monumental contributions to the understanding of the unconscious mental phenomena, a field completely ignored by his predecessors, and specifically his discovery that all dreams have a latent psychological meaning which is detectable by certain psychological procedures. He had to look straight forward, without diverting his sight to lateral issues. Only in this way could he discover the primary mental process and the dream work which, through substitutions and condensations and archaic symbols, as well as through visual representations of abstract thoughts, leads to an unrecognizable distortion of the latent dream content.

In any case, we repeat, the ego also participates in every dream, even if only as a passive perceiving agent. It also participates, as indicated above, in censoring the contents emerging from the id and, more or less, in exercising some secondary revision of the distorted contents. It reacts in various ways to the perception of the dream scenes. In this way, the secondary mental process is also in action during the dreaming activity of the mind. But since the ego is often functionally mutilated while dreaming, and often regresses to previous stages, these activities of the dreaming ego, and especially the secondary revision, may be very deficient or may not occur at all. It was again Federn who devoted himself to the study of the ego feeling (ego) in dreams. He noticed that in most dreams the body ego is missing, and that the ego perceives its dreams only as a mental ego. When bodily sensations and movements appear in some dreams they have a special significance. Furthermore, he pointed out that the dream may awaken the ego only incompletely and/or at different age levels. His findings and interpretations of the ego feeling in dreams will be the topic of a later discussion.

Realizing that schizophrenia and the other psychoses are diseases of the ego, we must recognize the great importance of the study of ego states during dreams in order to understand the psychotic process. The ego during dreams has many psychodynamic features in common with the psychotic ego, especially with the schizophrenic ego.

NOTES

(1) Nunberg, Herman. Principles of Psychoanalysis. New York, International Universities Press, 1955, p. 149.

XII

Divergent Ego Concepts of Psychoanalysis

EGO psychology became a field for psychoanalytic study relatively late. Before Freud the most important findings of experimental psychology were concerned chiefly with the physiology of the sense organs and the ways in which various stimuli were perceived under certain conditions. Freud's discovery of the vast field of the unconscious was a scientific achievement so new and so overwhelming that previous psychological knowledge could be almost ignored, for it contributed little to the understanding of normal and pathological mental phenomena.

With Freud's scientific discovery of this formidable subterranean dynamic source of conscious experiences, the unconscious and its ways of operation, light was cast on the perceived contents of the mind. Only then did we possess a scientific basis for understanding the psychology of these mental contents: the instinctive drives; the meaning and mechanisms of dreams and neuroses; normal psychological phenomena, such as, conscience, shame, humor, and love; the various kinds of interpersonal relationships; folkloristic, sociological and anthropological manifestations; myths and religion. The dynamic concepts of cathexis, as a movable or fixed charge of energy, and of a mental structure which can be observed in the developmental processes of the personality, are indispensable tools for the apprehension of mental functioning. Prepsychoanalytic psychology, which was merely ego psychology, did not develop such basic concepts; it lacked, therefore, a workable foundation for understanding the dynamic ego phenomenon itself. A new approach to the study of the ego, derived from the knowledge acquired in exploration of the unconscious, was the means for better comprehension of the ego itself, its ways of operation, and its various functions. But Freud was initially deflected from the study of the ego. He considered psychoanalysis as the science of the unconscious, and for a certain time ego psychology did not enter his field of interest.

It is true that Freud spoke very early of ego instincts. He distinguished them from the sexual instincts, but he did not go deeper into their analysis. At the time of his earlier concept of the drive dualism he recognized the importance of libido investment of the ego, namely, of one's own person, a condition which he called narcissism. Thus he distinguished, among the ego drives, the non-libidinal, the mere self-preservative, from the libidinal or the narcissistic. Alfred Adler, one of Freud's earliest followers, developed a theoretical system according to which he interpreted the meaning of all neuroses indiscriminately. His system was based on the exclusive consideration of those urges and tendencies which Freud classified as ego drives. According to Adler, these drives and their respective frustration were responsible for all neurotic suffering. He stressed the importance of the "will to power," mindful of Nietzsche's philosophy, the individual's striving to get "on top" of his fellow beings. He called the latter "masculine protest" which, in his opinion, determined also the masculine role of the sexual partner. Feelings of inferiority, to which he gave the name "inferiority complex," and of discouragement were the expression of failure in this aggressive striving. For the sake of social adjustment the urge "to be on top of the other," "to assert one's self in competition with the rival," has to be checked by "feelings of social community," according to which the same rights are granted to others. Adler distinguished very early (1908) the aggressive drives from the libidinal ones, on a quite different basis, however, from that which induced Freud later (1920) to revise his theory of the drive dualism into a distinction between life drives and death drives. In Freud's revised theory the death drives in their extraversion became aggressive object-destructive drives.

Freud at first accepted Adler's ideas as an important contribution and recognized that they were very conducive to the understanding of some character traits. But Adler soon eliminated completely the findings of Freud in the field of the unconscious and of infantile sexuality. He disregarded the oedipus and castration complexes, and his interpretation of various neuroses consisted in a monotonous repetition of the principles on which he based his whole theory. His psychology could no longer be called psycho-analysis, and its designation was, in fact, changed to "individual psychology." The secession of Adler and his adherents from the Freudian school occurred in 1911. One immediate consequence of this secession was that all ego psychology fell into disrepute and remained so for some time thereafter. There were two reasons for Freud's hostility toward investigation of ego phenomena: (1) He felt very much disturbed in his work by the consideration of scientific outlooks which diverged from the direction of his own studies. This is true for any original investigator. (2) Adler actually ignored the essential achievements of Freud's ingenious and laborious scrutiny.

Freud's initial formulation of the mental structure was made not in terms of id and ego, but in terms of "systems of the mental apparatus." These systems were not conceived as functionally different structures, as was his later concept of the mental substructures —the id, ego and superego. They were rather conceived as progressive stages in the mental process. The term "unconscious" had a descriptive and systematic meaning. The *system* unconscious (ucs.), ruled by the primary mental process, was that stage of mental phenomena which Freud later called the id. The secondary mental process characterized the *system* preconscious (pcs.) which, from a descriptive point of view, was also unconscious, although the preconscious mental processes could become conscious. The third stage of mental processes was called the *system* of consciousness, and perception (pcpt.-cs.). In order to designate the system in which a given mental process took place Freud proposed to use in writing the abbreviations ucs., pcs. and cs. Nosologically different mental disturbances were the effect of lack of ucs., pcs. or cs. cathexis in certain mental processes.

Later, when Freud turned his attention to the study of the ego, he considered it to be a mental structure which developed as a result of contact between the mental apparatus, or id, and the external world. In his opinion it was a differentiated part of the id, both genetically and topographically, analogous to the "ectoderm" (the ego) blanketing the "endoderm" (the id). This structure, he recognized, develops successively functions which enable it to deal with the external world and with the inner instinctual demands. Later, when the superego develops, the ego enters into relation with this mental structure also. These are the three classic relations of the ego: with the id, with the external world and with the superego.

We can now complete Freud's formulation of the ego given in the second chapter. In one of his last works,[1] he declared "Under the influence of the real external world which surrounds us, one portion of the id has undergone a special development. From what was originally a cortical layer, provided with organs for receiving stimuli and with an apparatus for protection against excessive stimulation, a special organization has arisen which henceforth acts as an intermediary between the id and the external world. This region of our mental life has been given the name of ego."

Not all psychoanalysts, however, agree with this view of the ego development. The original ban imposed on discussion of the ego may have been in part responsible for the many different ego concepts expressed by different psychoanalysts. Freud's closest adherents still hold the opinion that the ego develops from the id. Hartmann, Kris, Loewenstein, and others believe in an autonomous ego development.[2] In their opinion the ego does not emerge from the id, but rather, the id and the ego both develop independently from a common undifferentiated matrix. To use again the analogy of endoderm (id) and ectoderm (ego), in Freud's opinion this "ectoderm" develops from this "endoderm" through a process of differentiation. In the opinion of Heinz Hartmann and his followers, however, this ectoderm and this endoderm develop quite separately each from a common "germinal layer." For others the ego is only the sum of ego functions. Thomas M. French equates the ego with the integrative function.[3] For still other psychoanalysts the ego is seen only as an auxiliary hypothesis which enables us to understand better certain mental functions.

Anna Freud's concept of the ego[4] reminds us somewhat of that of Alfred Adler in so far as it considers the striving for self-preservation, self-assertion and self-defense as well as the inhibiting feelings of discouragement. But Anna Freud dealt with these ego manifestations in close connection with unconscious mental life and infantile sexuality, which were ignored by Adler, and her dynamic formulations were based on Freud's later drive dualism. In her approach the id and the ego (the latter in her particular conception) are examined in their inseparable interaction. In addition, she elaborated this ego psychology much further, proving the great importance of the processes of identification and externalization (projection) for the ego's adaptation to and defense against external and internal dangers, as well as for its obtaining vicarious gratification. But, like her father, she does not share Federn's concept of the ego. For example, she equates identification with imitation, disregarding the phenomenon of egotization, that is, inclusion within the ego feeling. But it is not possible to embark here on all the variations in ego concepts formulated by various psychoanalysts.

In order to explain Hartmann's concept of ego autonomy we want to consider the integrative function of the ego as it was presented in the third chapter. We said that the ego functions as an intermediary between the inner instinctual demands and those of the external world. No integrative function could develop if the ego did not have the capacity to postpone or renounce, to a certain extent, gratification of some urges and wishes, and if it were unable to resist, to a certain extent, some impositions of the external reality. This capacity of the ego is called by Hartmann and his followers relative autonomy. In fact, the ego is not mercilessly bound to satisfy immediately the demands of the id, nor to yield mercilessly to the stimuli of the external world. It is, to a certain degree, independent of the id and of the external world. As one of his followers, David Rapaport, expresses it, the ego has a relative autonomy in regard to the id, and also a relative autonomy in regard to the external world. It is questionable whether such semantics are of great help for our understanding. It is evident, further, that the ego will resist more strongly the demands of the id when external conditions become threatening, and conversely, that it will be less affected by external conditions when the id demands are irresistible. In the new terminology one would say, the stronger the ego's dependence on the external world the greater its autonomy will be vis-à-vis the id, and vice versa. At any rate, in this semantic form as in others one can usefully elaborate on observed facts and correlate various pertinent findings and experimental results to the ego's relative capacities to deal with the inner and external worlds.

Two words, "the self" and "narcissism," both pertaining to ego psychology, are used by different psychoanalysts in different senses. As mentioned above, Federn distinguished the ego as subject from the ego as object, using "self" for the latter. In his opinion the ego as subject is commonly expressed by the pronoun "I" and as object by the word "self," namely when it is the object of love or hate or the object of one's thoughts. Hartmann and his followers have chosen a completely different meaning for the word "self": To them it comprises the total personality which includes the id, the ego and the superego. This use of the word is linguistically correct, but common language ignores the existence of a "non-ego territory" in the personality. Commonly, one's whole mental and bodily personality, as distinguished from the external world, is equated with the ego, but in our psychoanalytic thinking we should not adhere to this equation nor equate mental life with ego. Hartmann comments on Freud's ambiguous use of the word ego, because Freud sometimes used it to indicate the whole personality, that is, the "self" (in Hartmann's sense), and sometimes to indicate the ego as a substructure of the "self" (again in Hartmann's sense).

A further implication of Hartmann's concept of the self derives from his suggestion that the word "narcissism" be used for the libido investment of any part of the personality, be it the ego, the id or the superego. In his formulation the counterpart of the external world is not the ego, but what he calls the self. His concept of narcissism is, therefore, broader than that of either Freud or Federn. Nevertheless, Federn himself, arguing against Freud's statement that the libido regresses in sleep to primary narcissism, once distinguished "structural narcissism" from "biological narcissism." Hartmann proposes to call "ego narcissism" the libido investment in the ego. Thus, he specifies this form of self-libido as distinguished from what one would call "id narcissism" and "superego narcissism." But Federn's biological narcissism is hardly more than a figure of speech, and Hartmann's id or superego narcissism should not be called narcissism at all. Freud would not have agreed with these terms. In fact, he characterized the narcissistic libidinous type as that in which the *structural* part itself, the ego, is most strongly libido-cathected. In contradistinction to the narcissistic type he characterized the erotic and the obsessional types as those in which the libido is concentrated on the id and the superego, respectively.

Therefore, to call the libido investment of any of the mental sub-structures other than the ego "narcissism" is at variance both with the myth of Narcissus and with Freud's concept of narcissism. And to call the total personality, in contradistinction to the external world, "self" disregards the characterization of the id as the inner *foreign* country.

As a matter of fact, the term "narcissism" is appropriate only when applied to the reflexive ego libido, the self-love in Federn's sense, since Narcissus fell in love with his mirrored image and suffered for being unable to possess himself as an object. In other words, he fell in love with his ego as object. It is true, however, that there were a few times when Freud used the word narcissism in a loose way. For example, he spoke of a regression of the libido during sleep to primary narcissism, and he also stated that in sleep the libido regresses to the state of intra-uterine existence. Yet, in his opinion neither ego nor narcissism exist during intra-uterine life, but rather the ego develops later in infancy. What Freud actually meant was that in sleep the libido is withdrawn from external interests into one's own person.

Let us return for a moment to Hartmann's stress upon what he calls an autonomous factor in the way in which the ego operates. Its functions—memory, perception, motility, etc.—develop independent of any immediate necessity to use them. He states that they develop before a conflict ever occurs. Also, as mentioned, Hartmann and his followers do not share Freud's opinion that the ego develops from the id, but believe in an independent disposition for the development of the id and the ego from a common matrix. This view seems, however, to be implied in Freud's earlier theory of the drives. In Freud's genetic description of the development of the ego from the id, he indicated that there is a special goal to be attained and this attainment is challenged or threatened by the conditions of the external world. In his earlier formulation Freud stated this goal in his concept of drive dualism. At that time he distinguished between the sexual drives and the ego drives, equating the latter explicitly with the self-preservation instincts. Thus, as he then formulated the drive dualism, the goal of self-preservation could be reached only by mastery of the threatening stimuli of the external world. And this striving for mastery constituted *the* motivating factor for ego development. Thus, the admission of two primordial, basically different groups of drives implied a primordial disposition to the development of two separate mental structures, the id and the ego. Contact with the external world could induce an ego development only if self-preservation instincts exist *prior* to its development. Hence, Hartmann and his followers labelled as relative ego autonomy the ability of the ego to function as an intermediary between the inner and external worlds.

Most psychoanalysts examine the mental substructure which they establish to be the ego from a behavioristic point of view, characterizing each of the three substructures according to its specific functions. Briefly, the id is the source of instinctive drives; the ego acts as the intermediary between the id and the external world, and the superego is the representative of conscience. Hartmann says that no psychoanalyst has tried to give a complete list of ego functions, and that such a list would be longer than that of the id or superego. Only the functions by which the ego operates can constitute a basis for its delineation, independent of the phenomenon of consciousness which is only one of its functions. The ego has also an unconscious portion. Freud considered the ego as "a coherent organization of mental processes," [5] and later added, "The ego does not envelop the whole of the id, but only does so to the extent to which the system pcs. forms its surface more or less as the germinal layer rests upon the ovum. The ego is not sharply separated from the id; its lower portion merges into it." [6]

The last sentence is at variance with Federn's concept of the inner ego boundaries which separate it from the id. In Federn's opinion only the ego feeling is permanently conscious, not the preconscious material over which it extends. He calls an ego state the mental material which—at one time or another—was or is unified by a coherent ego cathexis and has its own boundaries. Furthermore, Federn discovered that ego states, like id contents, can undergo repression. In such cases ego states lose their current ego cathexis, but remain preserved by a cohesive force intact in the unconscious. When repression of an ego state is lifted, as in dreams, in hypnosis or by psychoanalytic procedures, it is again experienced by the individual as a unity. The stratification in the unconscious of all former ego states, each having its pertinent boundary, constitutes, according to Federn, the unconscious portion of the ego which, however, does not include currently operating ego functions. Thus, Federn distinguishes the repressed id from the repressed portion of the ego. Both are ucs. in the systematic sense of the word. This topic will find a more exhaustive elaboration in Chapter XIX.

Federn did not try to establish what portion of the mind should be given the name ego. His efforts were directed to describing most accurately what everyone actually senses when he says "I." It seems strange that Federn's wise approach required a unique act of creativity on his part. His concept had long before been alluded to in such classical formulas as Descartes' *cogito ergo sum* ("I think, therefore I exist"). Federn recaptured such original, archaic, prescientific, and prephilosophic meanings of the pronoun "I" and applied to them common knowledge and understanding as the basis for his studies. As he emphasized, the Cartesian formula implied "that feeling my ego proves to me that thinking and being are mine." And so, every ego function and every ego defense is ego cathected. In the seventh chapter the extension of the ego feeling to the "we feeling" was discussed. This extension serves also the ego's need for integration and continuity. In the present author's opinion a peculiarity of the ego is related to this need: its sense of immortality—of being without beginning or end in time. Our reason and our critical faculties challenge this feeling, and many persons disregard or deny it, taking it for granted that self-experience begins at some point in time and ceases with death; yet the feeling persists and reveals itself in a number of ways. A child told of events that occurred prior to his birth sometimes objects, "No, I was there too," or "No, I have always been here." An elaboration of this feeling of eternal life is the belief in reincarnation or life after death.

Psychoanalysts who consider Federn's descriptions and findings as complicated, superfluous, and unproven forget that Federn's ego psychological concepts developed from his study of the psychoses. Their psychodynamics can be understood only through his formulations. Psychoses are ego afflictions. Freud's formulations of the ego and its defenses emerged from the study of the neuroses. Anna Freud derived her formulations from the analysis and observation of children. But the egos of neurotic patients, adults and children, are sufficiently intact and therefore they do not offer to the psychoanalyst the needed data for a deeper investigation of the ego. In any case, Federn could not have developed his formulations if he had not utilized Freud's psychodynamic concepts. Federn considered the concept of the ego cathexis, its flexible extension, quality, strength and function, as the "best argument" in favor of Breuer's and Freud's general theory of mental dynamics which depends on movable or fixed cathexes.

To conceive the ego as the integrative function does not necessarily contradict the concept of the ego as one's bodily and mental existence. One could ask whether one's own existence does not consist solely in one's own integrative function. But even if this were the case, one could not possibly equate the integrative function, considered from a mere behavioristic point of view, with the ego. The ego would have to be the subjective experience not only of the integrative function as such, but of the integrative—and we may add of the synthetic—processes which are maintained in continuous action. If these processes stop the individual dies.

In addition to the constant dynamic condition there are two important factors which determine the ego experience. (1) The experienced integrative and synthetic processes are not only in action, but they are unified within flexible boundaries. (2) The ego experience has the connotation of continuity. The ego feels extended in time and feels to be the same ego it was at all times in the past. In spite of passing through various ego states, the core of the ego remains always the same. Even upon awakening from a dream which has been experienced by the mental ego only in a state of great rational and mnemonic deficiency, the individual feels that it was he himself who had the dream, and that it was he himself who was in this deficient state.

In Chapter V we presented Paul Federn's metapsychological definition of the ego. Let us now consider two of his other definitions of the ego:

"1. *Descriptive Definition:* The ego is the lasting or recurrent continuity of the body *and* mind of an individual in respect of space, time and causality."

"2. *Phenomenological* (*i.e., subjectively descriptive*) *Definition:*

The ego is felt and known by the individual as a lasting or recurrent *continuity* of the body and mental life in respect of time and space and causality, and is felt and apprehended by him as a unity." [7]

We might ask whether any ego feeling can exist before the individual develops the capacity to discriminate between ego and non-ego, whether it is this capacity which gives origin to an ego feeling. In order to clarify this issue we may use the expressions "egotized span" and "de-egotized area" to outline the result of this development. If we consider ego and non-ego as a pair of opposites, then certainly no "ego" can be conceived of without its opposite "non-ego," just as the concept of light presupposes darkness. But in order to experience one's own existence it is indeed not necessary to conceptualize things existing beyond one's self. Federn's statement that the ego feeling is the discriminating factor between ego and non-ego does not hold for the earliest ego state in which no ego boundaries have yet been formed, or, in other words, when the whole universe of one's perception is egotized. As mentioned above, Federn calls this ego stage "ego-cosmic"; it precedes the ego's ability to discriminate between ego and non-ego. Freud himself alluded to this earliest stage of the ego in his book, *Civilization and Its Discontents.*[8]

Freud believed that the ego as a unity develops only at a certain age after birth and that the first stage of the ego is a mere body ego. Federn, however, traces the ego feeling back to a time preceding birth. In fact, his studies of psychoses induced him to postulate an ego feeling in the unborn fetus while it is swimming in the amniotic fluid. The contact of the individual, we do not say of the ego, with the external world causes a successive withdrawal of the ego boundaries, which coincides with a progressive discovery of the existence of an external world. Therefore, we realize that it is not the ego feeling per se, but the ego boundary feeling which serves to discriminate between ego and non-ego.

We have seen that consideration of the psychological processes of the ego has resulted in great dissension among Freudian psychoanalysts. The expositions of this section will enable the reader to follow in the successive sections more detailed achievements in the field of psychoanalysis.

NOTES

(1) Freud, Sigmund. An Outline of Psychoanalysis (1940). Translated by James Strachey. New York, Norton, 1949, p. 15.

(2) Hartmann, Heinz. Ego Psychology and the Problem of Adaptation (1939). Translated by David Rapaport. New York, International Universities Press, 1958. For a review of this literature, see the two articles by David Rapaport, The autonomy of the ego. Bull. Menninger Clin., 15:113-123, 1951, and The theory of ego autonomy: A generalization. Ibid., 22:13-35, 1958.

(3) French, Thomas Morton. The Integration of Behavior. Vols. 1-3. Chicago, The University of Chicago Press, 1952-1958. To be complete in 5 vols.

(4) Freud, Anna. The Ego and the Mechanisms of Defence (1936). London, Hogarth, 1937. See especially Chapter III.

(5) Freud, Sigmund. The Ego and the Id (1923). London, Hogarth, 1927, p. 15.

(6) Ibid., p. 28. See also the diagram on page 29.

(7) Federn, Paul. The awakening of the ego in dreams. In Ego Psychology and the Psychoses. New York, Basic Books, 1952, p. 94.

(8) Freud, Sigmund. Civilization and Its Discontents (1930). New York, Jonathan Cape, 1930, p. 11-12.

Section II

The Ego
and the External World

XIII

Pleasure-Pain and Reality Principles

FREUD'S formulations of the pleasure-pain principle and the reality principle resulted from psychological observations and were applied to commonly recognized facts. Their consideration is of great importance in understanding the ego's behavior. The discovery of a mental region subjected to the primary mental process, the id, required the formulation of these two principles since this region is, in fact, ruled only by the pleasure-pain principle. The mental processes of the id are not influenced by external reality directly but only through intervention of the ego when they are egotized. We shall see later an example of this intervention in the process of grief or mourning. The ubiquity of these principles is denied by Freud's conception of the death instinct which he presented for the first time in his classic work *Beyond the Pleasure Principle*.[1]

Everyone recognizes that we seek pleasure and attempt to avoid pain and that pleasure and pain determine to a great extent our mental activity, our actions, and our behavior. We desire food and drink because their intake is pleasurable; we avoid touching fire because it is painful. This guiding principle of mental life Freud called the pleasure-pain principle or, more briefly, the pleasure principle. If injuries were not painful and the satisfaction of hunger and thirst were not pleasurable, living beings would perish. Sexual enjoyment, similarly, is like a bribe of nature to ensure propagation of the species; and regardless of this ultimate biological purpose, the immediate psychological motivation for sexual activity is pleasure.

The experiences of pleasure and pain are thus indispensable guides to survival; yet in themselves these experiences are not sufficient. If one were to seek only pleasure and the avoidance of pain or discomfort, without regard to consequences, he could not survive. The possibilities for obtaining pleasure and avoiding pain are

72

limited, as we are all exposed to unavoidable sources of pain and suffering. Often a great suffering can be avoided only by enduring a lesser suffering. Frequently pleasure can be obtained only through distressing efforts and the acceptance of pain; and furthermore, some pleasant experiences will lead eventually to pain. All these relationships we learn by individual experience and register in our memory as a guide to appropriate behavior. A person who chooses to endure temporary pain in order to avoid greater distress, or one who denies himself some pleasure in order to avoid disagreeable consequences, can be said to be well adapted to reality. To say—as some psychoanalysts do—that this capacity of the ego is due to its relative autonomy from the id and external reality, respectively, seems redundant.

In the course of an individual's adjustment to reality the simple pleasure principle undergoes a gradual evolution beginning early in life. The infant seeks instinctively any pleasure immediately obtainable and is intolerant of any pain. Only with time and repeated experiences does he learn to adapt himself to reality, and by considering the consequences of his various pleasant and unpleasant experiences he becomes capable of accepting a certain amount of pain and renouncing a certain amount of pleasure. The principle of mental behavior whereby the individual chooses to endure pain which leads eventually to pleasure and to renounce pleasure which eventually produces suffering, Freud called the reality principle. Since both the pleasure and the reality principles operate toward the same ultimate goals, obtaining pleasure and avoiding pain, the reality principle must be regarded as a modified pleasure principle, evolved through the effect of foresight. It differs from the pure pleasure principle only with respect to the freedom and the urgency of the subject's reactions.

Conditioned responses are the effect of the reality principle, which has become an automatic reaction similar to a physiological reflex. Through repeated experiences of pleasure which always succeeds a pain sensation immediately, a reaction pattern develops by which pain is sought because of its associative connection with pleasure. Such responses to certain pain sensations materialize only if the experienced pleasure outweighs the preceding pain. These conditioned reactions have also been produced experimentally in animals which were consistently subjected to determined pain sensations just before being fed. They remind us of certain types of masochism. The psychodynamics of such a clinical picture rests on inseparable associative connections between pain and pleasure.

As mentioned above, we do not speak of varying degrees of ego autonomy in regard to the id, when, according to the reality principle, the ego has to renounce some satisfaction, or in regard to the external world, when it has to act against external demands. Rather, we must simply consider its strength or weakness in the exercise of its various functions. It is commonly said that an emotionally strong person can withstand renunciation and deprivation and can master and control emotions, such as anger, love, and grief, better than a weak person. The dynamic-economic point of view, which was presented in the preceding chapter, is of great theoretical, diagnostic, and therapeutic importance. In order to evaluate the strength of an ego in respect to some temptation, we must assess the intensity of the specific drive to be mastered. If several people are exposed to the same severe deprivation, mistreatment, punishment, or danger, it is common knowledge that some will endure the hardship more easily than others, that some can resist unharmed or with little damage, while others will break down. To evaluate the significance of the dynamic-economic events in these persons would require some means of measuring against the mastery-strength of each ego the intensity of the deprivation, fear, or rage that was felt by each. It is well known, moreover, that an individual may be strong in certain respects and weak in others. For instance, a person may show strong persistence in pursuing a given goal against certain odds, but may be weak in resisting some temptation. In biographies and in imaginative literature we find descriptions of personalities who are strong in many respects but have weak points. In his studies of the psychoses Federn correlated different forms of ego weakness to the scarcity of ego cathexis available to the individual for the exercise of various functions.

The reality principle forces itself upon the infant early in life. After an infant has experienced the relief of hunger by nursing at the breast, successive experiences of hunger provoke in him reactions directed toward a definite goal: repetition of the experience which brings relief. The easiest and quickest way to reproduce the satisfaction of nursing is hallucination. As stated in the preceding chapter, we have evidence to assume that the infant originally obtains satisfaction of his longings by means of hallucinations. His mind functions according to the absolute pleasure principle, as do the processes in the id. Such an immediate satisfaction without effort, were it efficient and lasting, would amount to omnipotence. Ferenczi, in fact, used the term "omnipotence of thought" to describe this first period of the infant's mental life. Hallucinatory appeasement, however, while causing the infant to forget his hunger for a while, does not remove it. The state of hunger is relieved only by the active consumption of real milk and not by an imaginary or illusory equivalent. Thus the infant has to make his first attempt to evolve the pleasure principle into the reality principle. And thus the experience of frustration, as the unavoidable sequel of the first illusory gratification, stimulates the infant to attempt to master the situation and relieve his state of tension in a more efficient way. Soon he develops the capacity to distinguish between an hallucination (the content of which is unreal) and the perception of reality; then the deceptive, hallucinatory satisfaction is renounced, and real satisfaction is immediately sought.

This new function, distinguishing reality from illusion, Freud termed reality testing. Considered in its fullest extent, it comprises all testing of thoughts and actions with reference to reality. This power of distinguishing between real and unreal, as mentioned earlier, develops initially through the performance of bodily movements. As the head is turned or the eyes are closed and reopened, real objects disappear and reappear, but hallucinated objects are not affected by such movements, since their appearance is due to a process within the mind. The motor system, furthermore, in addition to helping the infant to master the use of his sense organs, enables him to act directly upon the external world; through co-ordinated actions he eventually learns to produce what he needs.

Thus the ability to distinguish between inner and outer worlds and between real and unreal develops progressively with the acquisition of mastery over, and we would add, with the egotization of, the perceptive and motor systems. This mastery is achieved only gradually. It takes time, experience, and exercise before the infant learns to perceive adequately and to co-ordinate his movements properly in order to produce the intended changes of his body. The motivation for this progress has already been described. Since, according to Freud, the greatest single incentive for the adoption of the reality principle is the infant's realization that his tension of need persists during hallucination, hallucinatory satisfaction is normally discarded upon the development of motor control and persists henceforth only in dreams and fantasy, and in certain types of mental illness. In sleep, since contact with the external world is suspended and the motor system is out of function, no reality testing can take place. The acquisition of reality testing as a new function thus enables the infant to abandon the futile "omnipotence of thought."

The phenomenon of egotization was discovered by Federn; no description of it occurs in Freud's writings. As we shall soon see, the sense organs must be included within the external ego boundary in order to serve the ego in discriminating between real and unreal. Also the motor system must be egotized in order to be at the disposal of the ego. In the next section we shall examine more thoroughly the difference between reality testing and the sense of reality. Meanwhile, let us consider the progressive development of the reality principle.

As he frees himself from his early dependence upon hallucination, the growing child makes use of progressively more advanced and independent means of obtaining satisfaction for his needs. Through experience he learns that crying, originally only a spontaneous expression of pain due to frustration, summons the mother or other persons who take care of him and who produce what he is longing for. In his successive attempts to cope with hunger and other needs, therefore, he reverts to crying and calling, and later to asking; in this phase, crying and the use of language have an almost magic effect. Gradually, however, he achieves independence of other persons and gains more efficient means of mastering his problems. His intelligence progressively matures; the capacity to endure frustration and to delay satisfaction increases; and the ability to act in an appropriate way expands. Slowly he learns how to renounce immediate gratification of destructive aggressive drives and anti-social impulses, because such renunciation is constantly rewarded by approval and love from his parents and from persons who rear him, and because he anticipates punishment and rejection if he yields to wishes that are forbidden. The rearing of the child thus involves gradual substitution of the reality principle for the pleasure principle until in some cases all these renunciations become conditioned reactions.

Very few people (if any), however, succeed in adapting themselves completely to reality. The pleasure principle continues to express itself in wishful thinking and in the gratification (in daydreams or in fantasy) of ambitious and erotic aspirations. A well-known illustration of the human tendency to cling, in the face of reality, to the pure pleasure principle is the widespread belief that resigned acceptance of pain and suffering in this world ensures happiness in a future life. Since such a faith can produce many of the practical results of the operation of the reality principle, it can be of great assistance in the task of self-mastery. Anticipation of this compensation helps one to endure suffering; one accepts suffering in order to obtain later gratification. But since the rewards anticipated cannot be experienced and verified, being postponed to a life after death, no reality testing is possible. Unquestioning reliance on this "unassailable" faith, therefore, is clearly an expression of the pure pleasure principle.

"Autism" is the name given by Bleuler to the mental attitude of a person who neglects and falsifies the facts of reality and indulges in ideas constructed for his own complacency. Those who "shut their eyes," or "blindfold themselves," in order to deny painful reality are often compared, in common speech, to frightened ostriches burying their heads in sand. Such persons are often inclined to believe in magic. Autistic thinking and behavior is a sign of a particular "ego weakness."

To some extent biogenetic forces are advantageously prepared in advance for mastery of external difficulties. Strength of muscle, accuracy and ease of movement, and readiness of intellect contribute greatly to confidence and security, and in themselves lead to development of further capacity through exercise. Since the mere use of these capabilities brings pleasurable release of tension, humans indulge in all sorts of physical and intellectual activity. Exploitation of such abilities is sought as an end in itself. Special alloplastic devices are constructed for bringing external difficulties under more effective control, and situations and enterprises normally difficult or dangerous become means of enjoyment when brought within human capacity. Bicycle riding, motoring, flying, mountain climbing, hunting and the "dangerous" sports are familiar examples. A deeper understanding of these pleasurable activities requires, however, acquaintance with the psychology of drives. This topic will be treated in connection with precise study of the id, the great reservoir of the instinctive drives.

In addition to this power over external conditions, mastery requires control of emotions such as impatience, anxiety, and rage. Mastery is impossible when a person is overwhelmed by a state of grief, rage, or other emotion so strong that he loses contact with reality, becomes unable to care for his own needs or to consider the requirements of other people. In extreme cases the individual may have a sense of "disintegration," the feeling that he is losing his mind.

Emotional control is of crucial importance when external conditions are changed and the individual must face a suddenly altered reality. An example well known to everyone is the "natural reaction" of grief or mourning following loss: the loss of a loved person or of his affection, esteem, or confidence; the loss of an ideal, of one's freedom, or belief; the loss of hope. Such situations are too commonplace to call for comment in themselves; but since grief is recognized as a universal response to loss, it will be profitable to examine certain details as illustrated in mourning for the death of a loved person.

Confronted with such a loss, the mourner is torn between an uncontrollable longing for the loved one and recognition of the fact that the loved one no longer exists. His grief is an expression of conflict between an inner need, rooted in the id but egotized, and crude reality. Since instinctive drives arise in the id, they cannot be controlled at will. It is precisely for this reason—because the activating forces of longings and drives cannot be mastered—that grief follows loss. With time, however, respect for reality usually gains the upper hand, and the ego succeeds in giving up its longing for the dead person. As we have said, external reality influences the id indirectly through intervention of the ego. By affecting the id dynamically the ego can give up its longing.

Withdrawal of object cathexis in the id is accomplished by means of a number of changes. "Mourning work" is the term introduced by Freud to indicate the slow process of emotional adjustment to tragic reality, by which the mourner becomes gradually able to renounce his longing for the lost person. But something has to change in the id before he can accept the real world without the loved one. In severe grief this renunciation requires emotional reorientation to all details of the world of reality. At first the grief-stricken survivor must concentrate on every single detail and every situation associated with the loved one, until he can accept the fact of his disappearance. His longing for the lost person can be appeased, his emotional resignation achieved, only when the cathexis correlated to this longing is withdrawn, in the id, from the representation of this person. But such a withdrawal is preceded by a process in which each single memory and each single expectation concerning the lost person becomes focused in consciousness and over-cathected. One's attachment is often increased in a similar way when bidding farewell to a loved one who is departing for a long trip. The process by which one overcomes grief for a loss is a prolonged detailed mental activity. For this reason Freud called the process mourning *work*. Substitutions of the lost person by living persons and the mourner's identification with him (substitutive identification) are universal attempts to compensate for the loss, and they facilitate the ego's detachment from one who no longer exists. Mourning work must be considered also in its dynamic-economic implications, for it impoverishes the ego.

If love for a person has undergone repression, no mourning work occurs when this person dies. But when, through psychoanalytic intervention, such a repression is lifted, the patient's ego begins to mourn, even though this person may have died long before. This illustrates the way in which external reality affects id-cathexes only indirectly through the ego's intervention.

Not every loss can be accepted by means of mourning work without impairment of joy of living. Though humans are able eventually to adjust to their losses, for some the mourning work is not successful. Suicide is an extreme consequence. The mourner, unable to reconcile himself to his loss, frees himself from unbearable reality by taking his own life. Others, regressing to an earlier phase of hallucinatory gratification, retreat from the external world, lose contact with reality, and substitute delusion for real satisfaction. A mother who has lost a child, for example, may believe that he is still alive, keeping his room prepared for him, the bed ready, and his toys at hand, as if she anticipated his return to the nursery. She may wake startled in the night, thinking she has heard his cry. She may even wheel the carriage up the street, fancying the baby inside, or prepare the formula and fill the nursing bottle, all her behavior denying the death of her child. In melancholia and some obsessional neuroses many forms of pathological mourning are encountered. The case just mentioned is but one example of the tendency, under changed conditions, toward regression from reality to delusion. A prisoner, unable to endure his confinement, may develop a prison psychosis and become "stir-crazy." He may shake the bars of his cell and cry out, or he may become stuporous and withdrawn, as if unaware of his surroundings. Such reactions reveal particular weakness in the dynamic structure of the ego.

Psychologically, the goal of mastery, like the reality principle, is definitely related to the fundamental pleasure-pain principle. Mastery is sought for the feeling it gives of relief and pleasure, and the prospect of failure is shunned as something frightening. We shall return to this subject in the later presentation of the psychodynamic basis of anxiety. It should be clear that when any instinctive drive creates inner conflicts, as well as when there are external difficulties to be overcome, mastery must be the ultimate psychological goal, regardless of the nature of the problem.

Successful adaptation to reality, including the establishment of emotional rapport with one's fellows, occupies a considerable part of the life of a normal human being. The capacity to renounce or postpone one's desires cannot be attained in a short time. The experiences of childhood, however, play the most important role, and certain principles deserve special emphasis in the training of children.

For sound development, both excessive frustration and oversolicitude must be avoided. A child who is repeatedly thwarted in regard to food, or one who is exposed to prolonged physical discomfort without adequate care and affection from his mother, may fail to develop sufficient confidence to face difficulties in a hostile external world; consciousness of failure may result in traumatization of the ego. Conversely, if all needs are gratified at once, so that the child is not permitted any independent acquisition of mastery, he will be unable in later life to renounce his immediate wishes and will succumb to the slightest frustration. In order to acquire the greatest capacity for mastery, the child should meet, at each age level, "optimum" frustration. And this optimum varies from individual to individual.

Since, however, no young child easily postpones or relinquishes gratification, the adults who care for him should find a middle way, neither too permissive nor too strict. Toilet training should never be forced, nor should it be begun too early; as a general rule, it should be deferred until the child can sit alone. He should be allowed to feed himself in his own way, and even to put his hands into his food. By the free use of his sense of touch the infant learns much, over a long period of time, about the external world. Thumb-sucking has a special place in his development because it provides oral pleasure. He also discovers, and later explores, other areas of his body, his hands and fingers, his feet and toes, and the genital region. His own body normally serves as an object for the gratification of this drive. As we shall see later when we discuss the instinctive drives, the pleasure ("autoerotism") obtained by the child from different parts of his own body represents the first stage in sexual development. When such exploratory activity is restrained, anxiety develops and normal curiosity is repressed. All curiosity can be inhibited as a consequence, and the child may even become incapable of learning. The manner in which the child can be diverted from excessive autoerotic gratification is a special topic in the general area of sexual education.

Perhaps the greatest single general assistance to the child, in his efforts toward mastery, is consistency on the part of the adults who have charge of him. If the mother at times permits certain behavior and at other times forbids it, the child is confused, loses confidence in the mother, and becomes unable to accept the prohibitions imposed upon him by society for his own welfare. With consistent approval for good behavior and disapproval for bad, he feels secure in his relationships and consequently advances in his ability to overcome frustration, to adapt himself to the world around him, and to gratify, in ways that are socially acceptable and desirable, his instinctive drives toward the ultimate goal of pleasure.

NOTES

(1) Freud, Sigmund. Beyond the Pleasure Principle (1920). Standard Edition, 18:1-64. London, Hogarth, 1955.

XIV

Reality Testing and Sense of Reality

FORMERLY psychiatrists taught that the sense organs attach the "index" of reality to the stimuli of the external world which reach them. According to this simple theory sensory perception would be the basis for acknowledging reality, in fact, for the sensation of reality. By implication all the data for conclusions or testing in regard to the reality-value of given facts would be obtained, in their ultimate origin, by sensory perception.

Two psychological phenomena, however, contradict this view: (1) The contents of hallucinations of psychotic and dreaming egos are, as a rule, sensed as real, although these contents are not derived from perception by the sense organs but are only mental products. (2) In certain ego disorders the objects of the external world, although clearly perceived through the sense organs, are felt as unreal, an experience which is called "feeling of estrangement." [1] Therefore, the necessary conditions for normal perception, that is, for sensing as real only what one perceives through the sense organs, require special investigation, as does normal acknowledgment of external facts, based upon various conclusions and all kinds of "reality testing."

In the preceding pages we became acquainted with the idea that the original hallucinations of an infant are checked when his ego, by means of primitive testing with bodily movements, succeeds in discriminating between internal and external origin of perceived stimuli. This process of preventing mental stimuli from attaining sensory qualities is a highly dynamic process. A mobilized counter-cathexis stops mental stimuli from reaching the "perceptive system." Then, these stimuli either remain in the id, if they belong to repressed contents, or they become egotized and thus are sensed as unreal, that is, as belonging to the "internal mentality." When, however, the dynamic barrier erected toward such stimuli weakens, as is the case in dreams and hallucinatory psychoses, then these contents appear again in the form of hallucinations as they did in early infancy. This dynamic barrier is supplied from the reservoir of ego cathexis and constitutes the inner ego boundaries toward the id.

Healthy individuals are not aware of the potential ego boundaries of their bodies and minds. Self-observation in this respect requires, in the beginning, practice under proper guidance. Federn's concept of the dynamic ego boundaries is a new one, not contained in Freud's formulation of the ego. Federn's "geographical" description gave his readers the impression that he conceived the ego and its boundaries as static. Nothing could be more alien to Federn's teachings. Ego boundaries are, in fact, very flexible. The geographical connotation of the term "boundary" is unfortunate. It must be borne in mind that the concept indicated by this term is a distinctively dynamic one, and that Federn himself always emphasized the flexibility of ego boundaries.

The dynamic character of the ego boundaries can be experienced by anyone in the process of falling asleep. As sleep approaches the ego and its boundaries lose their cathexis, so that unegotized mental phenomena, entering through its weakened internal boundary, are able to reach the drowsy ego. Hypnagogic images ensue; one starts to hallucinate or dream. If, however, in this half-sleeping state one makes an effort to awaken completely, the ego boundaries are re-established to their full strength and the hypnagogic images disappear.

These ego boundaries do not exist at the very beginning of the infant's life. They establish themselves as a result of the ego's learning to discriminate the internal from the external origin of perceived stimuli. But once these boundaries are in full functional capacity, no reality testing is required for preventing hallucinations. Hallucinations arise again only when these boundaries weaken, not because of a failure in reality testing. They can be checked then only by strengthening the internal ego boundaries, not by any testing of reality. Their weakening during sleep is a normal occurrence.

Reality testing is based on healthy sensory perception. In the first place, seeing, hearing, touching, smelling, and tasting give evidence of objects and events of the external world. They play the most important role in our acknowledgment of external reality. But the perceptive function is not only a direct means of acknowledging external realities; it is also an indirect one. We may have different degrees of certainty or doubt about external facts. Thus, when a person tells us something which we have not perceived personally, the extent of our belief depends on the degree of confidence we have in him. Most of our information in every field of knowledge is conveyed to us by visual and auditory communication. Our conviction of the existence of countries we have never seen, of many world events which we do not witness, of the wealth of "known" historical and scientific facts, rests almost entirely upon what we have heard and read, that is, upon what we have been taught. Sceptical people believe only what they can see and touch personally.

Knowledge of external facts can be obtained also through thinking, the working patterns of which we shall not analyze further at this point. Besides, "obvious" logical conclusions or deductions from perceived data and remembered facts may force themselves spontaneously into one's mind without being the result of conscious conative thinking. This phenomenon is one of the proofs that the ego extends over the preconscious. The ability to apprehend some facts immediately, not through the data of direct sensory perception or conscious thinking, is commonly called intuition, although there is some divergence among psychologists regarding the meaning of the term and the explanation of the phenomenon which it indicates.

As with beliefs due to communications from others, we may have different degrees of certainty in the knowledge we arrive at through thinking or intuition. Experimentation and new "evidence," either in support of or in opposition to apprehended data, may lead to a rectification of "facts" which we formerly believed. In other words, assumed knowledge or opinions arrived at indirectly through sensory perception can be annulled or rectified upon more perfected testing.

The sensation of reality concerning certain facts and situations is not necessarily the result of reality testing. Only a healthy person's acknowledgment of facts of reality is dependent on, and can be rectified by, mental procedures, conscious or preconscious. A paranoid patient senses as real the contents of mental origin, without resorting to "testing" and even in spite of evident proofs to the contrary.

At this point we must elaborate more on an observation mentioned earlier, that the logical capacity, which serves the need for integration and which plays an important role in the function of reality testing, is at times of a high order in paranoid patients. But, since they sense as real what is only mental, the function of their logical thinking leads to mental activities, such as rationalization and secondary revision, which compensate for the omitted reality testing. The function of these activities is to establish an agreement between the contents of delusions, sensed as real, and the correctly acknowledged facts of the external world, which cannot be denied. The integrative task of the paranoid ego can be compared with that of a normal person who tries to reconcile facts which are in apparent contradiction. A normal person feels the need to solve the contradiction either by finding agreement between the facts or by exercising a more exact, "revised," reality testing which will deny one fact or the other. The paranoid patient, on the other hand, usually clings more firmly to the "false reality" than to the actually perceived or acknowledged facts of reality.

A paranoid patient had the delusion that a former friend belonged to a secret organization which wanted to capture him. Some facts, however, were at variance with his delusional fear. He realized that his friend behaved in a kind manner toward him, that he even displayed readiness to help him in a possible emergency situation. But instead of using his reasoning capacity to correct his delusion through reality testing, he used it to solve the contradiction while maintaining the delusion. The content of the delusion did not admit any doubt in regard to its reality value. This patient reached the conclusion, quite logical for him, that his friend was using psychological tactics in order eventually to "frame" him. As Federn demonstrated, such a patient's integrative efforts can be directed toward correct reality testing only when the delusion is of recent origin and when the guiding therapist has established a good rapport so that the patient has confidence in him.

A paranoid patient sometimes realizes that other people cannot be persuaded to the "reality" of his delusions and that they consider him insane or at least queer. In order to adjust himself to the behavior of "incredulous" people such a patient may resort to a deception: In the presence of these people he denies having his delusional ideas and behaves according to *their* "reality" and expectations. This attitude is called "dissimulation." In cases in which the patient is not dangerous to others or to himself and still maintains his delusions, the therapist may teach him how to dissimulate his ideas and thus help him to reach some kind of social adjustment.

Nor is reality testing always reliable, even in non-psychotic individuals. It can be impaired by emotions. But a healthy ego cannot easily ignore nor neglect strong direct evidence of unpleasant facts. The greater the ego's ability to substitute the reality principle for the pleasure principle, the greater will be its capacity to apply reality testing correctly in regard to painful realities. Even in scientific research an investigator may adhere unduly to the pleasure principle. He may be influenced by his wish to "prove" his ideas or his philosophical system. Sometimes the mental attitude of such scientists, who employ very complicated methods of "reality testing," reminds us of that of paranoid patients who resort to secondary revisions in order to construct an agreement between their delusions and the correctly acknowledged facts of reality. But these two types of mental behavior have only an exterior resemblance, for they are dynamically and structurally quite different. The "autism" of a healthy scientist is due to the prevalence of the pleasure principle for certain fields. The feeling of certainty of the paranoid patient in regard to the contents of his delusions arises from the breaking through of repressed contents into the ego from the id, i.e., from outside the internal ego boundaries.

Preconceived ideas acquired in early childhood, based on identification with parents and early environment, deserve special consideration. The parents constitute an absolute authority for the child, who himself lacks an efficient rational capacity. Without blind faith in them he would feel uncertain, at a loss; he would live in a continual state of apprehension and anxiety.

Therefore, to a very great extent the reality testing normal for the child rests on the opinions and teachings of his parents. In his dependent state he must accept *their* "realities." Absorption of the parents' ideas on social, moral and religious issues is the natural expression of the child's strong emotional attachment to them. Emancipation from their ideas would be equivalent to rejection of his parents. The belief in some "realities" constitutes an important superego feature. Accordingly, we should bear in mind that the superego also participates in the function of reality testing.

Perhaps no one is completely free from prejudices. But an ego with strong social, moral, or racial prejudices, or with religious convictions which arose from early mental absorptions, has a very impaired reality testing function in certain areas.

To illustrate the striking difference between the function called "reality testing," which has just been presented in its main characteristics, and the "sense of reality" discovered by Federn, let us examine the mental experience of an individual during the process of awakening from a fainting spell. The patient described his sensations in the following way: First there was a loud, uncomfortable singing in the ears. He could not say just when it began. . . . There were very faint, elusive, and almost imperceptible dream-like feelings, dim, indistinct dream-images, such as one sees when falling asleep, human forms moving and passing like shadows, voices from a long way off. These dim and hazy dreams grew gradually clearer, and then it dawned on him that it was he himself who was experiencing these sensations, that previously he had not existed. The singing in his ears grew fainter and finally ceased. It was succeeded by an agonizing sense of disorientation. Had the whole thing been real and not simply a dream? He felt weak, as if he were paralyzed. All his strength was gone, and he was unable to help himself. He suffered indescribable torment and was still not sure of his own identity or of how such a situation had arisen. Little by little he remembered what had happened just before he fainted. Then he no longer mistrusted the evidence of his senses, and his ego recovered its feeling of continuity. It was as if he had come into harbor in a world which had seemed dream-like, even dimmer and more unreal than a dream, but which had in fact proved to be real.[2]

It is a well-known fact that some of the most important normal functions of our organism were discovered, and could only have been discovered, through the study of pathology. In the field of psychodynamics Federn arrived at his findings through the study of the psychoses. The description given above of an ego's awakening from a state of non-existence illustrates many features of Federn's dynamic concept of the ego. It shows that the return of ego cathexis occurs in successive phases, and it shows the way in which the ego's identity and continuity is re-established after an interruption. But for our purposes here we want to note particularly the patient's transitory feeling (of estrangement or derealization) that the real objects of the external world, which he started to perceive through his sense organs, were not real but only mental products.

A dream-like sensation is not equivalent to the sensation of unreal. While we are dreaming we feel the dream events as real. The designation of dream-like for the sensation of unreality is due to our retrospective sensation, upon awakening, that the dream was unreal. But this is not the case with hypnagogic images which appear in our minds in the process of falling asleep. Not yet asleep, we feel distinctly that such images arise in our minds. Our patient in his description referred precisely to such experiences, which are sensed by everyone as mental in origin and unreal. He awoke in a world which he perceived for a certain time as unreal as hypnagogic images are; then he began to feel progressively that this was not a mental product but the real external world. This experience is proof that perception of stimuli through our sense organs is not sufficient to make us *feel* that they actually exist.

One might conclude in this particular case that the sensation of derealization was due to the patient's enfeebled perceptions, since he had this experience before he had revived completely. This case, then, would prove only that perceptive sensations must reach a certain degree of intensity in order to convey to the ego the connotation of their real existence. It is a mistake, however, to correlate intensity always with quality. There are cases of very intense sensory perception in which the ego feels the perceived world as unreal. Conversely, one may perceive the external world very feebly without any feeling of derealization. And, as Federn taught us, feelings of derealization or estrangement may appear in patients in different degrees, for varying lengths of time, independent of the perceptive intensity. Thus we recognize in the experience described above that a specific dynamic factor other than the perceptive intensity must have been responsible for the patient's feeling of derealization. It is true that he was not yet quite awake as long as he did not feel the external world real. But what was not yet awakened in him was the sense of reality, the main function of the ego's boundaries.

The phenomenon of derealization has been described and studied by a number of psychoanalysts: Tausk, Schilder, Nunberg, Fenichel, Wittels, and others. Their explanations, though interesting, were unsatisfactory because they considered the phenomenon as an effect of withdrawal of interest (libido) from the representations of objects rather than from the ego boundaries. As Federn has shown, feelings of derealization may appear also in regard to objects for which the individual still has a strong interest. As pointed out in the preceding chapter, stimuli from the external world must impinge on the well-cathected ego boundaries in order to be sensed as real. And visual, auditory, tactile, olfactory, and gustatory sense organs are parts of the boundary of the bodily ego. They may be considered to be embedded in the boundary like windows in a wall. We conclude, therefore, that the organs of perception per se do *not* attach the "index" of reality to the stimuli of the external world which reach them. If these organs are deprived of ego cathexis, the ego may still perceive the stimuli, but only with the feeling that they are unreal, like mental products. It is perception through sense organs participating dynamically with the ego boundary which attaches "the index of reality" to perceived objects. In our patient, during the slow process of reawakening from a state of unconsciousness, the sense organs awakened before ego cathexis could return to the bodily boundary. Therefore, when he first began to perceive, he felt the external world as unreal.

Federn describes accurately two monosymptomatic neuroses, in which the patient has only one complaint, a feeling either of estrangement or of depersonalization. With the latter, one's ego feeling itself is deficient or parts of one's own personality become de-egotized. Emotions and thoughts may also lose their ego cathexis, so that the patient has the unpleasant sensation that such contents or functions do not belong to him. In these neuroses the symptoms are usually more pronounced in the morning upon awakening. Ego cathexis is normally withdrawn during sleep, and in these clinical entities the cathexis delays in returning completely to the ego or to its boundaries.

In a paper dealing with the superego this writer reported a case in which the psychological mechanism of the feeling of estrangement, divestment of the ego-frontier of libido, was not determined by dynamic-economic factors only but occurred as a defense against an unpleasant reality.[3] The patient felt very guilty for a theft which he had committed. To quote from the published report: "When he had done the deed, it seemed to him for some time that the whole world was changed, i.e., unreal: Houses, people, vehicles, everything seemed strange, and voices and other noises had a totally different sound. Something in him refused to admit the perceptual world as actually existing; for the theft which he had committed was now an actual fact, followed by an inner tension (whose nature we must examine) which the patient could not endure; hence he had to deny the perpetrated act. If the perceptual world were not an actuality but merely a dream, then the theft also would not actually have taken place."

To this writer's satisfaction Freud advanced a few years later the same motivation for a slight feeling of derealization which he himself had experienced when he visited the Acropolis of Athens with his brother.[4] He described his feelings by saying: "By the evidence of my senses I am now standing on the Acropolis, but I cannot believe it." Then, " 'What I see here is not real.' Such feeling is known as a 'feeling of derealization.' " His explanation of this feeling, as a defense, is as follows: "It must be that a sense of guilt was attached to the satisfaction in having got so far: There was something about it that was wrong, that was from earliest times forbidden. It was something to do with a child's criticism of his father, with the undervaluation which took the place of the overvaluation of earlier childhood. It seems as though the essence of success were to have got further than one's father, and as though to excel one's father were still something forbidden."

"As an addition to this generally valid motive there was a special factor present in our particular case. The very theme of Athens and the Acropolis in itself contained evidence of the sons' superiority. Our father had been in business, he had had no secondary education, and Athens could not have meant much to him. Thus what interfered with our enjoyment of the journey to Athens was a feeling of *piety*. . . ."

With his characteristic psychological acuteness Freud uncovered the hidden feeling of guilt, connected with infantile and repressed attitudes, which called for a defense in the form of a feeling of unreality regarding the perception of an external situation. But he did not mention the metapsychological mechanism of such a defense, which he thought had still to be explored.

If a healthy ego directs its attention simultaneously inside and outside of itself, it senses clearly what is its body, its thoughts, memories or imaginations and what are objects and events of the external reality. The flexible dividing plane between one's self and the external world is precisely what Federn called ego-boundary. When the ego cathexis, experienced as ego feeling, withdraws from a part of the body or conscious mind, one loses the sensation that that part belongs to one's self. Furthermore, objects of the external world which are perceived by unegotized sense organs are felt as strange, as unreal.

There is, however, a great difference between the boundaries which separate the ego from the outer external world and those which separate it from the inner external world, the id. As stated in the preceding section, our body possesses a protective barrier (*Reizschutz*) against the afflux of stimuli from the external world. Only samples, as it were, of external stimuli can enter the ego's perceptive system through the physical sense organs which are normally located at the external dynamic boundary. Such samples are perceived with different qualities according to their nature and the specific sense organs which they stimulate, that is, as visual, auditory, tactile, or olfactory sensations, etc. In this way the ego is informed about the events of external reality. When the defensive barrier is broken through, a condition which we call a lesion or trauma, a powerful counter-cathexis is mobilized to isolate and to check the invading stimuli. This constitutes a second, a dynamic, defensive barrier against "the invaders."

The internal ego boundaries, however, are not supported by any anatomical barrier against id impulses. They consist of only a dynamic, though flexible, wall formed by counter-cathexes, which keeps the id stimuli separated from the ego. Moreover, the internal ego boundaries do not possess anything analogous to the sense organs. Accordingly, repressed contents in the id cannot possibly be perceived by the ego. They are located behind "a wall without windows." Normally id contents must first be egotized in order to reach the ego's awareness, and then they are sensed as internal factors, belonging to the ego. Since sense organs for id contents do not exist, a normal ego is ordinarily not aware of the inner external world. In fact, the existence of the id had to be discovered through scientific methods. As we have seen, however, the dynamic weakening of the internal ego boundaries, during sleep and in the psychosis, does permit the ego to perceive id contents. But it perceives them then as external realities in the form of hallucinations and delusions. This is proof of Federn's concept that the sense of reality is the function of both the internal and the external ego boundaries.

In psychotic states stimuli both from the unegotized id and from the external world reach the ego's awareness. The patient perceives external reality and also has hallucinations. Both kinds of stimuli impinge on the ego boundaries from without but from two directions, from the inner external world, from the id, as well as from the outer external reality. Contents of both kinds of perception are sensed as real, independent of any reality testing. I myself observed, however, that the ego perceives contents of mental origin differently from the way in which it perceives the actual external world. While dreaming such a distinction cannot be made, because the ego is then exposed only to dream perceptions which stem from mental stimulations alone.

With a schizophrenic patient I succeeded in establishing this distinction quite easily. We agreed that everything he heard was real, as he sensed it, but I proposed that he distinguish two kinds of reality. We called them reality A and reality B. Whenever he spoke about hallucinated voices I asked him to which reality they belonged, and he answered immediately that they belonged to reality B. When I spoke to him or when we heard other persons' real voices or the noise of a passing car, he immediately said, "This is reality A." But unless the patient was told to make this distinction, he would not reveal that the two sets of contents had a different character. I have also noticed that psychotic patients often have the sensation that hallucinated voices or de-egotized mental contents are produced in them by hypnosis, by wireless telegraphy or that they come from a "fourth dimension." As soon as such a patient realizes that other persons are "not sensitive to these vibrations," he can easily adjust himself, through dissimulation, to social rapport. He feels exactly which kind of voices are perceived by other persons and which are not. This capacity of some psychotic patients to discriminate between two kinds of things which they sense as "reality" can be utilized for therapeutic purposes.

The recognition of the difference between testing and sensing reality is essential not only for the dynamic comprehension of certain psychotic diseases. Primitive reality testing through movements is followed by the formation of internal dynamic ego boundaries toward the id. If delusional or hallucinating patients are taught by the therapist how to use reality testing correctly, their weakened inner ego boundaries are strengthened.[5]

NOTES

(1) German, *Entfremdungsgefühl*. This has been translated by "feeling of estrangement" (used by Federn to whom we owe the most accurate study of the phenomenon) and also by "feeling of derealization." This latter term, used by Strachey in his translations of Freud, was introduced by Sir David Henderson and the late R. D. Gillespie in the Fifth Edition of their Text-Book of Psychiatry (Oxford University Press, 1940).

(2) This description was published by the author in his Agoraphobia and its relation to hysterical attacks and to traumas. Int. J. Psychoanal., 16:59-83, 1935.

(3) A portion of this paper was read by the author before the Vienna Psychoanalytic Society on December 11, 1930. It was later published with the title Regression and projection in the super-ego. Int. J. Psychoanal., 13:449-478, 1932. The passage quoted is on page 452.

(4) Freud, Sigmund. A disturbance of memory on the Acropolis (1936). Collected Papers, 5:302-312. London, Hogarth, 1950. The passages cited are on p. 307, 308, and 311-312.

(5) This chapter is partly based on the author's article, Sense of reality and reality testing. Samiska, 4:171-180, 1950.

XV

The Dynamic Survival of the Ego

PHYSICAL analogies can illustrate a psychodynamic condition only partially and vaguely. They can never do justice to all details. Accordingly, the analogy of the wall without windows brings nearer to our understanding only the fact that the ego cannot possibly perceive the vast unegotized territory of the id in its actual nature, that is, as a field of mental life. Id contents can be perceived as such only when they obtain preconscious cathexis and are thus included (incorporated, as it were) within the ego itself.

There are no "windows" of any kind through which the ego can perceive id contents. These contents are either excluded from the ego and not perceived at all as inner mentality, or they participate in the ego as parts of it, through assimilation and synthesis. On the other hand, when these contents do reach the ego's awareness without being ego-cathected, as in dreams and psychotic states, then they are sensed (wrongly) as pertaining to external reality. Only those stimuli which enter the ego through egotized "windows," that is, through the ego-invested sense organs, are rightly sensed as belonging to external reality.

Our analogy does not take into account many other properties of the internal ego boundary. We learned that the internal ego boundary is a dynamic and not an anatomical barrier, that it is flexible and can have varying degrees of resistance toward pressures from the id. It can become stronger or weaker. Its consideration from an economic point of view requires some knowledge of the somatogenic sources of the cathexes and their distribution among the various functions of the mental apparatus. We shall discuss this issue in a following section. For the time being we may conceive a "reservoir" of ego cathexis, composed of various kinds of cathexis, from which the ego boundaries are dynamically supplied. Ego cathexis is experienced in the coherent ego feeling. The internal ego boundary is a selective barrier; it does not prevent those id contents and drive representatives which agree with the ego from being egotized and synthetized by it.

All memories and drive representatives arise from the id, either directly without disguise, or through a detour. Repressed memories and drives are substituted by distant, unrecognizable contents, an effect of the primary mental process, before they can find admission in the ego, if at all. It is difficult, indeed, to conceive the internal ego boundary, which is strengthened in some portions by systems of counter-cathexes, in terms of physical analogies. In the id, behind this "wall without windows," a very complex and strange mental activity must take place, from which all kinds of wishes and urges develop. Some are immediately egotized, some only in their distant derivatives, and some not at all. The fate of each repressed drive depends on its strength (called *impetus*) and on the organization and strength of the ego which tries to ward it off. If the pressure of a repressed drive outweighs the defensive strength of the ego, the ego's functional integrity is impaired or may even break down.

Laymen and pre-Freudian psychiatrists alike were puzzled by the way the ego in pathological conditions becomes driven by incomprehensible impulses and thoughts and the way in which it reacts. One might expect, therefore, that exploration of this invisible foreign country, which furnishes the ego with all its zest for life, would be fascinating to all intelligent people. But very early Freud learned from sad experience that only a very small minority was interested in his discoveries. We realize from this that the dynamic wall is experienced by most people as an insurmountable resistance against any learning about what takes place behind the wall. It is this resistance which maintains repressions. Findings from investigations of the unconscious are commonly met with denial, hostile rejection, or neutral interest. These attitudes are dynamic features inherent in the conscious experience of the internal ego boundary, especially the portions of it which are strengthened by counter-cathexes.

Survival of the ego depends on the supply of ego cathexis which maintains dynamically its coherent unity and its integrative and synthetic capacities. We have learned that, as a measure of defense against disintegrating or disturbing influences, the ego resorts to shifting of ego cathexis; that is, some areas are invested by ego cathexis and some are divested of it.

In the phenomenon of repression as described by Freud a mental content does not obtain preconscious cathexis or this cathexis is withdrawn from it. Preconscious cathexis is ego cathexis, and ego cathexis is also employed as counter-cathexis against the pressure exercised by repressed drives and memories. Moreover, according to Freud, the same cathexis which is withdrawn from a repressed drive can be used as counter-cathexis against its pressure. The phenomena of internalization (identification) and externalization (incorrectly called "projection" in psychoanalytic literature) consist, in Federn's description, of extension of ego cathexis over an object or its autoplastic duplication and in its withdrawal from a part of an ego state, respectively. Both phenomena can be used by the ego as defensive means against integrative difficulties, unbearable deprivations, as in mourning work, or against dangerous situations. Anna Freud found "identification with the aggressor" to be one of the ego's defenses against a threatening object. When the ego itself becomes the dangerous object it no longer fears it. A child may bark like a dog in order to overcome his fear of it. In the preceding chapter we explained the feeling of derealization which ensued when the ego tried to deny the existence of an unpleasant reality, as an effect of withdrawal of ego cathexis from its external boundary, specifically from the sense organs. Often in cases of derealization the surroundings are sensed as lifeless, like pictures on a screen. In the process of recovery the slightest increase of libido cathexis on the external ego boundary is recognizable. The perception of objects becomes warmer, and the phenomenon is ascribed by the patient to a pleasantly increased vividness of the objects themselves. Derealization ranges in degree from an ephemeral feeling of unfamiliarity to a permanent sense of unreality and lifelessness with respect to the whole world.

In the course of this presentation we shall describe some other types of ego defenses. We shall then recognize that all defense mechanisms of the ego consist in moving, weakening, or strengthening, in given areas, of the flexible ego boundaries.

But we must now realize that, irrespective of any defensive

motivation, an ego may have an insufficient amount of ego cathexis available for the maintenance of its efficiency. Disintegrative factors may impair its functions, and in extreme cases the ego may succumb completely. Its survival depends on a sufficient flow of powering cathexis. The ego cathexis in its complex composition develops in the organism in a continuous flow, and in waking life it is continuously used up in the preservation of the ego feeling itself, as well as in its various functions. Its production cannot keep pace with its consumption. The ego must therefore interrupt its activity at given intervals and for a certain length of time. Furthermore, every physiological organ can be dynamically restored to its full efficiency only through the suspension of its activity after a certain amount of functioning. Even heartbeat consists of systolic contractions and diastolic relaxations. During the latter the heart muscle regains its tonic efficiency.

The ego's need for sleep is a vital need for restoration of ego cathexis. During sleep ego cathexis is withdrawn from the ego, and thus its flow is temporarily suspended. Only in the state of sleep can the "reservoir" of ego cathexis be replenished to its full capacity, and the deeper the sleep the more efficient the dynamic restoration of the ego will be. People who postpone sleeping too long or who do not sleep enough experience symptoms due to scarcity of ego libido. They may suffer from feelings of derealization or depersonalization caused by insufficient investment of their ego boundaries. The external world may seem somewhat unreal, dreamlike; they may lose the full sensation of some parts of their bodies, or not sense them in their actual full shape.

Insufficient production of ego cathexis may have a constitutional basis, or it may be due to a specific disease process which is characteristic of the schizophrenias. The greater the constitutional factor the easier it is for this still-unknown disease process to set in. Prognostically more favorable are those cases in which a lack of available ego cathexis can be compensated by reduction of the patient's expenditure of ego cathexis through a rational psychotherapeutic intervention. All the excessive responsibilities put on the patient's ego and excessive demands which it has to meet must be lowered. Some dependent needs of 'weak' egos should be respected, and such patients should not be pushed into positions of mature emancipation. This orientation in dealing with dynamically poorly endowed egos becomes clear when we consider a typical defense mechanism of schizophrenic patients pointed out by Federn.

Patients afflicted by a schizophrenic process regress to a former ego stage in which they were more dependent on other persons and did not have to meet too severe demands. At that earlier stage much less ego cathexis was required. From an economic point of view an ego in such a stage can maintain its integration and keep its internal and external ego boundaries sufficiently cathected to prevent hallucinations, delusions, and feelings of derealization and depersonalization. But as soon as such an ego is driven into a more mature ego state, which implies a greater consumption of ego cathexis, it breaks down and disintegrates. Regression of the ego to an earlier ego stage is one of the characteristic preliminary features of an ensuing schizophrenic process. This phenomenon serves a protective purpose, while the other symptoms mentioned indicate that a dynamic lesion of the ego has already occurred.

Freud considered the schizophrenic process to be the effect of a concentration of libido on the ego, of a regression to a primary narcissistic state in which object interests were not yet developed. This implied, according to Freud, a withdrawal of libido (interest) from the external world of objects. Freud interpreted the ensuing hallucinations and delusions as an "attempt of restitution," in other words, an unsuccessful attempt to contact the "lost reality." In his opinion the actual reality became replaced by a "false reality" arising from hallucinations and delusions, just as the dream scenes are "unreal external realities." Federn, however, as we have just seen, came to the opposite conclusion. He saw the schizophrenic ego as suffering from insufficient ego cathexis and not from an excess. To him hallucinations and delusions are not the effect of attempts to make up for a lost external world, but the consequences of dynamic lesions, or more precisely lesions of the ego boundaries.

Psychoanalysts who accept Freud's later drive dualism assign the unifying and synthetic functions of the ego to the libidinal component of the ego cathexis. The ego is constantly felt to function as a coherent unity in space, time, and causality. The expressions "ego strength" and "ego weakness" are terms too general to indicate the specific areas in which the ego lacks adequate dynamic capacity. The internal or external ego boundaries just described may be an ego's weak point. It may also be the self experience itself, and in such cases Federn speaks of "ego atony" which leads to feelings of depersonalization. Through experience and practice, as we learned in the preceding chapters, the ego steadily increases its capacity for mastery and improves its ability to renounce or postpone gratification: The gradual evolution of the pure pleasure principle into the reality principle is a part of this development of the ego toward maturity. Every successful encounter with contingencies serves as an encouragement to the ego; and every failure brings discouragement. The ego may be strong or weak in its adjustment to reality under pressure from the drives.

Although no one can remember his earliest ego stages which have undergone deep repression, the feeling of one's continuity in time is an essential feature of the ego feeling, as was pointed out in Chapter XII.

In speaking of "coherence" of ego feeling or ego cathexis we must realize that a cathexis or a feeling cannot be coherent in the manner of a physical organism or an organic system within such organism. In a cathexis, which is experienced in the ego feeling, coherence is the property of investing simultaneously all of a given area so that the resulting experience is felt as a unit. It is only by means of such an investment of ego cathexis that the ego is apprehended as a unit.

In order to explain the body ego in dynamic terms we must first present the concept of the body image or body scheme, which should not be equated with the body ego. The body image is the basis of the body ego and consists in a durable, integrated aggregate of sensations. Schilder and Bernfeld regarded the body image as the nucleus of the entire ego, and some investigators have regarded the sense of equilibrium as the formative center for the nucleus of the ego. Every part of the body is directly felt and localized when touched, and all parts which can enter the field of vision are seen. We move our bodies at will, within anatomical and physiological limits; we sense intimately and directly our muscular tensions and relaxations and the flexed or extended positions of the joints. We can feel and localize also certain visceral sensations which manifest themselves to some extent as elements of our emotions. All these sensations are synthesized into a complete, coherent, three-dimensional mental image of the body. Paul Schilder made the greatest contribution to the study of the body image. He discovered that the image could be affected by lesions of certain coordinating parts of the brain, as well as by mental factors.

The body image is a constant mental representation, but only when it is completely ego-cathected does the actual feeling of the body ego correspond to the entire body image. Under normal circumstances no discrepancy is felt, and the body ego feeling corresponds, to a satisfactory degree, to the body image. More precise observation has shown that the ego feeling, although it is based on this constant image, varies in intensity, quality and extension. Thus it is obvious that the ego cathexis is subject to quantitative as well as qualitative changes. By such variations in this cathexis, areas of changing boundaries are coherently invested by it. Therefore, the ego cathexis can be called the "egotizing cathexis," and the ego itself comes into being through "egotization."

It is the medial libido component of the ego cathexis which Federn regards as responsible for the feeling that everyday life, with its sensations and its motor and intellectual functions, is not an empty, dull, or disagreeable experience, but a pleasantly familiar one. Body and mind combine to procure for the ego this enigmatic *joie de vivre* which is the "privilege of normal health." Every function of the ego, mental as well as bodily, carries some of the self-enjoyment of medial ego libido. Whenever the libidinous component is lacking, either because it is not supplied or because it has been withdrawn, the individual feels a disagreeable change in his vitality and in his self-unity. The integrative function of the ego remains, but the familiar feeling of an integrative balance is impaired. This is a subtle feature of a disturbance which was previously described as psychasthenia.

Persons of good introspective capacity describe changes of their body ego feeling, in normal as well as in fatigued or irritated states, by saying that some parts of their body are not felt in the same vivid way as the rest of it, or that they are felt more vividly than usual. Such variations are evidently the result of decrease or increase of ego cathexis, and they become marked deviations in certain kinds of disorders. People who live constantly in a state of mental fatigue, whether due to hormonal disorders or caused by emotional disturbances, report various kinds of de-egotization of the body or changes in the body ego feeling: Sometimes the ego feeling extends only as far as the knees or the legs or the neck; in severest cases only the area around the eyes and the mouth remains egotized.

This author has observed acute attacks of depersonalization which appeared in the form of hysterical seizures and had a psychological significance. They were caused by an emotional imbalance of the patient's ego. A girl of thirteen had an attack of this kind nine months after her first menstruation. She felt a tremendous change coming over herself and over her surroundings, and this gave her an indescribable sense of horror. The seizures consisted in a complete loss of the body ego feeling. It withdrew first from her feet, successively from her knees, thighs, abdomen, chest and neck. When the loss of ego feeling reached her head the patient began to scream in a state of paroxysmal anxiety. She fought against the loss of body ego feeling, determined to retain her own ego, but she could not. In her state of terror she grabbed the nearest person and clung with her arms around him in an attempt to hold on to her own body ego. With a cry of extreme terror the attack passed, and the ego feeling returned to her body. In this and similar cases the withdrawal of ego cathexis from the body had a psychological significance; it was due to overwhelming repressed desires. Without embarking at this point on the psychological analysis of this case, suffice it to say that the core of her conflict concerned strong identification with her mother in giving birth to a child.

In most cases, however, feelings of depersonalization are due to an economic deficiency of ego cathexis. If the individual directs his attention to the "unegotized" portions of the body, he feels them as external objects. Yet the body image is complete: The individual has the right conception of his body, but he does not feel it to the whole extent. No sensory or motor function is impaired, and the full ego feeling can be restored by willful effort or muscular activity in cases of minor variations. This special impairment of the body ego is attributed by Federn to decrease or loss of the medial libido component of the ego cathexis.

Quite analogous are the dynamic variations of the mental ego. Federn assumes that the mental ego, like the body ego, consists in a coherent mental cathexis. A range of mental phenomena, changing but always exactly defined, is *felt* as mental ego, and every single phenomenon in this area is invested with ego feeling. The mental ego embraces not only perceptions, feelings and emotions, but all conative acts, that is, volition, thinking, impulses toward movement, drives, memories and anticipations. It includes also representations of time and space, in brief, the formation of all concepts. It is evident that all these mental processes are indispensable for the integrative and mastery functions of the ego. This author conceives also a mental image analogous to the body image previously mentioned. The mental image is the mental representation of an integrated aggregate of those memories, feelings, desires, and instinctive drives for which the ego is alerted by hormonal stimulations. It differs, however, from the body image in that its features change according to the aroused and satisfied desires and drives. The body image is durable because the physical body changes only slightly during growth; its shape remains by and large the same. But drives and desires as well as emotional needs fluctuate continuously. When the ego cathexis does not invest a part of the current mental image, the ego feels dynamically "mutilated." In the present writer's opinion this phenomenon forms the core of some types of phobias.

Like the body ego, the mental ego has boundaries which may lose their libido component. With such a loss mental activities are felt to be estranged. Ideas, memories, the contents of one's own reading or writing, one's own voice, even well-known melodies and sometimes common words lose their familiar character, and thinking itself seems to be altered. True interest is lacking; ideas seem not to be one's own. This inner estrangement, mental depersonalization, is even more astonishing and terrifying than the corresponding estrangement of external objects, called derealization. The difference between the phenomenon of de-egotization which causes feelings of depersonalization and that which causes the repression of mental contents will be discussed in the next chapter. For the moment suffice it to say that in the first case an ego content becomes objectified, that is, turned into an object representation which, as such, remains conscious (or preconscious). In the second case the repressed content disappears altogether from the range of the ego; it is no longer available to the ego either as ego content or as object representation.

Federn regards the morbid ego feeling characteristic of depressive states as the most convincing proof of the existence of the death drive. In his opinion the pathological condition is due to a temporary failure of the supply of libido, so that "mortido" remains prevalent in the ego cathexis. In the most severe cases the patient is completely unable to enjoy anything, nor does he recall pleasant experiences of the past. He dislikes everything in his existence and is overwhelmed by the anticipation of ceasing to exist. This feeling is not a longing for peaceful relaxation, nor is it a masochistic urge to obtain pleasure through suffering. Severe melancholic patients are simply driven toward death for the sake of nonexistence and nothing else. "Mortido," unchecked by libido, prevails in active, passive, reflexive and medial forms. As Federn observed, it overflows into object relations, and the death drive becomes thus a destructive drive. The severe depressive is full of hate and reproaches everyone, including himself. A businessman in a state of depression, for example, may ruin the business of others as well as his own. All happiness around him vexes him and soon ceases. An atmosphere of death and despair flows from him and spreads around.

In the next chapter some disturbances of the thinking function and behavior due to insufficient ego cathexis will be illustrated.

XVI

Thinking and Acting

FOR a better understanding of the processes of repression, identification (internalization) and externalization, two aspects of the phenomena of egotization and de-egotization must be examined more closely.

Id contents, whether memories or representations of objects and goals of instinctive drives, are egotized if no opposing force intervenes. When egotized they are encompassed in specific affective or emotional ego states. We speak of repression when, by action of an opposing force, id contents are not egotized or become de-egotized after having been already ego-invested. Repressed contents conduct an "extraterritorial" existence, that is, an existence in the id, and their cathexes are blocked from affective or emotional discharge as well as from motoric discharge into muscular activity. As Federn showed, ego states also can be repressed, that is, excluded from the current ego. We shall give special consideration to this phenomenon in the next chapter.

We described as egotization also the ego investment of a perceived or consciously represented object or its autoplastic duplication. It is then felt as a part of an ego state. This phenomenon is called identification with or internalization of the object. And we described as de-egotization also the phenomenon in which a portion of the ego is turned into a conscious object representation. This is the phenomenon of externalization, improperly called projection in the psychoanalytic literature.

First we described the inclusion of an id content within the ego as an act of egotization; second we described the transformation of a conscious object representation into an ego content as an act of egotization. And likewise, we designated the phenomenon of repression, the exclusion of a mental content from the ego, be it related to an object or to the ego, as an act of de-egotization. And we designated also as an act of de-egotization the phenomenon of externalization, which is turning a part of an ego state into a consciously represented object. Distinguishing two aspects of egotization and de-egotization requires us to examine more thoroughly the contents with which the ego operates in its thinking function.

In the postulated ego-cosmic phase the ego experiences itself only in its medial aspect, as existing, as being. Every perceived content constitutes a part of an ego state. The whole world of its perception, of its visual, auditory, olfactory, and all other perceptions, is ego-cathected. Boundaries between ego and an external world do not yet exist. Only very slowly is a non-ego territory discovered through the continuous experience that some portions of the original ego state change, that they appear and disappear, chiefly in connection with physical movements which the ego learns progressively how to control. The ego cannot easily withdraw from the sensations of its body, from its instinctive drives, from its affects and emotions, but it does become able to influence the field of its sensory perception, and we repeat, especially through its bodily movements.

Under the influence of some drugs, the ego boundaries may suffer a minor or even a major rearrangement. In this case the intoxicated ego feels the contents of visual, acoustic, olfactory, or other stimulations as features of itself, as the ego-cosmic ego does. Freeman, Cameron and McGhie[1] gave a clear illustration of this phenomenon. They write: "Most vivid illustrations of this lapping over of the person into the surrounding environment are provided by the number of recent studies on chemical intoxication produced by such drugs as mescalin, hashish, and lysergic acid. One subject under mescalin, upon hearing mouth-organ music outside declared, 'I am music—I am climbing in music.' Another reported, 'I feel my body floating over without limit into the surroundings.'" Another such person revealed, upon re-establishment of his normal ego boundaries, that he had sensed the music which he was hearing under the influence of the drug as arising within himself, as affects and emotions do. He had lost the ability to discriminate the external source of the music from his "perception" of it. The music was a part of himself. In his own words, "I was music."

Some sensory perceptions procure for the infant indispensable gratification of his needs, some only minor or different degrees of pleasure, and still others cause him discomfort and suffering. In the progressive development of ego boundaries, which coincides with the discovery of the external world, that is, of the non-ego territory, the pleasure-pain principle plays an important role.

Let us now designate as de-egotization the process by which a newly discovered external world becomes separated from the original ego-cosmic self-experience. The ego requires certain coherent sensory perceptions for its comfort and survival; the more indispensable they are, the more tenaciously the ego keeps them within its boundaries, in other words, the more tenaciously will the ego *feel* them as belonging to its own experience unity. As stated in the preceding section, for a time the mother, and later only her breast, remains included in the child's ego feeling.

Freud described an early phase in ego development, called the "purified pleasure ego," in which pleasure is equated with one's ego and pain or displeasure with the world of objects. In this phase the ego includes within itself all pleasurable sensations and excludes from itself all unpleasant and painful sensations. Thus, in the process of severing the external world from the ego, not all sensations arising within one's self are necessarily and always sensed as parts of an ego state. We learned in the preceding section, for instance, that in dreams some ego states or parts of ego states can appear as objects. We gave the example of a dreamer whose own headache appeared in his dream as another person suffering from headache, and who recognized only upon awakening that it was he himself who was suffering.

The phase of the purified pleasure ego cannot be maintained over a long period of time. Reality adaptation, necessary for survival, makes the ego recognize and endure unpleasant factors within itself and accept pleasant qualities belonging to external objects.

We must now focus our attention on the relation of the perceptive function to different ego states. With the development of a dynamic dividing plane between ego and non-ego, namely the ego boundaries, the ego does not cease to have sensory experiences. But the perceived physical qualities, which appear in coherent combinations, lose their medial character and thus are no longer felt as one's own ego states. Before the external world of objects is discovered we cannot speak of a perceptive function but only of ego experiences. It is only through the acquisition of ego boundaries that the ego acquires its perceptive function. The ego then has *perceptions* in which different reactive, namely, affective or emotional, colors are inherent. The *perceptive function* as such remains egotized, but this is not true of all the contents captured by this function. This state of affairs can be brought nearer to our understanding by various modes of expression.

To say that extrospection, which we call simply perception, cannot exist in the ego-cosmic phase is a tautology; nevertheless it helps us in understanding how this physio-psychological ego function comes into being. The separation of the world of objects from the ego is the most spectacular developmental phase of the ego. Simultaneously the ego acknowledges objects and enters into various relationships with them. Prior to this development all experiences, whether produced by external physical stimuli or accessible through introspection, are of the same nature. Those produced by external stimuli are not yet correlated to something which is non-ego. But through the progressive de-egotization of the sensory field of experiences, which the ego continues to have, they develop into perceptive experiences. They convey to the ego the notion of external, that is, non-ego, objects and events.

Why does the ego continue to have sensory experiences after it has de-egotized the contents of these experiences? The answer to this question is given by our knowledge of the inner "windowless" ego boundaries and the external ego boundaries with their embedded "windows." One of the two fields of experiences does not disappear through de-egotization, because the stimulations which cause these experiences enter the ego through the "windows" which are the sense organs. Only in pathological cases, as in hysterical blindness or deafness, may the mobilization of a strong countercathexis prevent external stimulations from reaching the ego. This phenomenon is analogous to that of repression. But in normal circumstances the sense organs, included within the external ego boundaries, remain permeable by external stimulations, and the interposed external ego boundary turns the originally medial ego experiences into the perception of a non-ego field of phenomena. Inherent in every perceptive experience is a distinct feeling that such an experience is strictly dependent on external, non-ego events. In the further course of mental development the ego learns to distinguish its actual perceptions of objects from the notion of the independent existence of the objects themselves. In other words, the ego learns that the objects exist independent of whether it actually perceives them or not. This distinction constitutes the first and most important step in the development of the thinking function.

Quite different is the effect of de-egotization of contents arising from the inner external world, the id. When such contents lose their ego investment they become separated from the ego by the internal ego boundary which is not provided with anything analogous to sense organs; it is "windowless." The de-egotization of id contents is called repression, and repressed contents cannot be perceived as such. We learn about them only indirectly through their egotized derivatives. As was pointed out in the preceding chapters, id contents must be egotized in order to become accessible to introspection, but then they participate in the ego itself. In other words, these experiences are not felt to be related to something beyond the ego, and by this connotation they are clearly distinct from perceptive (extrospective) experiences. And we repeat, if unegotized id contents do enter the windowless boundary, as in dreams and in the hallucinations of psychotics, they are perceived as (false) realities of the external world. In other words, they appear "projected" from the id into the external world of objects.

We can now understand clearly the difference between the aspect of de-egotization which leads to repression and that which leads to externalization. The separation of the perceived external world from the ego is, on the perceptive level, that phenomenon which we described as externalization. The ego states consisting of medial sensory experiences are turned into perceptions of objects. No ego feeling adheres to the contents of such perceptions, but the ego feels that it is perceiving them. On the mnemonic and imaginative level, through de-egotization of their contents, which had occurred on the perceptive level, parts of ego states are turned into object representations. The ego can remember the de-egotized contents of its previous perceptions, or it can combine parts of them to new formations. Perception and representation of objects are related topographically to the ego boundaries. Every experience encompassed in the ego is a part of an ego state, as are perceptions as such. But every experience content derived from the entrance of unegotized stimuli through the internal or external ego boundary has object character.

It is interesting now to note that repressed ego states are again felt as ego states only when their repression is lifted, but when repressed ego states break through the current ego boundary without current ego investment, they are perceived as objects. Memories and representations of objects, that is, of de-egotized sensory contents, arise from the id and not by entrance through sense organs; they can therefore undergo repression, as representatives of repressed instinctive drives or sources of experienced traumas. In psychoanalytic literature one speaks of objects only in relation to the individual's needs and urges. Neither the character of objects in the ego experience nor the development of the perceptive function is considered. Accordingly, Glover defines an object as "that person or thing toward which instinctive urges are directed and on which they can be gratified." [2] We have learned now that the object character of mental contents and the perceptive function can be understood only with the knowledge of the bodily and mental ego boundaries discovered by Federn. But, of course, we distinguish the thought or perception of an object from the object itself existing in the external world.

Representations of objects and of external events in general, which have various effects on inner experiences, are elaborated in various ways through the secondary mental process. But we cannot embark here on all the complicated operations by which temporal, spatial, and causal (recognition of laws of succession) connections are established,[3] nor on the essential roles which verbal and nonverbal expressions, as well as the amount of available active ego cathexis, play in the thinking process. We shall elaborate only on a few details of this function and on some of its disturbances.

The coherent nature and the continuity in time of the ego feeling is clearly revealed in all ego functions. Thinking is preparation for action. The separation of the external world of objects from the coherent medial ego feeling leads to an important discovery: The body ego, originally only a medial experience, can also be perceived (with the exception of one's head and the back) through the sense organs and is felt to be shaped like the bodies of other persons who can be perceived entirely. In other words, one's own ego also attains *object* character. Federn's emphasis on the subject *and* object aspects of the ego is fully justified. The ego's identification with representations of other persons (who are objects) and the externalization of some of its states into these representations can be understood only through this knowledge. We explained in the preceding section how the ego interprets instinctively and automatically the behavior and expressions of other persons as manifestations of an inner life like its own. This prompt interpretation amounts almost to a "perception" of their inner experiences.

The mental ego is felt to be inside the body ego, and we both sense our body as a medial experience, to the extent to which it is ego-invested, and perceive it as an object. Our whole ego, in its mental and bodily aspects, can become the object of thinking, of loving and hating, or briefly stated, the object of many kinds of affects and emotions.

Through past experiences the ego becomes acquainted with the modes in which external phenomena succeed each other, and it maintains a coherent picture of the external events which influence each other. Thomas M. French in his analysis of the integrative process has introduced a very helpful terminology for the understanding of the integrative thinking process and thus of integrative behavior.[4] He says that "effective efforts to achieve a goal result only when motor activity is guided by insight or by a plan." He calls "integrative field" this practically effective knowledge that we must infer in order to account for a person's behavior. As a rule the ego can reach the desired end-goal only by reaching, in proper succession, a number of intermediary or subsidiary goals. If I want to visit a certain city, I have to consider the possible means of transportation, consult time tables, provide means to pay for the trip, and so forth. French calls "integrative span" or "span of the integrative field" all the knowledge included in the integrative field, which has a delimitation. If a necessary piece of knowledge for making a plan to reach an end-goal or the proper sequence of time of the single acts are not contained in the integrative span, the ego's plan will be deficient. In our example, if I ignore the fact that a passport is required for visiting a certain country before entering this country, my integrative field will have a defective integrative span.

The ego must be able to bring the pressure of its need under the control of the integrative field. The greater the pressure of the need and/or the broader the required integrative span, the greater must be the ego's capacity, "integrative capacity," to control all the single intermediary actions according to the plan. French calls "integrative task" the amount of pressure that has to be bound by an integrative field. For effective goal-directed behavior the integrative capacity must be adequate to the integrative task. When the integrative task exceeds the integrative capacity, the mechanism of goal-directed behavior disintegrates. The phenomenon of disintegration of an integrative field, as a result of the individual's loss of hope of attaining the needed end-goal, has a special importance in French's concept of the origin of aggressive cathexis. In his opinion no aggression can develop without frustration. As we shall learn in a later section dealing with various psychoanalytic theories of the cathexes, the occurrence which French describes as disintegration of an integrative field leads to a "defusion" of libido and destructive cathexis (in Freud's concept of the dualism of instincts) which, prior to the disintegration, were fused into a combination.

The terminology used by French to describe integrative behavior brings into evidence the coherence in time of the thinking function, which is an ego-dynamic manifestation. In order to maintain this function adequately a certain amount of ego cathexis must be available. Ego cathexis must be employed in different ways, however, in the thinking function. For example, connecting representations of objects and events with the pertinent verbal expressions is a dynamic task of the ego—although there is also a nonverbal mode of thinking. (French designates the latter as "practical grasp" as it is revealed in the activities of mechanical constructions.) Bleuler described a typical thinking disturbance of schizophrenics which consists in a sudden cutting off of an ideation. In such cases the patient cannot recapture the continuation of his thought. Again, in some cases an ideational content may become over-cathected in an integrative field, and some other indispensable elements may disappear altogether from an integrative span. This leads to startling behavior which we observe in schizophrenics. Federn explained

THINKING AND ACTING 113

the formation of abstract concepts in terms of a certain employment of ego cathexis. He came to this conclusion from the observation that schizophrenic patients lose progressively the capacity for conceptual (abstract) thinking.

NOTES

(1) Freeman, Thomas; Cameron, John L.; and McGhie, Andrew. Chronic Schizophrenia. London, Tavistock, 1958, p. 51.
(2) Glover, Edward, op. cit., p. 345.
(3) This is a position (arrived at on a purely psychodynamic level) which recalls the philosophical concept introduced by Immanuel Kant: The "I" constructs its empirical knowledge in function of time and space and the categories of quantity, quality, modality, and relation.
(4) French, op. cit., Vol. I.

XVII

Ego Economy in Thinking and Behavior

EGO cathexis, an exquisitely binding cathexis, is employed in various ways to maintain a coherent unity and a proper functioning of the field which it invests. This field is the ego.

No integrative field can be formed without cohesive cathexis. We speak of an integrative field, in French's terminology, when we consider a guiding plan for reaching a given end-goal. He explains further, ". . . when we reconstruct the motivational patterns of purposive behavior, we find not one integrative field only but a hierarchy of integrative fields in ever changing relations to one another." [1] But according to French, one is confronted at any given moment with need pressures, and their end-goals require a proper integrative field.

Different need pressures may occur simultaneously, and all the integrative fields pertaining to these various need pressures are, as French expressed it in his study of dreams, "fitted together into a close-knit logical structure." He calls this logical structure the "cognitive structure." [2] An end-goal of one field may coincide with a subsidiary goal of another field, or a single end-goal may satisfy more than one need. The cathexis responsible for the "functional readiness" and "integrative capacity" of French, which brings the need pressures under control according to the integrative plan, corresponds to the ego cathexis of Federn. The present writer confirms French's findings that "hope" is the most important single factor in preservation of integrative capacity and that loss of "hope" results in disintegration.

It is important to repeat here that ego cathexis is manifested in medial, active, passive and reflexive modes. The very complex composition of ego cathexis will be discussed in the third section dealing with cathexis theories.

We shall now discuss only the most important symptoms derived from deficiency of ego cathexis: separation of word representations from ideational contents, regression of the ego to earlier stages, and loss of capacity for conceptual or abstract thinking. Feelings of derealization and depersonalization, as well as delusions and hallucinations, have been discussed earlier in connection with the dynamics of ego boundaries. In the next chapter we will deal with devious or defective integrative spans and contamination of one span by another unrelated one, which brings about a disturbance in cognitive structure and spastic ego paresis.[3] One or more of these disturbances may appear in the same patient, and some of these symptoms may alternate at different periods. Conversely, a patient suffering from one of these disturbances may show other ego functions in perfect condition. For example, a person suffering from severe delusions and hallucinations may express himself quite coherently in speaking and writing.

Thus we must recognize that the mere dynamic-economic characterization—a deficient amount of ego cathexis supply—of all these various symptoms is an insufficient explanation for each single type of symptom. Perhaps the difference in symptomatology may be due to different points of minor resistance in different egos. Perhaps we may someday discover that the ego cathexis has a more complex composition than we know today. Much remains to be explored about the dynamic functioning of the most complicated structure of our mind which is experienced in our ego feeling. But for the purposes of this presentation a dynamic-economic consideration of the complex ego cathexis will suffice.

Let us now examine some mental disturbances caused by a deficient ego cathexis. Everyone understands the importance of verbal expressions for the thinking process. All representations and all perceived or understood events become firmly labeled by words. Words also express relations of the ego, of objects, and of various events to each other in time, space, and causality. "When," "if," "as long as," "since," "because," "between," "among," "later," "earlier" are such words. In the efficient thinking process the ego loses awareness of the mere phonetic character of the words of the language at its command. The word-labels are so firmly attached to the ideational contents which they express that they evoke immediately only the pertinent ideational contents. According to

Freud, word representations are the carriers of the preconscious cathexis. In the id words have only phonetic meaning and do not express anything else; in the id words are treated as object representations subjected to the primary mental process. But the fusion of ideational contents (mostly object or thing representations) with word representations, which thus become the expressions of such contents, puts an end to the primary mental process which rules in the id. This fusion establishes what Freud called the secondary mental process: The unconscious (ucs.) cathexis is fixed on the ideational contents by the preconscious (pcs.) cathexis. The secondary mental process, operating in the pcs., is responsible for the integration of all ideational egotized contents according to the mentioned categories of time, space, causality and so on.

We do not believe that the pcs. cathexis is limited only to word representations, for there is also non-verbal thinking. But all the word representations in their function of expressing ideas are ego-cathected, that is, preconsciously cathected.

Children sometimes concentrate playfully on the sound of some common words, turning their minds away from the expressive meaning. In doing so they get the impression that the sound of such words is very funny. This sensation is very similar to that of estrangement. The words seem strange to them. It is interesting to note that any withdrawal of ego cathexis, or separation of an ego-cathected content from a connection, produces either a feeling of derealization or depersonalization or some other feeling of estrangement. A different kind of playing with words is the pun. These examples demonstrate that word representations can be easily disjoined from the ideational contents which they express. The cathexis which makes the verbal expressions adhere to ideational contents is drawn from the supply of ego cathexis.

Among various kinds of defects of thinking, we find in the hebephrenic form of schizophrenia a progressive detachment of word representations from the pertinent ideational contents. In the most advanced stages of the disease these patients utter words without contents. The words follow each other mostly according to mere phonetic associations, and two or more words can be fused into one word. Freud remarked that in these cases the word representations undergo a process analogous to the primary mental process which is operating in the ucs. Thus according to Freud, both representations of objects (which are separated from their pcs. cathexis), and representations of words (which became disjointed from the ideational contents for which they were used as expressions) undergo the same effect, caused by a free-floating, unfixed cathexis. It seems that the ucs. and the pcs. cathexes have a binding effect on each other. This is the Freudian conception of the phenomenon.

The following example may illustrate speech in an advanced case of hebephrenia: The patient had an expressionless face, as if his look was focused on infinity. The interviewer had the impression that the patient was not looking at him. He asked him what his problem was. The patient answered in a monotonous tone, "My problem? It is very problematic. I am not to blame. This is it. Why? Who knows? O.K. O.K. You have your way, blah, blah, blah, blah." Then the interviewer drew a circle on a sheet of paper, held it in front of the patient's eyes and asked him, "Do you know what this is?" The patient answered, "A circle which has a radius. I have to take so much radiation, it is too hot, you know. In the radiologic institute they do such things. They think in a radiological exact manner. But who cares? There are many carriers of diseases. Am I sick? Who knows? O.K., O.K. . . ." The term used in psychiatry textbooks for such a speech is "word-salad." The patient seems unable to communicate anything. But on closer examination we can grasp a meaning in this patient's utterances. He reveals to the interviewer that he is aware of being sick and of being unable to think properly. "My problem is problematic" means "My disease is unclear, not understood." "I have to take so much radiation, it is too hot" means that he has unusual, unpleasant physical sensations of some kind. His allusion to other people's (radio) logical exact thinking reveals that he is aware of his own inability to think straight. He questions whether he is sick and shows again that he feels sick. He also wards off an accusation that he is responsible or guilty for his condition by saying, "I am not to blame." Perhaps he feels that it is useless to continue to talk, as expressed in the words "blah, blah, blah." His speech could, perhaps, be put into coherent language as follows: "I am sick; I cannot think properly and have all kinds of unusual, unpleasant physical sensations. My disease is not understood, and I should not be blamed for it. Be-

sides, I feel that it is useless for me to talk, because I am unable
to express myself in a way that other people can understand. For
them my speech is only blah, blah, blah, blah." It is doubtful whether
the patient was conscious of the meaning of his speech. In spite of
the phonetic associations—problem, problematic, blame, blah,
blah, radius, radiation, things, think, etc.—some intelligible ideas
did come through. But one also could see that the patient was re-
pudiating all attempts to solve the problem and, rather, was ridi-
culing the interviewer's questioning.

In other cases, through this kind of speech, schizophrenic patients reveal contents which are normally deeply repressed, and
they may also use a symbolic language which we find normally
only in the dream work.

Freud's interpretation of this characteristic speech of schizophrenic patients derives from the observation that the patient's
interest is withdrawn, *in the id*, from the objects of the external
world and is concentrated on himself, on his own ego. The patient
regresses to the condition of primary narcissism. Only the repressed
object drives, such as the oedipus complex, maintain their cathexes.
The schizophrenic patient loses progressively all his interest and
thus also his contact with the external world. He becomes apathetic,
withdrawn; all the previous object libido is turned into narcissistic
libido. For this reason, according to Freud, one cannot establish a
contact with these patients.

There is in these patients, however, a tendency for restitution of
the lost interest in the external world. They make efforts to re-establish a rapport with the external world. Freud considered the
hallucinations and delusions of psychotic patients as an attempt
to replace the lost external world by an hallucinated and delusional
one. But according to Federn hallucinations and delusions do not
arise from restitution attempts; they are, rather, the result of a deficiency, a dynamic lesion, of the internal ego boundary, as was explained in previous chapters.

Another attempt to re-establish a contact with the external world
is induced, according to Freud, by the patient's perception of external stimuli. In this attempt the ego tries to re-cathect object
representations from the perceptive system. We learned that object
interests, as well as every instinctual drive, arise from the id, and

that they become conscious after having obtained pcs. cathexis. We called this phenomenon egotization. Now, in Freud's concept the ego attempts in these cases to recapture, as it were, an interest in objects from the opposite direction, that is, from the perceptive system. And this attempt is doomed to failure. From outside stimulations the ego succeeds in cathecting the pcs., that is, it succeeds in catching words, but the object representations cannot in this way obtain cathexis in the id; the communication from the pcs. to the ucs., the id, remains blocked. Therefore the words become over-cathected without connecting themselves with the object representations which are the representatives of object drives and which can be dynamically powered, cathected, only in the id. Figuratively speaking, the ego captures the shadows but not the substance.

Federn did not express himself about this interpretation of the schizophrenic speech. But his concept of the schizophrenic process does not agree with that of Freud. In his study of schizophrenic patients Federn came to the realization that their egos are not over-cathected but, on the contrary, insufficiently cathected. Nevertheless, he accepted the characterization of the psychoses as narcissistic neuroses, but with the implication that they are due to a deficiency and not to an excess of ego libido. It is true that in the course of the disease schizophrenic patients withdraw emotionally from the external world of objects, but the schizophrenic process sets in before the patients lose interest in the external world. According to Federn, the progressive withdrawal of these patients from the objects is due to the ego's need to drain cathexis from the objects in order to direct it toward its own depleted functions. When an ego has to preserve its own integration and functioning, its own existence, in its struggle with a deficient supply of powering energy, it cannot afford to maintain object interests. The feeling of some psychotic patients that the world is coming to an end expresses the sensation, in an externalized form, that their ego is coming to an end, rather than that they are losing interest in the external world. But this loss is a consequence of fading away of the ego feeling.

We would extend to the phenomenon of the schizophrenic speech Federn's statement that hallucinations and delusions are not unsuccessful attempts at recovery, attempts at re-establishing an emotional contact with the external world, but are the result of dynamic lesions of the ego. In other words, we would say that the disturbed speech of schizophrenics results from an insufficient supply of ego cathexis for binding ideational contents with proper expressions. It is not the effect of an unsuccessful attempt to contact emotionally the lost external world from the reverse direction, that is, via perception and preconscious.

Among other disturbances of the thinking function Federn mentioned the difficulty that schizophrenic patients have in forming abstract concepts. Many authors have characterized schizophrenic language and thinking as a deficiency or complete absence of conceptual or abstract thoughts. Remembering a concrete object—*that* tree, *that* house, *that* desk—is the mnemonic reproduction of the exact perceptive experience of that object. An abstract concept is the idea of a given kind of object, for which we use an appellative, such as *a* tree, *a* house, *a* desk. Abstract concepts are formed from elements common to various experience situations. These elements must be isolated, sensed, recognized as such, and purified from all other additional contents of the concrete ego states which were their source. For this process of isolation and purification a certain amount of ego cathexis is employed. Deficiency of ego cathexis may deprive an ego of the ability to think of *a* tree, *a* house, *a* desk. Such an ego will be able to reproduce only the memory of single, concrete, really seen, trees, houses, desks.

Federn indicated three main pathological features of schizophrenia which are due to a deficient supply of ego cathexis. One is regression of the ego to former states, a protective economic measure against disintegration. As has been mentioned, functioning in a less mature ego state requires less expenditure of ego cathexis. But this measure is often inadequate. A variety of schizophrenic symptoms have their source in regression to the earliest ego stages and can be explained only through the study of these stages. We shall consider these stages briefly in another chapter. It is precisely the phenomenon of such regressions which induced Freud to characterize schizophrenic disorders as a regression to primary narcissism. In the present author's opinion the equating of earlier developmental stages of the ego with narcissism leads to a confusion in our concept of schizophrenia. The second main feature indicated by

Federn is invasion of the ego by false realities, hallucinations and delusions. As was explained before, these are caused by insufficiently cathected inner ego boundaries. The third is loss of the ability for abstract thinking.

NOTES

(1) French, op. cit., Vol. I, p. 118.
(2) Ibid., Vol. 2, p. 1-18.
(3) See Chapter XVIII, especially, pp. 132-133.

XVIII

Span Disturbances and Spastic Ego Paresis

EACH action and each inhibitory impulse of the ego results from various motivations. All these motivations are encompassed in a span which is held together by ego cathexis, forming the "cognitive structure" described by French. An individual may have aggressive urges; he may wish to please other people; he may have to earn his living; he may have love wishes toward other persons, and so on. Because giving in indiscriminately to his aggressive impulses may thwart his other goals, in certain situations he will control his aggressive trends.

At any given time each single interest has its own degree of intensity. For example, at a certain moment an individual may become so much enraged at someone that the impulse to give in to his aggressive urge is stronger than any other interest; he will then attack that person and neglect his weaker interests. Later, because of a decrease in his aggressive urge and an increase in the other interests, he may regret his action. This economic consideration can be applied also in assessing the proportionate strength of some id impulse and the superego (conscience) which condemns it. Or, an individual passionately in love might neglect all other considerations in order to reach his goal and so behave in a way which would ordinarily be thought quite unreasonable.

The behavior of schizophrenic patients often seems extremely foolish and incomprehensible to normal persons. As illustration, an athletic, twenty-two-year-old boy was walking one Sunday at noon on a pier in a small seaport where a crowd of people were promenading. Suddenly he undressed himself, threw his clothes onto a large boat anchored at the pier, and climbed naked to the top of a high mast. From there he began an incoherent speech to address the startled and laughing crowd below. Firemen had to be called to take him down. This was the first *manifest* symptom of schizophrenia. From his case history, however, it became evident that he had shown milder schizophrenic behavior patterns before, but that his family had not been excessively impressed.

Shifts of interest in healthy individuals in given situations can be easily understood. They are different and often typical for different "character structures." But the behavior of the schizophrenic patient described above cannot be understood as readily as our two examples of non-psychotic persons under the pressure of some strong recognizable urge. In the first place, we must understand what is the meaning to the schizophrenic patient of his climbing up the mast, naked and in the presence of a large crowd. If we could understand this, then we could apply the same economic criteria as we do to explain the "foolish" but understandable behavior of non-psychotic people described above. We may see in this behavior the strongly cathected exhibitionistic and athletic impulses of the patient. Analysis could detect some deeper meaning in his impulse to climb the mast, which cannot be recognized without investigation. But normal people cannot comprehend the strength of such impulses which neglect all feelings of shame, understanding of the inevitable consequences of such behavior, the ego's interest in not disgracing his family, etc.

In this patient's case we may also recognize that some important span contents are temporarily or permanently dropped. This is also a consequence of a deficient supply of ego cathexis necessary for maintaining egotization of all the interests and insights of a span. In behavior disturbances of schizophrenic patients the diminution or disappearance from the integrative span of important interests is often startling. To say that such diminution or disappearance is due to withdrawal of object libido, that is, of interest in the external world, is not always consistent with the observed facts, although such withdrawal may contribute to a deficiency in the integrative span. It is more important to keep in mind that all contents of an integrative span must be egotized, since no integration can take place without the secondary mental process. In the present writer's opinion it is precisely the disappearance of important elements from an integrative span which leads to the incomprehensibly strange behavior of schizophrenics.

We learned that our patient did care very much for his family and showed many kinds of object interests. We conclude, therefore, that his ego cathexis, not id cathexis, withdrew for a certain length of time from the mentioned interests in the external world and thus severely mutilated the integrative span. His single acts became incoherent.

An intelligent ten-year-old girl, who in later years became schizophrenic, threw her expensive doll to the floor without any apparent reason, reducing it to pieces. She laughed as if it were a joke. Later she regretted her action bitterly. The motivation for this bizarre act indicated that the girl maintained a strong object interest. She loved her mother dearly and was jealous because her younger sister was preferred. Hostility against her sister was displaced on her doll. This displaced hostility became so strongly cathected that her understanding and insight about the loss of the doll, as well as the reactions of the members of her family, were dropped for a moment from her integrative span.

Neurotic patients who suffer from obsessional impulses of criminal, disgusting, or shameful contents never give in to such impulses. Their defensive measures always maintain the upper hand. When they are frightened we may assure them that they will never commit such actions. But in cases of a schizophrenic affliction we cannot be sure. Defensive measures and insights regarding consequences may lose their ego cathexis and disappear from the span; then such patients actually can commit the fearful actions. A woman drove her car intentionally into a crowd of people waiting on an island for a bus. She explained that she could not resist the opportunity to catch seven people with one stroke of the car. Here the dynamic mutilation of the integrative span is very evident. An obsessional mother was afraid she might kill her children, whom she loved dearly. She was assured by her psychiatrist that she need not fear, because no obsessional neurotic ever had committed such an act. She answered, "But if I should do it, all you have to do is to change your diagnosis." Her answer illustrates the intensity of her fear, but she was not schizophrenic and never committed a crime.

Let us now consider the psychodynamics of the span mutilations described. What happens to the contents which "fall out" from an integrative span? Are they repressed either temporarily or permanently? Or do they perhaps lose their cathexis in the id, as actually happens with the object interests in more advanced cases of schizophrenia? Either of these vicissitudes may occur, in varying degree, with disappearance of ego or object ideational contents from an integrative span, but neither fully explains the phenomenon of span mutilation. Diminution or loss of id (ucs.) cathexis, as well as repression of contents, may facilitate or contribute to the schizophrenic span mutilation, but these are not the specific factors which cause it.

The only concrete fact which can be observed in the phenomenon of span mutilation is that essential contents do not appear integrated in an integrative span, and yet they reveal their presence, disconnected from the span, in some other way or at some other time. Thus we come to the realization that the binding function of the ego (pcs.) cathexis is twofold: (1) to fix (egotize) the id (ucs.) cathexis to the ideational content; (2) to bind the single contents to an integrative field, that is, to a unified mental field. Only the second portion of this function brings the secondary mental process into being. A weakening or an atonic condition of ego cathexis may be responsible for the failure of important ideational contents to become connected within an integrative field.

Although we have described only severe cases of span mutilation, similar mutilations of minor importance are frequent not only in the earlier stages of schizophrenia but also in some individuals who never develop a classical psychosis. Silly or incomprehensible acts or modes of behavior can be observed in egos which have such a morbid disposition, but these egos can be strengthened under favorable conditions. Some adolescents may at times burst into hostile, aggressive and quite unjustified attitudes toward parents or teachers, "without considering" the favorable treatment which they have received from them. But on other occasions they express their insight and interests in the contents which had disappeared from the integrative span.

The ego-cathexis function of isolating elements common to various ego states operates in the formation of abstract thinking. The present author observed another typical thinking disturbance in schizophrenic patients which revealed the importance of the function of keeping separated the ideational contents pertaining to different integrative fields. This function is essential for normal thinking and particularly in the discriminating activity. At the end of a psychoanalytic session with a patient who did not seem well integrated, the therapist began to make arrangements for the next session, whereupon the patient became perturbed. Asked the reason for his unexpected upset, the patient said, "What has this to do with the dream which we discussed?" When the therapist explained that arrangement for another interview had nothing to do with the dream, the patient was not satisfied but continued to argue that talking about the next appointment did not make the dream clearer to him. In another case a patient heard on the radio at home that the Russians had hurled another "sputnik." A little later when he entered his office he heard about the difficulties which the French were having in Algeria. He became confused because he could not figure out how the Russian sputnik could have provoked the nationalist movement in Algeria.

These examples illustrate the failure of the ego to separate one integrative field from another. The fusion of unrelated integrative fields or the mere contamination of one field with another leads to disorientation. We can easily understand that one of the most important ego functions is that of "boundary-formation." According to my own observation boundaries are formed between different integrative fields. This is perhaps another way of expressing Federn's statement that every single ego state has its own boundary.

Without a close and prompt interplay between integrative and boundary-forming (or synthetic and isolating) operations rational thinking and behavior would be impossible. Either or both of these partial functions can be disturbed by deficiency of their activating power, which is supplied from the reservoir or ego cathexis. The fact that these two partial functions act in opposite directions—the one to unite, the other to separate—could favor the idea that ego cathexis is composed of more than one biological component, as Federn maintained. Lack of one of these components could be responsible for the falling out of some elements from an integrative span, the lack of the other for fusion of unrelated fields or ego states. This issue will be better clarified in a later section dealing with cathexis theories.

Contamination of one field by another often induces an ego to make efforts to extricate itself from the resulting confusion. Such efforts have a great similarity with the process of secondary revision, which plays an important role in the formation of the manifest dream content and even more in the elaboration of paranoid delusions, as discussed in the preceding section. In my opinion the process of secondary revision not only takes care of distortions due to the primary mental process and of contradictions between a mental content felt as real and the actual facts of reality, but it also does take care of the effects of fusions or contamination of unrelated fields. The ego tries to combine into an integrative pattern the data of one field with those of another. In this case we might speak of "secondary integration." One school of psychiatry characterizes such delusions as "combinatory," and calls a paranoid clinical picture "paranoia combinatoria."

We come now to the phenomenon of "spastic ego paresis." For purposes of understanding this we must first consider the inhibiting function of ego cathexis which is most clearly manifested in repression. A repressed drive, as explained earlier, may exercise pressure of varying degree against the inner ego boundary in order to force its way into the ego. The ego has, therefore, to maintain a system of anti- or counter-cathexis against such pressures from drive cathexes arising in the id. Repression is the most common defensive act of the ego.

Before continuing we wish to clarify an issue concerning the ego concept. Many psychoanalysts have studied the ego only in its various defensive manifestations, an approach which leads to the belief that the ego develops from the defensive operations of the mental apparatus; in other words, where there is no conflict no ego could come into being. In his idea of the autonomous development of the ego Heinz Hartmann corrected this misconception, and he introduced the term "conflict-free sphere" for functions of the ego which do not serve any defensive purpose. Long before Hartmann, however, Federn's concept of the ego unequivocally contained the idea that the ego exists and develops before it has to cope with any conflict.

We return now to the dynamics of the process of repression. If a repressed content becomes strongly cathected in the id, the ego has to use up a great amount of its dynamic resources in order to maintain the repression. One can easily understand that such a repression constitutes an impoverishment of ego cathexis. In many cases, however, such a dynamic impoverishment is preferable to the entrance of the repressed drive into the ego. In other words, the task of egotizing a drive, of controlling and integrating it within its existing structure, may represent a greater risk for the ego than the loss of ego cathexis employed in counter-cathexis. A repression should not be lifted until changes in the ego structure have been promoted which will permit the previously repressed drive to be egotized and integrated.

When, in the course of a proper psychotherapeutic procedure, a repression has been lifted, the ego becomes strengthened in two ways, through two newly gained dynamic resources. One of these gains has long been considered in psychoanalytic literature: The ego cathexis which had been employed in the process of repression as counter-cathexis becomes freely available to the ego, thus increasing its tonus. The second source of dynamic increase of the ego stems, in the present author's opinion, from the drive cathexis itself which has been captured, as it were, by the ego via egotization. The increased emotional ego state results both from the freed (ego) counter-cathexis and from the afflux of drive (id) cathexis captured by the ego. The present writer came to this realization many years ago through the observation in two patients, a man and a woman, of the immediate effect of the removal of a repressive blockage.

Since the effect of this removal was very similar in both cases, a brief report of the experience of the female patient will suffice here. She was a depressed and anxious young woman whose physical sexual feelings were completely repressed, although she was attracted to men. Through treatment structural changes were produced in the ego so that her resistance against sexual feelings gradually diminished. Eventually during intercourse with a congenial partner she reached a strong sexual orgasm for the first time. Through this experience she felt as if she had become a complete woman. She described her sensations as the most pleasurable experiences that a woman could have, and her enthusiasm about it was limitless.

Her ensuing ego states were interesting. She said that she felt much more alive than ever before. But almost immediately she rectified this assertion. Indeed, she said, as a small child she had felt her own existence with the same vividness when she felt loved and protected by her parents. This vividness, however, progressively and imperceptibly receded. It was only after the unblocking of her feminine sexual drive that she again experienced everything with great intensity. Buildings, trees and flowers, people's voices, the noises of passing cars, all had obtained a pleasantly increased feeling tone. She could enjoy music much more than ever before. This invigorated ego feeling was felt by her as incompatible with depression or anxiety. This case illustrated that after unblocking of previously repressed drives the ego becomes more strongly cathected from release of counter-cathexis as well as through afflux of id cathexis.

When an increased ego feeling occurs suddenly without an accompanying economic decompensation of other ego functions, the behavior of the individual not only remains coherent and rational but may become even more rational and coherent than before. The ego has only gained and lost nothing. This was so in the case of the two patients mentioned in whom a proper structural change in their ego had paved the way for the unblocking of orgastic discharge. In a similar but milder form such an increase of ego feeling can be observed in many persons as an effect of a new pleasurable experience, especially an unexpected one: in young girls or boys who have the first date with one they love, in women who have given birth to the first child, in ambitious persons who reach great, unexpected success in life, etc.

We have to keep in mind, however, that a sudden "unexplained" great increase of ego feeling, in some respects similar to the example given, often constitutes the outbreak of a severe psychosis. Federn observed such outbreaks in severely neurotic patients who suddenly "recovered" from their neurosis without having gone through structural changes which could explain such a recovery. The present author had the opportunity to observe the essential difference between these two kinds of sudden increase of ego feeling. In increase of ego feeling before the outbreak of a psychosis the patient is unable to control the ensuing excitation, and he becomes increasingly less coherent. In the course of his agitation he may feel depersonalized and/or have feelings of derealization. He may then have vivid hallucinations and delusions, the contents of which seem much more real to him than the contents of things which he actually perceives.

A patient who suffered from severe obsessional thoughts, doubts and fears, upon awakening one morning felt completely free from obsessions. Simultaneously he experienced a very much increased ego feeling with the sensation of having solved all his mental problems. This sensation, which had the character of absolute certainty, was that the number one, the unity, was the natural and ultimate basis for all mental life and for the whole universe. His manic excitement about this "great, suddenly gained intuition" increased to such intensity that he had to be hospitalized and put under sedation. In actual fact the sudden "intuition," which removed all his neurotic symptoms, was the distorted awareness that his internal conflicts had suddenly disappeared. The unification of formerly repressed impulses with the ego was represented in his mind by the number one. Fortunately the discharge of the unblocked id cathexis took place in the form of great excitation and was absorbed by his great elation at the absolute certainty of his grandiose insight. The doubting neurotic ego was turned into an ego with indubitable certainties. After a few weeks he recovered from the acute psychotic state, and his obsessions returned in a milder form. His treatment had to be radically modified.

Another patient, an intelligent and cultured twenty-five-year-old college student, came, through his somewhat immature and not too rational behavior, into a situation which was too difficult for him to handle, a situation in which he had lost hope. One morning upon awakening from a deep sleep, he felt a greatly increased ego feeling. In his own terms, his vitality was increased. Soon he became agitated and began to hallucinate. Because of his incoherent behavior he soon required hospitalization, and his condition worsened until he had to be restrained. In the hospital he had acoustic and visual hallucinations, the contents of which bore the character of absolute certainty. He felt them as unmistakable revelations of God.

From this patient, in his own words, the present writer was able to obtain a description of his mental experience prior to complete breakdown: "I didn't feel in complete control of my 'expanding' self. A storm, wonderful, fearful, awesome, was coming, and the problem was to ride the storm wherever it took me." Describing the worst stage of his agitation, he said that he felt as if his expanding self continued to expand like a balloon until finally it burst, and then there was nothing. It was during this period of unconsciousness, when all ego feeling was gone, that he had to be restrained.

After three months he recovered from this acute agitation, but he still maintained the feeling that his extraordinary experience must have contained some real revelation, since he had never before experienced a situation which seemed as real to him as that one. Even after his complete recovery from the psychotic state he was convinced that this experience was not completely negative, although he recognized that it was pathological. He also spoke of a corrective function of his attack.

One feature of the state of agitation described reminds us of a detail of the healthy ego during the first strong orgastic experience: At the peak of the orgastic state the patients mentioned also could not control the emotional discharge of tension, as indeed most normal egos cannot. It was this detail that conveyed to them the unusual, never before experienced, character of the experience. We should add that neither of these two patients had ever before experienced a sexual climax; both had been unable even to masturbate. But for them this lack of control was limited to the brief orgastic experience, while in the psychotic patients the incapacity to control the discharge of the freed cathexis, progressing into agitation, extended over the whole period of their psychotic states. Furthermore, the psychotic patients' feeling, upon recovery from their agitation, that such a state had also a positive side, derives from the sensation that an unbearable tension had been lifted.

Another eighteen-year-old male patient, who had a psychotic breakdown of the type described, had completely repressed his sexual feelings prior to the psychotic episode of six months' duration. During his hospitalization he expressed in his state of agitation strong homosexual and heterosexual urges which were also contained in his delusions and hallucinations. After his recovery from the acute psychotic state he maintained normal heterosexual wishes, and he was then able to satisfy them in a normal relationship with a girl. In this case the liberation of his sexuality from repressing forces occurred through a psychotic breakdown.

It is easy to understand that the psychotic agitations described are due to a withdrawal of repressing (counter-cathecting), controlling and guiding ego cathexis. In the catatonic attack all barriers of shame, guilt and other insights disappear completely, as Nunberg[1] has shown. He pointed out that in such attacks the earliest states of libido development are revived.

The present author was struck by the analogy between such states of agitation and the neurological spastic paresis. This agitation is as uncontrollable as are the reflexes and movements in a spastic paresis. A brief exposition of the neuropathology of the flaccid and spastic paresis will help the non-medical reader to understand this analogy. The muscular apparatus is innervated by a central nervous structure and a peripheral nervous structure. Voluntary muscular action occurs by stimulation of the peripheral nerve cells in the spinal cord via central nerve fibers which descend from brain cells. Their function is not only that of stimulating the peripheral nervous cells from which the peripheral nerves depart to the muscles but also that of controlling and inhibiting the dynamic discharge of the peripheral cells. When the peripheral nervous structure is damaged or destroyed, the muscles which were innervated by it are paralyzed and flaccid. We speak in this case of a flaccid paresis. When, however, the central nervous structure is damaged or destroyed, these muscles can no longer function at will but are put into a spastic condition by the now uninhibited and uncontrolled peripheral nerve cells so that the muscular reflexes are exaggerated. We speak then of a *spastic* paresis.

The analogy, and it is only an analogy, of the central nervous structure with the ego and of the peripheral nervous structure with the id, may serve to bring the described state of agitation nearer to our understanding. When id cathexis is lacking, the ego is without zest, without initiative, "flaccid," as it were. But if id cathexis is in abundance, unchecked by repressing, controlling, and guiding ego cathexis, the individual enters into a state of great psychomotor agitation and loses the capacity to control the overwhelming discharge of id cathexis. Drawing upon the neurological analogy the present author introduced the term spastic ego paresis to express the dynamic feature of such a mental condition.

In the case of spastic agitation the inhibiting, controlling, and guiding portion of ego cathexis is withdrawn, while the ego feeling still resists the onslaught from the id. Moreover, the ego feeling becomes enhanced by the cathexes of the contents which have broken through, so that the hallucinated and delusional contents are felt much more vividly than the perceived ones from the real external world.

How can we explain the increased ego feeling which followed the disappearance of the repressing and controlling ego cathexis in psychotic patients? It would be logical to resort to the explanation given earlier for increased ego feeling which followed the lifting of a repression in non-psychotic patients. There was a change in the use of ego cathexis, and also a new afflux of id cathexis became egotized.

After therapeutic removal of a repression the increase of ego feeling results from that amount of ego cathexis which had been employed in its repressing function and also from the newly egotized id contents. But in this situation sufficient—and we may say abundant—ego cathexis is left for control, for repression of other disturbing id contents and for integration. In the case of spastic agitation, however, the ego cathexis is completely withdrawn from its controlling and integrating positions. Eventually, when the penetrating id contents exceed the extended ego cathexis employed in ego feeling, then the "balloon" explodes and the ego feeling disappears completely. Only after a certain length of time, when the inner tension from the id is sufficiently diminished as a result of the profuse discharge of cathexis, may a checking and integrating ego cathexis again establish itself and the ego come out of its state of agitation.

NOTES

(1) Nunberg, Herman. On the catatonic attack (1920). In Practice and Theory of Psychoanalysis. New York, Nervous and Mental Disease Monographs, 1948, p. 3-23.

XIX

Ego States and Ego Stages

THE coherent contents and the qualities of an individual's self-experience are in a continuous state of flux, depending on constantly changing internal and external conditions. Let us consider schematically the variations in the self-experience of a normal average man. In the morning upon awakening his ego feels rested, resourceful. This man is looking forward to his breakfast. He relates to the members of his family according to the feelings he has at this time for each of them. He is eager to face his tasks of the day.

In considering the way he feels we shall not speak of his "state of mind," because this term would include the conditions of his id and superego. The complex way in which he is actually experiencing himself is specifically his "ego state." We do not, however, ignore the fact that among the various factors which determine his ego state his attitudes toward the various pressures from the id and superego play an important role.

In describing an ego state it is important to consider the ego's relatedness to other individuals, namely, to other egos. In complete isolation from other living beings the human ego easily disintegrates.[1] Only in a postulated earliest, very short stage in ego development, in which the ego has not yet discovered an external world populated by other egos, can there be no relatedness to other beings. Most psychoanalysts do not consider such a stage as a phase in ego development. Their concept of the ego presupposes the distinction between ego and non-ego. Yet, Freud himself accepted Romain Rolland's "oceanic feeling" which is identical with Federn's ego-cosmic ego. Let us continue now with discussion of ego states.

After breakfast our man will go to his place of work. Other feelings, other interests will shape his ego state. He will relate to different people, and his behavior will be determined by different motivations. The same ego will find itself in another state. And so in the course of the day it will pass through different ego states which are determined by the changing egotized needs and by the external situations in which it finds itself at any given time. In describing an ego state we use all the same terms used by everyone to describe what is generally called a "mental condition" or an "emotional state." So we say that an ego is in a placid mood, that it is agitated, restful, angry, frightened, loving, hungry, depressed, sleepy, elated, playful, etc. These are descriptions of an ego state, and we understand that a complete description of an ego state requires a number of such adjectives. But in spite of its continuously changing states every ego feels that it remains the same. This feeling of "sameness" throughout the changes proves that the ego has an invariable core. In healthy egos the changing states maintain a coherence with the ego structure.

The ego remembers most of its states for a certain length of time, and it also knows that under certain conditions any one of the experienced states will return. But we also understand that the specific ego states which a given ego can experience at any age level are characteristic for its coherent structure. In other words, not every ego can enter into the state which only great artists experience when they feel the urge and the capacity to create; not every ego can experience pleasure in cruel acts; not every ego can experience a courageous mood in which it feels ready to meet the most dangerous situations. Therefore it is clear that we must distinguish between different ego states and different ego structures. A certain repertoire of ego states is correlated to any concrete ego. One ego is different from another if the structure of the one can agree with states which would be incompatible with the structure of another ego; or if certain urges, arising from the id, become egotized by one ego, and do not arise from the id of, or are not egotized by, another ego; or if some reaction patterns of one ego are different from those of another ego; or if some qualities of a state of one ego are never experienced by another ego. In the development of ego structure the importance of early identifications with other egos bears repeating here. Also, by the same token, later changes in ego structure result from changes in identifications, as in analytic treatment, by giving up old identifications and by acquiring new ones. In the most simple description of an ego we would speak of an honest or dishonest ego, of a realistic or unrealistic one, of a healthy, neurotic or psychotic ego, of a conscientious ego, of a heterosexual or homosexual ego, of a sadistic ego, of an artistic, strong or weak, sensitive, object-loving, or narcissistic ego, etc. We certainly understand that the indicated attributes are not constantly experienced but that an ego structure, manifested in different states, is characterized by them. Briefly, we describe different egos in the same way in which everyone describes the conscious personalities of people, description for which great writers have a special acumen and ability.

For a better understanding of ego disturbances we shall now consider the effects of alcohol and various other drugs on the ego experience. Very simple is the description of a drunken ego state in healthy egos, where tiredness and sleepiness dominate the picture. But in many drunken persons we observe a great variety of pathological ego states, which are alien to them in the state of sobriety. Some people become very elated, lose their judgmental capacity, and become very verbose. Some become sad, others violent; some present a picture similar to that of a schizophrenic or paranoid condition; some manifest sexual perversions which they did not experience in sober state. In all these cases the individuals harbor, more or less, a latent pathological condition which can be properly checked only in a state of sobriety. As soon as their resistance is weakened by some drug, which in addition stimulates, impairs or paralyzes certain ego functions, the "latent" condition comes to the fore.

Also of interest are the reactions of a "recovered" ego to the memory of such an unusual state which it cannot integrate with its structure of sober life. Very often the ego "forgets" completely how it felt and how it behaved during drunkenness. Actually the ego state is repressed, since in a subsequent state of drunkenness or in a dream it can be remembered. When the ego does remember some of that ego state, or is told how it behaved during intoxication, it becomes embarrassed. The ego state due to intoxication has its own boundary, and the clash between two differently cathected boundaries, pertaining to different ego states, produces this feeling of embarrassment. When in a later chapter we present the meta-psychology of the drives, we shall understand Federn's statement that "affects always develop between two ego boundaries acting on each other, and differ according to the kind of drive cathexis of the ego at these boundaries." [2]

In intoxication the ensuing ego states are alien to the ego as it is structured in state of sobriety. We must, therefore, consider such states as belonging to different, although transitory, ego structures. It should be noted that we are presenting this subject here merely from a descriptive point of view. A psychodynamic approach to study of change in ego states and ego structures requires an understanding of the drive dynamics and the ego defenses which will be discussed later.

Apart from effects of various kinds of intoxication, there are pathological cases in which ego structures, manifested in different states, appear alternately for varying lengths of time. In manic-depressive ego disorders the ego feels very different in each phase, not only in regard to its arising contents and its reactions, but also in regard to the medial and reflexive quality of the ego cathexis. In the depressive state self-destructive cathexis is predominant and determines the patient's uneasiness or even suffering for his very existence. In the manic phase the ego libido is exuberant, and the destructive cathexis is turned toward the external world. In many cases the ego cannot fully remember how it felt and acted in the other state. Slight oscillations of mood, however, can be observed in a great number of persons and therefore the concept of structural stability should not be taken in a very strict sense.

Very striking also are the rather rare cases of so-called double or multiple personality. Such an ego passes from one state to a structurally different state and remains in it for a varying length of time. In almost all cases the ego represses completely the unusual state as soon as it re-enters the previous one. For instance, a female patient who developed a chaste ego, which inhibited all emotional expressions, began at a certain age to change her behavior at irregular intervals, displaying deep feelings and becoming flirtatious. Each time after returning to her usual ego state she felt as if she had undergone a blackout, as if she had had an "attack of amnesia" concerning the period during which she was in the other ego state.

She had difficulty in accepting the report that she had behaved in the way described.

During psychoanalytic therapy one often has the occasion to observe regressions of an ego to former stages. What is an ego stage? We have said that an ego can remember the states it went through back to a certain time in the past. The older an ego phase is, the more faintly will the current ego remember it. The earliest ego structures cannot be remembered at all, although we have evidence that they exist in the repressed ucs. and are revived in severe mental conditions. A mature person can remember vaguely how he felt in adolescence, less well how he felt as a child, and not at all how he experienced himself in the very first years of life. A forty-year-old woman, for example, came upon a diary she had kept for a short time as a child and felt as if she were reading something written by a total stranger. An artistic boy of twenty found drawings he had made only five years before and had no familiar response nor any memory of them. An infantile ego experiences emotions, impulses, etc., which a mature ego cannot experience. Under hypnosis, however, ego feelings as they were experienced in the past can be re-aroused.

We call ego stages the ways the ego was experienced at different age levels. With growth and development, with the learning processes from new life experiences, the ego structure undergoes profound modifications. All the different ego states remain stratified in the repressed ucs. During psychoanalytic treatment, when the patient makes efforts to recapture past emotional states, slight or intensive regressions to former ego stages often occur, although in less degree than in hypnosis. On arising from the analytic couch patients often feel "dizzy" for a few moments. On the couch the patient was recapturing emotional experiences from the past. In so doing he reactivated the former ego stage in which he had had these experiences, and in a certain measure he lost contact with current reality. The feeling of dizziness which he experiences on getting up is due to the sudden re-establishment of full contact with immediate reality and to his return to the current ego stage.

This feeling of dizziness was explained by Sandor Ferenczi[3]: "Many patients have a sensation of giddiness on rising from the recumbent position at the end of the psychoanalytic session. The explanation—in itself rational—that this is the result of the sudden change of posture (cerebral anemia) proves on analysis to be a successful rationalization; in reality the sensation on change of posture is only the means of expression of certain feelings and thoughts still under censorship. During the session the patient gave himself up wholly to free association and its preliminary stipulation, transference to the doctor, and lives in the fantasy that he will always enjoy such well-being. Suddenly this (unconscious) fantasy is destroyed by the doctor's warning that the session is ended; he suddenly becomes conscious of the actual facts; he is not 'at home' here, but a patient like any other; it is the paid doctor and not the helpful father that stands before him. This sudden alteration of the psychic setting, the disillusionment (when one feels as 'though fallen from the clouds') may call up the same subjective feeling as is experienced in sudden and unexpected change of posture when one is unable to adapt one's self suitably by compensation movements and by means of the sense organs—that is to say, to preserve one's 'equilibrium'—which is the essence of giddiness. Naturally at the moment of this disillusionment, that part of the belief in analysis that did not yet rest on honest conviction, but only on a filial trust, disappears very easily, and the patient is again suddenly more inclined to regard the analytic explanations as a 'swindle,'[4] which word association may also facilitate the appearance of the symptom. This problem, however, is not solved, but merely displaced by this discovery, for the question at once arises, why does one call the deceiver a swindler, that is, take him for a person who knows how to rouse feelings of giddiness in others? Probably just because he is able to waken illusions that at the moment of disillusionment will call up the feeling of giddiness (in the manner just described.)"

The present author's point of view is much less complicated and complements Ferenczi's explanation. Careful inquiry has revealed to him that some patients feel strange, rather than giddy, although they complained in almost all such cases of dizziness. The strangeness (depersonalization) is the reaction of the mature ego stage to the regression to an earlier stage just experienced on the couch. Often this feeling of depersonalization is accompanied by anxiety. An adult female patient, who had recaptured on the couch an emotional state which she had experienced at five years of age, indicated quite decisively that she felt then emotionally five years old, and she became frightened that she might not be able to return to her adult ego feeling. These feelings, in less intensity, lasted for two days.

This phenomenon presents a number of problems of practical interest. Sometimes the emotions and emotional memories experienced on the analytic couch are afterwards not fully and immediately assimilated by the adult ego. Therefore, the therapist must avoid as much as possible reawakening a psychotic state which a patient may have experienced in the past. Federn warns the therapist not to take a detailed history of a patient who has had a psychotic episode in the past, because the recollection of that ego state may drag him back to the psychosis. Such a history should be taken only from the patient's relatives.

On leaving a theatre after having been deeply engrossed in the performance, one sometimes feels estranged from reality for varying lengths of time. Accordingly, it is questionable whether psychotic patients whose grasp of reality is limited should be permitted to attend theatrical performances. Tausk mentioned that often in dreams a theatre represents the analysis, or one's internal life, which is unreal, in antithesis to external reality.

A patient who dwells on an especially eventful and emotional period of his life, which may be puberty or a phase of his childhood, may regress to the ego stage of that period and remain in this stage for some time after the psychoanalytic session. In this case the patient does not feel strange after the interruption of the analytic session because he remains in the earlier reawakened stage instead of returning to the current one. But the reawakened ego succeeds in establishing a compromise with current external reality. The reawakened ego stage is revealed in emotions, expectations, affective attitudes, etc., which belonged to that past period of life and to which the ego now becomes susceptible. Such a regression is sometimes more conspicuous when the patient is analyzed away from home and returns home for a visit after several months or a year. During the period of analysis he is without the continuous control of permanent contact with his family; thus in the analytic set-up his ego can regress more freely to a former stage.

A twenty-two-year-old girl in analysis began to feel more viva-
cious especially when she returned home for a visit. In her analysis
she was recalling her emotional state during puberty. At home she
became more attentive to her parents with whom she had lost all
relationship, and on one occasion she caught up her mother and
started dancing with her as she used to do when she was fourteen
or fifteen. Such regressive behavior naturally bewilders the patient's
family and intimates.

In severe cases of schizophrenia, in certain mental conditions resulting from brain lesions, and in senile dementia the ego may
regress to very early stages. It is through observation of regressive
ego stages in these conditions and of infant behavior at various age
levels that we are able to gain our knowledge of the earliest stages
in human development.

Of course, not all psychotic manifestations can be understood
simply as the result of the ego's regression to earlier or earliest ego
stages. For example, the catatonic waxy flexibility, the stereotypies
and echolalia of hebephrenics, and other symptoms have a complex
psychological meaning. But we wish to consider here only the regressive aspects of the psychotic ego.

In the deepest regressive states the psychotic ego, like that of the
infant, does not acknowledge the external world. But while the infant is protected by adults and has neither the physical strength
nor the ability to move, the adult psychotic patient may injure himself through actions which ignore reality completely. In a state of
agitation he may scream, throw himself to the floor, run with his
head against the wall, hit solid objects or glass windows with his
fists. In these cases the destructive cathexis is evident. His soiling,
his smearing himself and everything around him with feces, his
loss of any barrier of shame or guilt or disgust, and his lack of
any consideration of the immediate effects of his actions are all due
to a regression to an earliest ego stage in which early drives, later
repressed with reaction formations, have again become egotized.
In a later chapter on the development of the drives some features
of such regressive behavior will be better elucidated. Such deep
regression is typical for severe catatonic attacks, as Nunberg has
described in the article mentioned.

The importance of the development of interpersonal relation-

ships for the normal growth of the ego has been made evident by
René Spitz's interesting observations and experimental studies of
infants at different age levels, and of different races, in private
homes, in hospitals, nurseries, and foundling homes.[5] Spitz has
shown that the infant has a vital need to be contacted by and related to his mother or her substitutes. Absence of the mother constitutes a dangerous lack of psychological stimulation: Mortality
rates are much higher among those children who are seldom in contact with a motherly person. In the first two months the infant
shows responses of pleasure and displeasure to physical stimulation.
In the third month the infant smiles in response to a human face. At
that age level no other object is yet recognized. Food is recognized
at the age of four or five months. The smiling response occurs when
the infant sees both eyes of another human but not when he sees
only one eye as in profile. The presence of the smiling response is a
criterion of the normal inception of the infant's later capacity for
social contact and social relations. Some time later the infant expresses pleasure and displeasure, not only in response to physical
stimulations but also to psychological ones, for example, to being
abandoned by his mother or her substitutes.

After the age of six months expression of anxiety is differentiated
from that of general expression of displeasure. In agreement with
Ernest R. Hilgard, Spitz assumes that a minimum of ego development is prerequisite for the development of anxiety. But his genetic
concept of the ego is different from that of Federn as presented in
the previous pages. Two months later the infant shows possessive
emotions toward toys. In his ninth and tenth months he manifests
anger, love, sympathy, friendliness, enjoyment, and a positive sense
of property. Interesting too are Spitz's studies of the development
of the child's expressions of yes and no. Such ego stages cannot, of
course, be remembered by adults nor even by children who have
learned to talk.

Very important are Federn's studies of the dreaming ego. In
deep dreamless sleep the ego loses its cathexis; the ego feeling
fades away. Its cathexis is withdrawn into the biological organism.
If we called this state, as Federn once did, "biological narcissism,"
we would abandon the structural concept of the mind. In fact, as
we said earlier, Hartmann calls narcissism the libido investment of

any part of the mind, be it the ego, the id, or the superego. His extension of this term implies an "egomorphic" concept of the whole mind and ignores the topographical position of the ego within the mind.

In dreams the ego is partially reawakened, sometimes only to some of its former stages. Many old and many recent memories, the ego's rational capacity, and other functions may remain dormant.[6] Federn's discovery that ego states undergo repression and are not altogether eliminated is also proved by the fact that they can be reawakened in dreams. In dreams one's body is often not felt and only the mental ego is cathected, a sensation which would be dreadful in waking life. Yet, in dreaming some affects and the will can awaken certain bodily sensations, although too strong or too persistent bodily feelings awaken the ego completely. Usually the dreaming ego perceives its dreams passively, while the will is, in Federn's opinion, the very concentration of active ego cathexis toward an action or thought and not a mere "foreknowledge" of the action, the thought or the planning that is going to occur.

In the process of awakening from dreamless sleep the ego recapitulates rapidly its whole genesis. In other words, the stratified ego stages from the embryonic stage on are instantaneously re-experienced until the ego stage of the actual moment is reached. In a dream the ego may be reawakened only to a stage of the past, and in such case it is only upon complete awakening that the ego realizes that it has experienced itself in the dream as it felt in an earlier period of its life. In the process of awakening from a dream the ego passes through the stages which followed the state in which it was dreaming. Since this phenomenon occurs daily with the coming of morning, Federn called it "orthriogenesis," a word coined from analogy with onto- and phylogenesis.[7]

Let us recapitulate Federn's finding: (1) The feeling of one's identity concerns only the mental ego, since upon awakening one feels one's self to be the same as during dreaming. (2) In dreams with complete absence of body ego feelings some dream figures always represent some parts of the dreamer's own ego. (3) Those portions or situations of the ego that are excluded from the dreaming ego (which has retracted boundaries) appear as external objects, i.e., they are projected on dream persons. As early as the *In-*

terpretation of Dreams, Freud recognized that some dream persons must be interpreted as the dreamer's ego or part of it. We would say only part of it, since another part at least is always that which perceives the dream persons.

NOTES

(1) There is some evidence that absolute loneliness (i.e., isolation) is in itself a powerful stress and can produce effects similar to any extreme stress. On this point, see the contributions of John C. Lilly in the symposium: Illustrative strategies for research on psychopathology in mental health (Group for the Advancement of Psychiatry. Symposium 2 [1956]). It must be recognized, however, that the literature cited by Lilly (dealing mainly with Arctic explorers and shipwreck survivors) implies the presence of other stress-producing agents in addition to absolute loneliness.

(2) Federn, op. cit., p. 334.

(3) Ferenczi, Sandor. Sensations of giddiness at the end of the psychoanalytic session (1914). In his Further Contributions to the Theory and Technique of Psycho-Analysis. London, Hogarth, 1926, p. 239-241.

(4) Ibid., footnote on p. 240: "German 'Schwindel'—giddiness as well as 'swindle'. The interplay here of meaning and sound is untranslatable . . . Translator."

(5) Spitz, René A. Hospitalism. Psychoanalytic Study of the Child, 1:53-74, 1945; The role of ecological factors in emotional development in infancy. Child Develm., 20:145-155, 1949; Infantile depression and the general adaptation syndrome. Proc. Am. Psychopath. Assoc. (1952), 42:93-108, 1954; The primal cavity. Psychoanalytic Study of the Child, 10:215-240, 1955; The smiling response. Genet. Psychol. Monogr., 34:57-125, 1946; No and Yes. On the Genesis of Human Communication. New York, International Universities Press, 1957.

(6) The author has summarized these findings of Federn in the introduction to Federn, op. cit.

(7) In classical Greek *orthrion* signifies the coming of day or daybreak in general, while *eos* is the word used to denote the appearance of dawn in the sky.

Section III

The Id
and the Instincts

XX

First Approach to the Study of the Id

WE are inclined to describe the internal ego boundary, which at certain places is strengthened through counter-cathexes, as a dynamic windowless wall that delimits the ego from the id. But such a description does not account for all its complex properties, nor are the functions of this dynamic wall yet fully understood.

How are the egotized contents which emerge from the id—the tendencies, drives, memories, etc.—related to the internal ego boundary? When they reach a certain degree of intensity, and if no resistance interferes, emerging mental contents are immediately egotized, thus fully experienced within the ego. When this occurs the existence of an internal ego boundary is not apparent. In its progression from the id to the ego a dynamic content obtains preconscious cathexis (ego cathexis) and the ego remains completely unaware of its unconscious origin. By psychoanalytic investigation, however, the origin of the content can be traced back to the unconscious, i.e., to the phase preceding egotization. Figuratively speaking, we can assume the existence of a potential ego boundary which the emerging contents have to cross in their progression from the id (ucs.) to the ego (pcs.). The line of demarcation is set by the process of egotization.

In those egotized contents which seem strange and incomprehensible to the ego, the clear separation of an egotized mental content from the unegotized process of its development is apparent. Such contents appear in perversions of the oddest nature, in bizarre tendencies and wishes, and especially in very absurd obsessional thoughts and impulses. Freud showed us that the unconscious meaning of such perversions, tendencies and obsessions underwent a distortion in the id before they reached the ego's awareness. Freud does not speak of internal ego boundary, but from the very beginning of his psychological investigations he distinguished topographically the unconscious (ucs.) from the pre-conscious (pcs.). As pointed out earlier, the ucs. is governed by the primary mental process, the pcs. by the secondary mental process. The distortion which makes some repressed ucs. contents unrecognizable before they become egotized is an effect of the primary mental process, which we shall examine more thoroughly later.

The dynamic phenomenon of resistance against unacceptable mental contents, which prevents their egotization, is undoubtedly one of the most important discoveries of Freud. Resistance is a manifestation of the ego and appears in various modes. It is now common knowledge that manifestations of resistance were the most formidable obstacles to the acceptance of Freud's discoveries in the field of unconscious mental phenomena. Resistance against understanding and acceptance of the ucs., and of the particular processes by which it is ruled, has a "multiple" motivation as we shall see.

We know that it is not enough to distinguish topographically the ucs. from the pcs., the id from the ego, in order to understand the phenomenon of hallucination. We must also consider the dynamically maintained internal ego boundary. Here it is useful to repeat that mental contents which are not egotized belong (with respect to the ego) to the "inner" external world. The ego lacks sense organs to perceive these contents in the same way it is able to perceive the visual, auditory, and/or olfactory quality of objects of the "outer" external world. We therefore describe the internal ego boundary as "windowless." When the internal ego boundary is weakened (as in a state of sleep or psychosis), unegotized contents are able to penetrate it and reach the ego's awareness. But in such cases they are perceived in their unegotized condition, i.e., they are sensed not as internal mental phenomena, but as external real ones, with all the qualities of external objects or events over which the ego has no selective or influencing capacity. The dreaming ego reacts to the dream scenes and the psychotic ego to hallucinated contents as they do to perceived contents of external reality. Therefore, the assumption of the existence of a flexible, dynamic internal ego boundary is a conceptual necessity for our metapsychological comprehension of many phenomena.

The internal ego boundary is that imagined "locality" in the mind where emerging mental contents become egotized. This flexible, internal, dynamic marginal portion of the ego has a multiple function. It "captures" emerging mental contents through egotization, thus including them within the integrating ego. It also averts unacceptable mental contents from "entrance into the ego"; it recoils from them. These unacceptable mental contents are also known as repressed contents. The refusal to egotize these unacceptable mental contents constitutes a dynamic exertion which is proportional to the pressure of the stimulated contents in the id. A counter-cathexis or anti-cathexis is mobilized from the available sources of the ego cathexis in order to balance the ucs. cathexis, that is, the pressure exerted by the repressed drives and memories. Freud called this consideration an economic appraisal of repression.

As we have seen, the ego's refusal or economic incapacity to egotize ucs. contents does not always prevent it from perceiving them. But such perceptions, often "unwelcome," have an hallucinatory character. As Freud demonstrated, particularly through dream analyses, the "latent" content of dreams (as well as hallucinations in general) undergoes a process of distortion in most cases before it reaches the ego's awareness as "manifest" content. Resistance may prevent unconscious contents from reaching the ego's awareness in their actual form (called the "latent content")—even hallucinatory states—although these contents are perceived as external realities. Only after the repressed contents have been disguised in the id (which makes them unrecognizable to the ego) does the resistance cease to prevent their appearing as dream scenes or psychotic hallucinations. Freud called the perceived contents "manifest." The figurative language which he used to describe this situation is very enlightening. He called the indicated manifestation of resistance the "dream censor," a function which "examines" the emerging mental contents for acceptability or unacceptability to the ego. When a given content is found unacceptable, it must first be disguised until the "censuring function" no longer objects to its appearance as a dream scene or an hallucinated content.

The desired goals and objects of some odd perversions and the contents of bizarre obsessions are egotized end-effects of distorting processes. The contents of dream scenes and the hallucinations of psychotics are unegotized end-effects of such distortions which impinge on the internal ego boundary from the id. In the latter case two sets of "distortion" take place: The first concerns the specific ideational content, and through the second the mental phenomenon is sensed as an external reality.

An understanding of these psychological mechanisms is also essential for a complete understanding of the effects of resistance. "Psychological or emotional resistance" was a familiar phrase long before the advent of psychoanalysis. And even today the man in the street is inclined to speak of emotional resistance whenever a person experiences a reluctance, repugnance, or disgust in doing something, in thinking of something, or in harboring some undesirable tendency or wish. But the resistance discovered by Freud is *unconscious* resistance, an entirely new, hitherto unrecognized phenomenon. In "resistance" in the non-psychoanalytic sense, the ego can immediately indicate against what it is resisting, but this is decidedly untrue of the resistance (in the psychoanalytic sense) which brings about repression. Here the ego is completely unaware of the mental content against which it is resisting. Indeed, Freud considered the ego's resistance itself to be unconscious. In Federn's concept of ego feeling, however, only the repressed mental content (relegated to the id) is unconscious to the ego, while the ego feels the resistance against the ucs. content.

A clinical example may illustrate one of the manifestations of repression-causing resistance. A twenty-three-year-old man consulted a psychoanalyst because he had lost all sexual desire some years before. The loss itself did not bother him, but he suffered from anxiety states and believed that these symptoms might be somehow related to the loss of sexual feelings. He believed he fully understood why he could not have sexual desire, and he did not think that any unconscious phenomenon could be responsible.

The patient said that he had been amazed to read of Freud's statement that a child's first sexual interest is directed toward the mother, because his own experience had been quite opposite. Remembering his past life from early childhood, he recalled that he had known the anatomical difference between the sexes from the age of two when he saw his mother changing the diapers of his baby sister, and that he had experienced strong sexual curiosity from an early age. When he was no more than two or three years old he had begun to have tremendous desire to inspect the genitalia of adult women which he imagined to be similar to those of his sister, although he was not interested in her because her anatomy was well-known to him. In the beginning his curiosity was directed toward all adult women, young and old alike; but there was one exception—his mother. He was strongly attached to her with feelings of tenderness and dependency, but he never experienced the slightest sexual curiosity about her. His love for his mother was incompatible with such feelings. She remained always an absolute exception.

In later years he became normally selective in his sexual craving, which had been very strong for as long as he could remember. He was attracted toward good-looking young women. But in his late teens when he began making sexual approaches to them, he found that he immediately lost interest. The breast of a girl was like the remembered breast of his mother; a girl's body hair reminded him of his mother's hair; and any resemblance to his mother's body immediately neutralized completely the sexual attraction he had felt at first. Gradually he came to realize that the anatomical qualities of all adult women were basically the same, and eventually he understood that his sexual feelings had had as object an unrealistic image of a woman built from misunderstood observations of statues and paintings. His sexual cravings were directed toward women with hairless bodies and breasts of muscular consistency. Once he recognized that such women did not exist, that all women were built like his mother, he could have no further sexual wish toward them, for his mother had never been an object of sexual attraction and could never be.

The patient gave this report in the first interview. From this he concluded that everything was conscious to him, and he had no doubt that his loss of sexual feelings was due to the erroneous picture he had built in his mind of woman. Once he realized that his sexual drives could have no object in reality, he explained, he had lost all sexual interest in women. In his opinion it was not necessary to resort to unconscious mental phenomena in order to understand this state of affairs.

The psychoanalyst remarked that, since the patient's mother was a woman too, he had previously distinguished two kinds of women. One kind belonged to the category of his mother, toward whom he could have tender and loving feelings but not possibly sexual interest. The other kind belonged to the category which aroused in him sexual longings. In order to settle on an acceptable object for his sexual excitation, he had to build in his mind a concept of a female body sufficiently different from that of his mother. But eventually he discovered that such women did not exist in reality.

He was not aware of any resistance against sexual tendencies toward women of the mother type. As a matter of fact, he was not opposed to sexual interest in the girls he had contacted even after the discovery of their actual physical nature. But they simply did not have the slightest "sex-appeal" for him; they were not the sexual objects which he desired.

Psychoanalysis revealed that the patient had very early repressed his sexual interest in his mother and the early ego states which encompassed it. At this point in our discussion it seems appropriate to distinguish two systems in the id: (1) the biological id in which sexual drives are neither ego- nor object-invested, and (2) the id in which the repressed object-related drives are encompassed. The repressed oedipal wishes of this patient belong to the latter upper stratum and not to the biological id. To avoid confusion I shall not pursue this distinction here but will continue to speak of the id as a single structure.

It was interesting to learn that, prior to his discovery of the actual physical aspect of all women, this patient's erotic dreams were often disturbed by the interference of his mother. Repressed contents broke through into the sleeping ego which reacted to them with feelings of horror and disgust. These feelings are those commonly designated as resistances. But before Freud we ignored the "reactive character" of these resistances. In other words, the repression-causing resistance was directed against an actual, but unconscious, sexual craving for his mother, which he ignored completely. Every time that this unconscious craving broke through, in an unegotized hallucinatory form, the dreaming ego reacted with feelings of horror and disgust. We call these feelings reaction formations to the pressure of repressed drives. They are powered by counter-cathexes mobilized as a defense measure against such pressure. Thus feelings of horror and disgust prevent the ego from sensing the repressed drives.

It is quite understandable that Freud's announcement of his psychological findings aroused the most violent public reactions. In the slow process of civilization man has built formidable emotional barriers against his primitive, antisocial, and cruel instinctive drives. These drives constitute our inheritance from earliest times, through vast periods of development from subhuman beings to civilized men who had progressively to integrate themselves into social life. To ask acceptance of all the psychoanalytic findings might seem to some people to ask them to undo all the repressive and defensive efforts which humanity has made to become civilized. But these discoveries were necessary in order to comprehend human nature as well as to understand mental and emotional disorders which could not have been explained otherwise. A healthy ego in our civilization must have the strength to accept psychological truth without feeling threatened in its ethical, cultural, and social integration. At the same time we must realize that psychoanalysis also explains the nature and sources of man's strong ethical values.

Another source of resistance against acceptance of the unconscious is man's pride, or narcissism as Freud calls it. Man wants to keep the illusion that he is master of his own mind. How can he then accept the knowledge that he is completely unaware of his strongest urges and drives? Further, the operating processes in the id ignore and defy the logical coherent way in which conscious ideation unfolds itself.

At the same time we can easily understand why for a period ego psychology fell into disrepute among Freudian analysts. When we consider how bitterly Freud had to fight to defend his pioneer discoveries in the field of the unconscious, we can also understand that any diversion from this field could have imperiled progress in the investigation of the unconscious. Psychoanalysis was then emphasized as the psychology of the unconscious—and nothing else. To be sure, many of Freud's pupils could follow him only to a certain point and for a certain length of time, for they could not well endure the impact of their own resistances. Some tried to arrive at more acceptable interpretations of dreams and the neuroses, but this was at the expense of scientific truth and depth. On the other hand, some of their correct and useful findings were ignored or neglected by the followers of Freud.

We should bear in mind, however, that a proper scientific attitude requires evidence for reported psychological findings. Moreover, as is true in the historical development of many sciences, some of the early psychoanalytic findings must often be corrected, refined, or even replaced by new facts derived from subsequent investigations.

In the next chapters we shall discuss the development of the instinctive drives and the psychology of the id in its interrelationship with ego psychology, the main functions of which we presented in the first two sections.

XXI

Instincts and Drives

FREUD, who was the first to undertake a systematic study of instincts, called urges and drives *Triebe* (literally, "impelling force"). Considerable confusion has resulted from the translation of this word by the English "instincts," essentially innate, co-ordinated sequences of impulses which lead to specific end-goals. They are to be found in all individuals of the same species in the same form. In animals the significant co-ordination of the sequence of instinctive actions is evident from the highest to the lowest species. Birds, for example, build their nests at mating time; and the acts of laying eggs, brooding, and the parental care of the young are all conative actions leading to the goal of propagation of the species.

Freud's scientific interest was directed primarily toward those impulses and drives (*Triebe*) which played the most important role in psychodynamic phenomena. Such drives are, of course, induced by instincts, but they may appear in different individuals in different forms and may have a different emotional color. In order to understand their immediate specific goals and the objects toward which they are directed, it is necessary to study the phenomena of the "great powerhouse"—the id. The specific paths into which instinctive forces are led are determined by the past experiences of each individual and the ways in which he has succeeded in coping with conflicts which have arisen. The study of the "instinctive drives" (as we shall call the *Triebe*) led Freud eventually to formulations regarding the basic drives of all living matter, and thus his explorations entered the field of general biology.

The physiological approach to study of instinctive drives led to some confusion, because some psychoanalysts mistook the working mechanisms of "biological tools" for the end-goal of the life process. But before examining this approach let us consider briefly the state

154

of knowledge in the field of instincts and drives as it existed before Freud.

Definitions and classifications of instincts and drives were often very loose. They were defined, often interchangeably, merely as "natural impulses." Some instincts were superficially classified according to the nervous areas stimulated, others according to the immediate goals to be reached. Hunger, thirst, pain, sexual desire, anger, or rage, all urges and drives whose tensions are released in the achievement of goals, and those which are felt as needs "instinctively" satisfied, were considered basic "instincts."

William McDougall listed a great number of such "instincts," among them fright or escape, pugnacity, repulsion, curiosity, self-display, submission, sex, acquisitiveness, and the parental, gregarious, and hunting instincts. Of these, some are interchangeable; others, like fright, are merely reflexes produced by certain stimuli and subordinated to the basic instinctive organization. By analyzing these instincts and identifying common components, the list can be reduced. One classification still very popular reduces the number of instincts to three: the self-preservative, the species-preservative, and the herd instincts. Another classifies "love" and "hate" as irreducible instincts and the basis of concepts used in different ways by different authors which can be traced back to Plato.

Let us now examine the physiological basis from which some psychoanalysts (and in certain measure Freud himself) tried to interpret the manifestations of the drives. Biologists call irritability the common property of all living organisms to react to external and internal stimuli. The chemical composition and state of dynamic tension of living matter are of very inconstant and unsteady nature and are continually disturbed by the stimulations mentioned. Their reaction to these stimuli tends to restore the equilibrium which existed prior to the stimulation. Fechner called "stability principle" the tendency of the tension inherent in physiological and correlated mental processes to remain at the same level and the constant reaction of the nervous system to every increase of tension resulting from stimulation in such a way that the former level is re-established. He explained the phenomena of pain and pleasure by means of the stability principle: Every increase of tension would be sensed as pain and every decrease of tension as pleasure. But, as we shall soon see, these phenomena are too complicated to be explained only by this consideration. It is not known on what factor the stability principle is based. This principle and the property of living matter to react, which we call irritability, constitute the riddle of life. The frequent reference in biology and psychology to such "principles" is an admission that no explanation can be made for the facts described.

Claude Bernard also recognized the stability principle, but he called it the "constancy principle." It was later applied to the study of all physiological phenomena by W. B. Cannon. This principle is in fact a general manifestation of the self-preservative instinct. The constancy level is that amount of tension most favorable for the process of life. It is well known, for example, that the temperature of warm-blooded animals is maintained within a very narrow range of variation regardless of the temperature of the external environment. If the organism is put into a cold environment, various physiological processes set in to forestall a decrease in temperature or to increase it to the former level if it has fallen. Conversely, if the organism is put into a warm environment, physiological processes operate in such a way as to reduce to normal the increased internal temperature. The chemical composition of the blood and lymph, called by Claude Bernard *milieu interne* and by Cannon "fluid matrix," is also subjected to the constancy principle. In *The Wisdom of the Body* Cannon analyzes the complex integrative operations of all tissues and organs in re-establishing, after disturbance, the chemical and physical equilibria within the body. The acid-base balance, the chemical composition, the osmotic pressure, and other qualities of the fluid matrix are always restored to the normal level after disturbance. Cannon called this physiological principle the "homeostatic principle" or, briefly, homeostasis.

Under conditions of actual life, nervous tension is continuously subject to stimulation and disturbance. Therefore, life activity is directed toward re-establishing tension at its prestimulation level. This principle, as we just mentioned, is the basis for Fechner's theory of pain and pleasure: Since every change in nervous tension must be experienced as something abnormal, any increase of tension over the normal level must be felt as unpleasant or painful, and any relief must be felt as pleasant. The intensity of pain and pleasure is assumed to correspond to the quantity and rapidity of increase or decrease of tension. This economic explanation of pain and pleasure is acceptable for a vast category of pleasurable or unpleasurable experiences, but not for all.

Various kinds of excitation and correlated cathexes, can be distinguished here from the following consideration: Though pleasure is caused directly by the discharge of tension, a state of tension may in itself become desirable for the pleasure to be derived from release. The quality of excitation (cathexis) which causes the tension seems to play an important role. Pleasure produced by certain kinds of cathexis is obtained by a level above constancy. Not only is energetic tension restored after a discharge but for effective mastery it is restored in excess of the minimal quantity required for survival. In this way capacity for mastery is developed in advance of situations for which it is required, and various processes for discharging the excess tensions—muscular exertion, intellectual activities, etc. —may be cultivated and are pleasurable.

It is a basic vital activity of the organism to restore the energy consumed in reaction to stimulation and discharge of tension. In earlier chapters dealing with ego functions we considered the restoration of ego cathexis.

A brief indication of Freud's instinct theories, which will be more exhaustively discussed later in this section, may be inserted here. If the restored energies are exhausted and no afflux of new "fuel" occurs, no amount of stimulation can produce a further increase of tension, and the organism dies of the very reactions by which it rid itself of all tension. In his later theories Freud formulated another "principle" which is manifested in all living organisms. He assumed on the basis of his observations that living organisms tend also to get rid of tension altogether, with the goal of returning to the inorganic state from which they are thought to have developed. Accepting Barbara Low's term "nirvana principle," Freud held that inherent in every living organism there is also a death instinct which acts in a direction opposite to that of libido, inhibiting and destroying production, assimilation, and even pleasure, and counteracting the restoratory processes induced by the life instinct which he called "Eros." This instinctual dichotomy would be responsible for the biological anabolic and catabolic processes.

The victory of exhaustion over restoration, catabolism over anabolism, causing the organism to age and die, is in Freud's opinion the most primitive effect of the death instinct. It is the life instinct which is responsible for the restoration of the level of tension most favorable for life. As a matter of fact, Freud's formulations of the principles of the life and death instincts were not clearly expressed and were both misunderstood and misinterpreted by some psychoanalysts. It seemed a fusion of the constancy and nirvana principles when Freud stated that "there is an attempt on the part of the psychic apparatus to keep the quantity of excitation present as low as possible, or at least constant."

That exhaustion of energy causes fatigue and discomfort, and that its restoration brings about re-invigoration and pleasurable sensations, should be interpreted, in the sense of Freud's theories, as reactions induced by the life instinct to the aims of the death instinct. The misunderstanding of Freud's concept of the death instinct is revealed by some psychoanalysts who consider states of rest and sleep as expressions of the death instinct. Quite the opposite would correspond to Freud's theories, for as Federn pointed out, rest and sleep are antithetical to the death instinct, since they serve the restoratory processes of energy by which life is maintained. In rest and sleep anabolic processes outweigh the catabolic ones. The assimilation of food could not keep pace with the speed of the consumption of energy if the organism did not periodically interrupt its work. Every function has periods of rest. Even the heart beat consists of alternating contractions and relaxations. In dreamless sleep, as Federn has pointed out, the ego "fades away," and the organism is relieved of the drain on energy exacted by the functioning ego. The sensation in retrospect that sleep was pleasant is due to the process of restoration.

It seems clear that the purely economic stability principle fails to account for all the facts concerning pleasure and pain. In particular, no answer is given to the question why certain states of tension are felt as pleasurable in themselves. One explanation considered by some psychoanalysts, including Fenichel, is that the anticipation of pleasurable discharge which accompanies the state of tension actually initiates the process of release. It is the factor of anticipation, in their opinion, that guarantees the integrative process by inducing the organism to discharge its tension. We are here reminded of French's emphasis on the importance of the role of "hope" in the establishment and maintenance of an integrative field. When there is no anticipation of relief, there is no discharge, and the tension is usually felt as frustration and pain. A hungry man can enjoy his hunger in the immediate prospect of a hearty meal. But relief through anticipation, as we have seen in our discussion of hallucinatory gratification, has its limits, and if he is kept waiting long, his sensation becomes one of frustration. Frequently conscious efforts are made to heighten pleasure by anticipation, as by increasing thirst before drinking, or by purposeful increase of sexual tension in order to increase the orgastic discharge of the tension obtained. But nobody would seek increase of physical pain even if he could have the certainty and expectancy of a quick relief of such a tension. It is therefore evident that there are excitations of different nature.

We have said that pleasurable phenomena are explained from the economic point of view by the heightened discharge following a heightened state of tension, so that the economic balance is preserved; but this answer contradicts those who, by their own testimony, enjoy the state of tension itself as well as the sensation of discharge. The latter is, of course, more conclusively enjoyable. It bears the sensation of having accomplished something. So far as the state of tension is concerned there is, of course, a limit which pleasurable tension cannot exceed. But this limit is well above the equilibrium level of the stability theory. Love and sexuality are enjoyed even before or in absence of discharge when their tension exceeds the level of constancy. The great pleasure of sexual orgasm generally occurs at the peak of tension, even before the critical discharge. The latter, it is true, is accompanied by the most conclusive pleasure; yet many people postpone this conclusion in order to prolong the enjoyable tension itself.

Thus it seems undeniable that in certain cases the state of tension is felt as pleasurable, as in love, sexuality, the phenomenon of ecstasy and many others. Conversely, we repeat, states of tension associated with apprehension, anxiety or discomfort, although their draining brings relief, are never in themselves enjoyable. In the pathological exception of masochism physical or emotional pain has become erotized in the id through associative connections which will be discussed later. Also in this case the experienced pleasure seems to be an expression of a special kind of excitation cathexis, called libido. Thus, we conclude, to obtain a satisfactory explanation of pain and pleasure we must supplement quantitative economic considerations with others, giving special attention to the quality of the relevant cathexes. If pleasure involving certain cathexes requires a level above equilibrium, it seems reasonable to seek the explanation in the nature of the fundamental instincts and the pertinent drives.

Federn, who fully accepted Freud's formulation of the death instinct, invented the terms "suffering" and "non-suffering" (in German *Leid* and *Unleid*) to express a principle of the operation of the destructive energy which he called "mortido." The "suffering-non-suffering principle" would act in opposite direction from the "pleasure-pain principle" (in German *Lust-Unlust*) for the operation of libido, the dynamic expression of the life instinct. In fact, in Freud's later writing the pleasure-pain principle (presented in Chapter VII) has validity only in respect to libido. In anticipation of a later more extensive discussion on this subject, we note here that in Freud's teachings libido and the destructive cathexis, both of which can be directed toward one's own individuality or toward objects of the external world, appear always fused together in varying proportions. According to Federn's "suffering-nonsuffering principle" the tension and discharge of mortido, directed toward one's own person, lead to suffering and to avoidance of nonsuffering and pleasure. The present writer, however, who has reached no conclusion regarding the instinct theories, disagrees with Federn's formulation of the "suffering-nonsuffering principle." In the present author's opinion the tension or discharge of a postulated death-drive cathexis would cause suffering and interfere with pleasure only in the presence of a still operating, but overwhelmed, libido. The libidinal portion of the ego would react with pain and displeasure to the operation of mortido. In absence of any libido-cathected portion of the ego, introverted mortido would kill the individual *without* pain and suffering.

If homeostasis alone were operative in a living organism, no changes, no development, no growth, no production, no propagation would occur. The organism would have only to restore the energy spent in the maintenance of the "energetic status quo" and to offset, with its reactions, the disturbances of energetic balance caused by external stimulations. But the living organism is also continuously stimulated by endogenous stimuli, and it also reacts to them according to the homeostatic principle. The endogenous, differentiated afflux of excitation or energy into a homeostatic system constitutes the biological tool or biological mechanism for work and production. It is precisely because of the effects of this internal, biological, stimulation that no "status quo" can exist in a living organism.

The selective effects of various kinds of endogenous stimulation bring about constructive activity, growth, and propagation. Freud always considered a specific hormonal source of excitation, in particular excess excitation, as the generating factor of libido. Physiological investigation of the immediate sources of the drives revealed that the physiochemical stimulations are so timed and integrated as to arouse in any given phase such drives as lead to self-preservation and preservation of the species. The secretion of different hormones occurs at the proper time for awakening those interests which induce the individual organism to perform the biological tasks in proper sequence. It seems that the different instinctive drives are related to the primary instincts as subsidiary goals are related to end-goals; and the achievement of subsidiary goals relieves the ego. We do not know what factors bring about these integrative processes; we can merely speak of "principles," in this case of "integrating" or "ordering" principles, running throughout all life, the origin of which is not understood. Without considering the nature of biological stimuli which set the homeostatic system into action, and the goals of this action, we could make no classification of drives and their pertinent cathexes.

Franz Alexander, who considers only the quantitative and not the qualitative manifestations of endogenous excitation, introduced the term "surplus energy principle" to characterize the interaction of the two factors mentioned: homeostasis, and the endogenous production of excitation which continuously and selectively raises the organic tension above the equilibrium level. He calls this endogenously produced energy "surplus energy." In his approach he does not intend to reach any formulation of drives. He makes only a distinction between those tendencies which comply merely with homeostasis and those which result from the "surplus energy" and its discharge in various activities. Alexander calls the latter "erotic drives." According to his theory, the discharge of all surplus energy, by which homeostasis is re-established, is pleasurable. His theory of pleasure and pain is thus in full accord with that of Fechner, presented above. Alexander equates libido with surplus energy.

C. G. Jung calls "libido" all vital energy of any kind. His concept of libido is similar to Bergson's *élan vital* or "vital energy" as it is conceived by the vitalists.

In the next chapter we shall present Freud's libido theory in its development and evolution, then the specific instinctive drives as they develop and are manifested in humans. Perhaps then we shall be better prepared to examine the different theories of the basic instincts and their pertinent cathexes.

XXII

The Libido Theory

WHEN an external stimulus causes an increase of tension in a living organism, the organism has to remove the stimulus or withdraw from it in order to restore the tension to the previous level. But when the stimulus arises within the organism, the organism has to deal with it in different ways. Life is characterized by continuous states of tension which are also manifested in the ego's various interests and urges. As was pointed out in the previous chapter, satisfaction of these interests and urges is reached when the state of tension inherent in them is lowered to the constancy level. In addition, the activities induced by states of tension caused by inner stimulation are directed toward the goal of removing the stimulation, but the individual cannot withdraw from it as he can from external stimulation.

This is true also in every physiological activity. Lack of oxygen and an excess of carbon dioxide stimulate the respiratory center. This stimulation is removed by oxygen intake and elimination of carbon dioxide. Lack of nourishment stimulates specific nervous centers, and the derived tension is experienced in the sensation of hunger which is satisfied by food intake. The specific actions toward this goal follow innate and learned patterns. The tension caused by accumulation of urine in the bladder and fecal masses in the bowel is relieved by acts of expulsion of these substances from the body. As we shall see, the latter urges play an important role in the development of erotic drives.

If we consider sexual stimulations, we realize that their biological goals can be substituted in many cases by different goals. States of sexual tension are produced by hormonal excitation of various kinds, but the individual cannot resort to any direct actions to remove the sexual hormones. The difference between this kind of stimulation and those of the urges mentioned is quite evident. States of

163

sexual tension are diminished through various kinds of discharging processes which can be bound, in different individual cases, to different goals and different objects. Through various processes and acts sexual cathexis in excess of the constancy level is pleasurably discharged. In all cases of endogenous stimulation we must consider also the quantitative factor. Whether the stimulation is caused by lack of oxygen and excess of carbon dioxide, or by lack of nourishment, or by the pressure of waste products, or by various hormonal actions, in all these cases the tension must reach a certain degree of intensity before the individual becomes aware of it. Then the increase of tension can be endured to a certain intensity, so that the enduring capacity varies for each kind of resulting need. Lack of oxygen and excess of carbon dioxide can be endured only for a very short time, lack of nourishment can be endured much longer, while sexual gratification can be postponed indefinitely without danger to the individual's survival. This consideration, among others, induced Freud to distinguish originally between self-preservative or ego drives and the sexual drives. He called libido only the cathexis pertaining to the sexual drives.

Freud's concept of sexuality or erotism requires further elaboration. In the pre-Freudian concept only one form of discharge of sexual excitation in healthy mature individuals was considered: the emotional, extremely pleasurable discharge in the form of a "crisis" called orgasm. In this "explosive" emotional state not only is the excessive sexual tension discharged in both sexes, and the semen expelled in men, but a chemical neutralization of the hormones, which produced the sexual tension, also occurs. Strong emotional states of any kind are accompanied by specific endocrine secretions, a phenomenon which became particularly evident in the study of psychosomatic disorders. In the state of sexual tension the heart beat is accelerated, the pupils enlarged, which indicates that the sympathetic nervous system is stimulated by specific hormones. After an orgastic discharge of sexual tension, specific vasomotor and vasosecretory phenomena occur—slowing down of the heart beat and narrowing of the pupils—which indicates that the parasympathetic nervous system, the antagonist of the sympathetic nervous system, is stimulated.

Sexual experiences appear in a great variety of forms, not only in that which is considered as the natural biological one of mature individuals. Physical erotic pleasure is not always bound to the genital organs, sexual desires are not always directed toward an individual of the opposite sex, nor are they always or only satisfied by the act of intercourse. Masturbatory acts and sexual perversions are known deviations from the "biological" aspect of erotism. Besides, sexual urges and tendencies are manifested in childhood, long before the inherent tension could be discharged in an orgastic manner. We call "erogenous zones" those parts of the body which give erotic pleasure on stimulation. The displaceability of erotization from one bodily zone to another, from one mental content to another, is another characteristic of libido.

Two more features are encompassed in Freud's libido theory. First, libido can be desexualized or de-erotized, as it were. This means that in cathecting certain objects and goals libido loses its sexual appearance and thus does not create any urge for an orgastic discharge. Freud called "sublimation" the phenomenon of substitution of originally sexual objects and goals by others which are not only accepted by society but also highly evaluated by it. Scientific and artistic interests, "platonic love," are examples. The second feature is an economic one which leads to the assumption that desexualized interests are powered by libido. The amount of libido which is produced in an individual at any given time powers a great variety of interests and urges. The more strongly one given position is invested by libido, the less libido is left for other positions. The more libido is invested in sublimated interests, the less of it will be used for sexual interests. The more an individual loves himself, the less he can love other individuals. Thus, the conclusion can be drawn that the same kind of cathexis is employed in a variety of interests. In other words, many emotionally different interests and urges are dynamically fed by the same source of cathexis, in much the same way that the same electric current can power different devices, a light, a motor, a bell, a refrigerator, etc. The more electric energy from the same current is used for one device, the more weakly will the others be powered. This analogy can be used only in regard to that libido quantity which is produced at any given time. Let us now summarize the tenets contained in Freud's *original* libido theory as follows: (1) Sexual cathexis (libido) has its own biological source of production; it cannot power self-preservative or ego drives. (2) Likewise, the cathexis of the ego drives (which was not called libido) cannot power erotic interests. (3) Libido can be displaced from one zone of the body to another, from one object or goal to another. The libido-economic point of view must take into account the phenomenon of desexualization of certain interests and urges.

We may now ask, how is desexualized libido discharged? An orgasm-like discharge is out of the question, but the answer is simple: Desexualized libido (interest) tension remains by and large on the same level, although it does oscillate. Tendencies, urges and interests which are powered by desexualized libido can be continuously and intermittently, but not explosively, satisfied. It is this kind of libido which makes life lastingly enjoyable. If desexualized libido does not find a way of satisfaction, the individual experiences boredom and frustration. Physical and intellectual activities are continuously sought, from infancy to old age, in forms of "diversions," play or valuable productivity, aimed to satisfy all kinds of interests beyond self-preservation. All are expressions of libido. On the other hand, if all libido were discharged only in an explosive manner, life would consist in a monotonous increase of erotic tension which had to be frequently discharged through an orgastic experience, after which a complete state of rest would follow, and no other activity or productivity would occur.

Freud's distinction of two basically different sets of drives, each powered by an economically independent source of cathexis, is called "drive dualism." It must be mentioned here that, in Freud's original concept, the self-preservative drives did not encompass only those which maintain or restore "homeostasis" but included the processes of normal development and growth of the individual. Alexander, however, considers erotic also every normal development and growth of the individual himself. As was mentioned in the preceding chapter, in his formulation of the "surplus energy principle" he considers as non-erotic only the cathexis employed to maintain or restore the status quo in the strictest sense of the word. Freud, on the other hand, considered the "surplus energy," without using this term, as essential in both kinds of drives, in the ego drives and the sexual drives. Therefore Alexander's new theory cannot be considered a return to the original Freudian formulation, in which a qualitative distinction between two basic instinctive drives was made. Alexander makes only a quantitative distinction.

In order to do justice to the theories of the instinctive drives and the pertinent cathexes, it is necessary to mention briefly some historical background. Freud maintained his earlier formulation of the drive dualism until 1920. In his classic monograph *Beyond the Pleasure Principle*[1] the earlier formulation of the basic drives was replaced by another, in which he postulated the existence of life and death instincts.[2] C. G. Jung from the very beginning denied any drive dualism, and in his "monistic" drive theory he admitted only the existence of libido, an animating, vital energy in all life phenomena. His theory was very disturbing to Freud at the time of his early discoveries. Initially Freud explained the phenomenon of repression as a result of a conflict between a sexual drive and those drives pertaining to the ego. Only later was repression recognized as the effect of incompatibility between an id impulse and the demands of the ego, particularly in its submission to the superego. In other words, only in a later stage of psychoanalytic progress was repression recognized as the effect of a structural conflict. Fenichel, who does not accept Freud's dualistic theory of instincts, writes: "When Jung denied this dualism of instincts and wanted to call all ego instincts libidinal, his unification at that time would have obscured the newly discovered fact of repression." [3]

In the early years of psychoanalysis much was elaborated on the relation between ego drive cathexis and libido. It was easy to recognize that the aims of the libido often followed the paths of the self-preservative drives. This became most evident in the study of erotization of bodily organs, as will be presented in the next chapter. In addition, desexualized libidinal interests find gratification in various activities by which also some means necessary for survival are produced. These libidinal interests are responsible for a more than absolutely necessary and for increasingly perfected production. When Freud presented his concept of narcissism, in its more elaborate form in 1914,[4] that is, of the libido invested in one's own ego, he distinguished clearly between egoism or selfishness and narcissism. Egoism, he explained, was an expression of the ego drives, while narcissism, self-*love*, was the libidinal complement to egoism.

In 1908 Alfred Adler made a clear distinction between libido and aggressive impulses, and considered the sexual perversion of sadism as an intertwinement (in German *Verschränkung*) of libido and aggression. He derived the aggressive impulses from his theory of the "will to power" of the ego, in other words, from the ego's urge to dominate his fellow-beings. The "masculine protest" was (in his opinion) another expression of this urge. When Freud arrived at his concept of a nonlibidinal aggressive cathexis in 1920, he derived it from an origin completely different from that contained in the Adlerian formulation. To Freud the primary expression of destructive cathexis is the tendency of an organism to die. But since this kind of cathexis can also be directed at objects in the external world and one's own individuality is spared the action of that amount of destructive cathexis which becomes "extraverted," aggression toward external objects is a secondary phenomenon. The difference between the Adlerian and Freudian concepts of aggressive energy is quite evident, although Freud's concept of the fusion of libido and destructive energy is reminiscent of Adler's intertwinement of libido and aggression.

The problem concerning the phenomenon of desexualization of libido is not yet solved. The existence of this phenomenon is proved by the undeniable fact that various sexual, as well as non-sexual, interests and urges are powered by a common economic unity of cathexis, as was pointed out above. Libido is in high degree displaceable. The importance of this phenomenon became particularly evident when the concept of libido, according to the second formulation of Freud's dualism of drives, was applied to the study of ego dynamics by Federn and Hartmann, each through different approaches.

It seems very probable that both psychological and hormonal factors of various kinds are responsible for different employment of libido. Freud had already considered endocrine phenomena when he formulated his earlier theory of the drive dualism. At that time he assumed that the hormones which produced libido had a different chemical composition from those which produced the cathexis of the ego drives. He also realized that, besides psychological factors, different kinds of sexual hormones also were responsible for different sexual tendencies.

It is well known that male hormones produce different physiological and emotional effects than female hormones. If we consider the observation that men who have lost their testicles after puberty, who have been castrated in the physiological (not in the psychoanalytic) sense of the term, can still have orgastic experiences, we shall realize how complex the sexual endocrine phenomena are. Benedek and Rubenstein[5] have demonstrated that estrogen, which is produced in the woman before ovulation, creates in her an active tendency toward the male partner, while progesterone, which is produced after ovulation, produces more passive-receptive tendencies. Physiology has demonstrated that there exists a very complex interaction between different endocrine glands, and much work is still to be done in this field.

The question now arises whether different hormonal excitations are responsible only for the direction which the libido takes or also for the generation of the manifested amount of libido. In other words, one may question whether undifferentiated libido has its own biological sources of production or is directly produced by excitation of specific sex hormones. In the latter case the sex hormones would be the dynamic generators of libido and would not have only the function of specifically channeling the libido. Such questions are pertinent to the libido theory. We may assume that both modalities may operate in different cases in different proportions.

Freud maintained consistently his belief in two different kinds of cathexis which fuse with each other in different proportions but which can never turn into each other. His libido theory underwent an evolution when he announced a new theory of drive dualism. The more he realized that libido is turned also toward one's own person (a condition he called "narcissism"), the more difficult became a strict distinction between self-preservative and species-preservative drives, or between ego instincts and sexual instincts. Eventually, on the basis of clinical observations, the study of sociological data, and theoretical speculations which were mostly supported by the phenomenon of "repetition compulsion," he came to the conclusion that inherent in living matter there is a primary tendency to die. Freud's formulation of the repetition compulsion and of the death instinct will be thoroughly dealt with later in this section. Many of his followers accepted his belief in a death instinct, though some of them dropped this belief after a time. Today while many Freudian psychoanalysts take the existence of the death instinct for granted, others have doubts about it, and still others reject the assumption on biological grounds. Here we want to consider only Freud's concept of libido in its development. With his announcement of the death instinct Freud dropped his separation of self-preservative and species-preservative drives. In his formulation of a new drive dualism, all constructive life drives, whether directed toward self-preservation or preservation of the species were powered by libido. Libido became the term for the dynamic expression of *Eros,* the life instinct.

Freud's extension of the libido concept to include the constructive and self-preservative ego functions was elaborated by Federn in his dynamic studies of the ego. As was explained in the preceding sections, Federn considered the ego cathexis, which is experienced in the ego feeling, to be composed of a fusion of libido and the newly "discovered" destructive cathexis which he called "mortido." In Federn's opinion it is because of the libido component of ego cathexis that one's own existence is felt as pleasurable. Conversely, joy of life is not experienced by egos which are cathected predominantly by mortido. This is actually so in severe cases of depression. These patients do not enjoy living but wish to cease to exist, to die.

Justification for admitting a libido component in the ego cathexis derives from the observation that the ego is dynamically fed from the same common source of biological energy as the sexual drives. Federn observed that people who indulge excessively in sexual activities, induced by purposefully sought stimulation followed by frequent orgastic discharges, experience then feelings of depersonalization or derealization. Since these feelings are due to scarcely cathected ego boundaries or portions of the ego, the conclusion is evident that too much libido has been discharged through orgastic experiences and too little is left for cathecting the ego. After a certain time of rest from sexual activities these egos regain their normal feeling.

Some psychoanalysts admit the presence of still other kinds of cathexis, but further discussion of the basic drives and cathexes will be resumed in this section after a systematic presentation of human sexual development.

NOTES

(1) Freud, Sigmund. Beyond the Pleasure Principle (1920). Standard Edition, 18:1-64. London, Hogarth, 1955.

(2) This will be discussed in detail in a later chapter.

(3) Fenichel, Otto. The Psychoanalytic Theory of Neurosis. New York, Norton, 1945, p. 57.

(4) Freud, Sigmund. On narcissism: An introduction (1914). Standard Edition, 14:67-102. London, Hogarth, 1957.

(5) Benedek, Therese and Rubenstein, Boris B. The Sexual Cycle in Women; the Relation between Ovarian Function and Psychodynamic Processes. ("Psychosomatic Medicine Monographs," Vol. 3, Nos. 1-2.) Washington, D.C., National Research Council, 1942.

XXIII

Infantile Sexuality

THE extension of the libido concept to include the self-preservative drives simplified our understanding of the nature of this cathexis and the ways it manifests itself. In the previous sections we learned that the ego's contact and relations with other egos is essential for its integration, development, and survival. One cannot overestimate the importance of the vital need of the child to be accepted and loved by his mother or her substitutes. For the most valuable information on this subject we are indebted to several psychoanalysts, including especially the following: Anna Freud, Paul Federn (who recognized the need for including a motherly therapist in the treatment of schizophrenics), Melanie Klein, Helene Deutsch, and Therese Benedek (who elaborated on the "mother-child symbiosis"). Harry Stack Sullivan also stressed the importance of the two basic needs of satisfaction and security, as well as of interpersonal relationships, for a healthy emotional development of the individual. More recently René A. Spitz has demonstrated that the infant's need for loving contact with the mother is a self-preservative need. All reached the conclusion that mother's love is essential for survival and normal development of the infant and the child, although we find among them divergent opinions in regard to some reactions and attitudes of children. The introduction of new terms by some authors has, however, increased our difficulty in properly evaluating and integrating their presentations.

In the study of the development of libidinal interests and drives many items must be considered: the phenomenon of erotization of different zones of the body; the specific tendencies arising from such erotizations; the transition from the "autoerotic" phase to object interest; conflicts between drives which are incompatible; specific innate fears which inhibit the ego from reaching some drive goal; compromise formations between, and replacement of, goals and

172

objects of some drives. In the limited space of this exposition, however, only the main features of sexual development can be presented.

The helpless infant must rely completely on his mother and mother-substitutes for satisfaction of his needs for food and care. Hunger must be satisfied at frequent intervals, and the organ through which this satisfaction is immediately obtained is the mouth; hence the "oral-receptive" attitude is already present, and the first attitude of the infant toward his needs is a "passive-receptive" or "passive-dependent" one. Yet food intake is not an exclusively passive experience; though instigated by reflexes, sucking and swallowing are movements and represent activity.

Although "erotic" pleasure of the mouth is phylogenetically and ontogenetically dependent on satisfaction of hunger, pleasurable sensations derived from the stimulation of the mucous membrane of the mouth become independent of food intake. Freud called "autoerotic" all erotic pleasure obtained from one's own body without relation to any object interest. Autoerotic too are later masturbatory acts which are not related to fantasies of objects but are practiced by the individual exclusively for physical pleasure. But the first manifestations of autoerotism occur at an early developmental stage before the infant has established any rapport with an object. Freud quotes the Hungarian pediatrician Lindner as the first scientist to emphasize the sexual nature of the pleasure that the infant derives from thumb-sucking, and the first to notice that indulgence in this pleasure is often accompanied by masturbatory acts. Thumb-sucking is an innate reflex which occurs in some cases even during late fetal life when food intake through the mouth is out of the question. When oral erotism extends over the upper digestive tract, and the sensation of swallowing and filling the stomach gives satisfaction independent of the physical need for food, the individual resorts to overeating and excessive drinking and smoking. But in the latter cases we realize that the transitory, tension-relieving effects of alcohol and nicotine also play an important role.

In the autoerotic phase the infant uses his own fingers and toes to gratify his oral tension. But very early satisfaction of hunger as well as of oral erotic tension leads the ego to recognize other objects and to enter into relationship with them. At first these objects are the mother's de-egotized breast and the mother herself. Melanie Klein traces the origin of the ego's relations to objects and its depressive states to the infant's earliest oral experiences. The infant distinguishes very soon the good, milk-giving breast from the bad, dry breast. He reacts to oral frustration with anger and hostility toward the "bad object." This attitude appears then displaced on later objects. Perhaps Melanie Klein's views have validity only in regard to the infant's need for nourishment and not in regard to his oral erotic needs which are independent of food intake.

In Chapter VIII the relation of "oral incorporation" to the process of primary identification was presented. From analyses of dreams and various neurotic manifestations as well as from the study of anthropological phenomena and folklore, the conclusion could be drawn that in our id (ucs.) we still harbor cannibalistic tendencies. A cannibal takes for granted that he acquires the qualities of the enemies and animals he eats; and among people of a certain cultural level it is a common belief that babies acquire the traits of their wet nurses and of those animals whose milk is taken as nourishment. As mentioned on previous occasions, the present writer prefers to avoid Ferenczi's term "introjection," commonly used in psychoanalytic literature, for the "oral embodiment of the object," the qualities of which are then autoplastically acquired. We repeat that internalization of an object consists in the ego's extension over the autoplastic duplication of that object or parts of it.

Karl Abraham, who related depressive and melancholic symptoms to a fixation of the libido to the oral level of organization, distinguished two phases of oral erotism. In the first preambivalent phase the infant has not yet established a rapport with an object. This view is at variance with the later statements of Melanie Klein and her followers who trace back the infant's relations to and internalization (introjection) of objects to a much earlier stage in which a destructive urge, a desire to kill the object by its ingestion, is manifested. In Abraham's teachings only with the eruption of teeth, accompanied by the urge to bite, does the oral-sadistic phase develop. At the time of Abraham's announcements Freud had not yet formulated his new concept of drive dualism. Abraham called aggressive and hostile drives manifestations of negative libido. The ambivalent character of oral erotism is most understandable if we consider that through eating of an object, however loved it may be, the object is as such destroyed. Substitutive identification is an expression of this situation. But, also, the ego becomes compensated for the loss of the love object through the erection, within itself, of a duplication of it (identification). As mentioned earlier, this phenomenon often accompanies a grief reaction to the death of a love object. Such a person often dreams, during the mourning period, of eating meat.

The positive erotic component of oral erotism is generally accepted as a partial manifestation of love. The child's first longing for an object or another person, the mother's breast and the mother, contains an oral urge. The word "mamma," Latin for the female breast, is extended to mean mother, in English "mama." The oral "love-goal" is preserved in the most natural and commonly accepted and understood form, in kissing. The cannibalistic implication of oral erotism finds expression in every language, as when a love object is said to be so sweet that one could "eat it up." And so, in calling a loved one "honey" or "sugar" or "lambie pie" we express our oral-incorporative tendencies under the guise of tender feelings and acceptance.

Oral-aggressive drives, often shown physically by grasping movements, are expressed in the urge to gain possession of something. This urge is frequently displaced to a need for understanding and learning. Our language expresses this oral-aggressive significance of intellectual drives by such phrases and clichés as "voracious readers," "meaty subjects," material that is "hard to digest," "biting off more than one can chew." Here again the connection between oral incorporation, identification, and absorption into the ego is clearly portrayed. Using Federn's metapsychological description of newly gained and well-understood concepts or ideas, which become integrated with formerly acquired knowledge, we shall say that the ego's boundaries extend over the new intellectual material. In this process some earlier conceptions are modified or dropped. It is clear that this metapsychological process is the same as that previously described of egotization in the act of identification. It is actually the ego cathexis which engorges new knowledge as well as autoplastic duplications of objects. We conclude that, from the ego metapsychological point of view, the phrases mentioned express an undistorted, actual process, and are not mere metaphors. We have only to add that it is not through the mouth but through ego cathexis that objects and contents become "incorporated."

One important factor which enhances skin erotism is the circumstance that vasomotor and vasosecretory phenomena stimulated by the endocrine system, such as sweating, blushing and paling, are sensed on the skin. Besides, the skin which surrounds and protects the body is exposed to all kinds of external stimulation and plays an important role in body erotism. The skin also belongs to the external protective barrier, called *Reizschutz,* which conveys the sensation of pain when injured. From the time of his first existence the infant experiences that the skin gives sensations of pain and pleasure, the latter being closely connected with feelings of love and protection. The contact of the infant with the warm body of his mother and the caresses she bestows impart to him a deep feeling of security. People who have a strong fixation on skin erotism suffer often and easily from loneliness. The great pleasure which the infant takes in his daily bath is known to everyone. Skin sensations enhance the infant's passive-receptive attitude; hence there is a psychodynamic explanation for the fact that after the bath the infant is fed and then is settled for his nap. It is common knowledge also that the tactile sensations experienced from warmth, water, or stroking lull the infant to sleep. The kinesthetic sensation derived from being rocked likewise increases the infant's passive-receptiveness and helps him to sleep.

In adults as well, skin erotism has considerable significance; it finds its gratification not only as a concomitant and forepleasure in sexual activities but also in many other situations. Back-rubbing is frequently used as a calming measure. In massage both the stimulating of the passive skin and the reduction of tension in the active muscles satisfy the passive need and are responsible for the soothing effect. Skin erotism is often combined with other drives, especially with exhibitionism and voyeurism. Both are frequently involved in conflicts which lead to their repression and the subsequent reaction formation. In the sensation of shame as well as in the emotional reactions expressed in blushing and blanching, such conflicts may be the provoking factors. Skin reactions are frequently the response to erotic tension in general as well as to its repression, since the skin has a rich nervous and capillary supply through which many emotions are discharged. Indeed, in many skin afflictions we find an emotional factor. Therefore the skin became an important subject of study for psychosomatic medicine.

Many so-called pregenital erotic manifestations, such as oral and skin erotism, sexual curiosity, exhibitionism and scoptophilia (voyeurism) play an important role as concomitant or forepleasure activities in mature genital sexual life which will be discussed in the next chapter. But normally they are subordinated to the genital organization, which begins about the third year of life and lasts into the fifth or sixth year. Then, in most cases, it is interrupted to be strongly revived with the processes of puberty. The phase of sexual lull, called by Freud the latency period, and the period of sexual revival at puberty will deserve special consideration. In normal sexual development the pregenital drives are preserved only to a certain extent, as sources of forepleasure or exciting concomitant additions to the genitally discharging processes of sexual tension. They are called component or partial drives (instincts). Normally they are not only subordinated to the genital organization, but they are also partially absorbed by it, as will be seen. In certain kinds of sexual perversions they constitute the decisive factor for discharge of sexual tension.

The mucous membranes and the sphincters of the anus, and the urethra also are erogenous zones, for they too, like the mucous membrane of the mouth, are exposed to frequent stimulation. When the fecal mass or the urine passes through its orifice, the individual experiences a pleasurable sensation combined with relief from tension in the rectum or bladder. As a result of such pleasurable experiences an erotic tension is established in these zones, independent of physical needs and sometimes even interfering with them. In this respect Freud reminds us that phylogenetically the urinary, the intestinal, the genital and the alimentary systems had one common opening, the cloaca, which is still a characteristic of some vertebrates—certain fishes and reptiles.

It seems that, because of this evolutionary history, erotic sensations remained inherent in the separate excretory openings. Tension in the lower end of the digestive tract stimulates the excremental function, and the fecal mass is sensed, originally, as an unpleasant object which has to be eliminated. But pleasurable sensations during the expulsion of the feces are probably present from the beginning of life. Therefore the stimulating presence of this highly uncomfortable mass is responsible for anal-erotism. An ambivalent attitude toward its stimulation ensues; it is undesired but at the same time desired. And the anal ambivalence becomes greater when the infant discovers that the withholding of excrement increases the pleasure of expulsion.

This anal-erotic ambivalence directed psychoanalytic attention to the fact that in oral erotism, similarly, ambivalent feelings toward love objects arise. Food is not only desired, but through the very act of satisfaction it is destroyed. Therefore, when oral gratification as a "love-goal" is instinctively applied to love objects which the individual wants to preserve, the erotic pleasure is limited to the mucosa of the mouth and lips, and the oral-destructive component has to be checked.

As every frustrated drive results in rage and hostility, so also do inhibited oral and anal drives. If the nipple or the thumb is taken from the child's mouth, he may react with rage or resentment, as he does when he cannot obtain enough milk from the breast. In like manner, toilet training prematurely imposed upon him precipitates rebellion and hostility. In order to obtain as much pleasure as possible from the incorporative, the retentive and the eliminatory acts, the infant (and the child) wants to control these functions himself. After all, this is his own bodily function, and he does not tolerate any interference with his "right" to regulate at will the single acts in this performance. Therefore, as a consequence of both oral and anal erotism, we are confronted with oral and anal sadism. (We should note that in psychoanalytic literature the word "sadism" is applied to any hostile and aggressive manifestation regardless of whether it appears in the goal desired for overt sexual gratification or not.)

The child's interest in the fecal mass is of great psychological importance. This interest is bound to the experience of anal-erotic stimulation produced by this substance. It is enhanced by the feeling that its delivery represents for the infant his first accomplishment. It is the first "present" he gives to the person he wishes to please and by whom he wants to be loved. But the normal child, though at first reluctant to separate this evaluated substance from himself, soon learns to reject his interest in the excreta, which he is taught to consider dirty and disgusting. For this important reaction formation to his interest and over-evaluation of the excreted masses, called "coprophilia," there is also an innate disposition. This source of ambivalence toward feces and defecation is very comprehensible. This is a clear example of repression of an original liking with the help of the reaction formations of disgust and aversion, common to almost every human being. This repression followed by reaction formations varies, however, in intensity and forms of expression in different cultures.

Already there is a voluminous literature which deals with the consequences and derivatives of the anal-sadistic phase and its implications in the development of specific character features which derive from it. These features are due to displacement of anal ambivalence from feces to other objects. Typical feelings and emotional attitudes are directly derived from anal-sadistic erotism. Others are due to its repression, which is enhanced by the child's rearing and later by his superego which takes over external attitudes toward oral and anal tendencies. It is understandable that reaction formations to an interest in the excrement of other people become much more tenacious than those to the narcissistic over-evaluation of one's own waste products.

The displacement of the urge to hold back the content of the lower intestinal tract appears in the morbid pleasure in accumulating other objects, and these anal-erotic and coprophilic components are especially evident when the collected and hoarded objects are quite worthless. More frequently, however, this element is hidden behind the desire to possess objects of general value. Even the urge to collect stamps and coins, as well as objects of art or scientific interest, frequently has an anal-erotic component. It is a common phenomenon that original objects and goals of condemned or rejected drives are substituted by objects and goals of highly accepted value. As was mentioned above, this phenomenon was called by Freud sublimation; it is considered as one "mechanism of defense." By the process of sublimation conflicts are avoided, and with socially acceptable objects anal-erotic drives can be maintained as sources of gratification. Most astonishing is the substitution of money for excrement, making it easy to rationalize the urge for retention because of the usefulness and value of the cherished bills and coins. Yet money is hoarded less for utilitarian reasons than for the satisfaction gained by the very act of accumulating and retaining. It is not without psychological interest that primitive man indicates possession by sitting on a desired object, and that the word "possess" is derived from Latin *possessum,* "sat on, occupied." And the squatter takes possession by squatting, or sitting, on his property.

From the earliest recorded time, in folklore and fairy tales, and in popular expressions and proverbs in all languages and cultures, money and gold are equated with feces and filth in general. Thus the ambivalent attitude toward excrement is quite generally seen. As we have said, feces are the child's first possession and are therefore esteemed as a precious substance which he presents to the persons he loves. Everyone who takes care of infants can observe that babies like to touch their excrements, to play with them, and even to put them in the mouth. On the other hand, through the expelled fecal mass hatred and hostility are expressed.

Clinical experience has revealed without doubt that the child's reluctance to have his eliminative function controlled by adults contributes largely to the character features of stubbornness and spite. But some character traits are also formed by reaction patterns needed to keep one's anal erotism repressed. Thus, as has been already pointed out, exaggerated cleanliness ensues as a reaction formation to coprophilic tendencies, as do orderliness and punctuality, all three of which may increase to a neurotic extreme.

An active as well as a passive disposition normally derives from the biological function of the anus. The expelling act is the active component of the anal function. This activity becomes more or less hostile; the infant soon feels that those who care for him do not like the unpleasant odor nor the mess but are nevertheless forced to clean it up. Yet defecation has also a passive-receptive component, of which the tendency may lead to the urge to be anally stimulated by the outgoing feces and later by entering objects. It plays a determining role in passive homosexual men, whereas in females it is later displaced on the passive function of the vagina. The use of enemas stimulates both anal components and their derivatives.

The urinary function is responsible for the localization of erotism in the urethra. One would expect to find in urethral erotism conditions analogous to those inherent in anal erotism, but clinical observation and psychological investigation have revealed some fundamental differences between the two. While skin, oral, and anal erotism are based on the same anatomical and physiological conditions in males and females, the anatomical differences in the urinary system of males and females are responsible also for diverging developments of urethral erotism in the two sexes. We shall present this "partial drive" in connection with the genital phase in the next chapter.

XXIV

The Genital Phase

BECAUSE of the anatomical difference between the sexes the act of urination has many complex psychological implications, and these have led to misevaluation and misinterpretation of the manifestations in the genital phase. The psychological reactions of the boy to discovery of the female genitalia, and those of the girl to discovery of the penis, for a long time obscured our understanding of feminine sexuality and the role of the sexual partner in sexual drives in both males and females. Freud called the last phase of sexual development in the male the "phallic phase." But since this phase occurs at an age when children believe that boys and girls should be genitally constructed alike and equally in possession of a penis, it is distinguished from the genital phase in which male and female genitalia are seen and experienced as different. Only at this later time can one speak of a "vaginal" phase for the girl, a term which has not found entrance in psychoanalytic literature. Phallic erotism is experienced by the girl in a very incomplete way on the clitoris.

In order to clarify some misunderstandings, we shall first consider urethral erotism. The act of urination is more erotized than the act of retention of urine. In the anal-erotic phase, as stated above, the act of retention of feces also plays an important role. In the male the act of urination has predominantly, but not exclusively, an active character which is later linked with the urge to penetrate into the female and to eject the semen. This active and erotic-aggressive character is inherent in the physiology of the penis, independent of any urge to urinate, and is clearly expressed in erection of the penis, a very early occurrence which can be verified by every mother and nurse who takes care of baby boys. On the other hand, urination may occur in a passive way upon refusal to control it, and it may result in a passive urge combined with skin erotism. Wetting himself or the bed, feeling the warm stream of urine on the skin of the thighs, gives the child autoerotic gratification, and therefore the later neurotic symptom of involuntary enuresis often is considered as masturbation on the urethral-erotic level. The passive urge for urination is of clinical interest because it has great significance in severe cases of premature ejaculation or even ejaculation in absence of an erection of the penis.

The control of the bladder sphincters is a difficult and absorbing feat for every little child; it determines the formation of important character traits in the individual. The child is proud of achieving control over the act of urination, and toilet training conveys to him the strong feeling that wetting himself constitutes a great disgrace. It was Alfred Adler who first discovered the connection between urethral erotism and pride, and between enuresis and ambition. He elaborated these observations into the frame of his general theory of the urge to show power. Ernest Jones (and subsequently other analysts) also called attention to the fact that the child has a narcissistic pride in his ability to control the urinary function. Children frequently compete with each other in the act of urinating itself as well as in their ability to perform through urination. The little "Gulliver" experiences a great satisfaction of his ambition when he excels over his competitors in such playfully done but seriously meant performances.

A spectacular psychological manifestation in children interferes with or retards the normal sexual development on the genital level. The girl's discovery of the boy's penis and the boy's discovery of the absence of this organ in girls give rise to the misconception that man is genitally favored and prepotent and that the woman is genitally mutilated. There is a voluminous literature on the many problems centered around the "castration complex," from which in individuals of both sexes typical fears and character traits are derived. However, in this writer's opinion (which is shared with other psychoanalysts), the "castration complex" in males and females is not a necessary phase for mature sexual development but is an almost unavoidable interference with the psycho-biological development of mature sexuality.

In Freud's opinion the castration complex plays an important role in every neurosis. Fear of losing his penis is the most intolerable fear of the male child and constitutes the greatest threat to his dynamic survival. His imagined dire consequences of sexual and other forbidden deeds stem from this fear, together with the fear of losing his parents' love. Through internalization of the parents into the superego these two fears are later sensed as "fear of one's own conscience." In Freud's opinion the child's fear of losing his penis is in part due to the threat by his parents that he will be deprived of his penis if he indulges in enuresis or other masturbatory acts. Often the child does not take such threats seriously, but the sight of the penisless female genitalia "gives him the proof" that one can actually be so deprived. Originally the child ascribes a penis to the mother; later he develops various mechanisms for denying that she does not possess a penis. (The concept of the "phallic mother" also is the subject of a vast psychoanalytic literature.) The castration fear has an innate disposition which plays a varying role in different cases.

This writer shares Freud's view that castration (loss of the penis) constitutes for the male the most severe "narcissistic injury." We know from clinical experience that patients can adjust themselves more easily to any other kind of mutilation, even to the self-inflicted mutilation of King Oedipus (the loss of eyesight), rather than to the loss of the penis. We find often behind a patient's paroxysmal fear of any mutilation his unconscious dread of losing his penis. This is quite understandable, since the penis is an indispensable masculine organ, strongly narcissistically cathected, and highly erotized from biological sources. It is endowed with the physiological function of orgastic discharge of a great erotic tension. It is my opinion that through egotization of the genitals (the feminine as well as the masculine) the ego captures the afflux of a huge amount of libido. There are additional implications in the loss of one's genitalia, which will be discussed shortly. As mentioned earlier, one cannot doubt that the castration fear has an inherited root.

Indeed, castration of captured or wounded enemies has often been the practice in war not only among primitive peoples, or in antiquity and the Middle Ages, but also occasionally among certain cultural groups even in our own day.

Sexual mutilation has been conceived by psychoanalysts mainly as loss of the penis. The concept has been applied to the woman to indicate her misgiving and her protest at not possessing a penis. The literature on the female castration complex, on the "masculine complex," and on castrating women who want to rob the man of his penis, is voluminous indeed. In the girl erotic sensations in the clitoris, an organ with erectile properties, intensify her belief in the boy's great advantage in having a penis—a real scepter in comparison with a small clitoris. This becomes evident, more or less, in the "phallic phase" of the woman. This misconception on the part of the female child leads to a reaction of great envy, the so-called "penis envy," and to emotional attitudes of "masculine protest," which extend to all masculine prerequisites. The boy who misinterprets the visible female genitalia frequently develops disrespect for women, considering them "mutilated individuals." While Alfred Adler interpreted the "masculine protest" from the point of view of his theory of the "will to power," "to be on top of the other," Freud derived the "masculine protest" from the castration complex.

Very interesting are the elaborations of Freud and other psychoanalysts on the processes of absorption of the pregenital or component drives by the genital function and genital erotism. These processes are based on displacement onto the genitalia of oral, anal and urethral trends and related fears and frustrations. For example, castration fear has predecessors in the pregenital phases. As was explained in our discussion of the development of ego boundaries, the infant includes for a certain time the mother's breast within his ego feeling. Every time the nipple is withdrawn from his mouth short of alimentary and erotic satisfaction, he senses this withdrawal as a mutilation. At the anal-erotic phase the infant also experiences that something, the feces, becomes separated from his body. These experiences corroborate later, through displacement processes, the child's fear of having his penis detached from him. Likewise, other traits inherent in oral and anal erotism appear displaced on the masculine and feminine genitalia. The erotic sensation of the passage of a column of feces through the anus appears displaced in the urge to penetrate with the erected penis a bodily opening, normally the vagina. Ferenczi called amphimixis the passing over of both, the anal-retentive urge and the urge to urinate, to the phallic organization. In his interpretation, in the act of intercourse these two tendencies, anal and urethral, compete with each other in rapidly alternating urges: the urge to withhold, to withdraw, and the urge to give, to urinate actively, to ejaculate, until the giving prevails. The vagina, also, absorbs oral tendencies of incorporation which are expressed in muscular sucking contractions. Accordingly in Freud's theories and those of other psychoanalysts, many traits of the component drives become absorbed and integrated into the genital function, but not completely.

Of particular interest is Freud's finding (obtained from analyses of dreams and neuroses) that in the unconscious id representations of a column of feces, of the penis, and of babies (who are expelled from the body like feces) are interchangeable. According to Freud's formulation the girl who cannot grow a penis comes to realize that she can borrow one from a man if she merely accepts him as if he were an appendage to his penis. Receiving the penis as a "present" (in terms of the anal-erotic equation feces = present) also satisfies her anal-erotic tendencies. Furthermore, she longs for a baby, as an equivalent of feces and penis. On the other hand, she is the giver of a "present" to the man, in the form of a baby.

The castration complex affects the oedipus complex quite differently in males and females. The phallic primacy is reached by the boy, as stated in the preceding chapter, about the second or third year of life, and is interrupted during the so-called latency period, which will be discussed later. The phallic phase plays a central role in the oedipus complex, i.e., in the boy's sexual desire for his mother and rivalrous attitude toward his father. But the oedipal situation constitutes a greater threat to the boy's phallic drives. His fear of being deprived of his penis ("castrated"), as punishment for his sexual wishes toward his mother, eventually makes him renounce the mother as a sexual object. The oedipus complex is first repressed, and then in normal development it is successively destroyed in the id. Freud describes this phenomenon as "the dissolution of the oedipus complex." The permanence of the oedipus complex in the repressed portion of the id constitutes a nucleus for a later neurosis. Many other implications derived from oedipal guilt, fear of the castrating authority (the mother may also be a castration-threatening person) lead to various psychopathological conditions upon which we cannot embark at this point.

In the development of normal sexuality in women the castration complex plays a quite different role. The little girl feels "castrated" and this is an important source of her feeling of inferiority. She cannot hope to receive a penis from her mother. On the contrary, she blames her mother for not having provided her with a penis like the boy. We have just mentioned how the girl overcomes her castration complex, according to Freud. Freud expressed himself in the following way: "We can indicate the ultimate outcome of the infantile penis-wish in those persons in whom the conditions for a neurosis in later life are absent: it changes into the wish for a man, accepting the man as an appendage, as it were, of the penis." [1]

This outcome of the girl's castration complex leads her toward her father. She expects him to furnish her a penis and a baby, in the manner indicated above. Accordingly, Freud concluded, the masculine oedipus complex is destroyed as an effect of the castration complex, while the feminine oedipus complex, sexual wish for the father and rivalrous attitudes toward the mother, is the very outcome of the castration complex.

All tendencies described, having arisen from various absorptions of traits of component drives into the genital organization, cannot, of course, account for all psychological factors which determine a woman's longing for a man and for children. Nor do these absorptions explain fully the most important traits of heterosexual relationships of men and women. In the first section we have considered the need for substitutive externalizations, and we shall now see how important this phenomenon is in the establishment of heterosexual relationships and in the wish for both men and women to have children. But from the mere point of view of the normal development of "genitality" we understand, through the expositions given, many psychophysiological traits of sexuality. The penis is the active organ, the vagina the passive organ; the male develops more sexual aggression than the woman; not only is the woman predominantly passive sexually, but a certain degree of masochism, related to the function of the vagina, is a normal occurrence. It is also important to realize that genital erotism, in the normal development of love or desire for the sexual partner, loses that ambivalent feature which is inherent in love in pregenital phases. True, some women develop oral aggressive tendencies, displaced to the vagina, with which these women want to capture the man's penis. But the subject of "castrating women" belongs to a discussion on psychopathology.

A modification of Freud's formulation, quoted above, of the "ultimate outcome" of the infantile penis-wish of the girl brings into sharper focus many emotional features of the woman's heterosexual experiences.[2] Instead of stating that "the infantile penis-wish changes into the wish for a man, accepting the man as an appendage, as it were, of the penis," the present author would prefer to say, the penis-wish is met by externalization of the desired ego state into an object representation of a person possessing a penis. Through this externalization the girl can then enjoy vicarious gratification of the function of a penis with a person corresponding to the externalized portion of that ego state. This is the actual motivation for a woman's wish for a man.

With this modification Freud's formulation can also be applied to a certain type of masculine homosexuality. Exposition of this piece of sexual pathology will help the reader to comprehend better the normal development of heterosexuality. A man can have feelings of genital inferiority for two reasons: (1) He may rightly or wrongly feel a phallic deficiency; or (2) due to early intimidation he may not dare to assert his phallic masculine drives and may even de-egotize his penis. If such a man succeeds in externalizing his penis and its function into the object representation of another man who possesses an efficient penis, his own phallic erotism is turned into the desire for such a man, as is the girl's penis-wish—and we shall see that the penis-wish of the woman is also biologically determined. The desired man constitutes, then, more than a mere "prosthesis" for one's own missing, defective or de-egotized penis. It represents the externalization of an indispensable emotional ego state. The strong erotic cathexis inherent in the externalized portion of that ego state gives rise to an intense longing for vicarious gratification. Ego libido is turned into object libido of the narcissistic type. Renunciation of such a love object is, for this type of homosexual, equivalent to castration, the intolerance for which has been described above.

We must realize that in the phenomenon of externalization the process is not limited to the bodily and mental content of externalized portion, but it involves also the cathexis pertaining to this por-

tion. In the process of externalization, an amount of ego cathexis is
turned into object cathexis. Accordingly, when an ego state encom-
passing the genitalia and their function is externalized, the biologically produced cathexis bound to these organs is co-externalized
with the content into the resulting object representation. When the
flow of cathexis becomes blocked (as happens in repression) the
ego feels dynamically mutilated. In the case of externalization into
an object representation the dynamic entireness of the ego is restored by a satisfactory relation of "resonance" with a corresponding object.

The externalization of a "penis-ego state," into a corresponding
object representation makes the ego susceptible and desirous of a
vicarious gratification with such an object. The goal of this "object
love" is precisely to arouse in the object those emotional experiences
which the patient's ego is lacking. By it his ego feels restored to its
sexual entireness. Thus in the process of externalization, the penis
of such homosexuals is not completely cut off through de-egotization (repression), but it retains its capacity for being revived (egotized) through resonance with the experiences of the object.

This way of recovering his penis is, however, for such a man
only a subsidiary goal to the normal sexual end-goal. But, as in
many forms of sexual deviations, by attaining a desired subsidiary
goal the libido tension is discharged, in most cases short of the biological end-goal. The end-goal becomes more or less lost. The subsidiary goal to restore the function of one's own penis through
resonance becomes the sexual end-goal. This is not always the case,
however. Some of these homosexuals can have intercourse with a
woman after they have stimulated themselves first in a homosexual
manner, by which they have revived their penis function. There
are also cases in which such a patient induced his girl or wife to
have intercourse with one of his male friends. In this case not only
the function of the penis but also the heterosexual relation is enjoyed vicariously.

Now we should like to understand the psychological mechanism
of the normal sexual development of the masculine ego which feels
sexually entire and efficient, a male who egotizes his efficient penis.
Why is he longing for a female partner?

To answer this question we must first compare the normal outcome of the girl's penis-wish with the type of masculine homosexuality described. It is interesting to note, from the way in which the girl overcomes her "castration feeling," that the ego can externalize a portion of one of its desired states, also, when this state encompasses a functioning organ which it does not anatomically possess or possesses only in a rudimentary form. Woman's anatomy is not equipped to discharge efficiently the masculine phallic cathexis inherent in her bisexual constitution. The clitoris is very inadequate for such a discharge. We can compare the normal solution, obtained through psychoanalytic treatment, of the pathological process in the aforementioned homosexuals with the normal outcome of the penis-wish of the girl as follows: In the process of recovery from homosexuality, the patient internalizes (egotizes) the penis which he actually possesses and which he had previously externalized into an object representation of another man. Conversely, the normal outcome of the penis-wish of the girl consists of the externalization of her phallic urges for which she is not properly equipped.

The concept of "bisexuality" bears elucidating here. In the common sense of the word, a person is said to be bisexual if he can enjoy sexual gratification with both male and female partners. Freud emphasized the "bisexual disposition" of the individual, first stated by Wilhelm Fliess. Bisexuality is not synonymous with hermaphroditism. Hermaphroditism in the biological sense, meaning the production of both female and male germ cells, does not exist in vertebrates. But secondary sexual characteristics of the opposite sex appear more or less pronounced in the individual. The erotism in the clitoris, for example, is a manifestation of masculine erotism in the woman. In fact (as stated above) in psychoanalysis we speak of the "phallic phase" including the erotism which is centered on the clitoris before the prevailing vaginal erotism is reached. Therefore, the normal woman has a need for satisfaction of both sexual components, the masculine and the feminine. We have just learned that she can satisfy her phallic urges, in the normal outcome of development, vicariously with the phallic function of the male. On the other hand, the feminine vaginal component is egotized by the woman and thus its satisfaction can be obtained only directly in the act of intercourse with a man. In those women whose feminine urges are totally egotized, and in whom the phallic erotic tension is totally externalized onto the object representation of a man—and when she cares for his satisfaction—we cannot see any bisexual attitude but only a heterosexual one. Thus the concept of the "general bisexual disposition" must be reduced to that of the presence, in the id, of both masculine and feminine urges. But normal egos are not bisexual, because the urges of the opposite sex are externalized and only those of one's own biological sex are egotized.

We can now also understand why a normal man is not satisfied only in possessing and egotizing his penis. He longs for a woman because he also has both phallic and feminine urges. The latter are already present in the pregenital, oral and passive-anal urges. In regard to the genital localization of passivity and activity it is worthwhile mentioning an important discovery of Federn. He found that there exists a fundamental difference between the sadistic and the masochistic sexuality of the male: The sadist feels the sexual genital sensation on the top of the penis, which is an active characteristic, while the masochist feels a passive genital sensation localized at the root of the penis or even at the scrotum and perineum, which is the location of the vagina in the female. The desire for and the lack of genitalia of the opposite sex lead to the need and desire to explore the other sex.

The study of feminine sexual sensations has met many difficulties. The vagina is an invisible organ and is consciously discovered by the girl much later than the penis. Furthermore, the strongest obstacle to correct understanding of the man's need for feminine organs is the boy's early misconception of the phallic mother and his consequent horror when he first sees the feminine genitalia. This writer does not believe, however, that the boy's misinterpretation of the superficial sight of feminine genitalia as a ghastly mutilation is a general unavoidable occurrence. The actual discovery of the female genitalia, and not only of the missing penis, excites the boy sexually and does not frighten him. The horror of the misunderstood sight of the external female genitalia, which is a recent phylogenetic occurrence, is superimposed on the longing for the not yet discovered and used ("known," to use the Biblical term) feminine organs.

Less attention has been given in psychoanalytic literature to the concept in both women and men of mutilation of feminine organs.

In fact, observations have been published of boys and men who wish to possess feminine genitalia and be able to give birth to children.[3] Furthermore, men may envy women. On this last point, however, we find more material in the literature of anthropology than of psychoanalysis. The phenomenon has been interpreted mainly in terms of mere feminine identification on the part of the boy rather than as a normal, innate feminine tendency contained in the id. Indeed, men who repress their feminine urges instead of externalizing them into a representation of a woman lose their interest in women and do not understand them.

This writer had the opportunity to study the pathological effect in women of repression or de-egotization of feminine vaginal drives. Such a repression or de-egotization is the equivalent of genital mutilation, but it is obvious that this mutilation cannot be called "castration," a term reserved for "phallic mutilation." Thus, we are led to the following conclusion: The more the ego egotizes the tendencies of its own sex (while those of the opposite sex are turned into representations of desired objects), the more it feels "complete." Conversely, the more it fails to egotize the features corresponding to its own anatomical and physiological organism and/or egotizes the features corresponding to the anatomy and physiology of the opposite sex, the more it feels mutilated. The normally developed man externalizes his feminine erotism and thus feels a longing for a woman. And he cares for the sexual experiences which he arouses in the woman. The union of the externalized portion with the egotized one, in mutual vicarious gratification, restores the bisexual unity, as it is aroused in the id by various endocrine phenomena.

Referring once more to the two strata of the id mentioned briefly in Chapter XX, we may say that the constitutional bisexuality would be located in the biological id. This normal bisexuality of the id cannot be conceived in the same way as an ego-invested bisexuality. Only an ego can be consciously or unconsciously homosexual or heterosexual. We cannot use these terms regarding the biological id because in this stratum the sexual drives are neither ego- nor object-invested. On the other hand, ego- and object-invested sexual drives can be repressed, but then they are encompassed in the other stratum of the id, not in the biological id. Again, to avoid complication, I shall continue hereafter to speak of the id as a single structure.

To conclude this exposition of the genital level of psychosexual development, I would like to cite as further support for my theory of bisexuality a myth found in Plato's *Symposium* which stated that there once was a third sex with four hands, four feet, two faces, and both male and female genitalia. Zeus divided this creature in two " 'like a sorb-apple which is halved for pickling.' After the division had been made, 'the two parts of man, each desiring the other half, came together, and threw their arms about one another eager to grow into one.' " [4] Freud, who used this Platonic myth to support his view of libido as a manifestation of the repetition compulsion, cites information regarding its origin furnished him by the historian of philosophy, Heinrich Gomperz. Gomperz traced the myth to a passage in the *Brihadâramyaka-upanishad,* the oldest of all the Upanishads, and dated no later than 800 B.C. The content of this passage is to the effect that the Atman (the self or ego) "felt no delight. Therefore a man who is lonely feels no delight. He wished for a second. He was so large as man and wife together. He then made this his Self fall in two, and then arose husband and wife. Therefore Yagñavalkya said: 'We two are thus (each of us) like half a shell! Therefore the void which was there, is filled by the wife." [5]

I have shown the mutilation which this myth underwent in the Biblical story (of Babylonian origin) of the creation of Adam and Eve.[6] The first human being who felt lonely was no longer a man-woman creature but a man, Adam. And his "better half" was reduced to a mere rib of Adam, the shape of which, like the crescent moon, is suggestive of the external female genitalia. But, although the woman became so much depreciated in a patriarchal culture, she was felt as the object of desire for the man who wanted to be restored to his original entirety. The feminine mutilation, which is not castration in the psychoanalytic sense of the word, was compensated by his longing for the woman.

These myths can be easily applied to the separation of masculine and feminine erotisms in the processes of egotization and externalization of masculine and feminine egos, whereby there arises in the remaining ego the urge to recapture the externalized countersexual part of the ego state and so to re-establish the bisexual unity of the id, which cannot be established in the ego.

As we see, in order to understand all the manifestations of the sexual and other drives it is not sufficient to examine merely the id impulses, but it is necessary to consider also the modes in which the ego responds to them.

NOTES

(1) Freud, Sigmund. On transformations of instinct as exemplified in anal erotism (1917). Standard edition, 17:125-133. London, Hogarth, 1955.

(2) These ideas were expressed in the following of my articles: Über eine noch nicht beschriebene Phase der Entwicklung zur heterosexuellen Liebe. Int. Z. Psychoanal., 11:429-443, 1925; The phenomenon of "ego passage." J. Am. Psychoanal. Assn., 5:267-281, 1957; Bisexuality and ego structure. Int. J. Psychoanal., 39:91-97, 1958.

(3) For example, Jacobson, Edith. Development of the wish for a child in boys. Psychoanalytic Study of the Child, 5:139-152, 1950; or Evans, William N. Simulated pregnancy in a male. Psychoanal. Quart., 20:165-178, 1951.

(4) Freud, Sigmund. Beyond the pleasure principle. Standard edition, 18:1-64. London, Hogarth, 1955. The passage cited is on p. 57-58.

(5) Ibid., p. 58, footnote 1.

(6) This is discussed in greater detail in my article Bisexuality and ego structure. See Note 2, above.

XXV

Narcissism and Object Love

IN the two preceding chapters some connections between erogenous zones and erotic longing for an object were presented. At the
pregenital levels the ego relates to the objects in an ambivalent manner. Ambivalence no longer adheres to object relationships at the
genital level. Freud called autoerotism all erotic tensions which
are not bound to an external object. In the erotic activity of thumb-
sucking the child uses a part of his own body to relieve the oral-
erotic tension. Likewise, passive skin erotism and active muscular
erotism can be satisfied by body movements as anal and urethral
erotism by retentive and eliminatory activities. All masturbatory
acts are autoerotic.

The infant's longing for the nipple or bottle can be considered
the first step toward an "object relationship," although on a much
lower level than the anaclitic relationship with the mother. Melanie
Klein and her followers attribute essential importance to the infant's
early experiences in his oral relation to both the milk-giving and the
dry breast for development of later object relationships. It is evident
that the infant reacts with feelings of satisfaction, of being loved,
to sucking at a milk-giving breast, a "good breast," as it were. Conversely, he reacts with disappointment, frustration, anger (hostility)
and even with feelings of being unloved or "hated," to sucking at a
dry breast, a "bad breast," as it were. These experiences influence
his later object relationships on higher levels. But Melanie Klein implies that the very act of or urge for "oral ingestion" leads or is
equivalent to "introjection" of the "good" or "bad" breasts. In her
opinion the processes of such an "introjection" and successive "projection" of the introjected good and bad breasts (internalization
and externalization in our terminology) occur after the first months
of the infant's life.

We realize that an ego's identification with (introjection of) the breast or bottle must be somewhat different from its identification with a person. In the latter case the person or some of his attitudes are autoplastically duplicated and egotized. And so we may well understand that in the phenomenon of "breast identification" ("introjection of the breast") the infantile ego assumes, from its own dynamic sources, a loving and/or hating and destructive attitude toward other objects as a result of the oral experiences mentioned. But to question whether the ego's "introjection" of the good and bad breast leads to the superego formation, as Melanie Klein asserts, is fully justified. In other words, not every identification produces a "split of the ego" into an ego and superego, to use Klein's terms, or to a formation of "a step in the ego," as Freud characterized the superego. An answer to this question will be given in the next section where the superego formation will be more thoroughly discussed.

We return now to the discussion of autoerotism and narcissism. The mythological figure Narcissus, distinguished for his beauty, was unable to love anyone, and became unhappy and lonely. One day he saw his own *reflected* image in a pool and fell in love with it. According to one version, he then pined away; according to another version he killed himself. He loved himself so much as an object (reflexive libido) that no love for another object was left in him.

Havelock Ellis introduced the term "narcissism" to indicate the sexual perversion in which one's own body is the sexual object. Later, Freud extended the significance of the term to include all ramifications and expressions of the ego libido. Freud recognized that libido, in its broadest psychoanalytic sense, always is invested in one's own self; that it is connected with the self-preservative drives, according to his later libido concept, and is also manifested in one's need to please one's self, to raise one's self-esteem, to enjoy one's prestige and popularity—in brief, in all kinds of evaluation, especially over-appreciation, of one's own person. And so the term narcissism came to embrace a much broader field than that of the sexual perversion first mentioned. The complete interpretation of the Greek myth of Narcissus has been made after 2500 years, as a result of the analysis of various clinical and characterological manifestations of narcissism, among which may be included suicide, depression, isolation, ecstasy, homosexuality, exhibitionism, and many other phenomena.

In psychoanalytic literature "primary" and "secondary" narcissism are terms which are ordinarily accepted and generally understood in the sense which Freud, their originator, attributed to them. Freud's criterion for distinguishing between primary and secondary narcissism was a genetic one. He considered as primary narcissism whatever libido is invested in the organism itself—not only in the ego—from the very beginning; and he recognized that originally all libido is narcissistic, namely, invested in one's self. Only gradually does the infant separate interest in the surrounding world of objects (object libido) from his narcissistic interest. But object libido can be returned to and re-invested in the ego. This occurs, as we have seen, when a loved object is internalized by the ego. Then the ego loves that object in its autoplastic and egotized duplication. In Freud's terms, the ego loves that object in itself, a condition which he called secondary narcissism. The narcissistic elements of the secondary narcissism, we repeat, do not belong continuously to the ego but become re-invested in the ego through internalization of (identification with) love objects. The process by which libido is withdrawn from objects for re-investment in the ego is called narcissistic withdrawal. Freud compared the way in which the libido expands over objects of the external world and withdraws to the ego, to the way an amoeba extends pseudopods toward something in an adjacent area and draws them back into its body.

Through the extension of the term "narcissism" to include all manifestations of ego libido the term has lost in many respects the meaning which is inherent in the love of the mythical Narcissus. The very existence of the ego is due to the action of ego libido, and precisely of that form of libido which Federn describes as medial libido. As already pointed out in Section II, the middle voice is rendered in English by intransitive verbs such as "I exist," "I live." Narcissus could not have fallen in love with himself as an object (with the "self" in Federn's sense) if he had not had an ego feeling, i.e., an ego. And no one can love himself or any external object if he does not experience his own existence. Yet the term "narcissism" is used to designate also the medial ego libido. In fact, Federn calls primary narcissism only the medial ego libido—"I am," "I exist," "I live" —and designates as secondary narcissism all the other forms of ego libido, also that reflexive libido—"I love myself"—which has never been turned toward an object of the external world. But in the course of his writings he increasingly preferred the term "ego libido" to "narcissistic libido." In my opinion the term narcissism should be used only to designate the reflexive libido, the love of one's ego as object.

Does the psychoanalytic term narcissism include also all auto-erotism? Freud was not consistent in the use of this term, and many of his close adherents consider all autoerotic libido as narcissistic, simply because it is not object libido. But in many passages Freud expressly limited the use of the term narcissism to the libido investment of the *substructure ego*. We learned that Freud did not believe that the ego exists in the individual from the very beginning of his life. In his opinion it develops slowly from the id after birth. In his classic paper on narcissism, published in 1914, he says: "We are bound to suppose that a unity comparable to the ego cannot exist in the individual from the start; the ego has to be developed. The auto-erotic instincts, however, are there from the very first; so there must be something added to auto-erotism—a new psychical activity—in order to bring about narcissism." [1]

Hartmann calls "the self" the whole personality which encompasses all three substructures, the id, the ego and the superego. He proposed to call narcissism the libido investment in any of these three mental substructures. Furthermore he designates as "ego narcissism" the narcissism in the strictly Freudian sense, namely, the libido investment in the ego.[2] But there are different kinds of libido investments even in the ego. Medial libido is different from active, passive or reflexive libido. And from the study of disturbances of various ego functions it became evident that each ego function is differently powered by libido, in kind and in intensity.

We shall now present some aspects and vicissitudes of narcissism in its strict sense of the word, namely, of the libido (love) directed to the self in Federn's sense.

Narcissus liked himself as he actually was; in other words, he could not possibly have harbored "feelings of inferiority." And usually a person is considered narcissistic when he loves himself as he actually is or as he thinks he is. A movie star may be in love with herself because she is aware of her appealing physical appearance, her ability to perform on the screen, and the enthusiasm she arouses in audiences. An artist or a scientist may be proud of (i.e., narcissistically pleased with) his artistic or scientific achievements, a moralist proud of his ethical standards and behavior. Everyone feels, more or less, a need to be a worthwhile individual.

Should we also now consider narcissistic a person who suffers from feelings of inferiority, who feels unworthy, undesirable and unloved? Alfred Adler invented the term "inferiority complex" to indicate the emotional condition of a person who suffers from such feelings. To call feelings of inferiority "a complex" is meaningless to Freudian psychoanalysts, but the Adlerian term has won wide acceptance in the vocabulary of the general public.

It is easy to understand that feelings of inferiority could be of no emotional importance if the ego did not have a "narcissistic need." A narcissistic craving may be satisfied or frustrated. The greater the craving, the greater will be the ego's satisfaction if it pleases itself and the greater its suffering if it displeases itself. Thus suffering derived from feelings of inferiority is the expression of what we call a "narcissistic injury," that is, a lesion of the love which one has for himself. Everyone is exposed to various kinds of humiliations in life. Every child is narcissistically injured whenever his parents or other persons reprimand, criticize, or punish him. Freud compares the ensuing feelings of inferiority to a scar formation. We must therefore distinguish "narcissistic craving" from satisfied narcissism.

Once more it becomes a matter of agreement as to whether the term narcissism (even to indicate merely reflexive libido) should be used solely to mean satisfied self-love or also to indicate a craving for self-love independent of satisfaction. If we accept the latter definition we would consider a person very narcissistic when he is dissatisfied with himself but gets hurt easily and suffers excessively from feelings of inferiority.

No one is completely without narcissistic needs. Freud indicated an important psychological device for offsetting feelings of inferiority.[3] Since everybody is exposed to narcissistic injuries and everybody's reality testing reveals to him his deficiencies, our narcissistic need is necessarily frustrated. Narcissistic tension can, however, be relieved by the formation of what Freud called "ego ideal," that is, of an image with the qualities which the ego would like to have. Reflexive libido is deflected from one's actual, real ego to the ego ideal. Narcissistic need may lead to the search for a person who corresponds to the ego ideal. Such an ego has the need to love and to admire an ideal person and feels narcissistically hurt when it is disappointed by this person. But, after the formation of an ego ideal the ego's narcissistic feelings are also influenced by its own qualities and behavior. In other words, when the ego feels too distant from its ideal it feels inferior, and the closer it approaches the ideal the more it is narcissistically satisfied. With the concept of the ego ideal Freud tackled for the first time (in 1914) the problem of conscience. He stated that the ego forms its ideal chiefly in the image of the father (or parents), and he postulated the existence of a special self-observing and judging "agency" which continuously measures the real ego by the standard of the ego ideal. Thus, originally, Freud conceived the phenomenon of conscience in terms of narcissistic need.

Only later (1923) in *The Ego and the Id*, did Freud call this censoring agency the superego. It develops, as he explained, from the "incorporation" or "introjection" (in our terminology, internalization) of the father. For a long time some psychoanalysts equated "ego ideal" with "superego." But these two mental institutions are by no means identical. The ego ideal is responsible for feelings of shame or pride, the superego for feelings of self-approval or feelings of guilt and need for self-punishment. There are also cases in which an individual would feel ashamed to behave according to the demands of his superego, and conversely, those in which he would feel guilty to behave like his ego ideal when it is disapproved by the superego. But, by and large, there are not often discrepancies between the demands of the ego ideal and those of the superego.

In regard to the origin of narcissistic scar formations, Adler asserted that in every case of "inferiority complex," to use his term, these feelings derive from an early "organ inferiority." One patient felt that he was of less value for not having good eyesight, another for not being good-looking, a third for having some other infirmity or physically crippling condition. Adler's idea of the importance of "organ inferiority" plays a central role in his psychological system. Freud disagreed with him.

According to Freud there are two sources of feelings of inferiority. One is specifically organic, the other psychological. He believed that not every kind of organ inferiority can cause feelings of inferiority, but that such feelings came from one (and only one) specific kind of organ inferiority: the awareness, feeling, or belief that one has an inefficient genital organ, or more precisely, that one has a deficient penis or that one is lacking a penis altogether. Only a genital inferiority, in this sense, could arouse directly a feeling of inferiority. Thus, a boy or a man who becomes aware, feels, or thinks that he has a small or incomplete penis (or a penis with an inefficient functional capacity), and particularly a girl or woman who, not having overcome the phallic phase, feels mutilated for not possessing a penis, reacts with feelings of inferiority. The other source of feelings of inferiority—also a psychological one—stems from the experience of being unloved or rejected, especially by the parents. This sensation of being depreciated as a person plays a great role independent of any organic deficiency. But, of course, if an organ deficiency of any kind is the cause for being unloved or rejected, then it is the indirect reason for ensuing feelings of inferiority. In Freud's opinion, children who, in spite of some crippling organic condition, feel unconditionally loved and accepted by their parents do not develop feelings of inferiority. We may say that Adler's emphasis on the factor of "organic inferiority" is exaggerated. On the other hand, Freud's exclusion of a direct causation of such feelings by organic deficiencies other than those related to the penis, may be an unjustified generalization. In fact, neurotic and especially psychotic reactions to feelings of inferiority consist in the arousal of an exaggerated need for excelling in any kind of positive qualities, achievements, or performances. And often such individuals succeed in their intents, the neurotic in reality, the psychotic in delusion. Such reactions are generally recognized in the so-called "feelings of superiority" of some persons. Persons who feel superior to others are often those who have had to fight against some underlying feeling of inferiority.

These observations lead to an important question. How does an ego realize when it is loved and in possession of all the prerogatives for which it is craving? The answer is simple if we consider only mature egos with a healthy sense of reality and a proper reality testing. It is true, of course, that "wishful thinking" handicaps, more or less, an objective evaluation of one's self and of one's prerogatives. Nevertheless such misevaluations of healthy mature egos cannot be compared with the "feelings of grandeur" typical of infantile and psychotic egos.

At a certain age, prior to the development of an efficient sense of reality and to the transition of the pleasure principle into the reality principle, the infant's ego has the illusion of being able to do everything through his thoughts. As explained previously, at an early stage of ego development thoughts are followed by hallucinations. Ferenczi called this phenomenon "omnipotence of thoughts." This and other unrealistic overestimations of one's own capacities are considered narcissistic manifestations which, in this extreme form, are normal at a certain developmental level. Progressively the child is forced to give up, bit by bit, too unrealistic overestimations of himself. The development of the function called "reality testing" implies an increasing interest in objects of the external world. And the more the child becomes interested in the external world, the weaker and more realistic become his narcissistic cravings. Thus his renunciation of his omnipotence becomes more and more tolerable the more the reflexive libido is directed toward the external world.

In delusional psychosis the ego regresses to the phase of "omnipotence of thoughts," and often such patients have the delusion of being selected by God for some high mission. This ego regression and the contents of these delusions are, according to Federn, the economic consequence of scarcity of ego cathexis necessary for efficient functioning of the ego. As pointed out previously, the ego can economize its cathexis through regression to an earlier stage and thereby maintain a better integration than it could on a more "expensive," more mature level. Such a regression, however, does not always guarantee efficient ego functioning but may represent only an attempt to conserve ego cathexis. We also learned that the sense of reality is economically maintained by well-cathected ego boundaries. To call narcissistic any employment of ego cathexis other than that manifested in self-love (reflexive libido) obscures our understanding of the psychotic processes.

Very often an increase in narcissistic craving, especially when it is combined with delusional gratification, is a reaction to a deficient amount of that ego cathexis which must be employed in the functions and integrative processes of the ego. On one hand an ego can afford to maintain object love when it feels secure in its "home," namely, in its own functioning unity. On the other hand, excessive object love depletes the ego of self-love. The narcissistic reaction to organic depleting processes was illustrated by Ferenczi in his explanation of megalomaniac delusions in patients suffering from general paresis. In his opinion the awareness of these patients, in the form of a vague sensation of the destructive processes in their brains, mobilizes a grandiose attempt to deny the dwindling of brain substance. This denying function is accomplished by the known megalomaniac delusions of these patients. And likewise, we should add, the increased narcissism in psychotic patients, i.e., the need for self-love (reflexive libido), also develops in an attempt to deny a deficient amount of ego cathexis necessary for adequate functioning.

We mentioned that the earliest form of object love develops in response to the infant's gratification of his vital needs. The better the infant's ego is cathected, the sooner and the stronger he starts loving the persons who provide him with such gratifications.

Various emotional needs arouse "object love" in the ego. Of particular importance for the ego's integration and development are the ensuing relationships with other egos—interpersonal relationships. We learned of two kinds of development of object libido, which Freud called "love according to the anaclitic type" and "love according to the narcissistic type." The urge to survive and to assert one's self, narcissistic craving, need for vicarious gratifications, longing for orientation, guidance, and security, and sexual urges, all these factors induce the individual to associate with other persons and to relate himself to them in various ways. Through deeper study of the psychology of the oedipus complex and the relationships between the single members of the family, we shall gain a first insight into the development of interpersonal relationships. In further pro-

204 STRUCTURE AND DYNAMICS OF THE HUMAN MIND

gression we shall study the psychology of extra-family relationships as well as of the formation of new families.

NOTES

(1) Freud, Sigmund. On narcissism: An introduction (1914). Standard edition, 14:67-102. London, Hogarth, 1957.

(2) For further details see Chapter XII.

(3) Op. cit., p. 101.

XXVI

Object Libido and Interpersonal Relationships

IN the beginning the ego pursues only gratification of its vital needs and becomes dependent on the persons who provide for it. As mentioned, the experiences of such gratifications are followed by "object love of the anaclitic type" for these persons: for the nursing mother, the protecting father, and for those who substitute for them. But the ego needs much more than food, care, and protection. From birth to death contacts with other people are indispensable to the ego. It must relate to other egos and must feel that other egos relate to it. The infant craves to be identified, accepted, and loved by other persons. For his psychological development he needs orientation, possibilities for learning how to behave and what to expect, as he needs milk to survive and to grow physically. Unless he perceives how other people behave and react no mental growth and structural development can occur. He obtains this mental and emotional "nourishment" from the persons who feed and protect him. Physical care alone is not sufficient to give him a sense of security, and the ego cannot survive without contact with and love from a mother or other persons who substitute for her in these functions.[1]

Originally the child's interest in the persons who take care of him in all these respects is merely selfish. He responds very early to the understood feelings of other persons. He comprehends that his fate and well-being depend on the emotional attitudes which the persons of his surroundings assume toward him. And he is very sensitive to any divergence of their interest from him toward other objects and objectives. This sensitivity leads to hostile feelings toward rivals.

The originally pure selfish "love" becomes successively and in varying degrees enriched by emotional resonance responses. The growing child cares for his mother's pleasure and pain experiences not only for selfish reasons; he participates in her emotional life to the extent within his reach. Resonance and internalization (identification) processes color the originally mere anaclitic love with other features. A child also identifies with other children and is sensitive to their experiences, provided these children do not interfere with his own interests. At an early age he becomes interested in stories and participates emotionally in the vicissitudes of the children of these tales. Every good or bad thing which can happen to other children can also happen to him.

Ambivalent and merely hostile feelings toward competitive siblings with whom he has to share parental love are never absent. The birth of a sibling is always more or less traumatic to the child. But "altruistic" feelings and tendencies likewise develop toward other children, especially toward those who enjoy less satisfaction than he himself. Pity and compassion, based on resonance identification, can be observed very early in children.

The feeling of envy acquires particular importance on the genital level. As stated above, the "penis envy" of the girl is of great clinical and characterological importance. For anatomical reasons the girl cannot obtain gratification of phallic erotism, while the boy can. On the pregenital levels the mother provides gratification of infantile erotisms in girls and boys alike. But the genital organization creates in the ego the urge for different relationships with an additional motivating power. Externalization of countersexual id urges are revealed very early in the child. They are constitutionally determined. Failure of the girl to externalize phallic urges leads to "penis envy." This is such a frequent occurrence that Freud was led to the belief that every girl passes normally through the "phallic phase." In my opinion it is the biological externalization of countersexual erotisms which is responsible for the boy's sexual attraction to the mother and the girl's sexual attraction to the father. This becomes most apparent at the age of three—and sometimes even earlier.

A fateful complication of the boy's love of the father and the girl's love of the mother arises from feelings of rivalry and competition toward the parent of the same sex. The boy resents the father taking mother away from him, and the girl resents the mother taking father away from her. The oedipus complex reaches its peak about the fifth year of life. Emotionally both boys and girls need both parents.

Normally the mother shows greater affection and tenderness, the father gives more physical security and orientation toward reality. Love of the anaclitic type develops in boys and girls, first toward the mother and later toward the father as well. Therefore the rivalry factor inherent in the oedipus complex and fear of hostile punitive reactions on the part of the parent of the same sex toward one's oedipal urges lead to a great complication in the child's relationship with this parent. In healthy development the libido and the hostile aggressive cathexis, inherent in the oedipus complex, become deflected from the object representations of the parents toward conflict-free objects. As we shall see they are also employed in a new substructure, the superego. But in many cases the oedipus complex is not "dissolved" in the id upon repression. It maintains a strong cathexis, and this "fixation" of the cathexis to the unconscious oedipus complex constitutes the nucleus for many or perhaps all ensuing neuroses. This fixation also determines various kinds of features sought in sexual relationships later in life. There are many important consequences of a still-persistent oedipus complex. One of these is a man's incapacity to integrate feelings of love, tenderness and respect with sexual desires toward a woman. This incompatibility is due to repression of sexual tendencies toward the mother whom he loves and respects. In this case the man seeks depreciated women for satisfaction of his sexual desires. Another consequence is the tendency to create, in one's love affairs, a triangular love situation. The individual feels sexually attracted only to a partner who is married to another person, thus duplicating the oedipal situation. We shall gain a better understanding of this trend when the phenomenon of "repetition compulsion" is presented. The choice of a sexual partner of a different race or culture ("exogamic choice") also expresses the resistance to feeling sexual toward a "mother-type" or "father-type" of partner. In Chapter XX a similar feeling was illustrated. Many other disturbances in sexual relationships are due to a fixation on the oedipus complex, among which, clinically very important, is a man's sexual impotence and a woman's sexual frigidity.

One very important vicissitude of an undissolved oedipus complex in men deserves special consideration. If in a boy's bisexual disposition the feminine urges are constitutionally strongly cathected and he develops an excessive fear of the father in his oedipal competitive attitude, he may give up his masculine claims on his mother and egotize his own feminine urges instead. Castration fear is constitutionally determined and can be enhanced by threatening experiences. The castration fear is the decisive motive for inversion of the externalization process: The masculine trends are externalized in such a boy, and the feminine egotized. In Freud's expositions the idea of losing his penis is equated by the boy with being turned into a woman. In my opinion the idea of losing his penis is equated per se with a horrible mutilation. Being turned into a woman implies not only the loss of the penis but also egotization of feminine urges.

Through renunciation of his phallic function and egotization of his feminine urges the boy offers himself to the father as a woman. In this way the boy tries to forestall the father's punitive and castrating reaction to his oedipal feelings, as if he would say, "Don't harm me. I shall submit myself to you as a woman, as mother does." In this attitude the mother may become the boy's rival in his passive feminine attitude toward his father. Freud called this result of defense against the oedipus complex the "negative oedipus complex."

This vicissitude of the boy's oedipus conflict is, of course, not recognized by him in the described psychological meaning. He does not verbalize this aspect in his thoughts, and the negative oedipus complex usually undergoes repression. To all realistic effects and purposes the boy maintains the concept of being a male. Nevertheless in his overt behavior toward his father and father figures many feminine traits in his behavior are apparent. Physiologically, he may maintain his sexual potency, although his ego assumes somewhat feminine attitudes also in its heterosexual relationships.

In the course of a psychotic process in which the ego loses its sense of reality and repressed contents break through into the ego's awareness, the negative oedipus complex may also be overtly manifested. This is most clearly illustrated in Freud's brilliant monograph on the Schreber case.[2] The patient had a delusion that the world was coming to an end. In his megalomania Schreber believed he had been selected by God for a high mission and showed complete submission to Him. His defiance was directed toward another father symbol, the sun, which spoke to him in human language and at which he yelled threatening words. The patient felt that he had to be turned into a woman, and he accepted this. The prospective transformation implied more than merely the loss of the penis. The patient imagined the great enjoyment which he would experience as a woman during intercourse. Accordingly, he egotized his feminine urges.[3]

Although the psychological contents of the patient's delusions were astutely interpreted by Freud, they do not explain the psychotic process itself.[4]

Beyond a certain degree and after puberty the negative oedipus complex is a pathological phenomenon. But the importance of the father for the normal psychological development of the boy cannot be overestimated. The father serves as an identification pattern for the boy. He conveys to the son a feeling of security and orients him toward reality. To be recognized and approved by the father is one of the most enjoyable and gratifying experiences for the boy. It is precisely the boy's "love" of the father that constitutes the greatest complication in the oedipal situation. The father is loved, emulated, and also feared and hated.

An important phase of ego development takes place in that period which Freud called "latency period." It precedes puberty and normally it begins at the age of five or six, sometimes earlier, sometimes later, and ends with puberty. During the latency period the ego is spared from strong sexual drives, and therefore it is relieved in its task of adjustment relative to one powerful source of problems, namely, the instinctive drives. It is precisely in this period that the ego can strengthen and develop reaction formations to unacceptable pregenital drives. During the latency period too the superego, the exponent of conscience, becomes more firmly established. Around the onset of the latency period the child starts to school for which he is emotionally properly prepared.

The latency period can, however, be disturbed, and this may have very serious consequences. Seductions to which the child may be exposed, seductive impressions from which he is not sheltered, impressions derived from different sources, from books, movies, or from witnessing sexual behavior of adults, may frustrate the ego's development during the latency period. Under such conditions, that is, when the child's environment does not respect his latency period, his ego is deprived of the necessary respite from instinctive activity and thus also deprived of a natural opportunity to develop and to strengthen. And when with puberty the instinctive drives become stimulated from biological sources, this ego is less prepared than a normal one of the same age to meet the demands of the external world in dealing with its impulses. In addition, the child's moral development may have suffered from those earlier disturbances.

Only in man is sexual development interrupted by a latency period which separates infantile sexuality from mature sexuality. With the beginning of puberty the endocrine processes which bring the reproductive organs to maturation re-awaken the sexual impetus strongly. Puberty it should be remembered is not only the initial phase of progressive sexual maturation but also the difficult period of ego adaptation to the newly arising integrative tasks derived from the increasing sexual demands and the conditions of society. The duration of puberty varies with cultural and ethnic conditions.

If the oedipus and castration complexes have not been overcome before the latency period or during it, they create minor or major emotional difficulties at puberty. But in healthy development the parental figures are replaced (with regard to sexual urges) by the desire for free partners, that is, non-incestuous ones. The processes of externalization of countersexual erotisms and egotization of erotisms of one's own sex are firmly established in puberty. The genital organization acquires new physiological functions. Although children may experience through masturbation incomplete orgasm-like sensations before puberty, only the fully developed reproductive organs can provide a complete orgastic discharge of sexual tension. Some pregenital drives always maintain the function of forepleasure and pleasure concomitant to the genitally discharging processes, but their persistent dominance leads to various forms of sexual perversions. During puberty the ego is confronted with many difficulties which have long been subjects of investigation by psychoanalysts. For example, we owe to Anna Freud a very accurate and lucid exposition not only of these difficulties but also of the means by which the ego endeavors to cope with them.[5]

The child observes many "facts of life" which he cannot understand by himself because he has not yet reached the psychophysiological maturation related to these facts. He becomes aware that his parents have some intimate relationship which is hidden from him. And when a child happens to witness or otherwise becomes aware of the sexual intercourse of his parents—the "primal scene"—he becomes traumatized and misinterprets this as a brutal assault on his mother by his father. His intellect poses the problem of how children are born; often he obtains either little or no explanation of the problem from adults, inexact explanation, or explanation that lends itself too easily to misinterpretation. Children must resort mainly to their fantasies in trying to solve the problems concerning the sexual relationships, the way in which impregnation of a woman occurs and the birth of children. Their conclusions are based largely on experiences at the pregenital levels. Among such fantasies we find the idea of oral impregnation through kissing or even through the man's urinating in the woman's mouth. They imagine that the ingestion of some substances make the woman pregnant, that childbirth occurs through the mouth too, or through the anus as feces are expelled, and the idea that the baby comes out through the navel is not infrequent. Fantasies of re-entering and dwelling within the mother's body (often combined with ideas of competition with siblings) are frequently encountered in psychoanalysis. Often the desire to return into the mother's body is a substitution for sexual intercourse with the mother, since the latter seems more forbidden to the child than the return wherefrom he came.

In the psychoanalytic exploration of repressed contents, which are manifested in a disguised or almost overt manner in neurotic symptoms and dreams, Freud and many of his followers have given much attention to various and sometimes amazing misconceptions by the child of facts which he observed or surmised without understanding them correctly. Such fantasies can become fixated in the repressed id and determine odd features and resistances in the ego's later relationships with the opposite sex. The study of such fantasies and their persistence in the ucs. id belongs to psychopathology. This topic was briefly mentioned here to complete the exposition of infantile sexuality.

Different needs determine different kinds of interpersonal relationships, and psychoanalysis investigates the deeper origin of the psychological factors operative in the maintenance of such relationships. It tries to explain the pathology of some forms of relationships and the inability of some persons to enter into healthy relationships with partners of the same sex and opposite sex and with individuals of different ages. The first interpersonal relationships develop in the child's rapport with his parents and siblings, and it is in the family situation that the child learns how to cope with feelings of rivalry and ambivalence. The socially important "we feeling," which is an extension of the ego feeling over other persons of a group, has its "boundaries" also, the "social boundaries." The ego feels strengthened through the "we feeling" and can even obtain narcissistic gratification in this extension. Ambitious successes of parents and siblings are often felt as aggrandizements of one's self. One's own family is originally delimited from people who do not belong to it, but fixation of the "we feeling" to one's own family limits the ego to relationships within the family and deprives it of feelings of closeness, understanding and consideration toward friends and love partners. To be more exact, failure to divert sufficiently one's object libido from parents and siblings deprives the ego not only of the emotional capacity to integrate its sexual needs with emotional closeness to a partner of the opposite sex, but also of an efficient rapport with its peer group. This rapport plays a decisive role in the process of emancipation from parental authority and in the development of community feelings toward persons outside one's original family.

We find in every neurosis an impairment in the patient's capacity to establish healthy interpersonal relationships. It is evident that failure to solve one's emotional problems toward parents and siblings leaves the ego unprepared for its task of relating adequately to other people. And when such an individual builds a new family, relating himself also sexually to the marital partner, the unsolved emotional problems create adjustment difficulties. The importance of interpersonal relationships for a normal emotional development was emphasized by Harry Stack Sullivan, who elaborated on the earliest experiences of the infant and child in contact with the mother and other persons and on the ways of mutual communication between single individuals.

A relationship is "differentiated" when it is based on various emotional interests of two individuals toward each other. The relation of a small child to his mother is less differentiated than the relation of the mother to the child. The child is interested only in being loved and cared for by his mother; the mother is interested not only in the child's well-being but also in many other of his needs and in his future development. To give another example, a man's relationship with a woman whom he uses only for sexual purposes is certainly not a differentiated one. Only men who understand the specific feminine needs, through externalization of their own countersexual traits and knowledge gained from contact with mother and sisters, can integrate these "humane" feelings with sexual ones. And these men will likewise choose women who understand and care for masculine aspirations in men. It is common knowledge that a woman feels depreciated when she feels that she serves only a man's sexual needs and is not valued as a human being.

Only in a harmonious and highly differentiated relationship can one speak of "love," which must be understood as an affective attitude different from that inherent in the mere desire to satisfy one's own drives through it. It is questionable whether a merely selfish emotional attachment to a "love object," chosen according to the anaclitic type, deserves the name "love." Love implies the sharing of the object's own experiences and gratifications, without disregarding any of its essential needs. Some of the needs must be surrendered to another suitable person; and so normal parents wish their children to find a proper love and sexual partner. And as stated above, apart from early sexuality, children soon develop an interest in their mother's needs, which is the forerunner of and basis for object love.

One of the most fascinating and controversial topics of psychology, philosophy, ethics, and esthetics is the relationship of sexuality to love. While biological observation supports the view that love is based on sexuality, esthetic observation emphasizes the absolute lack of connection and even the contrast between them. Celestial love and earthly love are said to be quite different, the first coming from the soul, the latter from the body. For the religious mind the former is given by God, the latter is the temptation of the devil. An idealistic philosopher, Otto Weininger, went so far as to say, "Whosoever covets a woman to enjoy her sexually has never known what love means." The French poet, Alfred de Musset, on the other hand, calls the sexual union of two lovers, a "three times holy communion of souls."

In my opinion it is proper to distinguish between "drive object" and "love object," which do not necessarily exclude each other. In neurotics one may exclude the other, but in healthy mature sexual relationships the love object is also drive object. According to Federn, love rests on the sexual drive, consciously or unconsciously, and he defines love as "imbuement of both the mental and bodily ego by the sexual desire concentrated on the chosen person." [6]

A proper feminine attitude by the mother and normal masculine behavior on the part of the father are most important identification patterns for the child and the best safeguards for sound psychosexual development in both boys and girls. Disturbances in personal relationships can be fully understood only after a consideration of the oedipus complex. As pointed out above, this complex has a different pattern for the girl and for the boy.[7]

NOTES

(1) See Note 5, Chapter XIX.

(2) Freud, Sigmund. Psychoanalytic notes on an autobiographical account of a case of paranoia (Dementia paranoides) (1911). Standard Edition, 12: 3-82. London, Hogarth, 1958.

(3) My own inference.

(4) Freud did not consider this case from an ego psychological point of view, although he did express his opinion that the patient's libido was fixated on a homosexual level. From sublimated homosexuality the libido had later regressed (in his opinion) to a narcissistic position as revealed in the patient's megalomaniac delusions and withdrawal from the external world of objects. This latter condition was expressed in Schreber's feeling that the world was coming to an end. We should note that Federn's ego psychology leads to a different interpretation of the psychotic process; however we cannot embark on a discussion of this at this point.

(5) Freud, Anna. The Ego and the Mechanisms of Defence. London, Hogarth, 1937.

(6) Letter dated January 6, 1948, Paul Federn to Edoardo Weiss.

(7) To make this difference more precise, some analysts have adopted the term "electra complex" when speaking of the oedipal problem in the female.

XXVII

The Cathexes

THE nature of the dynamic factors which operate in mental functioning is a very important subject in psychoanalysis, and a very controversial one. Moreover, since these factors are operating in all living matter, it has become a subject of general biological interest. To express the dynamic connotation of the concept of "mental energy" we borrow the term "energy" from physical science. It is more appropriate, however, to use the Freudian term "cathexis" to indicate the psychological dynamic factors.[1]

In physics, "energy" is defined as the capacity for doing work; there are two states of energy, "potential" and "kinetic," but no different kinds of energy. Physical science does not consider aims or purposes, nor "meaning" of any "work done." Only life phenomena are considered from the perspective of their "meaning" or "sense," terms which imply a goal and the intention of reaching one. Such a goal can be reached by various means. When a change of environment presents obstacles to achievement of the goal by the means first adopted, the organism resorts to new means for attaining the same goal. The ability to find proper means, to act selectively and to time single actions so as to attain the goal, is called integrative capacity. Our scientific approach to understanding mental phenomena is, in this respect, the same as that used for the study of biological phenomena in general: It is finalistic, or teleological.

A striking illustration of the approach which at times has even crept into the exact sciences is the interpretation formerly made by astronomers of straight and geometrically regular lines observed on the planet Mars. Assuming that these lines represented canals made for the purpose of connecting large bodies of water, they regarded them as the work of intelligent beings. Where goal-directed phenomena can be found, we must assume that there is life present. We realize, however, that physical energy must be employed also for "goal-directed work" and that life phenomena store up, autoplastically,

215

physical energy which is selectively released through processes of combustion. It is a chemico-physical task of biology to investigate the sources and the production of physical energy in all biological processes. This physical energy is not "cathexis." Cathexis implies the concept of need or instinct.

As indicated in Chapter XXI, many "principles" have been formulated by biologists, but to date none can be reduced to physical laws. Such a basic principle is homeostasis. What causes the state of dynamic tension in an organism to remain at a constant level and to return after disturbance to the "constancy" or "stability" level? If one answers this question by saying that the constancy level is the best level for survival, one must ask again, "What chemico-physical conditions are responsible for the tendency to survive?" The biological integrative processes cannot be explained so far by physical laws. Furthermore, we can easily understand that the admission of an absolute chemico-physical determinism in all phenomena is incompatible with the existence of organic integrative processes, with any goal-directed activity, briefly with any "meaningful" creation by living beings.

Cathexis is defined as the goal-directed employment of physical energy and the dynamic expression of needs and drives, which constitute the pressure toward attainment of goals. After the death of an organism the accumulated residual physical energy (no longer used in form of cathexis) can be utilized alloplastically by still living organisms. Purposeful alloplastic utilization of these is an outlet for satisfying our needs. And the needs and drives are themselves aroused by chemico-physical stimulations of selective portions of a living organism, in which "life goals" are inherent. The experience of hunger is more than the mere physical effect of specific chemico-physical stimulations, because hunger "pressures" the individual to attain a goal. Hunger is a cathexis, and the cathexis called libido is the dynamic expression of all erotic, self-preservative, and constructive drives.

It is not always easy to distinguish in a living organism pure physical energy from cathexis, since the very discharge of energy constitutes a need. The cathexis arises from physical energy which causes a pressure toward a goal, even though this goal may be only the reestablishment of the constancy state of tension which had been al-

tered. But we may ask why physical energy is anabolically produced by the organism in excess of the amount necessary for meeting
one's immediate needs. Is it produced and stored up in different tissues for the "purpose" of keeping the organism ready and activated
for obtaining gratification of future prospective needs? When this
excess of energy is not used up for the attainment of utilitarian
goals, it is discharged pleasurably in what seem to be "superfluous"
activities. Consideration of this fact leads to the concept of "surplus-
energy." French[2] has traced this concept back to the German
poet Friedrich Schiller who considered that all playful activity results from the discharge of surplus-energy.[3] This theory was later
elaborated by Herbert Spencer in 1878. French also mentions Karl
Groos's criticism of this "surplus-energy theory" to the effect that
playful activities of children and animals are expressions of inherited instincts which emerge in the course of early development and
have the function of inducing the individual to practice and to perfect his ability in the use of his organs before they are needed for
self-preservation. According to Groos, there is a proper instinct for
playful activities with the specific goal of preparing the individual
to meet efficiently future self-preservative tasks in situations in
which a great functional capacity will be needed. Some energy
is drawn or produced just for this purpose. In this case the energy
appears as cathexis.

This view does not take into account all forms of erotic pleasure.
In our discussion of the pregenital phases we recognized that different parts of the body convey erotic pleasure by stimulation and
that various activities are sought for their own sake. It was precisely
the acknowledgment of this fact, pleasure for its own sake, that induced Freud to formulate his libido theory.

As pointed out in Chapter XXI, Alexander calls "surplus-energy"
not only the energy which is manifested in every playful activity but
also every excess of energy and growth beyond homeostatis, that is,
beyond the status quo. Even cell division in unicellular organisms
and the propensity for the preservation of the species in multicellular organisms are considered by him to be the result of surplus
energy. He declares "The psychological equivalent of propagation
is love." [4]

French, on the other hand, considers two interacting components.

One is "the activating pressure that corresponds to some need of the organism as a whole," the other "the functional readiness of the activated organs." In his opinion the discharge of surplus energy implies a comparison. He asks, "Which of these two components is in excess of the other?" When the functional readiness or functional energy of the activated organs exceeds the activating pressure of the needs of the organism as a whole, behavior takes on a playful character.[5] Alexander does not distinguish the pressure exerted by the needs or instinctive drives from the functional energy of the organs activated by this pressure. He considers only homeostasis and calls surplus energy whatever energy, need or growth develops beyond homeostasis. French, however, calls surplus energy the energy over the need pressure, even if this pressure leads to a growth or development beyond the status quo. Erotic and playful activity which the individual enjoys for its own sake is, in French's opinion, the result of an energy in the activated organs in excess of the activating needs. But when the activating pressure is in excess of the functional readiness of the activated organs, the result is frustration, disintegration, and the appearance of aggressive destructive tendencies. French, who does not share Freud's belief in a separate death and destructive instinct, derives every aggressive and destructive manifestation from frustration of the integrative field.

The divergence between French's and Alexander's concepts of surplus energy finds the most clear expression in their interpretations of sadism. Alexander considers sadism as a "short-circuit type of discharge" in sexual activity of surplus aggressive and hostile impulses, but he does not consider these impulses as being derived from qualitatively distinct drives as Freud does. In French's view the aggressive impulses are not manifestations of surplus energy in excess of what is needed. He considers them as the result of frustration, of activating pressures in excess of what can be absorbed by the functional activity of the bodily organs. He says further: "The sexual discharge is an attempt to absorb and neutralize, to 'erotize,' the disturbing pressure; but the fact that the sexual impulse continues to take such a destructive form is evidence that this attempt at erotization is successful only to a very slight degree."[6]

A person may exhaust all his energy in reaching a goal toward which he felt pressured. This goal may constitute an achievement beyond the status quo, but in French's theory he will have no surplus energy left. This individual will feel the need for rest in order to give the anabolic processes the possibility of restoring the used up energies. If, however, he reaches his goal before his store of energy is exhausted, he will feel the urge for additional, as it were, "superfluous" activities in order to discharge the residual "surplus energy." This is Freud's economic explanation of states of triumph and elation. In French's terms these states are evidence of a "surplus energy" over the integrative task or over the need pressure.

The investment of mental contents by cathexes arouses affects and emotions appropriate to the aims of the instinctive drives. Any need pressure is felt emotionally in a way characteristic for any specific need, and the approaching of the respective aim, as well as the frustration of the efforts toward attaining it, are experienced as pleasurable and unpleasurable sensations, respectively. The phenomena of pain or discomfort and pleasure, and also the phenomenon of fear and anxiety are psychological expressions of goal-directed biological processes. In Chapters XIII and XXI we reached the conclusion that pleasurable and unpleasurable states of tension cannot be fully explained from an economic point of view, that is, only from the point of view of increase or decrease of tension. A state of tension itself may be pleasurable or unpleasurable, even before it is reduced to the previous level, depending on the kind of stimulation which is responsible for the increase of tension. But, before considering whether there is evidence for the admission of qualitatively different kinds of cathexis, we want to examine the phenomenon of fear and anxiety.

The basic goal of any living organism, a goal to which all other needs are subordinated, is mastery of any dynamic challenge to its existence. Stimulations in excess of the capacity of the organism to bind them cannot themselves be bound or discharged either. Such excitations can be compared with intruding forces which have first to be caught before they can be expelled. Thus control of stimuli becomes the dynamic task of any organism. In Chapters XIV and XV we spoke of a traumatic state when an organism becomes flooded by an amount of excitation beyond its capacity to bind it. In these chapters we also spoke of the concepts of the external defensive barrier against excessive external stimulation (*Reizschutz*), and of the internal dynamic wall formed by mobilized counter-cathexis. A trauma follows a lesion or a breakthrough of either barrier by stimuli.

It is commonly understood that fear and anxiety are responses of the ego to the perception of danger, and we consider danger to be any threat to the individual's integrity or well-being. In psychoanalysis one considers "danger" in dynamic terms: Danger exists only when the ego feels or perceives an impending threat of being exposed to a stimulation so uncontrollable that homeostasis could no longer be maintained or re-established. A trauma is precisely such a disruption of homeostasis. And the ego reacts with fear and anxiety to the threat of a traumatic condition. This is the danger.

In psychoanalysis we speak of "fear" when the danger threatens from external reality. Freud called this reaction "realistic or objective anxiety" (*Realangst*). The term "anxiety," on the other hand, is reserved exclusively for the ego's reaction to an internal danger, one originating almost exclusively in uncontrollable drives. The formation of the superego furnishes a third source of anxiety, namely, "conscience anxiety" (*Gewissensangst*), which continues to play an important role throughout life. As long as the ego can maintain reliable defenses and protections against injuries or disintegrative processes it does not feel threatened. When the inner defenses are felt to be inadequate to the dynamic task with which the ego is confronted, neurotic anxiety develops. It has been pointed out that repression of ego-alien drives requires quantities of ego cathexis, employed as counter-cathexes. Therefore it is evident that, by diminishing the amount of available cathexis, the maintenance of repressions impoverishes the ego and makes it more vulnerable to traumatic excitation. Physical and mental exhaustion, various preoccupations, and difficult tasks weaken the inner *Reizschutz* when they become too numerous or too intense. In brief, there are many conditions which can make the ego more vulnerable to anxiety.

The phenomena of pain and pleasure and fear and anxiety are the most significant (emotional) evidence that there exists a goal-directed striving in every individual. While the energies forming the defensive barriers deserve the name "cathexes" they are, in fact, counter-cathexes, because they serve a defensive purpose. Even when an individual is deprived of satisfaction of his strong needs and intense desires he uses counter-cathexes to master the tension due to deprivation. A child who is abandoned by his mother cannot master his unsatisfied longing for her; he is, therefore, traumatized and experiences anxiety. The first anticipation of a possible traumatic condition is followed by what Freud called "anxiety signal," namely, by a low degree of anxiety which does not disturb but actually enhances the functions of the ego. This "anxiety signal" induces the ego to activate its functions and to act promptly in order to forestall the danger or to escape from it. All available ego cathexis is mobilized as a defense against the threatening stimuli. But when the situation gets out of control, full anxiety—called panic or terror —disables the ego so that it cannot act in a proper way, at times even cannot act at all. Such acute anxiety paralyzes the motility and other functions of the ego and is accompanied by a disturbance of the ego feeling itself, usually in form of feelings of derealization and depersonalization. These phenomena are due to a full mobilization of great amounts of ego cathexis for the desperate attempt to bind the excessive stimulation, while other ego functions become divested of cathexis. We shall soon see that, in explaining the described conditions of the panic-stricken individual, those psychoanalysts who believe in the death instinct consider another factor in addition to this economic factor. In the next chapter we shall consider the physiological manifestations of fear and anxiety and the clinical picture of traumatic neurosis in connection with the most important phenomenon of living matter discovered by Freud, namely, the "repetition compulsion."

In the presentation of Freud's libido theory in Chapter XXII, we considered the libido as a cathexis belonging to an economic unit. All the drives with varying intensities, powered by libido, oscillate in time. The libidinal interests are activated by internal endocrine stimulations and also by external stimulations. But at any given time the distribution of the amount of libido, as revealed in the pressures toward different goals and also in the activated organs, the "organ cathexes," can be studied from an economic point of view.

The most controversial issue among psychoanalysts concerning the nature of the cathexis or cathexes centers around the question whether there is only one economic cathexis unity, or two or more.

If there is more than one unity, the different cathexes must be related to different *basic* instinctive goals of which one cannot be substituted for another, of which one may even be opposite to another, but which can enter into combination with one another.

In Chapters XXI and XXII the action of different hormonal stimulations in arousing specific urges was discussed. Male and female hormones, the latter estrogen and progesterone, not only cause specific somato-physiological effects, but also they arouse in the individual specific libidinal interests. Many other known and still-unknown endocrine phenomena are responsible for various emotional needs. It is therefore evident that displaceability of libido from one content to another has physiological limits. A feminine urge cannot be substituted by a masculine one, nor a passive urge by an active one. Accordingly, it would be correct to speak of different ranges or spheres, each pertaining to libido from a given source. This libido could be displaced from one goal to another only within its range.

It is also very probable that the ego's capacity to egotize certain instinctive drives and externalize others (the latter phenomenon leads to the individual's search for corresponding objects) has a physiological regulatory system. But such a system, as well as endocrine phenomena, can be influenced to a certain extent by psychological factors, as proved by psychotherapeutic interventions.

The question has also been raised whether specific endocrine phenomena have only a directive action on the libido or whether they are the exciting factors for the very arousal of the amount of libido manifested in the impetus of various drives and the intensity of various interests. Furthermore, the employment of a certain amount of cathexis, or the production of such a cathexis, for the establishment of ego feeling and for the dynamic maintenance of the ego boundaries, as well as for the ego functions, must be regulated by physiological processes. We called the cathexis thus employed "ego cathexis." But in spite of all these complications a "libido-economic" point of view in our dynamic orientation of mental processes is fully justified.

Psychoanalysts who deny the existence of a death instinct consider all instinctive drives (and all living processes in general) as expressions of the homeostatic principle. Stimuli which alter the constancy level induce the living organism to react in a way so that the equilibrium is re-established. Interest in the external world is due to the fact that conditions and objects of the external world provide satisfaction of the needs arising from various stimulations. To satisfy his hunger, which is aroused by specific disturbances of the constancy level, the individual feels pressured toward food intake. In the opinion of these psychoanalysts, stimulation which induces goal-directed activity with the aim of restoring the disturbed equilibrium—relaxation following satisfaction and the return to the state of rest—is the common basis of all instinctive striving and of all processes of life in general. They consider as impossible the existence of any striving induced other than by the principles mentioned. To them, aggressiveness is not a drive derived from a different principle, but only a mode of striving for instinctive goals of the basis mentioned. Aggressive drives are seen to arise from frustration in efforts to reach satisfaction of these drives. Some psychoanalysts believe that aggressiveness can also arise independent of any frustration, as a dynamic condition of removal of obstacles to achievement of needed satisfaction. We want only to note here that without a preceding state of frustration no tendency to obtain a satisfaction forcefully (aggressively) can develop. Frustration of libidinous goals permits putting forth aggression which, if properly used, is applied toward obtaining satisfaction of that libidinous pressure and thus ending the state of frustration. Only where frustration is neurotically (pathologically) determined is aggression unable to serve the libidinous aim.

Regardless of whether or not a basic death instinct exists, the homeostatically oriented psychoanalysts mentioned have bypassed Freud's concept of the basic drives. Freud's approach to the origin and the nature of instinctive drives and of life processes in general goes deeper and beyond the acknowledgment of the constancy principle. With correct understanding we realize that Freud's approach to this study aims at the explanation of the stability principle itself or at the answer to the question whether there also exists some other biological principle as well as the stability principle operating in the phenomenon of life.

NOTES

(1) In Chapter V, above, Edward Glover's definitions of the two concepts of cathexis were given. Here, however, the term "cathexis" is used only to indicate "investment of an idea with instinctive energy giving rise ordinarily to interest and to affect appropriate to the aim of the instinct," rather than in the other sense, namely, "an unconscious process fully experienced in consciousness only when there is no unconscious obstacle to the emergence of the impulse."

(2) French, op. cit., Vol. 1, p. 151.

(3) In his Briefe über die ästhetische Erziehung des Menschen, written in 1793; rewritten and first published in Die Horen in 1795. A recent English translation entitled On the Aesthetic Education of Man in a Series of Letters was made by Reginald Snell (New Haven, Yale University Press, 1954).

(4) Alexander, Franz. Psychoanalysis revised. Psychoanal. Quart., 9:1-36, 1940; see also his Fundamentals of Psychoanalysis. New York, Norton, 1948.

(5) Some critics of this dynamic formulation by French claim it to be merely a paraphrase of Freud's earlier libido theory (as maintained by Fenichel). But this is not so: French's formulation is essentially a structural-dynamic one, seen from the point of view of the integrative function. From a behavioristic point of view it is somewhat analogous to Federn's distinction between drive and ego cathexis.

(6) For a more exhaustive discussion of this issue, see French, op. cit., Vol. I, pp. 148-151.

XXVIII

Instinct Dichotomy

FROM certain observations of emotional experiences of patients during treatment, and of typical human behavior patterns in general, Freud conceived a principle which he called "repetition compulsion." And from an accurate study of various biological phenomena he came to the conclusion that the repetition compulsion constitutes the basic distinction between organic (life) and inorganic (non-life) processes.

In the process of elaborating a psychological technique for bringing to the patient's consciousness the repressed emotional contents of his childhood, Freud noticed that the patient rather repeated as a current experience the emotional events of the past, instead of recollecting them. With unwelcomed fidelity the patients reproduced fragments of their infantile sex life, of the oedipus complex, and related emotional experiences. Freud called transference the patient's re-experience of his infantile emotions and expectancies in their displacement from the original parental figure to the person of the psychoanalyst. Only when this re-experience, unknown to the patient as such, could be turned into a conscious recollection of the repeated contents, through skillful and timely interpretation, could a therapeutic result be obtained.

Freud recognized the great importance of the repetition compulsion in many other psychological and biological phenomena. Only a few of them may be presented here. In the case of a traumatic neurosis (which is due to the ego's incapacity to bind the excess of invading stimuli), the patient re-experiences in dreams, night after night whenever he succeeds in falling asleep, the same situation which traumatized him. He awakens in severe panic and needs time to regain waking control over the excitation which overpowered the dreaming ego. When the ego loses control over an inner situation, the latter is compelled to continuous repetition, while the ego, in fear and even in panic, endeavors to mobilize counter-cathexes in order to bind the excitation. By his repeated reliving of the traumatic experience, and his repeated survival of it, the individual may eventually be enabled to master and integrate it. The repetition compulsion is independent of the pleasure-pain principle; the past event is repeated regardless of whether it produces pleasure or pain to the individual.

After continuous or fatiguing work, physical or mental, such as long, tiring trips, mountain climbing, exciting meetings, or gambling late at night, one dreams and keeps dreaming of such fatiguing or exciting situations at the expense of one's rest and refreshment. After a day of arduous climbing one may repeat again and again the same experience during sleep; the urgent wish to relax and forget does not keep one from dreaming of the same efforts and struggles, fighting the battle of the previous day once more in the dreams of the night. Such dreams show the inefficiency of the pleasure principle, since in fact one wishes to be rid of these situations. A more thorough "economic analysis" of such dreams and some apparent exceptions to this rule will be presented in the section about dreams.

According to Freud physiological manifestations of fear and anxiety (e.g., palpitation, trembling, respiratory difficulties, increased bowel activity) correspond to the individual's actual experiences during his birth. In the experience of being born the individual is passively and helplessly exposed to an overwhelming influx of excitation; he becomes traumatized. He has to start breathing, his heart has to adapt itself to an increased function, the lungs have to provide oxygen, and the body enters from a warm into a cooler environment. These physiological experiences are automatically repeated later in life whenever the individual becomes aware of a danger. The fixation to the "birth trauma" explains the physiological concomitant phenomena of later fears and anxiety. This reaction pattern is, however, inherited from all our ancestors.

People in general unconsciously and with a cunning ability bring about repetition of situations which they were unable to master. This is particularly true in a form of the character neurosis called "fate neurosis." Such patients involve themselves over and over again in the same or similar situations, each time suffering the same kind of defeat, without being able to learn from their experiences to avoid such a "fate." For example, a man repeatedly falls in love with women who sooner or later betray or abandon him; another associates himself over and over again with business partners who lead him to complete failure, or engages in enterprises which are beyond his capacity, thus insuring loss and humiliation. Repressed memories of traumatic situations determine in the individual the urge to re-experience and re-enact them with striking fidelity. In repeating a situation of childhood adapted, however, to the changed life situations, the individual does not recall it while re-experiencing the earlier emotional involvements; he ignores the reasons for his bizarre behavior. This process plays a significant role in human behavior and thus represents an important factor in shaping the "destiny" of the single individual. The repetitive behavior is complicated by unconscious motives and accompanied by old emotions: It is called "acting out." In acting out the persons who were involved in the original situations, for the most part parents and siblings, are replaced by other individuals of the current environment according to their suitability for representing the original persons. Often this acting out consists in a determined affective attitude of the individual toward the person who becomes the representative of the original one, as was mentioned in the phenomenon of transference. Desires, expectations, and emotions of the past are thus "transferred" to a representative without any rational motive but merely out of an urge to re-experience the former unmastered situation. Transference feelings can be considered an "emotional acting out." As indicated above, once the transference is turned into a conscious recollection of the traumatic situation the patient becomes enabled to check the repetition.

Freud emphasizes the fact that instincts are historically conditioned. He defines instinct as *an urge inherent in organic life to restore an earlier state of things* which the living entity has been obliged to abandon under the pressure of external disturbing forces; that is a kind of organic elasticity, or, to put it another way, the expression of the inertia inherent in organic life." [1] "Certain fishes," he continues, "undertake laborious migrations at spawning-time in order to deposit their spawn in particular waters far removed from their customary haunts. In the opinion of many biologists what they are doing is merely to seek out the localities in which their species resided but which in the course of time they have exchanged for others. The same explanation is believed to apply to the migratory flights of birds of passage . . ." [2] Heredity too is a repetition, or rather a reproduction, of the features of the generators by the germ plasm, guided in a certain unknown way by the function of the genes. And every single individual repeats very briefly in his embryonal development all the phases through which the species has gone. Ontogenesis is known to be a repetition of phylogenesis. Memory itself is a very complex function; it presupposes, however, an act of reproduction of past experiences. In the act of "recollecting" the ego is well aware that what enters the mind is unreal and that the contents are related to bygone events. The sense of reality, a function of the internal ego boundary, prevents the hallucinatory re-experience. Nevertheless, without repetition compulsion, which is essential for remembering anything, no mnemonic function could come into being. Thus, the mnemonic function, heredity and life in general cannot be conceived without the biological principle called "repetition compulsion." Freud arrived at the final, though speculative conclusion: "If we are to take it as a truth that knows no exception that everything living dies for *internal* reasons—becomes inorganic once again—then we shall be compelled to say *the aim of all life is death*, and looking backwards, that *inanimate things existed before living ones.*" [3] By what operation of force lifeless matter was awakened to life is still completely unknown. The tension aroused in the previously inanimate matter strove to attain an equilibrium, and the first instinct was present, the instinct to return to lifelessness, that is, to re-establish the abandoned condition.

Before presenting Freud's further elaboration of this theory, I would like to mention my objection to it, published in 1935. [4] As long as one considers a state x in which the living matter found itself at some time in the past and to which it strives to return, it is permissible to assume the existence of a drive to re-establish the state x. Such a drive would be the expression of the repetition compulsion. As stated above, Freud calls this compulsion "a kind of organic elasticity" or the "expression of inertia in organic life," which is precisely the distinction between animate and inanimate matter. But it is not permissible to extend the conclusions, gained from the phenomenon of the repetition compulsion, to states which existed prior to life. Such a procedure is called extrapolation. Since the inanimate state existed prior to life, namely, before a repetition compulsion could come into being, the present author considered an extrapolation Freud's ultimate conclusion from the repetition compulsion that a death instinct exists. Nevertheless a death instinct may exist, but it cannot be deduced from the repetition compulsion; we must have other proofs for its admission.

How did Freud explain the existence of the self-preservative instinct, called Eros? And what interesting biodynamic conditions are implied in the admission of two basic tendencies in living matter, which are in opposition to each other?

One may ask why living matter does not die immediately upon its enigmatic formation, according to the repetition compulsion. In Freud's opinion, in the beginning living matter did die shortly after its formation and was continuously rebuilt. The short duration of the first organisms was determined by their chemical structure. And Freud assumed that decisive external influences must have caused a delay in the dying process of the living organisms. For external reasons, not internal, the primitive living matter could not reach its goal in a short time, that is, could not die as quickly as it did initially. Freud failed to explain, however, how the evolution of the earth, and its relation to the sun, could have kept living matter longer in a state of life, thus making it more complicated for it to return to the inorganic state. We would certainly postulate an inherent self-preservative tendency in living matter to account for its adaptation to changed external conditions. But Freud considered the delay in dying, imposed on the living matter from without, as a factor impelling it to undergo changes in order eventually to die. Thus the original danger to which living organisms were exposed was not that they could not survive but, on the contrary, that they could not die. To render Freud's train of thought we could speak of a "life tension." And the newly arisen organism reacted, according to Freud's speculative conjecture, against any increase of such a tension as if it signified increase in "living state." In the opinion of most biologists the "constancy level" is the most favorable dynamic state of tension for the life process. But Freud writes: "The dominating tendency of mental life, and perhaps of nervous life in general is the *effort to reduce,* to keep constant, or *to remove internal tension* due to stimuli (the Nirvana principle, to borrow a term from Barbara Low)—a tendency which finds expression in the pleasure principle; and our recognition of that fact is one of our strongest reasons for believing in the existence of death instincts." [5]

Freud implies that the "stability principle" (Cannon's homeostasis) is a preparatory principle in the direction of the death instinct. He declared, "The tension which then arose in what had hitherto been an inanimate substance endeavoured to cancel itself out. In this way the first instinct came into being: the instinct to return to the inanimate state." [6]

We understand that the behavior induced by instincts differs from that due to intelligent striving. If we want consciously to reach a given goal, our intellect tries to find the shortest way of reaching it, while aims which are striven for instinctively are reached through a succession of fixed steps. And so the still surviving substance was compelled, according to Freud, to resort to ever more complicated and circuitous ways in order to reach the inanimate state, death. All instincts are in Freud's opinion conservative, and the paths to death are faithfully retained deviations, imposed by external conditions, toward this goal. Only through the repetition of all the steps and changes through which living matter had to pass in order to die, through a repetition of an always-longer course of events, could it eventually cease to exist as living organism. What impresses us as an evolution or development is not viewed by Freud as a result of any progressive drive but, on the contrary, as the effect of external influences which made it increasingly more complicated for the living matter to become inanimate again. In Freud's words: ". . . The organism wishes to die only in its own fashion. Thus these guardians of life, too, were originally the myrmidons of death. Hence arises the paradoxical situation that the living organism struggles most energetically against events (dangers, in fact) which might help it to attain its life's aim rapidly—by a kind of short-circuit." [7] These self-preservative instincts would be only part-instincts induced by the repetition compulsion. Their aim is to prevent the organism from dying prior to repeating all the stages through which it was compelled to go before it could die. We realize thus that the repetition compulsion prevails not only over the pleasure principle, but also that it is more powerful than the instinctive aim to return to the inanimate state. Since the repetition compulsion is a characteristic of life, one could deduce that living organisms adhere more to this characteristic than to the aim to die, a conclusion that was not made, however.

Freud indicates three factors responsible for the self-preservative instincts, as follows: (1) the repetition compulsion which forces the organism to relive all past impediments to its dying and the changes which it had to undergo in order to die; (2) the libidinous drives, Eros, with which we shall deal shortly, and (3) the extraversion toward external objects of the death instinct, a factor which can be the cause of great destruction and of wars, as will be pointed out. As an intermediary link between his first and second instinct theories, Freud considered as ego instincts the silent, not openly revealed, death instinct itself as well as its myrmidons, which impress us as self-preservative instincts. These kinds of instincts are in opposition to the sexual instincts which we shall consider now.

Freud's earlier distinction between ego instincts, which he equated with self-preservative instincts, and sexual instincts had a very superficial structural implication. One could only say that the self-preservative instincts determine an "egoistic" attitude of the ego. But self-preservative striving per se is a general biological trend which extends beyond the mental substructure "ego." When Freud then drew a parallel between the death instinct (including its "myrmidons") and the life instinct on one side, and ego instincts and sexual instincts on the other side, as a link between his earlier and his later instinct theories, the structural implication of the two kinds of postulated cathexis was lost altogether.

The fact that living organisms propagate themselves made it clear that besides the postulated death instincts, life instincts must also exist. In multicellular organisms new individuals come into being from the mingling of male and female germ plasm. Protozoa, unicellular organisms, multiply through cell division and are thus potentially immortal. Freud considered the assumption that these life instincts might have existed from the very beginning, but he did not abandon the hypothesis of death instincts. Instead he conceived the idea of a "fusion" of life and death instincts. In my opinion the assumption that life instincts must have existed from the very beginning is in line with the fact that the repetition compulsion (if it is characteristic of life, as Freud himself asserted) prevails over the "short-circuit death," as was mentioned before. And these *life* instincts, not the death instincts, must have been responsible for the adaptation of living matter to changed conditions in its environment.

Freud connected the individual's striving for life with the observed strengthening and rejuvenating effect of the copulation of two equal unicellular organisms. This effect occurs even without a subsequent partition of the combined cell. Through this conjugation, as well as through certain experimentally produced chemical or mechanical stimulations of the cell, in certain cases the "life extension" is increased in it. But then the inner tendency to lower tension thus increased proved to Freud the existence of death instincts.

The mingling of two unicellular organisms is the prototype for the later mingling in multicellular individuals of two differentiated cells, a male and a female one. But some infusoria are potentially immortal and can increase, through cell division, to a limitless number even without any act of copulation. According to Freud who characterizes these cells as "narcissistic," in them the life tendency, in an inseparable fusion with the death instinct, is prevailing over the death tendency. He holds, however, that this striving for life stems from an original striving for a union of one cell with another.

Freud compares his concept of co-existence in an organism of both life and death instincts with Weismann's distinction between two substances in living organisms: One part, the germ plasm, is potentially immortal because in favorable conditions, in union with countersexual germ plasm, it can produce a new individual. The other part is constituted by the cells of the body which age and die. On the other hand, Freud distinguishes two kinds of goal-directed striving in the living organisms, (1) toward life and increased production through union, and (2) toward death. It is because the narcissistic germ plasm absorbs more "life cathexis" (libido) than the cells of the body, that it is potentially immortal. He also sees in the biologic metabolism, in the constructive anabolic and in the destructive catabolic processes, an expression of both life and death instincts. To put into better relief Freud's theory of instinct dichotomy we could make the following statements:

When the individual has traveled for a time along the path toward death, the germ plasm, which has narcissistically captured and concentrated the life cathexis on itself, detaches itself from the body. In favorable conditions it starts the journey all over again, and, compelled by the organic elasticity, it repeats in proper succession all phases through which the species went. It detaches itself from the body, which is going to age and die, because Eros rebels against the death instinct. And this interminable cycle is due to the titanic struggle between the life and death instincts.

The life instinct strives toward unions into increasingly greater formations. Why this should be so Freud did not know. He tried to find a tentative and very speculative solution of this problem, based also on the repetition compulsion. In this connection he mentions "the theory that Plato put into the mouth of Aristophanes in the *Symposium,* and which deals not only with the *origin* of the sexual instinct but also with the most important of its variations in relation to its object." [8] This theory was discussed in Chapter XXIV in connection, however, with the bisexual disposition and the phenomena of egotization of the urges of one's own sex and the externalization of those of the opposite sex. Freud takes from this Platonic theory the cue for asking the question whether ". . . living substance at the time of its coming to life was torn apart into small particles, which have ever since endeavoured to reunite through the sexual instincts?" [9] He then asks whether "these instincts, in which the chemical affinity of inanimate matter persisted, gradually succeeded, as they developed through the kingdom of the protista, in overcoming the difficulties put in the way of that endeavour by an environment charged with dangerous stimuli—stimuli which compelled them to form a protective cortical layer? that these splintered fragments of living substance in this way attained a multicellular condition and finally transferred the instinct for uniting, in the most highly concentrated form, to the germ-cells?" [10] At this point Freud broke off. He recognized the highly speculative character of his constructions, and he himself did not know how far he believed in them.

All speculative thought aside, however, the application of the new instinct dichotomy to the understanding not only of many neurotic and psychotic manifestations but also of normal psychological behavior patterns, particularly of the "aggressive" severity of the superego, strengthened Freud's belief in the death instinct. Whatever conclusion the reader may reach from this presentation, he must become acquainted with Freud's concepts of fusion and defusion, as well as of the introverted and extraverted manifestations of the two opposite cathexes, in order to understand fully Freud's position and that of some of his well-known followers regarding the instinctive forces. Three of his classic works deal exclusively with his theory of Eros and Death, a theory of which he had some doubts in the beginning, but of which later he was fully convinced.[11]

In the last chapter of this section we shall present a detailed discussion of Freud's ideas related to the death instinct, their application to a better understanding of normal and pathological mental phenomena, and opinions of some psychoanalysts who dissent from him.

NOTES

(1) Freud, Sigmund. Beyond the pleasure principle (1920). Standard Edition, 18:1-64. London, Hogarth, 1955. The passage cited is on p. 36.

(2) Ibid., p. 37.

(3) Ibid., p. 38.

(4) Weiss, Edoardo. Todestrieb und Masochismus. Imago, 21:393-411, 1935.

(5) Freud, op. cit., p. 55-56. My italics.

(6) Ibid., p. 38.

(7) Ibid., p. 39.

(8) Ibid., p. 57.

(9) Ibid., p. 58.

(10) Ibid., p. 58.

(11) I.e., Beyond the pleasure principle (see Note 1, above), Civilization and Its Discontents (1930) (New York, Jonathan Cape, 1930), and Why War? (1933). (Collected Papers, 5:273-287. London, Hogarth, 1950). The last is Freud's contribution to an exchange of open letters between him and

Albert Einstein arranged and published under auspices of the International Institute of Intellectual Cooperation of the League of Nations (the forerunner of UNESCO). The pamphlet containing these letters appeared simultaneously in English, French, and German (Paris: The Institute, 1933). Einstein's contribution is not reprinted in Freud's Collected Papers.

XXIX

Diverging Concepts of Drives

IN Chapter XXI we noted that Freud, in his studies of the "impelling forces" operating in living organisms, used the German term *Triebe,* a word which has been translated into English as "instincts." [1] These impelling forces (the *Triebe*) are more properly rendered by the English words "instinctive drives" or simply by "drives." A drive is an urge or an inner impulse to reach a particular goal, this goal being a decrease of tension to the prestimulation level according to homeostasis. Increase of specific tensions is produced by various physiological processes. And through the discharge of the excess of tension, directly or indirectly, productive processes and propagation occur.

In Freud's thesis, as we pointed out, the increase of tension stems from a union of one individual (or one cell) with another, but there is also in the organism an enigmatic urge to establish such unions, thus prolonging and strengthening life and creating new individuals. Freud called this basic "drive" *Eros,* and its dynamic expression, its cathexis, libido. This Latin word was used by A. Moll in 1898 in his *Researches on the Sexual Libido,* to designate the sexual urge, in the strict sense of the word, however. But, the urge to be stimulated is not the same as the effect from being stimulated whether there was such an urge or not. In the concept of those psychoanalysts who disagree with Freud's dualism of drives, only the latter condition is considered a drive (instinct), namely, the effects of particular physiological stimulations.

We learned in the preceding chapter that, in Freud's opinion, there is also in the living organism the opposite striving toward an opposite goal, that is, not only to lower the increased tension but to bring the tension to extinction altogether. As we have seen Freud accepted Barbara Low's term "nirvana principle" to designate this latter striving. It is evident that those psychoanalysts who conceive a drive only as the occurrence of a physiological stimulation and the discharge of the increased tension cannot accept the existence of a "drive" aiming at the avoidance of any stimulation and at the cessation of all life tension, that is, at a lifeless state. The drives as they are conceived by the dissenting psychoanalysts are considered by Freud as drive components in the service of the two basic drives, Eros and Death.[2]

If we consider the part-drives derived from physiological stimulation, we may ask how the individual knows in what manner he can reach their goals. Inherited instinctive actions, as we see them particularly in animals, are not sufficient means to reach satisfaction. True, the individual puts food "instinctively" into his mouth, he sucks, chews, and swallows. Likewise sexual acts are performed automatically according to inherited patterns. But the problem of how to reach the needed objects and conditions must be solved, by men and animals, through a learning process from experience. If an individual is unable to learn how to reach a special drive goal, he becomes also unable to bind and discharge the inner drive tension which has arisen. This condition may lead to a traumatic state like those described in Chapters IX and XXVII, due to a lesion of the protective barrier against excessive stimulation. The individual is flooded by stimulations which he cannot master. And such stimulations may derive also from physiological drive sources. French[3] has given clear expression to this conception of the traumatic experience in his expanded concept of psychic trauma. He defines a trauma as "any situation or event that more or less permanently interrupts the process of learning by experience." This definition requires clarification. For various reasons an ego may be unable to "learn" how to get rid of excessive external or internal (need) stimulation. A conflict which it cannot solve is one reason. Then if the afflux of excessive stimulation into the ego is too sudden, as in sudden accidents, the ego has neither the necessary time nor the needed resources to free itself from the invading stimulations. Furthermore, an ego may lack the endowment necessary for finding a solution to its problem, or it may have deficient (diseased or underdeveloped) organs for coping with the situation. French's definition implies that in all these cases the ego's "learning process by experience" is interrupted. And he defines the drive as "a latent inherited orientation that predisposes an organism to learn ways of achieving a particular goal. Its basic goal, we postulate, is a negative one—to avoid or put an end to a particular disturbing kind of physiological state, which we call the 'drive stimulus.' Its positive goals must be learned —ways of 'satisfying' the drive, i.e., ways of putting an end to this specific drive stimulus." [4]

We see again that Freud's concept of the drive differs basically from definitions given by psychoanalysts who do not accept a death instinct. In their opinion a drive could aim, directly or indirectly, only at the removal of physiological states which are disturbing some life condition. A drive could never aim at abolishing life altogether. This would amount, in their opinion, to pouring out the baby with the bath, the baby being the most favorable conditions for life, the bath the excess of tension. In Freud's view the adversary of the death instinct is Eros, and he did not attribute the same position to the repetition compulsion. He assigns to the latter, however, the determining factor both for the "death's myrmidons" and for the historically motivated force of the erotic drives which strive for union and re-creation.

The most important implication of Freud's instinct dichotomy is the assumption of two separate economic units. According to his earlier instinct theory libido could take various forms of expression, and the more libido is employed in one position the less is left for another position. For instance, the more libido is directed toward sublimated goals the less is available for the arousal of unsublimated sexual drives, and the more libido is turned toward objects the less remains for narcissistic interests. In Chapter XXII it was pointed out that the displaceable libido, manifested in various interests and drives, constitutes a proper economic unit. Ego drives or self-preservative drives (still according to Freud's earlier theory) could never be turned into libidinal interests and thus could never have any part in the libido economy.

According to his later instinct theory, however, Freud considered as libidinal all constructive life drives, retaining the term libido to designate their dynamic expression. And he maintained that the urges toward death and destruction were powered by a proper cathexis belonging to their own economic unit. Libido could neutralize a death drive cathexis but, still in Freud's later view, could never be turned into death drive cathexis or vice versa. We are aware, however, that the recognition of different libidinal interests, each elicited by different kinds of hormones, makes it difficult to conceive all libidinal drives from different hormonal sources as pertaining to one and the same economic unit, in spite of the implied restrictions of displaceability. In any case all libidinal components of all sorts of drives would strive for life, union and (re-)production.

In his earlier drive theory Freud assumed that the sexual drives and all their derivatives were produced by hormonal activities which were basically different from the physiological sources of the ego drives. Sexual urges (libido) and hunger, for instance, arise from basically different physiological sources. In his later drive theory, however, he never raised the question whether the death drive cathexis could be the effect of physiological phenomena different from those generating libido. But he became quite positive in his assertion that the death drive cathexis constituted an economic unit per se, although he did not introduce any word for its designation. Federn invented for this cathexis the term "mortido" from the Latin "mors" for death. The present author,[5] who did not find that the existence of a death drive was proved and still admitted that two separate kinds of cathexis might exist (the constructive libido and a destructive cathexis), proposed the term "destrudo" for the latter kind of cathexis. This term would not imply that every aggressive tendency be the result of extraversion of an original striving for self-annihilation.

Psychoanalysts who believe in the death drive, however, reject Federn's term "mortido" as a designation of death-drive cathexis. In general we do not find in psychoanalytic literature the terms "mortido" and "destrudo." And even the classic term "libido" is slowly disappearing from the publications of some psychoanalysts who prefer to speak simply of "cathexis" to designate any biological or mental driving force. Furthermore, the uncompromising terms "libidinal" and "aggressive" drives or cathexes are frequently used also by authors who do not believe in a death instinct.

In the following description of the vicissitudes of the two basic cathexes postulated by Freud, we shall use Federn's term "mortido" for the death-drive cathexis. The ways in which these cathexes can manifest themselves can best be described by the modes made familiar to us by grammar: medial, active, passive and reflexive. As pointed out in Chapter V, the ego feeling, thoroughly studied by Federn, is the experience of medial libido and mortido. Medial libido, which Federn calls "primary narcissism," is experienced in the pleasurable feeling of one's own experience and can be expressed by phrases such as "I live joyfully," "I enjoy my existence, my thriving," etc. The silent death drive, postulated by Freud, is normally revealed in one's aging and dying. According to Freud the two cathexes never appear isolated but are always fused together, though in varying proportions. But Federn[6] reports clinical cases of very severe depression in which mortido appears alone in the ego feeling. From his observations Federn concluded that a death drive must exist. And he found that the clinical cases mentioned are more reliable proofs of the existence of this death drive than the theoretical speculations presented in the preceding chapters. There are depressed patients who have only the desire to cease to exist. The occurrence of suicide would seem to prove the existence of a death drive especially when the patient, having first been unsuccessful, tries over and over again to kill himself. In taking the history of a depressed male patient I learned that the patient's mother had committed suicide in her first melancholic attack. She had poured gasoline over her clothes, ignited them, and then resisted all attempts to save her. She really wanted to die.

In Federn's opinion the pathological condition of such patients is due to the temporary failure of the supply of libido, so that only mortido remains in the ego cathexis. In such a state the patient is completely unable to enjoy anything, nor does he recall pleasant experiences of the past; he dislikes everything in his existence and is overwhelmed by the anticipation of ceasing to exist. As stated in Chapter XV, this feeling is not a longing for peaceful relaxation, nor is it a masochistic urge to obtain pleasure through suffering. Severe melancholics are simply driven toward death for the sake of nonexistence and nothing else. In Federn's description mortido, unchecked by libido, prevails in active, passive, reflexive, and medial forms.

At variance with Federn's concept, some psychoanalysts who believe firmly in the death drive also consider the need for rest and

sleep as an expression of this drive. Nothing could be more contradictory than such a view, since rest and sleep, during which the
exhausted energies are replaced and waste products eliminated, is
always enjoyed by the individual. During rest and sleep the anabolic processes prevail over the catabolic processes. On the other
hand, we may ask whether a destructive drive directed against one's
own person really proves that this drive is inherent in the living
organism and is not, rather, the result of an originally outward-
directed drive which became introverted as the consequence of a
hopeless state or as an effect of a severe sense of guilt. The latter
condition will find an exhaustive elaboration in the next section. In
any case, the clinical pictures described prove that a self-destructive
tendency, be it primarily or secondarily directed against one's self,
may prevail over the self-preservative drive. This occurrence alone
would certainly speak in favor of the existence of destructive drives
in opposition to life drives. Again we would like to understand under what circumstances an original death drive (if such a drive exists) can lead to a "short-circuit" goal and not to a goal reached
through the repetition of all stages which Freud describes as the
myrmidons of the death instinct. One may wonder why a person
does not simply age and die more rapidly—as happens in some
cases when the individual has lost all zest for life—instead of taking a short-cut exit from life. We realize, however, that in the process of aging and dying the destructive factor, mortido, operates in a
medial form, while in the case of suicide it operates in a reflexive
form; in other words, in the latter one's own person becomes the
object of the destructive cathexis.

Freud would not have resorted to the speculative deductions
published in *Beyond the Pleasure Principle* had he not been deeply
impressed by clinical material and specifically the realization that
some patients show an insurmountable resistance to recovery. Common sense suggests that in cases of extreme weariness of life the
afflicted individual must find himself in such a state of physical or
mental distress that to not exist seems preferable to living. Such
situations can be imagined by everyone. One would also think that
such individuals would wish to live if they were relieved from their
unbearable distress. But thorough investigation of some cases by
psychoanalysis revealed to Freud that a patient may harbor an in-

vincible urge to keep his neurotic suffering in spite of all prospects for a life which to others would seem desirable. In most of these cases an unconscious feeling of guilt, produced by an extremely destructive superego, keeps the patient from renouncing his neurosis which he senses as deserved punishment for his guilt. This is also true whenever the patient's guilt feelings are found to stem from childhood thoughts and deeds which can no longer be felt as guilty by an adult. If such a destructive sense of guilt or any kind of self-destructive tendency is powered by an amount of destructive cathexis constitutionally greater than the amount of libido, there is nothing the psychoanalyst can do to free the patient from his neurosis. Such self-destructive resistance may derive from repressed hostile feelings mostly toward the parent of the same sex in connection with the oedipus complex. And, in general, there are diseases in the course of which the individual reveals the tendency to destroy himself with an uncontrollable force. Such an intense destructive cathexis is postulated also by Nunberg in his classic study of the catatonic attack.[7]

The direction of either cathexis, libido or mortido, has the most far-reaching implications. We have just mentioned that the medial mortido is manifested in one's aging and dying. The reflexive mortido leads to suicide. We come now to the realization that one's own person can be spared from the destructive effect of mortido if this cathexis is directed toward objects of the external world. A similar state of affairs was described in our presentation of the libido theory. The greater the narcissism is, the less a person is capable of loving others and vice versa. An individual can be so strongly in love with another that he himself becomes depleted of libido; his self-value can sink to a low degree. Similarly, a person can maintain the desire to live not only when his ego is sufficiently libido-cathected but also if enough mortido, in medial or reflexive form, is averted from self-destruction and directed toward objects of the external world in form of aggression, hatred, and hostility. Freud holds that this is also true of any social unit. If members of a family feel very loving and close to each other, they will be more distant, even unfriendly or hostile, toward persons outside the family. People who love persons outside the family easily and become close to them are likely to live in discord and quarreling with members of family. Freud detected this phenomenon among different kinds of social groups, nations, classes, religions, etc. Through racial, religious, and national prejudices people create targets for their aggressive drives, thus safeguarding unity within their groups.

The degree of hostility and aggression which must be directed toward external individuals, groups, etc., depends on the varying amounts of libido and destructive cathexis biologically produced at any given time. Freud ascribes the main motivation of wars to the biological necessity of social and national groups to avert self-destruction by diverting the destructive forces toward external groups. He ends his book *Civilization and Its Discontents* with the following paragraph:

"The fateful question of the human species seems to me to be whether and to what extent the cultural process developed in it will succeed in mastering the derangements of communal life caused by the human instinct of aggression and self-destruction. In this connection, perhaps the phase through which we are at this moment passing [1930] deserves special interest. Men have brought their powers of subduing the forces of nature to such a pitch that by using them they could now very easily exterminate one another to the last man. They know this—hence arise a great part of their current unrest, their dejection, their mood of apprehension. And now it may be expected that the other of the two 'heavenly forces,' eternal Eros, will put forth his strength so as to maintain himself alongside of his equally immortal adversary. But who knows what the ultimate outcome will be?"

The occurrence of unprovoked aggressive and destructive manifestations in individuals, which can be easily observed even in small children, and particularly the horrifying aggressive and cruel actions of entire groups of people as recorded in history from earliest times to the present, strengthened Freud's belief in the destructive cathexis. Many psychoanalysts believe, however, that such aggressions do not derive from a proper destructive instinct but rather that they are means for the achievement of necessary goals, either selfish or unselfish. Others hold that no aggressive tendencies could develop in any individual, man or animal, if he were not exposed to any kind of frustration—but this is practically impossible.

Another issue must be mentioned here. We learned that a child must reach a good and healthy rapport with his parents and siblings in order to be able as an adult to establish a healthy social integration and close relationships with his peers, authority figures, and love partners. Does this acknowledgment not contradict the view that a close relationship of love among the members of a family can more easily be maintained if the aggressive cathexis is directed toward people outside of the family? Not necessarily. One could say that a child who reached a healthy relationship with his parents and siblings becomes psychologically (not necessarily dynamically) equipped for the establishment of good relationships with other people. But this psychological prerequisite must be dynamically supported in order to lead to closeness to and understanding and consideration of an increasingly broader group of individuals. Eventually this group would include more and more heterogeneous individuals. According to Freud's concept of drive dichotomy, the aggressive cathexis must at some point be diverted from its action within the group, be it small or large, toward outsiders, if the unity within the group is to be preserved.

Thus according to Freud, the destructive cathexis spares one's own person or one's own group by being extraverted against objects of the external world. We must add here that any extraverted cathexis, be it libido or mortido, can be again introverted, thus becoming manifested in a reflexive form: in self-love or self-hate and self-destruction, respectively.

The theory of the instinct dichotomy contains still another aspect. It is not necessary that all mortido be directed against the external world in order to lose its destructive effect on one's self. If it becomes "fused" with libido, neutralized by libido, its destructive quality is thwarted. To explain the phenomena of fusion and defusion of libido and mortido, some psychoanalysts have used an analogy with two chemical elements or substances. An acid, for example, can be neutralized by a base. This chemical combination is called a salt. Or, one metal can be alloyed with another metal, resulting in a fusion which has characteristics different from the two. If these two metals become again separated from each other, we can speak of a "defusion." But one may ask, as other psychoanalysts have done, whether it is permissible to compare a cathexis with a chemical element or substance.

The analogy is indeed confusing. Let us, therefore, describe and illustrate by concrete examples Freud's concepts of "fusion" and "defusion" of drives. A cathexis is a goal-directed force. What can be the vicissitudes of two cathexes, each directed toward an opposite goal, if they manifest themselves in combination? The result of such a combination will be different if libido prevails over mortido or mortido over libido. Besides, we understand that a fusion, in varying proportions, can appear in a medial, active, reflexive, and passive form. In the last the individual has the urge to become the object of someone else's active cathexis. The drive itself is active, but the drive goal is a passive one.

In the opinion of those who believe in the death instinct, fusion of the two basic drives can best be acknowledged in cases in which the destructive drive prevails in the fusion. For example, in sadism mortido is fused with a smaller amount of libido, but it is precisely the libidinal component of the cathexis which conveys to the individual erotic pleasure in harming or destroying the object. In masochism the destructive cathexis is also fused with libido, but in this case libido does not completely neutralize the self-destroying effect of mortido. Thus, the masochist experiences pleasure in suffering, physically or mentally. It depends on the proportion of libido and mortido how dangerous, that is, how destructive the mortido is in any single case of either sadism or masochism. Freud called primal masochism the deeply hidden portion (medial, to use Federn's term) of the self-destructive drive, which implies that the original death drive also appears always more or less fused with libido. Still in the opinion of the psychoanalysts who believe in the death instinct the manifestations of the pregenital sexual drives show an incomplete fusion of the life and death drives, since they have a clearly ambivalent character. In the occurrence of ambivalence some amount of love, libido, appears side by side with a free amount of mortido, but they do not neutralize each other. For example, they explain, food is desired, but it is destroyed through ingestion.[8] Oral erotism is equated with cannibalistic love. The ambivalent character of the anal-erotic drives was described in Chapter XXIII.

To the extent to which the sexual organization has reached the genital phase, ambivalent feelings toward the love partner subside and complete fusion is obtained. Then the man's loving "aggression" does not harm his female partner, nor does the passive "masochistic" component of the woman's sexual drive lead to any self-damaging consequences.

In all kinds of constructive activities certain objects are destroyed as such but for the purpose of new creations, of valuable constructions. One could conceive such activities as the result of a "constructive collaboration" of destructive and constructive drives. If the resulting new construction has a greater value for one's self and/or other people than the utilized, thus destroyed, material or objects, one could consider such cooperations of destructive cathexis and libido as the effect of a fusion of these cathexes.

When the genital organization is not firmly established it can be abandoned under certain circumstances. A labile consistency of the genital organization is due to a fixation of the libido and mortido to a pregenital phase. In this phenomenon some amount of cathexis remained attached in the id to a certain pregenital phase, while only an insufficient amount of cathexis progressed to the mature genital phase. In the case of fixation of the cathexis on the oral or anal-erotic phase the remaining genital cathexis may regress to the point of fixation when the individual suffers some deprivation or frustration. Such a regression to a previous phase of development, facilitated by a precedent fixation, leads to a defusion of the cathexes employed in the genital organization. That amount of mortido which had been bound by libido becomes free and finds expression in destructive tendencies. But under many other circumstances an ensuing aggressive attitude of an individual can be interpreted as an effect of a defusion of the two basic drives which has occurred.

Some psychoanalysts who do not believe in the death instinct explain every kind of aggression as the result of a state of frustration, as mentioned. In French's formulations aggressive and destructive drives develop as an effect of what he calls "physiological disintegration" of an "integrative field." If an individual cannot succeed in conceiving a proper plan of action for achieving the goal of a need, and if all his hopes of reaching this goal must be given up, the cathexis employed in the failed attempt to reach that goal can no longer be contained within an integrative field. In this case the discharge of the goalless cathexis acquires a destructive aggressive character. In other words, the cathexis which activates an integrative field becomes destructive when the integrative field is frustrated. French does not attribute its destructiveness to a proper cathexis, but he maintains, rather, that a cathexis which can no longer be contained in an integrative plan as goal-directed energy becomes aggressive and destructive because it cannot be so contained. In Freud's view, however, frustration leads to a defusion of libido and the destructive cathexis. In this process the latter is set free. In his opinion, frustration would lead simply to uneasiness, pain, and sadness, and any useful activity would cease if no destructive cathexis, as a proper cathexis directed toward death and destruction, were contained in man's (or animal's) striving. Perhaps no striving, no life, could exist without such a cathexis.

In Federn's dynamic concept of the ego and its functions, libido and mortido are fused in the ego cathexis, and each of these two components has its proper function. In muscular activity, in thinking, in the function of attention and particularly in the act of volition closely connected with muscular activity, mortido plays an important role in his opinion. In the case of defusion the ego destroys itself or objects of the external world. It is interesting to learn that Federn did not fully accept Freud's instinct dichotomy which implies that no other "mental energy" can exist besides libido and destrudo.[9] He declared: "Like other authors, such as Monakow, Driesch, and [Kurt] Goldstein, I assume that a third source of energy results from the living process of the organism, and in regard to mental activities, especially from the processes of the central nervous system. Jung evaded this problem by changing his concept of libido."[10] So, one would say that in Federn's view there are "living processes" which are not powered by either libido or mortido. One must ask, then, is "living" in itself not the expression of some biological energy? Federn, however, did not offer us further details of this third "neutral" kind of energy, that is, energy which is neither constructive nor destructive. Since he did not consider it as the dynamic expression of a proper instinct, this "mental energy" could not well be called a "cathexis."

Ives Hendrick,[11] on the other hand, conceives of a specific "instinct to master." This was suggested to him by Freud's occasional references to a *Bewältigungstrieb* ("drive to overcome or to master"), reminiscent of the ego instincts in his original formulation of the drive dualism. In Hendrick's opinion, not only the discharge of libidinous and aggressive tensions but also the exercising of neuromuscular functions, of thinking, of perceptive functions, etc., is pleasurable per se. In agreement with this view is French's concept of the "functional readiness" of the organs which can also find an outlet in play activities. It also corresponds to Alexander's concept of the "surplus or erotic energy."

Special consideration must be given to Hartmann's concept of "neutralization" of libido and destructive energy. His concept of "neutralization" differs from that of Freud. In Freud's theory an aggressive or destructive cathexis can be neutralized through its fusion with libido. But according to Hartmann each of these two cathexes must be "neutralized"; that is, the libido must be "desexualized" and the destructive cathexis "disaggressivized," in order to be employed in the various ego functions of motility, thinking, perception, etc. And this kind of "neutralization" is, in Hartmann's opinion, one of the main functions of the ego.

It is very difficult to summarize the different concepts of various psychoanalysts of the "Freudian School" regarding the qualities of drives and cathexes, since they differ essentially from one another. The closest adherents of Freud take for granted that all the instincts derive from two basic instincts: the sexual or life instincts and the death or destructive instincts. Other analysts exclude the possibility of a death instinct on various grounds. One may say that there is actually no logical reason why a death instinct, namely, an impulse toward fulfilling a cycle from lifeless state through life to a lifeless stage again, could not exist. It can be all the more easily admitted since we know that this is only one cycle, the other being the eternal re-creation of the living cell. Thus we observe that multicellular forms of life follow a brief cycle, an eternal process about which we know little. Some opponents of Freud's death instinct aim to deny what seems to them a pessimistic outlook on life. Other psychoanalysts do not find that Freud's death instinct leads necessarily to such pessimism. Still others remain noncommittal. Furthermore, among those who do accept the Freudian instinct dichotomy we find diverging interpretations of psychological processes as expressions of these two basic instincts. A number of analysts are not entirely convinced that there are only these two groups of instincts. Many others prefer to avoid altogether any formulation of an instinct theory. Thus, we find Alexander's concept of the "surplus energy principle" (presented in Chapter XXI). French, on the other hand, offers a very valuable dynamic orientation of human behavior by distinguishing pressures exerted by needs and drives from the functional readiness of the organs. But he fails to formulate any basic theory of instincts, although he does define a drive (as mentioned earlier in this chapter).

It is my opinion that the study of libidinal and aggressive (or destructive) drives aids us greatly in understanding many behavior patterns and many destructive mental diseases. I am not convinced however, that a proper aggressive or destructive cathexis (destrudo) must necessarily originate from a death instinct inherent in living matter.

NOTES

(1) In the Standard Edition of the Complete Psychological Works of Sigmund Freud (Translated from the German under the general editorship of James Strachey, in collaboration with Anna Freud and others, and usually cited as Standard Edition) the English "instincts" is retained as the translation of the German *Triebe*.

(2) Freud never used "Thanatos" for the death drive in any of his published works, but only in conversation. The term was introduced by Stekel (who used it in a different sense) long before Freud formulated his new instinct theory.

(3) French, op. cit., Vol. 3, p. 30.

(4) Ibid., p. 430.

(5) Weiss, op. cit.

(6) Federn, Paul. The reality of the death instinct, especially in melancholia; remarks on Freud's book Civilization and Its Discontents (1930). Psychoanal. Rev., 19:129-151, 1932.

(7) Nunberg, op. cit.

(8) The author disagrees with such indiscriminate generalizations. Only food which is desired can be assimilated through ingestion. Indigestible food is not desirable. Thus there is no ambivalence in hunger because our only goal in longing for food is to ingest it and not to preserve it as such.

(9) Federn sometimes used this term (which was introduced by the present author).

(10) Federn, Paul. Ego Psychology and the Psychoses, p. 227.

(11) Hendrick, Ives. Instinct and the ego during infancy. Psychoanal. Quart., 11:33-58, 1942; The discussion of the "instinct to master," Ibid., 12:561-565, 1943.

Section IV

Superego and
Related Drive
Controlling Factors

XXX

More About the Reality Principle

THE "integrative task" is a threefold task of the ego: (1) to take into account all motivating factors for its behavior; (2) by acknowledging the conditions of external reality, to find proper ways and means to achieve goals which it cannot dispense with; and (3) to avoid frustration. Some motivations for behavior may be quite compatible with one another and others may be in sharp contrast, thus presenting to the ego a difficult integrative task, a difficult problem to be solved.

In the preceding section we discussed the instinctive drives as motivating factors in human behavior. Here we shall present those factors which may interfere with indiscriminate satisfactions of some drives and which must be included within the "integrative span" for the elaboration of realistic plans of procedure. One guiding principle for integrative behavior, which Freud called the "reality principle," was presented in Chapter XIII. The ego learns through experience that indiscriminate achievement of some satisfaction leads to unpleasant and painful consequence, and that some desired goals can be reached only by strenuous efforts and endurance of unpleasant situations. Sometimes the ego must submit even to great discomfort and pain in order to avoid greater discomfort or pain. For example, a person will undergo a painful surgical operation in order to avoid worse suffering or even death. And sometimes one must struggle for years renouncing many sources of immediate pleasure in order to achieve desired abilities and knowledge. As we pointed out above, the "reality principle" is not in contradiction with the "pleasure principle," but represents rather an evolution of the latter, an evolution imposed upon the ego by the conditions of "reality." The final goal of the reality principle is eventual experience of pleasure and eventual avoidance of pain and discomfort.

Not only must drives, needs and knowledge of external conditions be included in the ego's integrative span, but provision must be made for inner psychological factors other than drives. Some of these internal factors have obtained the evaluating connotation of "ethical" or "moral," the most important of which derive from "conscience," a function ascribed to that "mental substructure" (in Federn's description that "ego state which has its own boundary") called superego. As a matter of fact, many emotional factors besides those related to the functioning of the superego may impress us as "ethical" in nature, e.g., attitudes which one has toward a person one loves, or feelings of pity and compassion as well as emotional attitudes related to the phenomenon which the present author calls "psychic presence." As we shall see later, psychic presence may constitute a developmental stage or a regressive expression of the superego, but it is not necessarily either. There are psychic presences which lack the main characteristics of the superego and are rather related to the ego's feelings of pity and compassion.

All factors which could impress us as "ethical" are related, in one way or another, to the ego's emotional participation with his fellowman. *Religere* is the Latin for connecting one's self to or binding one's self with one's fellow-human beings and the community. The word *religio* (and hence the English word religion) is derived from *religere*. But in the usual concept of an "established religion," it is, rather, the ego's relation to divine objects of worship or to God which is emphasized. Motivations determined by established religions are the result of various components. Some are closely connected with what one believes to be external consequences in so far as the individual seeks, through his behavior, to avoid divine (external) punishment and to assure happiness for himself. Other factors inherent in religious feelings are expressions of one's superego or rather of its projection onto God, the "heavenly father." In the study of the dynamics of different kinds of internal emotional factors of human behavior one should avoid moral evaluations of single factors, since this study does not offer a basis for such an evaluation. It is, however, important to acknowledge that those psychological factors which have a controlling function over selfish and destructive drives of the single individual are essential for social integration. Deficiency or lack of such factors leads to what is called asocial or criminal behavior.

In every individual several kinds of drive-controlling agents are in operation, though in different proportion. In this chapter we shall elaborate on motivations deriving from the reality principle, or to be more exact, deriving from the principle which takes into account only external conditions. Consideration of external conditions to the exclusion of all interest in the welfare of one's fellow-beings is not commonly evaluated as "ethical" or "moral." People with scant development of psychological controlling factors, among which the demands of the superego deserve special consideration, renounce satisfaction of some drives and refrain from committing forbidden and condemned actions only in order to avoid unpleasant external consequences for themselves. Enforcement of the law and punishment for criminal actions constitute for them the only control over their urges and drives.

In some individuals absence of inner drive-controlling factors can be acknowledged only under unusual circumstances, such as arise from situations of war and revolution. Many persons who were considered to be highly "moral" individuals have committed ferocious crimes, have killed and tortured human beings, stolen, raped, etc., when they have felt secure from punishment, revenge, or other kinds of retaliation. But it would be a mistake to ascribe all criminal acts committed by some individuals only to lack of psychological controlling devices. In some individuals, who do behave according to social standards in one environment, these standards are not firmly established but change easily with the change of community by which they happen to be absorbed. When such an individual becomes included in a group formed by conditions of war or revolt he conforms emotionally to the standards of that group. His "moral feelings" are merely an expression of his indiscriminate relatedness to the fortuitous group which encompasses him. Identification of the single individuals of a group with each other leads to collective standards, to "we standards," and constitutes an essential phenomenon in social behavior. Conversely, some individuals have standards so firmly established and resist collective influences so strongly that they react with fear, horror, and dismay to the sight of criminal behavior of the members of the group within which they became included by chance. These emotional factors will be presented in the following chapters.

Among the various needs and drives which are to be satisfied through external reality, dependent needs and narcissistic craving for being loved, admired, and highly evaluated by others deserve special examination. These drives or needs are certainly related to the ego's consideration of his fellow-beings and of the community, but the ego's particular mental attitude toward other people depends on various psychological factors. A person who is interested solely in achievement of external gratification, in the sense of the reality principle just formulated, will not care about other people's needs, welfare, rights, or suffering. In his behavior, aimed at dependent gratification, at being loved, and so on, he will enjoy such achievements regardless of whether or not he feels that he deserves love, appreciation, etc. The sensation of deserving love or admiration as a condition for fully enjoying them derives from psychological factors other than adherence to the reality principle. This will be clearly shown in the presentation of the phenomena of "psychic presence" and of the superego. A behavior based solely on calculations of the expected external results—an intellectual attitude which is foreign to higher animals in their behavior toward each other and toward their human friends—is a product of pure reality principle; it contains deceptive devices. In everyday language we often use the expression "diplomatic" to describe such an attitude.

People whose conduct is highly determined by consideration of other persons' feelings and/or by imposition of their conscience, are unable to identify with individuals whose behavior is controlled solely or largely by the reality principle. This difficulty is similar to that which well-integrated egos encounter in their attempts to understand psychotic behavior. Various motivations may induce an ego which is considering reality to challenge external dangers. One ego may risk external dangers in pursuing satisfaction of forbidden instinctive drives or in perpetrating condemned actions. Another ego may expose itself to dangers or other unpleasant situations in complying with the dictates of conscience and/or in desiring to benefit other persons for whatsoever motive. Some individuals venture into hazardous enterprises in their attempts to reach some goal of ambition or genuine scientific interest. All these individuals, driven by various motives, may take the most dangerous risks again and again after painful defeat, trying to learn from their experiences. In all these behavior patterns the economic factor plays a decisive role; that is, the intensity of the motivating impulse versus fear of unpleasant consequences.

A person who has been caught and punished after having committed actions condemned by society has learned from this experience how to be more cautious in future attempts to commit similar actions. He may also have come to the conclusion that "crime does not pay," in other words, that renunciation of such gratifications is preferable to taking the risk of increasingly more severe punishments. But punishment per se suffered by an adult for antisocial or criminal behavior does not elicit in him a development of internal conduct-controlling factors which would be effective irrespective of external consequences of his behavior. It is true that there is a specific neurotic behavior pattern through which the individual seeks punishment unconsciously. In these cases the ego betrays the fact that it has committed the criminal action, thus thwarting any possible escape from punishment. His unconscious feelings of guilt are thus clearly revealed. But we do not wish to expand here on this type of criminal behavior. Still, one may wonder whether experiences of punishment or any painful consequences for certain behavior could not eventually result in the establishment of internal inhibiting factors. After all, the reality principle leads not only to consciously directed behavior, but also to some automatic responses. "The burnt child fears the fire." On this principle are based all conditioned behavior patterns of men and animals. But, when the painful consequences of a certain behavior are fully and consciously understood by the ego in their essence and origin, as punishment and revenge are, this understanding becomes included in the integrative span of the ego. These well-comprehended consequences do not lead to conditioned behavior, but rather they enrich the ego's integrative span. This acknowledgment is of essential importance for the psychological treatment of asocial or criminal egos.

The conditions are different, however, in regard to the child's ego. The ego's cognitive capacity develops slowly, and only when it reaches a certain degree of development does it enable the ego to grasp fully the external implications inherent in unpleasant external consequences of certain behavior patterns. Therefore intimidations do establish in the child's mind lasting and rigid connections between drive and action on the one side and the experience of evil consequences on the other. Unfortunately, some natural and harmless instinctive drives also may be victims of experienced painful consequences. It is too difficult for the child to comprehend the realistic nature of his experiences and to manipulate intellectually the comprehended data in such a way as to master the problems arising from forbidden drives and fear of the experienced consequences. Indiscriminate emotional connections between indulgence of instinctive drives and the derived painful experiences presents to the ego a much easier integrative task. Forbidden behavior becomes blocked by established inner inhibiting factors, thus diminishing the ego's resources for modified behavior. As we shall learn in discussion of the superego, some of these inhibiting factors appear as functional expressions of those internalized persons who originally did threaten and punish the child.

Two important psychological phenomena are partially linked to, but not exclusively due to, the establishment in the child's ego of internal inhibiting factors, the superego formation and defense mechanisms. All defense mechanisms are subservient to the ego's integrative task; and through Federn's dynamic ego concept we can understand how the defenses are operating. All defenses are performed through mobilization, shift, withdrawal, and concentration, in different modalities, of ego cathexis. These dynamic-topographical processes were explained in the phenomenon of repression, internalization (identification), and externalization, and also in the defensive device of feelings of derealization presented in Chapter XV. As we shall see, the linkage of automatic responses to internalized persons is due to libido investment of these "introjects." [1] But not all conditioned responses become expressions of internalized objects, and many behavior patterns induced by the functioning of the superego have not the character of conditioned reactions.

Some examples may illustrate reactive formations in children which are not linked to internalized objects. A child was playing with water contained in a large vessel. He fell into it, was detected and saved just before he lost consciousness. After this traumatic experience he became afraid of water, and only slowly and by great encouragement could he be put again into the bathtub. Another child rejected a favorite food one evening when his mother had prepared it especially for him. He felt nauseated, and his mother soon realized that he was sick with fever. The doctor made an immediate diagnosis of scarlet fever, the onset of which is usually accompanied by nausea and vomiting. The unpleasant (we may even say "traumatic") experience of such sensations remained closely associated with the taste and smell of that dish even after the child's recovery from scarlet fever. From that time on he could no longer tolerate the smell or taste of the dish which had been his favorite previously, and later it was also learned that he could not even remember having once liked the dish.

We may now ask why the child's experience of the strong sensation of nausea had traumatized him. According to our dynamic concept of a traumatic experience we would say that he was traumatized because he felt completely powerless vis-à-vis that sensation. The memory of his liking that dish would have re-activated, through the close associative connection, the traumatic experience itself. By withdrawal of the ego cathexis from that representation, in other words, by repression of that memory, the ego protected itself from the reactivation of the trauma. These kinds of repression, like conditioned responses, are not due to the operation of the superego. They are vicissitudes of the reality principle which leads to the formation of internal psychological inhibiting and controlling factors. They occur in childhood when the ego is still incapable of mastering certain experiences through its intellect and force of endurance. And we repeat, punishment of adult egos does not "condition" their behavior in this way. Proper psychological procedure elicits internal controlling factors in the adult ego, not "conditioned" factors, and this is not accomplished by punishment or retaliation.

Adequate restrictive and demanding attitudes of parents toward their children, which induce the children to learn how to renounce indiscriminate satisfaction of impulses and to comply with necessary demands, do not traumatize the children but convey to them a feeling of security. A child who feels quite free to behave in any way he desires develops anxiety. He feels insecure because he is aware of his inadequacy to understand all external situations and the reactions of other people, and he does not have the strength on his own to renounce many urges. Conversely, when the child senses that the parents love him and that what they forbid and demand is not only for the sake of other people but also for his own sake, he soon feels that he cannot dispense with firm guidance by persons he trusts. Such restrictive experiences may eventually result in a partial automatization of certain behavior patterns. But if we consider also these patterns as "conditioned" responses, we cannot fail to note the difference between the effect of a traumatic experience and that derived from restrictive and demanding attitudes toward the child of persons by whom he feels loved and protected. The inner behavior-controlling factors of the latter origin have a different character and implications than those derived from mere traumatic experience. In our analysis of the superego we shall discuss this difference further.

A presentation of the most important issues concerning the reality principle cannot be concluded without consideration of some aspects of what is called in psychoanalysis "ego ideal." Originally (in 1914) Freud [2] linked the phenomenon of "ego ideal" formation to the development of conscience. The ego's narcissism is exposed continually to injuries derived from all the reproaches and criticisms which it meets as a child and as an adult, as well as from the realization of its own inadequacies. These narcissistic injuries lead to feelings of inferiority. As a defense against such injuries self-love becomes partially substituted by love of an image of what the real ego would like to be. This image is called by Freud "ego ideal." The more closely the real ego approaches its ego ideal, the more is its narcissism satisfied, and the further away the real ego gets from its ego ideal, the more is its narcissism frustrated. Freud postulated originally the existence of an internal agency which continuously measured the real ego with the standards of the ego ideal. Later, upon deeper investigation of this agency, he equated this agency with the mental substructure called "superego." He attributed the "voice of conscience" to the functioning of the internalized parental figures.

In the present author's view the ego ideal, representing a narcissistic goal, should be considered along with all other needs and instincts of the individual. The actual behavior induced by the ego's desire to correspond as closely as possible and in reality to one's ego ideal depends on the specific characters of the ego ideal. It does not necessarily include respect for and interest in other people's welfare and rights. Some individuals develop an ego ideal of power and utter disregard of other persons' interests. Even cruelty may be a dominant feature of an ego ideal. History gives us many examples of persons who have committed the most atrocious crimes in compliance with their ego ideals. Only if the ego ideal encompasses "moral" standards does the ego feel morally inferior when it does not comply with them. Some psychoanalysts consider such feelings of inferiority as guilt feelings, but they are of a different nature than the actual feelings of guilt induced by the superego.

Ego ideals can be independent of the superego, and there are even cases in which a person's superego is at variance with his ego ideal. Only when the ego ideal encompasses principles highly evaluated by society does it have a socially integrative value as well as a narcissistic one, and only in this case may it contribute to one's conscience. In any case, the ego ideal per se represents a set of goals which the ego endeavors to achieve in accordance with the reality principle.

NOTES

(1) The author introduced the term "introject" (as a noun) in his paper Der Vergiftungswahn im Lichte der Introjektions- und Projektionsvorgänge. Int. Z. Psychoanal., 12:466-477, 1926 (English abstract: The delusion of being poisoned in the light of introjective and projective procedures. Archives of Psychoanalysis, 1:226-228, 1926). At the time he also used "introjection" to mean "internalization" and "projection" for "externalization." The use of introject as a noun (which later became widely accepted in psychoanalytic literature) was intended to indicate that portion of the ego arising from the internalization of a specific object. The author now (1959) prefers to speak of internalized objects rather than use the simple but incorrect term 'introjects."

(2) Freud, Sigmund. On narcissism: An introduction (1914). Standard Edition, 14:95-97. London, Hogarth, 1957.

XXXI

Resonance Identification

THE previous chapter dealt with the ego's efforts to integrate its needs and instincts with the recognized conditions of the external world. Among its instinctive needs we considered those which are narcissistic and dependent. We understood that punishment and retaliation, which the ego has to take into account according to the reality principle, constitute external factors. But, among the internal factors which the ego has to integrate in its behavior we must recognize not only its instinctive needs but also internal pressures of different origin. They originate from three sources, from "resonance identification," from "psychic presences" and from the super-ego. All these factors derive from the ego's relation to and interest in other persons. They occupy in the ego a position which is different from that of instinctive drives, because they provide the inhibiting and controlling, as well as the inciting, internal motivations of behavior. In this chapter we wish to expand on the phenomenon of resonance identification.

We have compared the phenomenon of mental or emotional resonance to a musical chord struck on one instrument and echoed on another. We said that resonance identification takes place when those inner experiences of another person which are duplicated in one's own ego continued to be emotionally acknowledged by it in that other person. In order to describe this phenomenon more correctly we have to bear in mind that every form of identification implies egotization of a content. We can, therefore, speak of resonance identification only when the resonance content is egotized. This statement is important since an autoplastic duplication of another person's experiences, which continue to be acknowledged in him, can be egotized in varying degrees of intensity or even not at all. In the latter case we cannot speak of resonance identification but only of resonance duplication.

Empathy, sympathy, pity or commiseration, and compassion develop from different dynamic and topographic processes. All have in common resonance duplication, but not necessarily resonance identification. They play an essential role in personal interactions. The process which Anna Freud describes as "altruistic surrender," which leads to vicarious gratification through the experiences of another person, is based on resonance identification.[1]

We called "egotization" the inclusion of bodily and mental contents within one's ego feeling. "Objects," which can be perceived or recalled, are unegotized contents; they impinge on the ego boundaries from the outside. If a part of an ego state becomes de-egotized, or depersonalized, it may be turned into an object representation. The perception or thought of another person, however, encompasses also his *inner* experiences. As pointed out in Chapter VI, we "perceive" inner experiences of our fellow-beings because they behave and act in a manner identical or similar to the way we behave and act when we have certain experiences. And we are unable to understand those elements of the inner life of another human being when we cannot reproduce them by resonance. But if we do reproduce them, the resonance product obtained may be more or less included in our own ego feeling. If it is not, we cannot speak of identification. The resonance duplication is then included only in the object representation, remaining outside of one's own ego boundaries. In this case we speak of "empathy."

This phenomenon requires further clarification. An ego perceives through its sense organs the external aspect of other persons, that is, the physical aspect, and it recognizes through resonance duplication their inner, that is, mental experiences. Tautologically we may say that the broader and more accurate the resonance duplication in one's mind, the greater will be the "empathic" understanding of the inner life of that person. Resonance duplication is thus an equivalent of perception through sense organs. In empathy both the physical and the mental qualities of the other person are encompassed in the obtained unegotized content of the representation or perception. Such a content is called "object." Empathy occurs irrespective of the ego's emotional reaction to the perceived and understood personality of the other individual. When we understand another person empathically we say, in effect, "I know, I sense how you feel." Such a perceived unegotized resonance content has object character, and the ego does not identify itself with it.

We locate the original experiences, which are only duplicated in us, in the external object, where they actually belong. In this way we obtain a correct understanding, a correct "perception," as it were, of the emotional experiences of the object. This is precisely the meaning of the word "empathy." In every kind of comprehensive treatment the psychotherapist must understand the patient empathically. Cases of ego disturbances, as we find them particularly in the psychoses, present great difficulties to the therapist in understanding the patient's inner experiences empathically, and only a few persons succeed.

To have a fuller understanding of the role of mere resonance duplication in empathy, let us digress for a moment. Federn demonstrated the importance of investment with the ego cathexis unity for the sensation of "I-ness" inherent in all ego experiences. He described accurately not only cases of de-egotization of portions of the body but also of mental contents, particularly of feelings and emotions. This is the phenomenon of depersonalization. Melancholic patients may reveal feelings of love, grief and consideration for other people through their behavior and actions, but without having the sensation that they actually experience such feelings and emotions. In a self-accusatory attitude they complain that they are no longer able to feel love, sorrow, or any emotion toward anybody. This failure of the ego to feel emotions is not due in these cases to an actual lack of emotions but to withdrawal of ego cathexis from them.

The withdrawal of ego cathexis from instinctive drives and emotions, which this writer calls "dynamic or emotional mutilations," plays an important role in certain phobias. This phenomenon is not the same as repression, although it may lead to repression. Every repressed content is de-egotized, but not every de-egotized content is repressed. The experience ensuing from depersonalized feelings is very unpleasant, but there is a great difference between withdrawal of one's ego boundaries from those feelings and emotions which originate in one's own mind and which exert a pressure toward a dynamic discharge, and the absence of ego cathexis from resonance products. Only in the first case does the ego feel "mutilated"; in the second case the resonance contents are encompassed in the perception or representation of the object, and every object lies normally outside one's ego boundaries. The object does not appear mutilated but as a complete bodily and mental unity, acknowledged through one's sense organs and proper resonance. Unegotized duplication is not identification.

The ego's affective responses to and/or partial egotization of "perceived" experiences of the object go beyond the phenomenon of mere empathy. When an ego is "affected by the state of another with feelings corresponding in kind," we speak of "sympathy." Common language uses this term mostly in regard to grief and suffering. Nietzsche used a neologism for the resonance experience of pleasure, analogous to *Mitleid* (compassion), *Mitfreude* ("con-pleasure"). Compassion, pity, and commiseration are different forms of sympathy, which can be differentiated from each other from a metapsychological point of view. But we must also consider the ego's reactions to another person's suffering and pleasure which do not correspond in kind. One may react with enjoyment to the suffering of another person, a feeling which we call "sadistic." One may also react with misgiving to the pleasure experienced by another person, as in envy and jealousy.

Egotized and unegotized resonance duplications play an important role in the satisfaction of certain instinctive drives. Whenever an ego feels the need for a specific vicarious gratification through the experiences of another person, it seeks or tries to provoke corresponding feelings and emotions in him. The best examples of this kind are those given by Anna Freud in her description of a form of "altruistic surrender." [2] Another person must enjoy the satisfaction of those needs and desires which an ego cannot experience itself. Then at least it enjoys the other person's satisfaction through resonance *identification*. This is a very frequent kind of surrendering which is most evident in an adult's emotional participation in the experiences of a child. The role of vicarious gratification in normal heterosexuality was pointed out in Chapter XXIV. The girl renounces the personal possession of a penis by surrendering its function and derived sensations to her male partner, and the male surrenders his feminine needs to the woman.

But when the resonance duplication is completely unegotized, sympathetic participation in the joy and pain of another person is absent. The opposition of the "I" to the "you" or "he (she)" may be very sharply established; in other words, a strong boundary of one's own ego may separate it from an unegotized resonance product which is fully encompassed in the object representation or object perception. This resonance product may lend itself to all kinds of instinctual gratification, particularly to sadistic satisfaction. An ego which has a strong need for extraverting an excessive destructive cathexis, of whatever origin, must feel very distinctly "this is he, not I," in order to obtain sadistic gratification from the "perceived" suffering of another individual. The boundary of the ego which separates itself sharply from a resonance duplication varies very much in strength and intensity from one individual to another, from one group to another. The frenetic enjoyment of the Roman public in the very cruel performances in the arena was not shared in the same measure by the Greeks. When the Romans tried to introduce these performances to Athens, Athenian spectators repudiated such undignified forms of enjoyment. Enjoyment in extremely cruel public performances of humans and animals occurred until very recent times, in Europe until the beginning of the 19th century, not to mention the less cruel bullfights which are still practiced in Spanish-speaking countries.

Social integration among the Romans could not have been maintained if their sadism had not been restricted by their laws (which became the fundamental principles for all later legislations) and thereby permitted only in actions against enemies, slaves and subdued nations. Organization and discipline, in which the Romans excelled, were impositions dictated by the reality principle. They constituted powerful practical measures of social preservation and integration and can be considered only vaguely as equivalents to the moral principles enunciated by the Greek philosophers and moralists, such as Solon, Socrates, Plato, and Aristotle. The ethic of the ancient Greeks and Romans was not bound to their religion, as is the Judaic-Christian ethic.

It is evident that a need for extraversion of aggressive cathexis induces an integrated ego to make the proper choice of object for such a gratification. A love object must be excluded and so also must an object which provides necessary emotional contents for a desired vicarious gratification. In these cases the resonance duplications are egotized and thus obtain identification character. In addition we have also to consider the inhibiting action of the superego. In anticipation of a later more detailed presentation of this action, only the destrudo-economic factor involved will be mentioned here. It is evident that the more destructive cathexis is directed by the superego reflexively, namely, toward one's own person, the less will be left for extraverted needs. Destructive cathexis is never directed quite indiscriminately against any other individual. In the employment of destrudo an ego must seek proper objects and also find "justifications" for its superego in order to have sadistic enjoyment.[3] The understood suffering inflicted on other living beings rebounds, through identification, onto one's own ego. And a sadistic enjoyment forbidden by the superego is followed by feelings of guilt. Often an ego can enjoy harming other people only if it "feels the right" to do so, as for example, when it feels justified in taking revenge for wrongs suffered or when it has the permission and even the participation of the group to which it belongs. Otherwise the ego may be indifferent to the harm it does to others. An ego's emotional participation in kind to the suffering of another being is called pity or compassion. The dictionary does not make a strict distinction between these two ego states, yet there is a subtle difference. Both are based on resonance duplication, but they differ from each other in the degree of egotization of or identification with the resonance product. The pitying ego identifies itself less strongly with the suffering of the other being than the ego which feels compassion; it regards the other's suffering in the way it looks upon an object. It feels sorrow for the conditions of the object and acts to diminish his sufferings. Pity is thus an active state opposite to a sadistic one. In compassion the ego's identification with the sufferer is stronger; the resulting ego state is more passive than that of pity. Pity and compassion are vicissitudes of an ego's empathic understanding of the suffering of other living beings. There are two important factors that lead to these reactions: (1) the absence or exhaustion of an amount of destructive cathexis pressuring toward an extraverted goal; and (2) the ego's realization that it can itself become victim of the same misfortune, a realization which can be expressed by the words, "But for the grace of God, there go I."

There are many reasons for lack or absence of extravertible destrudo. In the first place the amount of cathexis of every form varies constitutionally from one individual to another. Then, too, frustrating experiences from childhood on may have aroused excessive aggressive needs in the individual. Furthermore, the sterner the superego, the more aggression becomes introverted into reflexive activity. But pity and compassion can also develop side by side with a still existing sadistic urge. An ego which has to solve such a conflict, which may be heightened by the superego's condemnation of such an urge, often resorts to repression of its sadistic tendencies. Then feelings of pity and compassion become intensified and build a defensive barrier of counter-cathexes against the forbidden sadistic impulses. Most psychoanalysts interpret all exaggerated feelings of pity and compassion, and also exaggerated interest in preventing cruelties to humans and animals, as reaction formations against repressed sadistic impulses. We can appreciate highly the ethical and social value of such reaction formations as long as they do not assume an obsessive and irrational character.

Exaggerated feelings of this kind may, however, have a quite different dynamic origin than that of a reaction formation against repressed sadism. The following realizations will make this point clear.

Clinical experience has revealed without doubt that destructive psychological factors can produce somatic destructive processes. This has been proven particularly by research in psychosomatic medicine. But there are somatic diseases which are not produced by or not mainly the result of introverted destrudo. In this case the destructive pathological organic process may bring about a satiation or even an oversatiation of the destructive need inherent in the individual. Such excessive and unsought "destrudo satisfaction" can lead to psychological disorders as can be illustrated by two examples.[4]

A patient who suffered from a severe form of anorexia and had lost a great deal of weight in a short time, presented at the beginning of this state of progressive weakness an intense feeling of pity for every living thing that had to suffer. This feeling reached such a degree that he felt horrified by the very thought of anyone killing a fly and even revolted at the thought of hurting an ant.

Another patient of this writer upon completion of his analysis was tortured by the mere thought of suffering and felt compelled to look at the world in a manner which brought into sharp focus every type of suffering inherent in life and every sort of injustice and cruelty to which living things were exposed. In his abnormal pity the most torturing pictures constantly forced themselves into his mind, e.g., a poor calf led to slaughter, tied up, reduced to impotence, its throat cut, the blood flowing out in a stream, and the calf looking around for help in a heart-rending way. Just one week after the patient had given me this pitiful description he developed a hemorrhagic sore throat with fever which was soon diagnosed as an acute leukemia. He was taken to the hospital and there had to experience his own slow extinction. I visited him every day, and the patient looked at me in a strange helpless manner, hopelessly seeking aid, an attitude which perfectly reflected his mental picture of the calf being slaughtered. In this case, because his mental condition was a result of a somatic state, the psychoanalysis had not detected a psychological reason for the patient's exaggerated feelings of sorrow for suffering living things.

As a rule, one who suffers becomes less and not more sensitive to the sufferings of others while engrossed in his own troubles. Both of these patients showed little or no feelings of pity for others once they became keenly aware of their own suffering. The defense by de-egotization and externalization of some ego state into object representations worked only in the beginning. Pity-provoking images forced themselves upon their minds, like obsessional ideas, as a vicarious cause for their own suffering. Through externalization of a part of an ego state one kind of suffering was replaced by another. This is a kind of defense mechanism which occurs frequently during sleep when the dreamer externalizes some of his own ego states into dream persons. In several papers (particularly in "Instincts and Their Vicissitudes" [5]) Freud described such processes of externalization and the projection of contents onto other persons, occuring in an early phase of ego development. The child projects, in that stage, every unpleasant sensation of his own body onto the external world, while he internalizes every source of pleasure from the external world. He equates ego with pleasant, and the external world with unpleasant, which leads to what Freud called "the purified pleasure ego."

The clinical pictures described require a clarification on one point. These patients struggled against egotization of their own suffering, i.e., suffering originating in themselves. Through externalization of these sensations into object representations they obtained the illusion that they could free themselves from suffering for others, e.g., from pity and compassion, if only they could prevent those other people and animals from suffering. The process of resonance identification is quite different. In this case the attempts to free one's self from feelings of distress by preventing or diminishing the perceived suffering of the objects are not illusory, because one's own distress, one's own pity and compassion, are really only effects of resonance of the ego states of other objects.

The less sadistic an ego, and the more it is inclined to react with pity and compassion to the suffering of others (even if this inclination is increased as a reaction to repressed sadism), the more helpful and socially constructive will such an ego be.

We wish now to establish the position of resonance identification with reference to the reality principle. In point of fact, this phenomenon is not antithetical to the reality principle, but constitutes a special motivating factor for an ego's realistic behavior, a factor which is considered of moral value. In every ego different kinds of "moral" motivations are operating in varying proportions. In my opinion there are different "ethical types" according to the prevalence of one or the other kind of "moral motivation." For the sake of clarity let us describe a hypothetically pure "resonance type" of moral personality. Let us imagine an ego motivated in its behavior only by its instincts, by the reality principle, and by resonance identification, but entirely lacking in other "moral" factors which will be presented in the next two chapters. Such a hypothetical person could commit all kinds of actions condemned by society if he could only be sure of avoiding undesirable consequences for himself according to the reality principle, and also if he did not cause suffering to his fellow-human beings, especially to those whom he loves. The latter consideration aims not only at forestalling hostile reactions of the injured parties but also avoidance of his own "resonance suffering" independent of other undesirable consequences. Such an ego is not reliable; it can lie, steal, and betray. A married man (or woman) with such an ego, knowing that his actions would cause great pain to his spouse, could lead a promiscuous sexual life without feeling guilty if he had reasonable guarantee only that his spouse would never learn of his activities, in other words, if there were no danger of his resonance suffering as a result of her suffering. Such an ego could steal without remorse, if it could not be detected, as long as it was not aware of causing distress or pain to concrete individuals, with whose suffering it would feel resonance suffering. Nevertheless an ego's interest in not causing pain and suffering to others whom he can perceive or imagine has still a certain restraining and controlling effect over his instincts and urges.

Perhaps a pure "resonance type" does not exist. It was our purpose here to consider this kind of inner control only as one among others, each of which appears in varying proportions in single individuals.

NOTES

(1) For psychoanalysts who distinguish two basically different kinds of cathexis, libidinous and destructive, it is important to establish whether a resonance content is one of love and pleasure or of hatred and suffering. In the first case the ego would mobilize libido for such an emotional duplication within itself; in the second it would mobilize destructive cathexis. Thus vicarious gratification of a love experience would contain libido, while on the other hand, feelings of pity or compassion would contain an excess of destrudo (Federn's mortido) over libido.

(2) Anna Freud borrowed the term "altruistic surrender" from Edward Bibring. In marginal notes to Anna Freud's Ego and the Mechanisms of Defense, Paul Federn noted that he preferred to call vicarious gratification derived from another's experience "egoistic or narcissistic surrender."

(3) This holds true even if this cathexis is conceived only as the effect of a frustrated plan for achieving a goal. We would also like to mention at this point that we do not consider in this context an ego's overpowering or destroying other living things without perceiving or caring for their inner experiences, as in hunting, fishing, or the slaughter of animals for food.

(4) We speak of a psychosomatic disorder whenever certain psychological conditions are specific factors in the etiology of an organic disease. Similarly, we could use the term "somatopsychic conditions or disorders" for psychopathology of essentially somatic origin.

(5) Freud, Sigmund. Instincts and their vicissitudes (1915). Standard Edition, 14:109-140. London, Hogarth, 1957.

XXXII

The Psychic Presence

WE described the behavior of a hypothetical person, adjusted to reality, whose only "moral" restricting and inciting factors would be feelings of pity and compassion for suffering beings. He could commit forbidden acts when he could avoid actually hurting others. We shall now describe a psychological phenomenon which constitutes a formidable controlling factor of our behavior and is not based simply on resonance identification. This factor cannot be called superego because it does not rest on identification; it is not an ego state. This was a phenomenon accurately described for the first time in 1931 by the present writer in a paper read before the Vienna Psychoanalytic Society,[1] and in his later publications was called "psychic presence." After discussing this phenomenon in its various manifestations we shall try to explain it in metapsychological terms.

The following observation awakened my interest in the phenomenon. A young man succeeded in convincing himself that under certain circumstances it would not be reprehensible to defraud the government of some money. He rationalized that he would harm nobody by his action. We know how a person tries to get rid of the inhibition of his conscience in order to be able to commit a forbidden deed—by explaining it away—and we know too that the psychoanalyst must analyze the unconscious meaning of the committed act because it does not always represent the real repressed motives for the action. But here we want to consider only the inhibitory factor involved. The young man thought he would be able to commit the crime without a sense of guilt. While he was arranging the details of the theft, the reproachful image of his father appeared in his mind with almost hallucinatory vividness. He thus became aware of the feeling of guilt which he had wished to ignore. This was an image of an object; the representation of his father was not egotized. (This patient was also mentioned in Chapter XIV, when the phenomenon of derealization as a defense mechanism was described.) Although his judgment told him that his father would never know about his crime (in fact, it always remained secret except for his psychoanalyst who advised him how to make restitution) the image of his father watching him forced itself upon his mind while he was carrying out the crime. In an earlier chapter the ensuing feeling of derealization, by which the ego tried to deny the reality of his action, was described.

Later when the patient met his father he experienced that inner uneasiness which we call "sense of guilt." His father, who suspected nothing, was as affectionate to him as before; the patient knew that nothing was more remote from his father's mind than any suspicion of his theft. It distressed him greatly that his father was giving him love and respect to which he had "no right." True, he regarded this feeling as irrational; for this special case of theft, committed in very peculiar circumstances, did not appear to him as anything wrong or despicable. But his father would have been very indignant with him and would have despised him for it. The patient retained his father's respect only because the latter knew nothing of what had happened, and the feeling of being an impostor was unbearable to him. The only solution for his mental discomfort would have been to have his father learn of the theft. He would then have understood the act, committed as it had been "in peculiar circumstances," i.e., he would not have disapproved of it; but even if he could not have helped condemning it at first, at least a reconciliation would have followed. The patient felt that his father's love and respect must be based on truth and frankness, i.e., must be merited. So, he became very confused in his relationship with his actual father, as if the earlier image of his father watching him had merged with the real person of his father. He felt as if his father had actually watched him while he was committing the crime.

This example illustrates clearly one form of "psychic presence." The father, watching reproachfully while the patient committed the reprehensible deed, was mentally present. We realize that the intensity of the image was due to the young man's transgression of his father's expectations. We can understand too that the intensity of a psychic presence is due not only to the gravity of the committed act but also to the degree of emotional attachment to the offended person. But the appearance of another person's image is not necessarily aroused by an action committed against him or an action which would have been disapproved by him.

A girl, for example, was cleaning the house in her mother's absence just the way her mother would have liked it, and had in her mind the pleased facial expression of her mother. Immediately upon her mother's return she had a feeling of great satisfaction as if her mother had already known of her accomplishment even before she actually noticed it. In this case also, the psychic presence of the mother had merged with the idea of the actual mother.

An important issue now draws our attention. True, the psychic presence is an object representation; the reproachful image of the patient's father was an unegotized mental content. But the young man's feeling that the father's love and respect must be based on truth and frankness, and that it must be merited in order to be accepted, is an egotized content. The sensation of being an impostor was unbearable to the ego of this young man. Are these feelings not related to the demands of conscience? Must we not assume that these are moral principles conveyed to the young man by his father and mother? Because this man had egotized the understood mental attitude of his parents, in other words, because he had internalized (introjected) them, did he experience these principles as expression of his own conscience, a function of the superego?

We cannot deny this. In fact, the patient's superego, as an inner agency distinct from the psychic presence, may well have contributed to his unpleasant experience. But, examining the single factors which control our behavior, we realize that more than one factor may participate in a given situation. If we try to examine the dynamics of the psychic presence, we must isolate its manifestations from those of the superego, which will be discussed in the next chapter. It is appropriate to ask whether the patient's feeling that his father's love and respect must be merited can be only a manifestation of his superego, of the internalized father, not the imagined father, or whether it can be also a direct manifestation of the psychic presence, i.e., of the imagined father. After all, the imagined father had witnessed the crime and had merged with the real father. The latter became contaminated by the former, and only through sincerity and truth could the real father be maintained free of contaminations. As we shall see, the phenomenon of psychic presence casts great light on the root of our relatedness to our fellow-beings, not only to our parents who implanted the first basis for our superego, but in general to all persons, of both sexes, of every age, and even to animals. We carry with us a mental duplicate of the persons to whom we feel close; changes in the real persons are transmitted to their psychic presences, and what the psychic presences know is, as it were, communicated to the real persons.

Observing the behavior of a dog this writer recognized the importance of psychic presence. When this dog had misbehaved in its master's absence (it had once stolen food from a cupboard which it had succeeded in opening) it ran away when he returned or cowered as if expecting a beating, even before the master had detected the "crime." In this way the dog betrayed itself. Was its sense of guilt a manifestation of superego or of a merging of the master's psychic presence with the actual master?

Knowledge of this phenomenon permits us to understand the meaning of many dream images, and, finally, provides us with valuable instruments for psychoanalytic intervention. In further discussion of the psychic presence we shall indicate some analogies in the genesis of this phenomenon with superego formation.

Artists have frequently exploited the phenomenon of psychic presence. In cartoons, pictures, dramas, and novels the guilty person is often represented as being tortured by the vivid image of the injured one. We are reminded of the Erinyes of Greek mythology. And, just as a psychic presence can have an accusatory or an approving attitude, the ancient Greeks likewise acknowledged both bad and good Erinyes. In motion pictures this phenomenon is sometimes represented by a kaleidoscopic succession of reproachful faces of the persons whose esteem and love the guilty person cannot relinquish. Very often in waking life the psychic presence is intensified when the guilty person looks at a picture of the offended or murdered person. We may even see occasionally that a person who feels guilty behaves toward a picture of a loved person in the same way as he would behave toward the real person. In some types of obsessional neurosis this is especially clear. The aggressive impulses of one person toward another are vented upon the picture of the latter. On the other hand, it sometimes happens that a husband or a wife cannot "betray" the partner in the presence of his or her picture. In a cartoon in a humorous magazine a woman allowed a man to kiss her after first covering the eyes of her husband's picture on a nearby table.

Murderers often feel haunted, when awake as well as in dreams, by the image and hallucination, respectively, of the murdered person. We think, for instance, of Macbeth's vision of Banquo who had been killed at his order. The most impressive example of this kind is found in Zola's *Thérèse Raquin*. In the crime described there one sees clearly the re-enacting of the oedipus fantasy. The lovers Laurent and Thérèse drown Camille, Thérèse's weakly husband, and marry each other. Zola makes us acquainted early with Laurent's character. He is a young man who anticipates his father's death with delight because the latter refuses to send him money. Laurent tries to paint pictures of saints to earn a few pence, but for so very mediocre a painter this affords extremely meagre income. After the murder of Camille the passionate love of Thérèse and Laurent dies. They become more and more estranged, avoid each other, and are terribly tormented by the image and, indeed, the hallucination of the murdered man. With the murder of Camille they have slain their passion.

We realize that the psychic presence of the murdered man was incompatible with gratification of the love which in life he would have prevented. We call this a deferred obedience. There is a close analogy between the operation of the psychic presence and that of the superego, as we shall see more clearly in the next chapter. The psychic presence, as distinguished from the superego, is an unegotized mental duplication not only of the physical features but also of the mental attitudes of the person in question.

To continue with Zola's example: Laurent continues to try to paint. A friend, a connoisseur of art, sees the heads of two women and three men painted by Laurent. They are masterpieces, and he can scarcely believe that Laurent is the artist. But, he points out, all five pictures resemble one another. True enough, all resemble the murdered Camille. Laurent realizes that he has looked too long at the drowned body of Camille in the morgue; the impression has been printed too strongly on his mind. He destroys the pictures and tries to paint heads of old men and girls, but all resemble Camille. He then makes up his mind to paint angels and virgins with haloes, caricatures with distorted features, Roman warriors with helmets on their heads—all in vain. He is not master of his hand when painting; it always reproduces, in a thousand forms, the features of Camille. Finally Thérèse and Laurent are driven to suicide by the psychic presence of Camille. While libido, in the strong ambivalent attitude toward the memory of Camille, was completely directed toward him—in fact, Laurent's hand tried continually to give him new life, to reproduce him—the destructive cathexis, withdrawn from him, was directed reflexively against the murderer himself. This employment of destrudo or mortido is clearly found in the operation of the superego. As we shall see, this sequence of dynamic processes—first the killing of the ambivalently loved person, then posthumous love without ambivalence, and then his mental resurrection and the introversion of the destrudo which was withdrawn from the feeling toward him—played the decisive role in the phylogenetic development of the superego, as Freud deduced from his studies of primitive society. And it is interesting to learn that actions against a loved person, which can be committed only in his absence, are often sensed as equivalent to killing him; in fact, one desires to remove the presence of that person in order to be able to commit the act. Upon satisfaction of the forbidden desire the longing for that person increases. Thus in one's superego formation, one repeats, ontogenetically but only on a mental level, the process of a phylogenetically acquired substructure and ego state. This sequence seems to play a role also in the occurrence of psychic presence.

The psychic presence of a person against whose will we have acted may also announce itself acoustically. A patient once told me that, when he was quite a young man, he was one day taken by some companions to a house of prostitution. When he arrived there he thought he heard his mother weeping.

We shall now distinguish the psychic presence and the superego. First of all, we repeat, psychic presence has object character, while the superego is an ego state. Secondly, a psychic presence changes immediately with learned or perceived changes in the attitudes, expectations and demands of the real person whose psychic presence appeared in one's mind. It is for this reason that feelings of guilt related to a psychic presence produce a strong need to confess one's guilt to the wronged one. The forgiveness of the latter removes the feeling of guilt. But when such a guilt-ridden ego does not hope to obtain forgiveness from the offended person, and especially when it expects to arouse anger and disapproval of the real person, it may refrain from confessing the crime. Furthermore, the psychic presence does not always represent a parental figure, identification with which gives rise to the superego formation. It may represent any person to whom one is emotionally bound, such as a friend or a child. An example will illustrate the fact that one "chooses" the psychic presence of a person in whose appreciation and love he is most interested: Of two men who felt guilty while indulging in extramarital affairs, one had the psychic presence of his wife, the other of his father.

In the personality development of the child the phenomenon of psychic presence precedes the superego formation. When during the latency period the psychic presences of the parents become egotized, the child's superego, which then and thus comes into being, replaces in varying degrees the psychic presences. And once the psychic presence is converted into an ego state, namely, into the superego, no changes in attitudes of the actual parents can affect this substructure as they did the psychic presence. Anna Freud stated that in children "the superego has not as yet become rigid, but is still accessible to every influence from the outside world." [2] In my opinion the flexibility of the child's conscience is due to the fact that the parental figures have not yet been egotized but appear more as object representations in the child's mind. Psychic presences are, as it were, the mirrored images of real persons. If the real persons change, the mirrored figures must change also. Sometimes the superego can regress to the psychic-presence state.

It has sometimes happened that a murderer has surrendered to authorities after a lapse of many years because he felt driven to do so by the "ghost" of his victim. In this case it is evident that the murderer's guilty conscience was induced by a psychic presence and not, strictly speaking, by his superego. Not all cases of psychic presence obtain such a distinct form in waking life. In the waking state (never in dreams) the psychic presence can be replaced by an intellectual elaboration of it. The most important elaboration is the disguise of the psychic presence in a conditional thought. The guilty person says, for instance, "I am worried about having done that, because my father (or someone else) *might* be grieved or become angry or even cease to love me *if* he knew it." The conditionality of this sentence is purely formal because the guilty person expresses himself that way even if the father or the other person is dead. This thought is a compromise formation between the psychic presence and the perception of reality which denies the material presence of the grieved person. The conditional thought absorbs the imaginative features of the psychic presence. Another mode of expression is, "He would turn over in his grave if he knew this."

In dreams the psychic presence is always hallucinated. A patient (already mentioned in Chapter XX) reported dreams he had during puberty. When he was about twelve he made the discovery that sometimes while dreaming he was aware of the fact that he was dreaming. Once he thought he could satisfy his strong and unbearable sexual longings in these dreams. He could assault sexually the women he met in a dream without danger if only he were aware that he was in a dream world. And, indeed, he sometimes did find himself dreaming and not only knowing that he was dreaming but also remembering this purpose. Once when a woman appeared to him in a dream he set about to approach her with aggressive sexual aims, but his mother appeared to him at the same time, staring at him in a reproachful manner, exactly as she used to stare at him in his infancy when she discovered in the morning that he had wet the bed. The appearance of his mother in the dream inhibited him in his sexual intentions as if she had been really present and not only a dream person. But when he awakened he became angry with himself for having ignored, in the dream, the fact that the mother was as unreal as everything else in the dream. The mother who appeared in his dream maintained reality character in spite of the boy's awareness that he was dreaming. Thus we realize that the dreaming ego did not acknowledge its dreaming state to the full extent. And the dream mother in particular did not surrender her reality character because she represented the psychic presence of the mother which exerted an inhibiting and intimidating influence in the boy's waking life. For this reason the dreaming ego's false perception of the hallucinated mother as the real mother was psychologically valid.[3]

The phenomenon of psychic presence is an expression of the mental omnipresence of the persons to whom we feel emotionally close. The infant and the small child cannot long endure the mother's absence. Not seeing her is for him the same as her not existing. Slowly he acquires the knowledge of her existence independent of his immediate perception of her, and this knowledge leads to her psychic presence. Only then does he become confident, even when he does not see her, that he will receive from her what he needs, and also when he does not see her he tries to behave according to her wishes.

In recent years many psychoanalysts have become interested in the role which the mother plays in the ego development of the infant and child. In Chapter XIX René Spitz's experimental studies in this field were mentioned. And in Chapter VII it was pointed out that the child acquires the feeling of his identity by being recognized by his mother, by being called by his given name which distinguishes him from other persons. His experience of being loved is the most important prerequisite for the development of ego strength. This writer has found that some patients suffering from severe anxiety states with feelings of depersonalization feel a strong need to be identified by their mothers in order not to lose their feeling of identity. Even if they themselves do not know who they are, the mother knows. In some cases the psychic presence of the mother assumes this role. The egos of these patients must behave so that they can be identified not only by their actual mothers but also by their mental images of their mothers. This mental omnipresence manifests itself successively also in respect to other persons to whom one feels attached.

Still another factor contributes to the occurrence of the psychic presence of persons with whom we cannot dispense. We acknowledge and understand the phenomenon of death only intellectually. And our ego adheres so strongly to this intellectual understanding that it becomes unaware of the fact that the emotional realization of someone's death is beyond its reach. A paraphrase may convey this idea accurately: We cannot possibly understand a dead person empathically. The realization that a living person can be transformed into a lifeless body is very traumatic for everybody. But such a realization is often repressed or ignored or dealt with in various defensive ways. As pointed out in Chapter XII, inherent in the ego feeling is the sensation of one's eternal existence. And this sensation, though denied by our intellect, cannot be removed. Both of these psychological facts, the impossibility of grasping the mental extinction of another person and the feeling of our eternal existence, strengthen the phenomenon of psychic presence. Everyone of us, after all, has experienced the absorption of the feeling of the mental continuation of a dead person by a conditional mental attitude. "To honor and preserve the memory" of a love object we act and behave in a way which would meet the agreement of the love object if it could be aware of it.

Children and adults are affected by the psychic presence of parental figures in varying degrees. Some children feel a great urge to confess when they have stolen candy or committed some other misdeed. Other children feel freer to behave in a reprehensible way when they are not observed and may even lie in self-defense with great determination. This does not always mean that they do not feel guilty. Every behavior pattern has to be considered also from an economic point of view. Behavior which arouses feelings of guilt may be due to the strength of the inner urge and to the prevalence of the reality principle over the influence of the psychic presence. We might expect that children who are less motivated in their behavior by the psychic presence of their parents will develop a less effective superego. But this is not always the case. There are adults with a strong superego who in childhood lied and deceived their parents whenever it was convenient. Freud has explained the fanatic urge of some persons always to tell the truth as a reaction to their infantile masturbation which they succeeded in keeping secret.

The study of criminal behavior has revealed that some egos may develop a "thick skin" with respect to a guilty conscience, be it determined by a psychic presence or by the superego. The consequences of repression or disregard for feelings of guilt lead to clinical pictures and to the elaboration of therapeutic procedures which cannot be dealt with at this point.

In normal development the ego reaches the integrative capacity

THE PSYCHIC PRESENCE 281

to respect the "rights" of its fellow-man while still maintaining its own "rights," that is, without surrendering them to unjustified expectations and demands of others. With this capacity a person becomes aware of a psychic presence only when he behaves in a manner which he senses by his own standards as doing wrong to someone else.

If we now consider a hypothetical ego whose behavior would be determined only by the reality principle and the phenomenon of psychic presence, we see very clearly the difference between it and the hypothetical individual considered in the preceding chapter, whose behavior is determined only by resonance identification. The latter is interested only in preventing the love object from suffering, and in order to obtain this "moral goal," while giving in to his desires, he may deceive and lie about his misdeeds without feeling guilty. The former, on the other hand, is driven to confess his misdeeds and feels very ill at ease when he has to hide them.

What is commonly sensed as feelings of guilt arises only from a discrepancy between some behavior or wish and the psychic presence or the superego. We are now prepared to return to the study of the superego and to deepen our understanding of this substructure of the mind which (as Federn demonstrated) is also an ego state with its own boundaries.

NOTES

(1) Weiss, Edoardo. Regression and projection in the superego. Int. J. Psychoanal., 13:449-478, 1932.

(2) Cf. Anna Freud's abstract of her Zur Theorie der Kinderanalyse, a paper read at the Tenth International Psychoanalytical Congress, Innsbruck, 1927, Int. Z. Psychoanal., 13:477, 1927.

(3) Weiss, Edoardo. The psychic presence. Bull. Menninger Clin., 3:177-183, 1939.

XXXIII

More About the Superego

IN Chapter VIII the origin and functions of the superego were presented only superficially. Our acquaintance with the phenomena of resonance identification and psychic presence will now help us gain a deeper understanding of the features and modes of operation of the superego. The psychic presence is an unegotized mental content, i.e. an object representation, which affects our behavior as the real object would affect us, though usually in a milder degree. The superego, on the other hand, is an egotized mental content, that is, an ego state. We learned that it develops from identification processes different from resonance identifications. The superego comes into being from lasting identifications which then operate independent of the objects with which the ego identified itself. We wish to examine now more closely the differences between resonance and permanent identifications.

In resonance identification the ego acknowledges that emotional contents which arise in another ego are only echoed within itself. And these contents resound in one's ego only for the duration of their perceived or imagined existence in the other ego. This implies also that only someone's current ego states can be captured by resonance identification. In the case of permanent identification, on the other hand, reaction patterns and attitudes of another ego are duplicated and egotized in one's own ego in such a way that the traits thus acquired obtain the lasting feeling of "I-ness" and are not, or not only, "perceived" as mental contents or dispositions of the other person. These lasting identifications induce one's ego to react to various situations in the same way as the other person would react. The other ego with whom a person originally identified himself no longer has any part in his reactions. The other ego may even be dead. To make this issue clear we may say: When one feels pity or compassion for a person who suffers, or rejoices perceiving a happy person, we speak of effects of resonance identification. But when someone himself reacts with feelings of satisfaction or disapproval to certain events in the same way in which, to his knowledge, the other person would react—whether the other person is present or not—we speak of lasting identification. The ego itself acquires qualities and emotional and behavior patterns of the other person.

Not all lasting identifications lead to the superego formation. We can easily understand that lasting identifications play an essential role in the structuralization of the ego in its development. As pointed out in previous chapters, our speech, our nonverbal expressions, our behavior, our gestures, our gait, the way we eat, and many of our emotional reactions develop from permanent identifications with the persons of the environment in which we grew up. All these acquisitions are felt as parts of the "I." And once they are egotized, we no longer feel that they originated from autoplastic duplications of the perceived manifestations of other persons. Such an identification is called "primary identification," as mentioned previously, and does not lead to superego formation. Thus we realize that the superego develops from specific lasting identifications. But not even all secondary identifications participate in the superego; some may conflict with it. This became particularly evident after Freud unveiled the psychodynamics of the clinical picture of classical melancholia.

In this clinical picture one can easily distinguish two ego states which are in opposition to each other: One ego state is the accused one, the other the accuser. Through identification with a love object to whom the patient was bound by strong ambivalent feelings, the accusations against it are turned into self-accusations. The accusations stem from the superego; the points of accusation derive from the ego's identification with a person whose behavior is disapproved by the superego. In fact, many acts and crimes of which the patient accuses himself were not committed by him, but by the internalized person. And it is evident that this person within the patient's ego, who is attacked by the superego, cannot be encompassed in the superego. Nevertheless, both parts are ego-cathected. Therefore, the ego accuses itself of all kinds of misdeeds. One ego state rages against another ego state; the first is the substructure called "superego," the second comes into operation through a lasting identification with an ambivalently loved object which is, however, unfit to participate in the structuralization of the superego. Later we shall examine this clinical picture more thoroughly. Only the initial stage is indicated here.

What kind of lasting identifications give rise to the superego which forms a separate structure within the ego? Freud characterizes the superego as a "step within the ego" (in his German expression *eine Stufe im Ich*). This term conveys clearly the idea of the unevenness existing between the ego and the superego. The latter is an ego state which elevates itself above the rest of the ego. It was Freud's great discovery that the superego develops from identification with the father or with both parents as the child conceives them. The product of such internalization ("introjects," this writer would have said in earlier terminology) cannot be integrated by the child with the feeling of his own ego. The child feels weak, ignorant, utterly dependent on his parents, whereas they are strong, omniscient, powerful, and perfect. He loves and fears them; without them he could not survive and develop. It is precisely because of his difficulty in assimilating the parents' prerogatives with the feeling of his own authentic ego that his identification with them leads to a special differentiation within his ego. Thus the portion of the ego which resulted from the internalization of the parents (phylogenetically of the father) lives an autonomous existence, as it were, and, as Federn has shown, develops its own boundaries which separate it from the rest of the ego. The superego relates, however, to the rest of the unified ego which also became structuralized by many other internalized personalities.

This substructure, the superego, has a phylogenetic origin. From study of anthropological data (particularly those found in Frazer's *Golden Bough*), Freud found support for his reconstruction of the earliest phases of prehistoric tribal society, a reconstruction which he had already formulated from his observations of neurotic patients. At some early stage of social development only the father had access to all the women of the horde. He was not only protective of all the members of the group but was also stern and punitive. Whenever a maturing son dared to make sexual approach to any of the women in the horde, all of whom were in the father's exclusive possession, the father's vengeance was inexorable, including even the amputation of the transgressor's penis. Freud introduced the term "castration" for this kind of mutilation, and the "castration fear" of our present-day males, which finds clear expression in neurotic patients, has an inherited root.

In further social development brothers united for the purpose of killing the despotic father who deprived them of female sexual partners. Together they succeeded in accomplishing what they could not do singlehanded. This historic event must have occurred at a state in which men were still cannibals. Freud interpreted the "totem feast" of primitive society as a symbolic repetition of the murder of the father and his actual "oral incorporation" by the sons. The totem animal stands, in Freud's interpretation, for the father of the primitive horde.

After the elimination of the father new difficulties arose, however. There was nobody then to protect the sons from one another's competition and aggression. Increasingly they felt a longing for the father. Their former aggressive drives, consumed in the act of patricide, were no longer directed toward the memory of the father. A protective idealized father-figure arose in the sons' minds. The murdered father was revived more powerful than before. In his article, On the Psychology of the Revolution: The Fatherless Society, Federn presented a very interesting study on the psychological implications of this phase of social development.[1]

The mental resurrection of the murdered father shows two aspects: One is revealed in the internalized father, namely, in one's superego; the other appears projected into the image of a deity. The latter has psychic-presence character, as the "heavenly father." Later we shall learn more about the transformation phenomena of internalized figures, when the process of the "ego passage" is presented. Freud showed that ontogeny repeats phylogeny also in the psychological development of the child. The oedipus complex is *in nuce* the ontogenetic repetition of the prehistorical events described. The boy's sexual longing for the mother, his wish to remove the father, and finally his identification with the father, are inherited dispositions derived from primitive man's desire for the father's women, the murder of the father and the father's resurrection as an internalized structure in the ego. Superego formation is the outcome of the oedipus complex. Libido and destrudo (Federn's mortido), which determined the emotional, ambivalent commitment of the child to his parents in the oedipus situation, power then the functions of the superego. One's own aggressive drives are employed in the exertion of the inhibiting and punitive functions of the superego. Thus one's aggression is turned into reflexive, self-inhibiting, and self-punitive actions. The original castration fear and the fear of losing parental love are transformed, upon superego formation, into conscience anxiety. In Freud's genetic concept the superego is the "heir of the oedipus complex."

The oedipus complex is at its height in the child between the third and fifth years of age and the superego reaches its full development during the latency period, i.e., between the fifth and twelfth years.

Melanie Klein believes that the origin of the superego can be traced back to the first year of life when the child "introjects" only partial objects: the good, giving breast and the bad, frustrating breast. But in my opinion, although these early experiences play an essential role in the child's emotional development, they cannot lead to the superego formation as Freud conceived it. Only through replacement by identification of persons who exercise a controlling function over the child's behavior can his superego be structuralized. And it is precisely the replacement of the parents by the ego's identification with them that brings the oedipus complex to its resolution. This view is consistent with Freud's idea of the archaic root of the superego formation.

Now, the analysis of the superego structure of different individuals reveals that some persons have a predominantly fatherly and others a predominantly motherly superego. And there is no doubt that the mother-child relationship, the source of so many personality traits and emotional dispositions, also contributes to the superego development in a high degree. In Freud's opinion it is the relative strength of the masculine or feminine component in an individual's bisexual disposition which determines whether his superego will become more motherly or more fatherly. But one has certainly to consider also the specific influence that the father and the mother assume in the rearing of the child.

Whatever the origin of the superego may be, its operation is experienced by almost every individual in a characteristic way.

This experience is different from that of resonance identification (pity, compassion, etc.) and also from the way one is affected by a psychic presence. The moral standards and views of the parents, and of other authority figures who became associated with them, are felt as moral standards and views of one's self. The individual's own ego approves a certain kind of behavior and urges and disapproves and condemns certain other kinds of behavior and longings. It is he himself who senses what is morally right and what is morally wrong. At the same time he feels that such sensations, approving and disapproving attitudes, derive from a given section of his ego, which is called "conscience." True, the functions of conscience are egotized, yet they are exercised by a distinct section of the ego. Thus both expressions are psychologically correct, whether one says, "I approve of this and I disapprove that," or whether he says, "My conscience approves of this and my conscience disapproves that." Once the superego is firmly established, the actual parents can themselves become targets for moral approval or disapproval by one's superego, when they behave according to or against the standards which have become internalized in the superego.

Many psychoanalysts emphasize the importance of the peer group for certain acquired identifications of the adolescent. It is true that the peer group affects the ideals and behavior patterns of the growing individual, and in some respects it has a beneficial influence on the ego development. Often this influence is in a direction opposite to principles taught by the parents. The effect of the peers, reminding us of the archaic brother clan which rebelled against the father, may forestall too great a dependence by the maturing youth on too strict or narrow-minded parents. And the possible evil effects of more or less delinquent peers are nowadays well known.

We have noted that ego boundaries are enlarged by the peer group and may be strengthened through homosexual cathexis insofar as they concern the oedipal content. It is well known that homosexuality is often a reaction to excessive oedipal strivings. The peer group serves to strengthen the ego against growing demands of the id; the "I" enlarged to the "we" is better able to deal with these demands which become much stronger during puberty. In a sense, then, the group might be said to strengthen the superego, also. But the father image will become stronger only if it is revered by the peers.

In my opinion opposition between parents and peers plays a much greater role on the psychic-presence level than on the superego level. A firmly established superego cannot easily be shaken. But other psychoanalysts consider the psychic-presence phenomena as manifestations of the superego and do not make such a distinction. When someone acts against the dictates of his superego (his own conscience) he feels guilty in a different way from one whose feelings of guilt are related to a psychic presence. The former accepts and even seeks punishment, the latter tries to avoid it. The employment of destructive cathexis in the functions of the superego constitutes a socially very useful diversion of this cathexis (Federn's mortido) from aggressive behavior against one's fellow-beings. The more of this cathexis that is invested in restriction of hostile drives and in self-punitive behavior for moral transgressions, the less is left for extraverted discharge.

In many of his publications Freud [2] elaborated on his findings that some patients have a neurotic breakdown when they achieve a long-desired goal. But the nature of such an achievement implies a guilt which the patient cannot endure. The feeling of guilt thus aroused can be appeased only by self-deprivation of the expected enjoyment. Every psychoanalyst becomes acquainted in his practice with the strength of the need for self-punishment to which some patients fall victim. In Chapter XXVIII we mentioned that the most convincing clinical proof for the existence of a proper destructive cathexis (whether or not it derives from a death instinct as postulated by Freud) is the prevalence of destructive over self-preservative trends, as found in severe mental diseases. And in Freud's opinion the superego operates in some cases as a kind of "transmuter" of aggression extraverted into self-destruction. In some rare cases the inexorable constitutional strength of destrudo, unchecked by available libido, constitutes an insurmountable obstacle to a successful outcome of psychoanalytic treatment.

In Chapter XXIX it was mentioned that initially (1914) Freud conceived the phenomenon of conscience as the narcissistic need to behave in conformity with one's ego ideal. After Freud's formulation of the superego the ego ideal often continued to be associated with superego and conscience. Because the function of conscience has been assigned to the superego, and since one's need to approach as closely as possible one's ego ideal aims at a narcissistic satisfaction, one may ask whether the superego formation does not also serve this narcissistic need. In truth, the individual forms his ego ideal originally from the image of his admired father and mother. The child accepts his father and later other authority figures as models, as "identification patterns." Yet the child is not allowed to behave in all respects like his father. In an early stage the prohibition against replacing the father in all his actions and prerogatives is inherent in the oedipus complex. Only upon the son's maturation and his choice of a non-incestuous woman, in other words, upon the dissolution of the oedipus complex, can the father constitute for the son a complete identification pattern, thus structuralizing not only his superego but also his ego ideal. Nevertheless a distinction must be made between ego ideal and superego; they serve different functions.

The child learns very early how mother and father want him to be and how they want him to behave. In order to obtain parental love and love, acceptance and admiration from other people in his surroundings, the child tries to shape himself according to the ego ideal which was conveyed to him by his parents. Only by being and behaving the way the parents want him to be and behave can the child hope to secure for himself love and protection from them. Initially he cares for approval from his external parents, successively also from his internalized parents, namely, from the superego. Mental attitudes for self-encouragement and self-consolation in conditions of need and suffering stem from a loving, protecting superego.

The structuralization of a person's ego ideal is also influenced by his peers in adolescence and by all acquired experiences (including reading) which supply him with specific goals for his ambition. All these factors may lead to modifications of his ego ideal which may diverge more or less from the picture of an ideal person portrayed to him by father and mother; in other words, some features of the "rectified ego ideal" may conflict with the superego. In these cases unconditional adherence to one's ego idea may cause feelings of guilt, and, vice versa, behavior in disagreement with one's ego ideal may result in narcissistic frustration, mostly felt as feelings of shame. When a person's conduct, way of life, choice of profession, etc., satisfy both his ego ideal and the demands of his superego, the individual's task of finding a conflictless way of living is much easier than when his ego ideal has acquired traits from sources other than the teachings and behavior patterns of his parents.

Let us now consider a hypothetical person whose moral behavior would be determined exclusively by a strongly developed superego and not by feelings of pity and compassion nor by any psychic presence. It is evident that such behavior would depend upon the specific demands of that person's superego. The superego of one person may demand a strict, honest behavior toward all fellow-human beings and authorities; the superego of another may command loyalty to family and/or friends and disregard unrelated people. The superego of one person may stress sexual fidelity to one's legal marital partner more strongly than that of another. In psychoanalysis we also speak of "criminal superegos." In considering a person's moral attitudes at different times and situations in the course of his life we may distinguish different facets of the superego and call them the "sexual," "professional," or "social" superegos, etc. The superego of one social group may contain discriminatory preconceptions about different races or religions, while that of another group will convey feelings of equality to all human beings, believing that everyone should enjoy the same rights. The latter attitude is the result of gradual moral evolution of mankind, but one which has not yet affected very many people in our present civilization. This moral achievement of Judaic-Christian origin is commonly called "Christian love." The Freudian psychoanalyst can easily interpret the "God of Love" as man's adherence to Freud's "heavenly force" *Eros*, Love, versus his death instinct or, if one does not accept the concept of a death instinct as such, versus the destructive and aggressive component in our strivings.

Thus we realize that the superegos of different individuals and of different cultural groups may differ markedly with respect to their moral impositions, demands, and prohibitions. Yet every individual experiences his superego and conscience in the same way.

This experience is one's own feeling of what is right and what is wrong. The ego feels that it can find moral peace of mind only if it behaves according to these feelings of right and wrong; and it feels ill at ease when it gives in to temptations which are disapproved by what it feels to be its own conscience. One type of maladjustment consists in a person's difficulty in resisting and controlling the impact of some wishes and instincts according to the demands of his superego. And every time he acts in disagreement with the demands of his superego he accepts and even seeks punishment. It was mentioned that the urge for atonement is often manifested in a patient's resistance to giving up his neurotic suffering.

Our hypothetical individual, whose moral behavior would be controlled exclusively by his superego, would not refrain from cruel acts against other persons when these acts were required by his superego. Feelings of pity and compassion would be neutralized by his inner satisfaction for having complied with the demands of the superego. And such an individual would not be tolerant of other persons' behavior which he sensed as "unethical." In pursuing the norms of his superego he would not become aware of any psychic presence in his actions against the interest of other persons as long as he could feel his behavior sanctioned by his superego.

We have considered different hypothetical egos in order to make clear the operations of various "ethical" factors. We don't consider "ethical" the mere adherence to the reality principle. But various kinds of resonance identifications, restrictions and actions induced by some kind of ego ideal, by psychic presences and by the superego can be considered as "ethical" according to the common evaluation of our society. We realize, however, that perhaps nobody's behavior is controlled by only one of these factors. This writer speaks of different "ethical types" in considering the proportions in which these factors are operative in single individuals. In psychoanalytic treatment one usually considers the conflicts which have arisen between objectionable drives and the superego. But it is also very important to assess some conflicts arising between pity or compassion and the superego, between a psychic presence and one's acquired ego ideal, between one's ego ideal and the superego, and even between a psychic presence and the superego when the appeasement of the superego does not completely absorb the tension caused by a psychic presence. In brief, various "ethical factors" may conflict with one another.

All these factors can undergo modifications in intensity and content during the individual's life. One of the main psychological mechanisms for such changes will be discussed in the next chapter.

NOTES

(1) Federn, Paul. Zur Psychologie der Revolution: Die vaterlose Gesellschaft. Der österreichische Volkswirt, 11:571-574, 595-598, May 1919. See also Note 6 to Introduction.

(2) E.g., in his article, Those wrecked by success (1916). Standard edition, 14:316-331. London, Hogarth, 1957.

XXXIV

The Phenomenon of Ego Passage

WE have discussed the various inner motivations that control one's instincts and desires: consideration of experienced and understood real consequences of certain actions, resonance identification, demands of psychic presences and of the superego, and the narcissistic need to conform more or less to one's ego ideal. We may now ask whether or not the specific demands of psychic presences and the superego can be modified in the course of one's life. We recognized that a healthy ego develops criteria in regard to its own rights and those of others. Thus, when an ego senses that it has the right to behave in a certain way even though its behavior is against the wishes of a person to whom it feels emotionally close, it does not feel guilty in behaving this way. It may, however, renounce some satisfactions as a favor to someone whom it loves and respects or simply as a practical expedient to maintain the relationship intact according to the reality principle. But when such an individual does not renounce satisfactions to which he feels entitled, he will not experience "psychic-presence guilt." Furthermore we noted that an individual who becomes aware of changes in another person's attitude automatically transmits these changes to that person's psychic presence which is the "mirror image" of that person. The superego cannot change in this way because it is independent of external persons.

Another important process which may have a modifying effect on the demands of a psychic presence is the intellectual "absorption" of it. As pointed out, our intellect denies the existence of psychic presences. Only in hallucinatory psychoses and in dreams may they appear with full visual and/or acoustic vividness. Nevertheless, psychic presences are felt by normal egos in waking state, and they exert a controlling action. We have considered a compromise between a feeling of a psychic presence and its intellec-

293

tual denial. This compromise consists in an intellectual act which is in fact a rationalization, namely, in the formulation of a conditional thought: "I don't do this because he would mind if I did it." Often there is no consideration of whether the other person may possibly learn about a given action, and this makes very evident the rationalization character of the condition expressed. It is as if someone opened an umbrella on a sunny cloudless day and explained: "I do this because I would get wet if it should rain." This pseudo-intellectual act is sufficient to deny the existence of a psychic presence in complying with its demands. The cathexis which activates or maintains the psychic presence is employed in this intellectual operation. We can also say that such an intellectual operation absorbs the psychic presence. Nevertheless, in this case the behavior remains controlled by the "absorbed psychic presence." In other cases intellectual absorption may tend toward the removal of its controlling action altogether. The young man discussed in Chapter XXXI, to whom the image of his disapproving father appeared while he was perpetrating a crime, also tried to appease his psychic-presence conscience by reasoning. He did not succeed in forestalling the psychic presence, but we can understand that it would have been much more threatening to him had he not resorted at all to such reasoning.

In some cases reasoning may be consistent and appropriate to free one's self from the pressure of unjustified demands of a psychic presence. In the course of his life an individual goes through various learning experiences, and the maturation of his intellect, his increased understanding of human nature and behavior, free him from naive concepts about honesty and sincerity and teach him the right of personal privacy; they also furnish him mental devices for absorption of inopportune and inhibiting psychic presences. In some cases the roughness of life induces an individual to form a "thick skin" in transgressing justified or unjustified impositions of other persons and society, as mentioned earlier. Conscience and feelings of guilt may also undergo repression, a process which is bound to lead to neurotic difficulties.

An individual may deal with the demands and impositions of the superego in an analogous way, although these are much more resistant to absorbing devices than are those of psychic presences.

Criminal behavior accompanied by feelings of guilt is more frequent on the psychic-presence level than on the superego level. This is also shown in descriptions of criminal personalities in dramas and novels. A much more radical change in the demands of the superego follows the process of "de-identification." The importance of this phenomenon can be fully understood when we consider the grandiose structuralization of the ego as the result of various identifications. We learned that not all identifications ("introjections," as they are called in psychoanalytic literature) are encompassed in the superego. In their substitutive function many identifications, including the earliest ones, structuralize the ego itself. They may even encounter the condemnation of the superego. In the words of Freud, "When it happens that a person has to give up a sexual object, there quite often ensues a modification in his ego which can only be described as a reinstatement of the object within the ego, as it occurs in melancholia; the exact nature of this substitution is as yet unknown to us. It may be that, by undertaking this introjection, which is a kind of regression to the mechanism of the oral phase, the ego makes it easier for an object to be given up or renders that process possible. It may even be that this identification is the sole condition under which the id can give up its objects. At any rate the process, especially in the early phases of development is a very frequent one, and it points to the conclusion that the character of the ego is a precipitate of abandoned object cathexes and that it contains a record of past object choices. It must, of course, be admitted from the outset that there are varying degrees of capacity for resistance, as shown by the extent to which the character of any particular person accepts or resists the influences of the erotic object-choices through which he has lived. In women who have had many love-affairs there seems to be no difficulty in finding vestiges of their object-cathexes in the traits of their character. We must also take into consideration the case of simultaneous object-cathexis and identification, i.e., when the alteration in character occurs before the object has been given up. In such a case the alteration in character would be able to survive the object-relation and in a certain sense to conserve it." [1]

The present author[2] described the phenomenon of externalization (in psychoanalytic literature this process is given the misleading term "projection") of a previously internalized object. The sequence of this phenomenon is as follows: (a) An object representation is internalized by the ego, thus becoming an ego trait or ego state. (b) This ego trait is at a later time externalized, becoming again an object representation. I called this phenomenon the "passing of an object through the ego" or simply the "ego passage" of an object. In this way an ego frees itself from an identification, in other words, it "de-identifies" itself from that object.

Through the "ego passage" object representations undergo changes. The re-externalized representations are not identical with the original ones. In the article mentioned I studied this phenomenon in cases of heterosexual love objects. The male child identifies himself, within the limits of his capacity, not only with his father but also in varying degrees with his mother. This process leads to what Freud described as secondary narcissism: The ego loves in itself the internalized object. At a later stage—during or after the latency period—the internalized mother-representation is, in the course of normal development, re-externalized. To the extent to which this does not occur, the male individual maintains a feminine identification. But in the case of re-externalization, a representation of a woman as a desired love object develops, having not only characteristics of the mother but also of the individual himself, mostly of his own feminine traits inherent in his bisexual disposition. It becomes quite evident that the internalized image of the original mother does not maintain its original features exactly, but during its stay in the ego it absorbs and integrates features and tendencies of the individual himself. The main normal modification of the mother image which underwent ego passage is its rejuvenation, in adaptation to the age of the son.

The process of externalization, that is, the transformation of a part of the ego into an object representation, is often expressed in dreams and myths by acts of birth or by a symbolic representation of birth, such as acts of liberation (rescue) of a girl by a young man from an enclosure or from a dangerous situation. In mythology this action constitutes the first heroic act of a growing youth, after which he becomes a mature man. If we consider that an adolescent can assert his masculinity after he has externalized his feminine features, we can understand the deep meaning of the sequence; he frees a girl and consequently he becomes a masculine hero. The young princess in the Tale of the Sleeping Beauty was 100 years older than the prince, her liberator. This is a common exaggeration, frequent in myths and fairy tales, for the indication of a former generation. The mother of the prince had been internalized by him, and upon her externalization (ego passage) she was revealed as only as old as the prince himself.

An analogous process of ego passage can be observed also in the psychosexual development of women. The ensuing masculine image shows characteristics of the father (brother) as well as of the girl herself, chiefly of her own masculine traits.

The phenomenon of ego passage does not appear only with regard to the countersexual part of an individual but also with regard to all internalized objects, feminine and masculine. Even the superego can be externalized again; it can be turned into an object representation which has been modified by the ego passage. One can easily understand the importance of ego passage in the process of de-identification, whereby the ego loses some previously acquired structural components. This can be recognized most clearly, however, in the case of externalization of the countersexual part. I recognized for the first time the implications of the process of de-identification in 1920, during the psychoanalytic treatment of a case of bronchial asthma.[3] A forty-year-old male patient entered psychoanalytic treatment because he suffered from deep depression and was also a homosexual. He had had very slight asthma attacks in early childhood but never again until they reappeared in the middle of his treatment. He had identified himself very early with his mother, and from his twenties on he enjoyed occasional homosexual relationships in feminine identification, though with great conflict. When during the course of his analysis his early positive feelings toward his mother were lifted from deep repression, he began to feel interested in a woman, and at about that same time a very severe bronchial asthma developed. It became clear that the asthma attacks were reactions to his fear of separation from his mother—or her substitutes—to whom he felt strongly attached in a passive dependent attitude. The asthma attacks were repressed crying spells. A few years later when I understood the phenomenon of ego passage, I could have made a better formulation of the psychodynamic processes involved. The woman with whom he felt in love was of his age and had both some traits of his mother and some of his own features. The patient married her, and when she became pregnant his asthma attacks worsened considerably. When she gave birth to a boy, they became even worse. Evidently the patient felt threatened by the birth of his son, fearing that his wife might feel closer to the child than to him. During one severe asthma attack when his wife was assisting him, he made a slip of the tongue and called her "Mother."

We may ask why this patient was free of asthma attacks from his earliest childhood until the age of forty-one when he de-identified himself from his mother. The answer is simply that the psychoanalytic process had provoked this psychosomatic disease. The patient felt this and became very negative toward his treatment. Through early internalization of his mother he had "erected this love object within his ego." The internalized mother could not possibly have estranged herself from him because she was a part of an ego state of his own. A very effective defense mechanism indeed! But once he had been deprived of this defense, in other words, after the externalization of his mother into an object representation —modified by ego passage—he became again dependent on her, this time as an external object. He had found then the modified externalized mother in an actual woman whom he married. It was interesting to note that this patient had lost many of his feminine traits when he became interested in this female partner. But still the fear of losing her or her affection was reactivated and produced the asthma attacks. At this stage of the psychoanalysis a severe neurosis was replaced by a psychosomatic disease.

As we have seen, externalization turns all kinds of internalized objects into representations of external objects. The superego itself may be turned into a psychic presence—of a special character, however, since the original parental figures have undergone modifications through ego passage. Such psychic presences are often indistinct, like the Erinyes of Greek mythology or god-eyes. As we shall soon see, there are many other implications of the externalization of the superego which can be observed in persecutory delusions of paranoid patients.

Freud believed that through identification one can give up a love object. We would now like to understand the "psychological purpose" of the process of de-identification. So far we recognized that externalization of a previously internalized object revives the desire for and the interest in that object. In Freud's theory a part of "secondary narcissism" is turned again into "object libido." It would appear that one can continue the renunciation of a love object only as long as one remains identified with it. But it also seems that an ego cannot resort indefinitely to this kind of defense against deprivation of love objects.

In the process of identification we must distinguish two dynamic accomplishments of the ego: (1) investment of the autoplastic duplication of an object with ego cathexis, and (2) integration of the internalized object with the existing ego structure. If we conceive ego strength in economic terms, namely, as the amount of ego cathexis available for the ego's functioning, we can well understand that the stronger an ego, the greater will be its capacity for identification with other objects. Therefore weak egos do not develop strong and reliable superegos either. Psychosis and psychopathy are ego deficiencies. Since the phenomenon of psychic presence is not based on identification, "psychic-presence conscience" prevails over "superego conscience" in immature and weak egos. An ego can give up identifications for different dynamic reasons. De-identification can be the result of the weakening of an ego which then lacks the necessary strength for maintaining certain identifications. But when de-identification from an internalized object is the expression of a biological need to recapture an object relation, this does not necessarily mean that the ego was too weak to maintain that identification. In any case, what Freud calls "secondary narcissism" is an ego exertion, and through the process of de-identification (in other words, through the return of object love), the ego becomes relieved of a dynamic effort. The phenomenon of de-identification as a consequence of ego weakness can be best observed in dreaming and psychotic ego states. Both are weak ego states.

As mentioned at the end of Chapter V, a man dreamt that someone suffered from severe headache, and upon awakening he realized that it was he himself who was suffering. True, the headache was not due to any identification, but every externalization is dynamically the same process as de-identification. As a matter of fact, one may also say in this case that the ego "has de-identified itself" from its headache in the dream. In re-awakening the ego cathexis flow was re-established in its full strength, and the headache again became egotized. The following example may illustrate the giving up of an identification in a dream:

A girl in her late teens met in a dream her aunt who had died some years before. Surprised to see her, she said, "Oh, so you are not dead!" The day before this dream she had had a date with a boy who tried to go "too far" in his physical affection, but she resisted because she didn't trust men easily. After he had taken her home, however, she regretted not having been a little more accepting of his advances and resolved to give up some of her resistance on the next occasion. The aunt of whom she dreamt was a very reserved person in her relationships, and the girl had often heard her say that girls should be cautious with men and not trust them too easily. Accordingly, in waking life this girl had identified herself with the standards of her aunt, shared but not so clearly expressed by her mother; in the dreaming state, however, she had given up this identification and her aunt had appeared as an object in the dream instead. The dreamer's saying, "Oh, so you are not dead!" is related to the girl's resolution to give up such standards on the next occasion. The dream revealed that she still adhered to them; in terms of externalization "the aunt was not dead." This is another example of the function of identification in substituting the object which has to be given up. Deeper meanings of this dream may be disregarded at this time; it was reported here only to illustrate the regression from identification to an object representation. Externalizations of identification products into dream persons and also into inanimate objects is very frequent in dreams. Schizophrenic patients who have lost some behavior patterns acquired through identification speak often of persons having those traits which they themselves could no longer maintain. Such persons may also appear in their hallucinations (mostly auditory) and in their persecutory delusions.

The great importance of ego passage for the establishment of interpersonal relationships in healthy egos deserves special consideration. In successful mourning work the ego succeeds in renouncing a concrete love object through identification with it.

But the substitution of an identification product—of an "introject" —for an object relationship constitutes a burden for the ego. The ego has a natural need for establishing object relationships. In normal development substitutive identification is only a transitory device of adaptation to a suffered object loss. The superego (which becomes a permanent substructure of the mind) is an exception, however, although forms of re-externalization of the superego can be observed, as mentioned, particularly in dreams and in psychotic states. As far as the loss of a needed love object is concerned, we realize that not every love object can be renounced through mourning work; there are cases of permanent grief for such a loss. But in successful adaptation of the loss of a love object through identification with it, sooner or later the ego's need for relating to such an object induces it to externalize the internalized object. The thought of the re-externalized object, modified through ego passage, is no longer directed toward the concrete object which was renounced, however, but constitutes a type of object which the ego endeavors to find in the external world.

So, the sequence of the whole process is as follows: (1) The ego has to renounce a needed object. (2) If the mourning work is successful, the object is internalized. This is a transitory appeasement of the id. (3) The need of a relationship with such an object increases and induces the ego to re-externalize the object with which it had identified itself. In doing so the ego no longer feels emotionally committed to the original concrete object but is driven toward a new object which resembles the original one modified in the process of ego passage.

We have seen that the process of externalization frees object interest. How can we then explain the fact that schizophrenic patients, who so easily externalize previously internalized objects, are losing and not gaining object interest? Is the withdrawal from the external world of objects not one of the most apparent symptoms of schizophrenia? As Federn taught us, this withdrawal is not a primary manifestation of schizophrenia, as Freud believed, but a secondary manifestation of the disease. It is precisely because of the ego's depletion of, and not increase in, ego cathexis that the schizophrenic individual cannot afford to maintain strong object cathexes. For this reason the ego also tries automatically to curtail its production and, as Federn has shown, it regresses to previous, more economic ego stages in order to maintain its integration. Thus, in answering our question we must consider the different dynamic reasons for externalization previously mentioned. It is helpful to repeat that externalization due to an ego's need for object relations has different implications than externalization caused by the ego's diminished dynamic resources for maintaining identifications. In the first case the "purpose" of de-identification is to gain object interest; in the second case the ego endeavors, through de-identification, to unburden itself from an excessive integrative task. In the first case the cathexis withdrawn from internalized objects is turned into object cathexis; in the second case the withdrawn cathexis is utilized for the imperiled integrative process of the ego itself. The schizophrenic ego cannot spare much cathexis either for object interests or for identifications with objects. Object representations of schizophrenic patients, arising from de-identification, can be well compared with emotionally unused products of this process.

This author[4] observed also the instinctive reluctance of schizophrenic patients to form new identifications. A forty-two-year-old paranoid patient told me that his enemies extracted certain humors or substances from corpses of dead people, perhaps also from the bodies of living persons (he was not sure in this respect), particularly from their excrements, and would mix these humors or substances in his food. Upon ingestion of the thus-contaminated food he would acquire similarities with these persons: their facial expressions, their voices, even their thoughts. This example is chosen here to illustrate the reluctance of schizophrenic patients to be overburdened by identifications. It also illustrates the relation between identification and oral incorporation. We may disregard at this time a detailed analysis of this complicated delusion in which some superego aspects were externalized into enemies. Likewise, an ego endeavors to free itself from previously acquired identification when a diminution of its cathexis forces it to economize the use of ego cathexis.

Ego cathexis adheres more tenaciously to internalized objects ("introjects") than to externalized ones invested by it. In melancholia, for example, the tenacity with which ego cathexis adheres to internalized objects is evident from the melancholic's superego, which remains strongly cathected.

Freud explained the self-accusation of the melancholic patient as the result of ambivalent feelings toward the love object which he internalized. This explanation, however, is incomplete. We may ask, for example, why the patient's ego cannot maintain an ambivalent love relationship with a still existing object, and why it must identify with the object itself.

At this point it seems profitable to compare the reactions of the paranoid schizophrenic with those of the melancholic. In paranoid schizophrenia the portion of the ego which maintains identifications is projected by the patient onto his enemies. To this type of patient his enemies are persons who compel him to be like other people. The melancholic ego, on the other hand, does not resort to such a projection but instead feels the presence of the internalized objects ("introjects") as if they were intruders, parasites, or usurpers. Indeed, these internalized objects bind a certain amount of cathexis which the melancholic ego needs very badly for its own functioning. Its hostility against internalized objects (which it feels to be itself) derives from this feeling of unwelcome intrusion. This factor is the dominant one in determining the patient's self-accusations. The negative feelings contained in the melancholic's ambivalent attitude toward objects become justified by the negative aspects of the introject. All patients suffering from classical melancholia have one point of accusation in common: They consider themselves as intruders and impostors and reject expressions of love and consideration by others. This attitude clearly reflects the motivation for the hostility against themselves.

The effects of ego passage will be further described in the next chapter when the "structural splitting process" is presented.

NOTES

(1) Freud, Sigmund. The Ego and the Id (1923). London, Hogarth, 1927, pp. 36-37.

(2) Weiss, Edoardo. Über eine noch nicht beschriebene Phase der Entwicklung zur heterosexuellen Liebe. Int. Z. Psychoanal., 11:429-443, 1925.

(3) ———. Die Psychoanalyse eines Falles von nervösem Asthma. Int. Z. Psychoanal., 8:440-455, 1922.

(4) ———. Der Vergiftungswahn im Lichte der Introjektions- und Projektionsvorgänge. Int. Z. Psychoanal., 12:466-477, 1926. See also Note 1 to Chapter XXX, above. This patient had formed a strong positive transference to me and always looked forward to our conversations. But since at that time I still believed that schizophrenic patients are unable to establish a transference relationship, I called the patient's transference manifestations "pseudo-transference."

XXXV

Structural Split

CERTAIN portions of ego states can be externalized and various objects or parts of them can be internalized and successively externalized again, undergoing modifications through ego passage as mentioned. Some ego states must be externalized in normal emotional development as, for instance, countersexual features and tendencies, the externalization of which then arouses in the ego a longing for a countersexual partner. In addition, former ego states are normally externalized, creating in the ego the desire for children and enabling it to participate vicariously in the experiences of younger individuals. An ego cannot function adequately in social integration if it does not feel sufficiently a need for various kinds of object relationships and if it does not develop the capacity to find proper love objects in reality. Furthermore, as emphasized often, the enlargement of the "ego feeling" to a "we feeling" is of essential importance for community life of the individual.

We are also aware that an ego which has had to give up too many essential love objects, adapting itself to their loss by means of identification, becomes impoverished in its longing for object relationships. In addition it becomes overburdened by the task of maintaining these identifications and integrating them within its coherent unity. But under the pressure of the need both to establish object relationships and to free itself from the "identification exertion," it re-externalizes the internalized objects with the described implications. The ego is then no longer emotionally committed to the original concrete objects but feels compelled to search for other objects of a given type, determined by ego passage.

The superego occupies a special position in mental functioning. It has its own boundaries, and its formation is phylogenetically determined. Strength and character of individual superegos are due to constitutional factors and to the specific persons who have be-

305

come permanently internalized in the superego structure. There is no "natural need" to externalize the superego, although some forms of superego externalization are well known. The most common is the superego externalization (projection) into a physical or merely "spiritual" image of God. In this case the externalized superego acquires psychic-presence character, and its demands and impositions can be modified by the ego's learning that God has changed His mind. "God's forgiveness removes guilty conscience." As explained earlier, this is the way in which the "laws" of psychic-presence conscience can be modified. The belief in God is in itself a demand of those authority figures who have been internalized as superego. It is precisely their imposition which induces the ego to replace first the parents themselves, then their identification (the superego), by an immensely elevated, unreachable psychic presence. Perhaps the parents' replacement by God, on their own demand, makes their internalization superfluous. One psychic presence is substituted for another, and the ego is spared identification exertion.

The important therapeutic task arising out of the need to modify unjustified and unreasonable demands of a patient's superego must be approached from this understanding. If the patient is induced, by the personality of the therapist and confidence in him, to develop a parental transference on him, this is often followed by externalization, in varying degrees, of the patient's superego onto the therapist. Unfortunately, however, this does not always occur; if the personality of the therapist and his approach cannot compete with the patient's superego, then the patient cannot free himself from an overly strong neurotic feeling of guilt. On the other hand, it is not always necessary to externalize the superego into a psychic presence in order to modify its demands and impositions. Internalized objects are subjected to modifications even before they are re-externalized. After all, the ego passage modifications take place during the object's stay in the ego, and such modifications become evident only upon its externalization.

In certain psychopathological conditions the difficulty encountered by the ego in its efforts to integrate incompatible internalized objects within its coherent unity is very evident. Conflicts between such identifications are very similar to conflicts between the superego and unacceptable drives. As we shall soon show, "inter-identification conflicts" often develop into structural conflicts, in the course of melancholic depressions, i.e., into conflicts between condemned drives (id) and the superego.

This writer distinguishes neurotic from psychotic melancholic depression. In the first the ego's sense of reality and reality testing remain intact, while in the second the ego loses, more or less, its capacity to discriminate between real and unreal. The dynamic mechanism of classic melancholia, discovered by Freud, can be clearly recognized in the psychotic form; to detect it in the neurotic form deeper analysis is required. One important avenue for exploration of neurotic afflictions has not yet been utilized because of misunderstanding of the psychotic process still prevailing among psychoanalysts who ignore Federn's findings. This avenue is the direct observation of neurotic symptoms in psychotic patients. The integrative efforts of a healthy ego, as found in non-psychotic neurotics, obscures the dynamics of the neurotic affliction. These efforts function as an impenetrable wall behind which the neurotic process takes place. Only through deep analysis of the unconscious processes can the dynamics of some neurotic symptoms be revealed. But in the psychosis this wall is broken, and thus the internal psychological events can be observed through breaches in the integrative wall, caused by the psychotic lesions.

There are different forms of neurotic depressions which present different clinical pictures and which have different "cathexis-economic" causes. In the melancholic form the patient depreciates himself without accusing himself of crimes which he has not committed. He feels guilty easily and is very unfair toward himself. He ignores or disregards his positive qualities and fails to consider his valuable accomplishments. But his behavior is integrated, and he does not suffer from delusions or hallucinations. Only through deep analysis can one discover that he has detached himself from a love object—or loved environment, usually his family—toward whom (or which) he had felt very resentful. Instead of condemning the other person or the environment, he depreciates himself. His depression expresses his identification with ambivalently loved objects. In the psychotic depression this mechanism is clearly revealed, since the patient accuses himself in his delusions of crimes and misdeeds which he himself has not committed but which were committed, often to a minor extent, by the love object with whom he has identified himself. In both the neurotic and psychotic conditions one ego state is in conflict with another ego state. The accused ego state is that which arises from the identifications mentioned; the other is the mental substructure, the superego.

The melancholic conflict can be resolved when one of the two conflicting ego states is externalized, thus re-establishing peace in the ego's home. We shall see, however, that the superego presents greater resistance to its externalization than other internalized objects, and once re-externalized it cannot easily be internalized again. We shall soon indicate the biological reason for the fact that some other internalized objects can be much more easily externalized and internalized again, with all the signs of ego passage.

Clinical experience shows that melancholic states can be turned into hypomanic states of elation. Here again it has to be borne in mind that there are different forms of emotional exultation, each caused by a different economic factor. For example, in our description of "spastic ego paresis" we noted that withdrawal of the inhibiting action of the ego, due to a specific lack of ego cathexis, frees previously checked urges and impulses which then overflow the ego until it breaks down into unconsciousness. After a long-desired achievement ego cathexis may remain in excess of a need for employment, and a state of elation called "feeling of triumph" ensues. But at this point we are interested mainly in the dynamic process which puts an end to a melancholic depression. The most common form of resolution of this internal discord consists in the ego's de-identification from the criticized internalized objects. In my 1926 article on paranoid delusions,[1] I distinguished the "persecuted introject"—the ambivalently loved internalized object—from the "persecuting introject"—the superego. In melancholic depression both "introjects" are maintained by the ego. Therefore the ego persecutes itself or, more correctly, one ego state persecutes another. Such a state of inner tension creates a strong urge for resolution. When a very aggressive superego overpowers the ego the patient is driven toward suicide. An ego can more easily endure a severe conflict between itself and some other person than between two of its own states. In the clinical picture of manic-depressive psychosis, the resolution mentioned is a typical outlet of this conscience conflict. This condition consists of periodic or irregular processes of internalization and externalization of the "persecuted introject." In the hypomanic phase the patient often becomes suspicious of other people, but he does not fear them as his personal persecutors; rather he himself becomes a persecutor of "evil-doers." He is ready to find faults in others; he may accuse them of being immoral, perverted, of plotting against the government and the nation, of being antireligious, of corrupting youth, etc. In such cases it is evident that the patient has de-identified himself from the "persecuted introject," but his superego has remained egotized; in other words he has kept, as a persecutor, the identification with those authority figures who have shaped his superego. His whole ego functions as superego, not toward himself but toward others.

It is erroneous to diagnose such patients as paranoid, as some psychiatrists do. These patients are rather hypomanic. Even when the initial state of agitation subsides, many such patients remain persecutors characterologically. Also in this phase we can distinguish neurotic from psychotic hypomanic afflictions, and the criterion of distinction between the two is again the intactness or impairment of the ego, chiefly its perception of reality. The single afflictions vary immensely with regard to the intensity and duration of the two phases. In some cases the depressive or the hypomanic phase can persist as a chronic condition, as a lasting character trait of the ego, though usually in an attenuated form. The hypomanic neurotic form is seen in people who feel that they are always right in their evaluation of other people's behavior and whose preferred theme of conversation is to criticize and accuse "evildoers." People of such a character often become investigators and find great satisfaction in detecting individuals who are, in their opinion, harmful to society, who engage in revolutionary activities or are disrupting public morals. But, while they are condemning and persecuting other individuals, onto whom they have externalized their own "persecuted introject," they themselves do not always conduct an irreprehensible life. Such a person does not feel guilty for his own dishonesty and selfish actions, however, because his ego, fused, as it were, with his superego, directs its condemning and punitive function toward external objects. In the psychotic form the contents of the patient's accusations of other people stem from his delusions.

Observation of psychotic melancholic states revealed to the present writer the importance of ego passage for the specific self-accusations of such patients. If we listen carefully to the self-reproaches of a psychotic melancholic patient, we discover that not all of his reproaches are actually related to the internalized love object. Some seem justified; they pertain to objectionable actions of the patient himself and were not committed by the internalized person. A melancholic woman accused herself of having stolen, cheated at cards, etc. These accusations should have been directed against her husband. But she reproached herself also for having been promiscuous and having indulged in sexual perversions, which she actually did in a preceding hypomanic phase. This example illustrates the fusion of an internalized object with some traits of the individual himself. Often the contents of the self-accusations consist in previously repressed condemned tendencies of the patient himself. There are also cases in which only the self-accusatory and self-punitive attitude of the ego is manifest, while the contents of the accusations change constantly. Often the internalization of an ambivalently loved object can be inferred only from the reproaching attitude of the patient's superego for any crime or objectionable tendency in general of which the patient accuses himself. The original object has disappeared altogether; it has been "digested" by the ego. In other words, it seems that in some cases the process of internalization of a love object, toward whom the patient had ambivalent feelings, had brought about a great strife between the ego and superego. Such an internalization acts as a catalyst, as it were, in the development of a strong dissension between these two mental substructures. This writer calls "structual split" the externalization of either the superego or that portion of the ego which is condemned by it.

In the publication mentioned I communicated another observation which I made in the study of the course of melancholic afflictions. Some patients who had been hospitalized in a severe melancholic state, with strong self-accusatory and self-punitive attitudes, developed after weeks or many months not a hypomanic condition but a persecutory paranoia. It became quite evident that the melancholic state had been overcome by externalization of the superego and not by externalization of the "persecuted introject."

Instead of "persecuting" themselves, they felt persecuted by outsiders; thus they no longer felt guilty. Freud recognized this projection in paranoid afflictions in 1914 [2] before he introduced the
term "superego" to designate the "special psychical agency which
performs the task of seeing that narcissistic satisfaction from the ego
ideal is ensured and which, with this end in view, constantly
watches the actual ego and measures it by that ideal." He considered then this agency to be what we call our "conscience." He
continues: "Recognition of this agency enables us to understand the
so-called 'delusions of being noticed' or more correctly, of being
watched, which are such striking symptoms in the paranoid diseases and which may also occur as an isolated form of illness, or
intercalated in a transference neurosis. Patients of this sort complain
that all their thoughts are known and their actions watched and
supervised; they are informed of the functioning of this agency by
voices which characteristically speak to them in the third person
('Now she's thinking of that again,' 'Now he's going out'). This complaint is justified; it describes the truth. A power of this kind, watching, discovering and criticizing all our intentions does really exist.
Indeed, it exists in every one of us in normal life." In this publication Freud characterized such delusions and auditory hallucinations as a regressive form of the agency mentioned. He wrote: "For
what prompted the subject to form an ego ideal, on whose behalf
his conscience acts as watchman, arose from the critical influence
of his parents (conveyed to him by the medium of the voice), to
whom were added, as time went on, those who trained and taught
him and the innumerable and indefinable host of all the other people in his environment—his fellow-men—and public opinion." [3]
    It was not until 1923 that Freud formulated the concept of the
superego which he equated for some time with the ego ideal. In
what Freud called a regressive form of the internal controlling
agency, we recognize now the phenomenon of externalization. This
externalization becomes more evident in those cases of paranoia
which have developed from a preceding melancholic state, as this
writer has observed. And some features of the persecutory manifestations of paranoid patients are due to the phenomenon of ego
passage. While in the hypomanic phase (which does not always
follow a melancholic condition) the ego "usurps" the function of

the superego, in paranoid afflictions (which usually develop independent of a preceding melancholic state) the superego or some of its functions are externalized.

It cannot be emphasized too often that the processes of internalization and externalization do not explain the psychotic symptoms of delusions and hallucinations. Delusions and hallucinations are due to dynamic lesions of the ego, to a depletion of ego cathexis at the ego boundaries; and they are not due, we should remind ourselves, to withdrawal of interest (of libido) from the external world. The processes of internalization and externalization—called "introjection" and "projection," thus creating confusion in the correct conception of these phenomena—consist merely in egotization and de-egotization of contents. Through egotization a content becomes included within one's ego feeling; through de-egotization a part of an ego state is turned into an object representation, not necessarily into a delusional or hallucinatory content. A healthy ego senses the object representation as such; to use Federn's term, it senses it as a content of "internal mentality." The quality and intensity of the object cathexis which has arisen from externalization of an ego state determines whether an ego then is longing for such a real object or tries to avoid it in fearful apprehension. When an ego with well-cathected boundaries externalizes the superego, temporarily or permanently, it does not experience hallucinations or delusons, but it will develop a quasi-phobic neurosis. In replacement of superego inhibition the phenomenon of psychic presence will become accentuated in him. Such a patient becomes cautious and anxious in dealing with other people who may criticize him; he will be preoccupied with fear of arousing disapproval in public; in brief, he will have an increased social anxiety. Such "phobic" patients can easily become paranoid with delusions and hallucinations if they use certain drugs, for instance, when they start smoking marijuana. These drugs produce these psychotic symptoms by altering the ego feeling chemically, by affecting displacements of ego cathexis and diminishing the cathexis supply at the ego boundaries. Upon recovery from such toxic effects, which may take some time, the ego usually loses its hallucinations and delusions. Likewise, paranoid persecutory psychoses are due not only to externalization of the superego, but, as we suppose, also to certain unknown hormonal deficiencies. The maintenance of normal cathexis strength in the various functional portions of the ego can well be due to specific hormones with which not all individuals are provided in the same measure. This would explain the individual differences in vulnerability to mental stress, overexertion, frustration, and traumatization.

Adequate consideration of all the implications of structural splits would require an exhaustive discussion of the paranoid psychoses. Here we can mention only the most important vicissitudes of superego externalization. In its neurotic form fear of being judged and criticized by other people may oscillate with feelings of guilt. Externalization of the superego may not have reached a state of stability. We also observe that the externalized superego may at times assume a positive attitude toward the subject. This is particularly clear in some forms of psychosis. For example, this is the case in delusions in which the patient believes himself to be especially chosen by God for some very important mission. One of the most important vicissitudes of superego externalization arises from a male ego's endeavor to appease a masculine superego by submitting itself to it as a woman. We saw this form of defense in our description of the negative oedipus complex. Such a defense is more readily found in psychotic egos because they can easily egotize the countersexual part in their bisexual disposition. In my opinion this may have been the dynamic mechanism of the homosexuality in Freud's Schreber Case.

We must now try to answer an important question: Why can the "persecuted introject" be externalized and internalized again so easily in manic-depressive psychoses, while superego externalization is more permanent? We usually expect a melancholic or a hypomanic phase to subside. When the hypomanic patient re-internalizes the "persecuted introject," he becomes melancholic again. Paranoid afflictions are known to be chronic ego states. In order to find an answer to our question we have to realize that the "persecuted introjects" are continuously fed by the id, since they become fused with one's own condemned drives. The superego, on the other hand, stems from the external world only, and once it has been externalized it has re-acquired its original form (parents and their substitutes) existing in external objects only. Since the drives from the id exert a continuous pressure to be egotized, so the externalized "persecuted introjects," which through ego passage have acquired demands of one's own instinctive drives, also exert a pressure to be egotized, that is, to be internalized again.

This chapter cannot be concluded without a brief summary of Freud's early concept of paranoia, which he presented in 1911 in the study of the famous Schreber case.[4] Freud published these "Notes" before his investigations were directed toward the dynamics and the functions of the ego. At that time he was interested mainly in the psychological understanding of the specific contents of delusions and hallucinations, in which he recognized a distorted "return of the repressed" as revealed in dreams and all neurotic symptoms. Psychoanalysis was at that time still only the psychology of the unconscious. But we now realize that the phenomena of hallucinations and delusions themselves cannot be explained by psychological interpretations of their specific contents. In Freud's opinion these phenomena were due to the patient's libidinous withdrawal from the objects of the external world and to an increase of narcissistic libido, i.e., of ego-libido. This narcissistic withdrawal would occur via homosexual tendencies, since the patient would love himself in a person of the same sex. Freud interpreted the delusional and hallucinatory contents of the patient as effects of the patient's efforts to deny his unconscious homosexual urges[5]: "In taking the view, then, that what lies at the core of the conflict in cases of paranoia among males is a homosexual wishful phantasy of loving a man, we shall certainly not forget that the confirmation of such an important hypothesis can only follow upon the investigation of a large number of instances of every variety of paranoid disorder. We must therefore be prepared, if need be, to limit our assertion to a single type of paranoia. Nevertheless, it is a remarkable fact that the familiar principal forms of paranoia can all be represented as contradictions of the single proposition: 'I (a man) love him (a man),' and indeed that they exhaust all the possible ways in which such contradictions could be formulated.

"The proposition 'I (a man) love him' is contradicted by:

"(a) Delusions of *persecution;* for they loudly assert:

" 'I do not *love* him—I *hate* him.'

"This contradiction, which must have run thus in the unconscious, cannot, however, become conscious to a paranoiac in this form. The mechanism of symptom-formation in paranoia requires that internal perceptions—feelings—shall be replaced by external perceptions. Consequently the proposition 'I hate him' becomes transformed by *projection* into another one: '*He hates* (persecutes) *me*, which will justify me in hating him.' And thus the impelling unconscious feeling makes its appearance as though it were the consequence of an external perception:

"'I do not *love* him—I *hate* him, because HE PERSECUTES ME.'

"Observation leaves room for no doubt that the persecutor is someone who was once loved.

"(b) Another element is chosen for contradiction in *erotomania*, which remains totally unintelligible on any other view:

"'I do not love *him*—I love *her*.'

"And in obedience to the same need for projection, the proposition is transformed into: 'I observe that *she* LOVES ME.'"

Since Freud's concept of paranoid afflictions, as just quoted, has not been modified I believe it is important to discuss it.

Federn, in his accurate investigations of psychotic patients, came later to different and in some respects opposite conclusions from those of Freud. Although this divergence from Freud's concept of the psychotic process was clearly expressed in the publications of his findings, Federn felt strongly constrained against taking a definite position, in his writings, toward Freud's ideas as expressed in his analysis of the Schreber case. Nevertheless some unpublished marginal notes of Federn's on this work of Freud's do reveal his dissension.[6]

As quoted above Freud stated: "The mechanism of symptom formation in paranoia requires that internal perceptions—feelings —shall be replaced by external perceptions." In his notes Federn comments on this point as follows: "This is no mechanism of symptom formation, but the consequence of reality attributed to thoughts. Therefore the association chain of thoughts is perceived as a chain of causes: My idea (of him), i.e., 'he makes me hate,' is sensed as 'he forces hate upon me,' 'he hates me.' A second way to conceive this delusional mechanism is: 'He does not love me' is felt as 'he hates me' because for a lover no love return is by contrast hatred. I observed in one case a third mechanism: To the beginning

paranoid patient his overt homosexuality is not welcomed. Therefore the object of the patient's own homosexuality is felt to be homosexual itself and to provoke in the patient homosexual feelings.
So, the patient's ego conceives the idea that the love object is persecuting him. Hatred is in this case the consequence, not the cause
of feelings of persecution." To the last sentence of Freud's quoted
above, Federn comments: "The mechanism is: 'She makes me think
of her, she introduces in me love thoughts, so she must love me.' "

A brief summary of the dissenting views may be inserted at this
point. In Freud's opinion the psychotic patient has an excess of ego
libido; the ego, having withdrawn libido from objects, regresses to
primary narcissism. Federn came to the opposite conclusion, as
stated in the preceding chapters. In his opinion the psychotic process is due to a decrease of ego cathexis (including ego libido), and
for this reason the ego's functions can no longer be dynamically
maintained. For economic necessity, then, cathexis is automatically
withdrawn from objects, because object cathexis can no longer be
afforded in great measure. Because of the need to economize
cathexis the ego also regresses, in a self-protecting attitude, to earlier, more economic ego stages. To Freud, delusions and hallucinations are attempts on the part of the ego to substitute an unreal
external world for the dwindling interest and contact with the real
external world; they are unsuccessful attempts at restitution.
Furthermore, the delusion of the paranoid patient that the world is
coming to an end corresponds (according to Freud) to the patient's awareness that the external world can no longer be cathected
by him. Federn, on the other hand, denies that hallucinations and
delusions correspond to unsuccessful attempts at restitution. He
holds them to be symptoms caused by a specific lesion of the ego,
loss of cathexis at its boundaries; he sees them as repressed contents reaching the ego's awareness as external realities (as false realities, to be sure), which are perceived by the ego with a feeling
of certainty that they actually exist. The ego's feeling that the world
is coming to an end stems from a projection onto the external world
of the sensation of its own dwindling. Freud himself, as a matter of
fact, also considers this mechanism. But Federn also considers the
feeling of derealization, caused by insufficiently cathected external
ego boundaries, as an important factor for the ensuing feeling of the

end of the world. In Freud's opinion the psychotic ego has delusions and hallucinations because the function which he called "reality testing" is broken down. To Federn, on the other hand, the psychotic patient does not feel any need to use reality testing, because he is certain that what he perceives in his delusions and hallucinations is real. Instead, the ego's "sense of reality," the main function of the ego's boundaries, is no longer dynamically maintained. The existence of the "sense of reality" as a sense of direct perception is not even acknowledged by psychoanalysts who ignore or disregard Federn's findings.

NOTES

(1) Weiss, op. cit., p. 474-475.

(2) Freud, Sigmund. On narcissism: An introduction (1914). Standard Edition, 14:67-102. London, Hogarth, 1957.

(3) Ibid., p. 96.

(4) Freud, Sigmund. Psychoanalytic notes on an autobiographical account of a case of paranoia (Dementia paranoides) (1911). Standard Edition, 12: 3-82. London, Hogarth, 1958.

(5) Ibid., p. 63.

(6) I am indebted to Paul Federn's son, Mr. Ernst Federn, for permission to publish these marginal notes found in his father's copy of Freud's Gesammelte Schriften.

Section V

Ego Defenses

XXXVI

The Concept of Ego Defenses

WE conceive the ego as a coherent experience unity, a unity which is continuous or re-established after interruption. The contents and states of the ego change continually. At times an ego state may consist merely in the feeling of the ego's own existence. Federn's description of the ego implies that it does not develop from the id nor from arising inner conflicts. Hartmann, as stated in Chapter XII, whose ego concept differs essentially from that of Federn in other respects, states explicitly that the id and the ego develop independently from a common matrix. Hartmann also introduced the term "conflict-free sphere" to indicate those ego-operations which unfold independent of any conflict. It is indeed erroneous to assume that the ego owes its existence to the necessity of settling internal conflicts.

The ego is a coherent unity but not in itself an integrated unity. Integration is the most important function of the ego, a function in which it may be more or less successful. The scope of the ego's integrative task comprises three territories: the id, the external reality, and the superego or, rather, the moral factors presented in the preceding section. One can understand the total *gestalt* of an ego through exploration of its strength and structure, exploration of the instinctive drives which are activated in the id and the ways the ego deals with them, and also through insight into its "moral type." All three of these mental territories develop both from constitutional dispositions and from the experiences which the ego has gone through since birth. The physiological stimulations (mainly hormonal) are directed by the concrete occasions which are offered the ego for the satisfactions of the ensuing drives and by its efforts to adapt itself to the conditions of the external world. The moral factors are shaped by the ego's emotional attachments to the persons of its surroundings, particularly to the parents, and by

the "way it was brought up." We learned that the ego's identifications with other persons play the most important role here.

In every psychotherapeutic orientation we must consider not only
the instinctive drives which the ego tries to ward off in its integrative efforts, but also the specific motivations which induce it to
ward them off and the methods it uses. If we frustrate an ego's defensive efforts, which are always performances of its integrative
function, we deprive it of necessary means of establishing integration. It is essential for every psychotherapy to produce in the patient's ego what we call a "structural change" which alone enables it
to integrate within its coherent unity the instinctive forces which are
keeping it in a traumatic state. The goal of every psychotherapy is
to detraumatize the ego.

Unskilled therapists may induce a worsening of the neurosis or
even bring about a psychotic breakdown in a weak ego by lifting
some repressed instincts in the patient before he becomes able to
integrate them into his ego structure. Usually a "workable" transference rapport of the patient with his therapist, together with the
therapist's proper attitude and reactions to the patient's emerging
instinctive urges which have been previously warded off, induces
in the patient an emotional re-orientation in his evaluations and
emotional attitudes toward his instincts. Fears and feelings of guilt
which the patient has acquired from his parents and other people
of his environment become modified by the therapist's attitude
when the patient finds in him a re-externalized parental figure. Alexander introduced the expression "corrective emotional experience"
for the therapeutically effective new experience of the patient in the
therapeutic situation. But every structural change takes time, depending on the depth and duration of the mental attitude which
has to be "corrected." Often the personality of a therapist cannot
compete with the parents as they were felt and evaluated by the
patient in his childhood. In any case the therapist must always try
to understand and evaluate properly the patient's "resistances"
to acceptance of tendencies previously warded off. In many cases
one must respect the ego's resistances in order not to disturb its integration.

From the very beginning of his new psychoanalytic procedure
Freud recognized that the patient manifested great resistance

against thoughts which could bring repressed instincts and wishes into his consciousness. This acknowledgment was the basis for development of psychodynamic concepts. A patient with a sufficiently strong ego maintains his resistance until his emotional insight into repressed mental contents can no longer disrupt his ego's integration. Such patients continue to resist rather than expose themselves to the danger of a breakdown. For this reason there was no great risk of severe breakdown in the great majority of patients when psychoanalysis adopted the rule of free association and the therapist's interpretation of the unconscious meanings of dreams and symptoms as well as of some transference manifestations. Nevertheless, some deep interpretations are sometimes followed by a transitory worsening of neurotic symptoms and anxiety states. Untimely interpretations often delay the psychoanalytic process by eliciting an increase of the patient's resistances. And in some cases, when the classic psychoanalytic method has been applied to weak, i.e., "psychosis-near," egos, this has precipitated a psychotic breakdown.

Federn has shown that not only single instincts and wishes undergo repression but also ego states. He found that patients who had had a psychotic episode could easily fall back into the previous psychotic state when they were induced to recall and to describe such a state retrospectively. Therefore he warned the psychiatrist against taking an anamnestic history with such a patient. A patient's repression of the memory of his feelings in a psychotic state is a necessary defense which must be respected. Likewise, the unconditional lifting of ego-alien drives into the ego is fraught with danger. In some cases it is necessary to "let sleeping dogs lie."

The author made a similar observation. There are some patients who have had in the past episodes of "criminal behavior" of varying duration, during which times they felt very uncomfortable and anxious. (This is a specific form of transitory ego weakness.) Later when such a patient enters psychoanalytic treatment he shows a strong conscious resistance to thinking retrospectively of the previous "criminal ego states." Even when the therapist succeeds in convincing such a patient that he is interested in these memories for therapeutic purposes, that his intention is only to help, and that he will never reveal what he may learn, the patient still feels very reluctant to speak about these past ego states and his behavior during them. We realize then that such patients are not afraid that the therapist may denounce or reject them; they simply cannot tolerate the memory of the criminal ego states which they have overcome.[1] In a proper mental-hygienic attitude toward a patient his recovered ego should not be identified [2] with a former sick ego state. And if the same attitude could be maintained in the patient's surroundings, he would be better protected against a relapse.

In the beginning Freud described only the phenomenon of repression as a defensive mechanism. Later he considered many other such mechanisms, and today we recognize a great number of such "ego defenses." Let us start now with the phenomenon of repression for our discussion of many basic issues concerning the "defensive activities of the ego" in general. Freud came to realize that resistance itself, which is an ego manifestation, is unconscious. In his opinion the ego is unconscious both of the repressed dynamic id contents and also of its own resistance which prevents them from entering the field of consciousness. Thus the task of the therapist is twofold: (1) to interpret the defensive unconscious actions of the ego, the specific forms of defense; and (2) to interpret the meaning of the repressed contents, of which the ego perceives only some derivatives in its symptoms and dreams. This was very lucidly described by Anna Freud in 1936.[3]

Let us compare the ways by which the ego defends itself against external dangers with the ways by which it defends itself against dangers threatening from the id. If we inadvertently touch a hot object, we withdraw our hand from it in a reflex-like manner. If we see a man or animal approaching us with aggressive intentions, we try to escape or defend ourselves. In all these cases the danger is consciously perceived, and our defenses are performed by proper muscular actions. But we cannot defend ourselves in the same manner against dangers which are threatening us from the id because the id is an inseparable and basic part of our own mind. We have learned under what conditions id impulses can be threatening to our ego. In Freud's description of mental functioning the ego alone normally has access to the outlets for discharging cathexis-tensions into feelings and emotions, as well as to the voluntary muscular apparatus. Thus the drives and wishes which reach a certain degree of intensity in the id seek entrance into consciousness (first into the preconscious ego) in order to reach an outlet for their tension into feelings and emotions and to gain access to muscular actions aimed at satisfactory goals. But some urges conflict with the demands of the superego, or for some other reason cannot be integrated into the coherent ego. Their acceptance would interfere with the ego's integrative efforts and thus cause states of anxiety. Therefore the entrance of such drives or traumatic memories constitutes a danger. As Anna Freud correctly stated, the ego senses in every instinct an enemy.

One important question now comes to mind: Does not every person occasionally experience conscious conflicts? We all know that we can master consciously many disturbing instinctive drives. Why can we not always defend ourselves merely by resisting their satisfaction? The ability to resist temptations was ascribed by Hartmann to the "relative autonomy" of the ego with regard to the id and the external world, as pointed out earlier. But such an "autonomy" has been implied in every ego concept, and it found a clear expression in Freud's formulation of the "pleasure and reality principles." We may add, however, that sometimes the ego feels disturbed in its self-esteem or feels guilty for merely harboring certain wishes and drives even though it has the capacity to control and withstand them. And why is it that the ego represses some instincts and wishes but is quite unable to do so in regard to other dynamic contents, as it is unable to choose at will its instincts and desires?

In Chapter IX it was pointed out that the exclusion of memories and instincts from consciousness, as a measure of defense, occurs first in childhood when the ego is not yet strong enough to control them. In this initial process, which Freud called "primal repression," the preconscious ego cathexis simply withdraws from "dangerous" mental contents or it does not invest them at all, because their very presence in the ego has unmasterable traumatic effects. Primal repression constitutes then the condition for all later repressions. The later repression is called "repression proper." As stated in the chapter mentioned, only such mental contents undergo repression proper as are either derivatives of or enter into associative connection with those contents which had undergone primal repression. In other words, repression proper is due to a pulling and a pushing force.

The repressed contents in the id exert a pulling action on their conscious derivatives, and simultaneously the resistance of the ego pushes these unwelcomed contents down into the unconscious id. Similarly, as Freud discovered, every adult neurosis has its roots in an infantile neurosis.

We come now to an important dynamic structural process which has not been dealt with before. How does an id content gain access into the ego? This process can best be described in Federn's terminology. We have said that an id content may be egotized, thus becoming a part of an ego state. But by what means does an id content force the ego to egotize it? In raising this very crucial question we think at once of the internal ego boundary which separates the id from the ego. For a better understanding of the nature of the pressure which id stimuli exert on the ego in order to be egotized, it is helpful to consider separately two factors in this process: (1) The ego protects itself from perceiving id stimuli as external realities. (2) It also captures and thus includes these stimuli within itself so that it can lead their tension to a discharge. In normal mental functioning both factors operate simultaneously.

We learned in Chapters XIV and XV that id contents which impinge from the "id-side" on the internal ego boundary with such a force as to reach the ego's awareness are perceived by it as external realities, as the contents of dreams and hallucinations are perceived. Therefore, the ego employs a certain amount of its cathexis to strengthen its internal boundary so that id stimuli are unable to enter it. In the state of sleep mental stimuli pass the weakened internal ego boundary, and so they are perceived by the dreaming ego as dream images, i.e., with the character of external reality. But in waking state the ego has to act on the reality; it could not survive if it remained unable to discriminate between "internal mentality" and "external reality." Acting as the sense organ for such a discrimination is the most important function of the ego boundaries, as we have seen. In the chapters mentioned we characterized the internal ego boundary as a dynamic windowless wall and the external ego boundary as a dynamic wall at the periphery, in which windows, the sense organs, are embedded. When unegotized contents reach the ego's awareness (regardless of whether they impinge on the ego boundaries from the external world or from the id) they are always perceived as external realities. We have reason to surmise that the infant hallucinates instead of remembering and thinking until his internal ego boundary has acquired sufficient strength.

The first act, namely, the dynamic blocking of id contents from awareness, does not yet solve the problem of how the tension of these contents can be discharged. If no discharge can take place, the pressure exerted by the id stimuli must steadily increase until they break through the internal ego boundary, thus frustrating the ego's efforts to keep its sense of reality functioning. No testing of reality can then prevent the ego from hallucinating. As we see, the ego's integrative function consists of defenses. The ego defends itself from the danger of hallucinating when it has to behave in an integrative manner. The defense against an increase of tension in id contents consists in egotization of these contents, in turning them into parts of ego states. As explained in Chapter X the coherent ego cathexis captures, as it were, id stimuli; it binds them, so that they no longer constitute external forces which can impinge on the id-side of the ego.

Very early in his investigations Freud called this binding process the "secondary mental process" which makes rational thinking possible according to concepts of space, time, and causality. He did not explain the process of egotization in the way it has been presented here, nor did he speak of ego boundaries; and he did not acknowledge a "sense of reality." In his description the preconscious cathexis binds the unconscious cathexis—which we call id cathexis —to the single representations, thus stopping the "primary mental process" which rules in the system ucs.—the id. We want to keep in mind what the two main functions of the internal ego boundary are, as we have described them. In normal functioning these two acts occur simultaneously. Through egotization of dynamically charged id contents the ego becomes enriched of ego states, and the ego feeling itself may obtain increased vigor, depending on the nature of the absorbed id cathexes.

Study of the integrative processes of the ego must necessarily include the exploration of its defenses, because defenses are the ego's means for integration. In primal repression only the first of the two "defensive" acts mentioned takes place. A mental content, be it a traumatic memory or a dangerous drive, is kept from the ego's awareness. This means that it does not enter the ego as an hallucinated content. Only the second act, its egotization, does not take place. This is a defensive inhibitory act. If such a content were egotized it would present the ego with a task too difficult to master. And Freud realized, we repeat, that later in life only those id contents undergo repression proper which are attracted by a nucleus in the id containing the primary-repressed contents. As far as the other unwelcome contents arising from the id are concerned, when they reach a certain degree of intensity their egotization occurs automatically and cannot be prevented. To protect its integration and to ward off dangers the ego must resort to other defense mechanisms which will be presented later in this section.

NOTES

(1) Here we shall consider only one particular form of "criminal neurosis," one with a specific psychodynamic structure. We cannot embark at this point on a discussion of the special therapeutic procedures which must be used in such cases and which cannot be applied to forms of "criminality" or "psychopathy" which are dynamically different.

(2) "Identified" is used here in the sense of "considered to be the same."

(3) Freud, Anna. The Ego and the Mechanisms of Defence (1936). London, Hogarth, 1937.

XXXVII

Unsuccessful Repression

WE learned that in Freud's concept the repressing and resisting activities of the ego are themselves unconscious. Yet, "unconsciousness" of repressed mental contents must be conceived in a different way from "unconsciousness" of these ego "activities." In order to clarify this issue let us return for a moment to Federn's view that the ego feeling is conscious in its whole extension. In his opinion only ego feeling is always conscious in waking life, and it extends itself as a coherent unity over the whole preconscious field. But while this feeling in waking state is continuously conscious, only a very small portion of the mental contents encompassed by it becomes conscious at any given time. The continuous change of contents of consciousness regards only the concrete data invested by ego feeling, not the ego feeling itself. It is precisely the investment of *all* preconscious data by the conscious ego feeling that makes integration possible and conveys to the ego the sensation of confidence in its behavior. The metapsychological basis of the ego feeling is the coherent ego cathexis. When some important preconscious knowledge temporarily falls out from the permanent ego feeling, the ego becomes uncertain and even panicky, even before it has to face an actual situation the handling of which requires that knowledge. A common experience of this kind is stage fright.

In the phenomenon of repression we must consider two circumstances: (1) In a defense against an external danger the ego perceives or understands the nature of the danger, while it is completely unconscious of the nature of danger threatening from the id. (2) The ego's repressing action, its failure to egotize a given content, occurs automatically and not by a conative act. Some muscular defenses also occur automatically. For example, if an object approaches too close to our eyes we shut them as a reflex action. In common language such an automatic movement is often called "unconscious," to indicate that a muscular action occurred without conscious or deliberate intention. Our muscular apparatus is the tool of defense against external dangers. The flexible ego cathexis, which can be shifted, withdrawn and condensed at certain points, is the tool of defense against id dangers. These two circumstances —that the ego is unconscious of mental contents which it does not invest, and that its resistance to invest them is an automatic manifestation—give us the impression that these ego "activities" are unconscious. But can we call these manifestations "activities" of the ego? The correct phenomenological statement of repression is "Repression of a content occurred" or "A content underwent repression," not "The ego repressed a content." It is difficult to establish whether the ego's resistances mentioned are really unconscious to the ego. What is certain is that the mental contents left behind in the id are unconscious. Some psychoanalysts have the incorrect idea that all defensive actions of the ego against the id occur without audible or visible signs. Actually such defensive attitudes can almost always be observed by modulations in the patient's gestures, speech, and posture. If the resistance becomes strengthened by reaction formations, then the ensuing reactive emotional state is very conscious to the ego, although it continues to ignore the existence, in the id, of the repressed instincts and thoughts.

When the impetus of repressed instincts reaches a certain degree of intensity, the ego faces a traumatic situation. But only in psychotic (weak) and dreaming egos can they force their way through the internal boundary to the ego's awareness. Then the ego perceives them as external realities; it hallucinates or has delusions. A waking ego which has a strongly cathected internal boundary resists the impact of repressed dynamic contents, so that it does not become aware of them. The discharge of the dynamic tension in the id must find other forms of outlet without interfering with the sense of reality. A neurosis is the effect of such deviously discharged processes together with the ego's efforts to check them and also its reactions to them. But not only an unsuccessful repression, which is responsible for "the return of the repressed" in a disguised form as revealed in neurotic symptoms and dreams, but also all other kinds of defense mechanisms may fail in their purpose, thus giving rise to special kinds of neuroses, each presenting a different clinical picture due to the repressed contents and the mode of defense.

It is not my intention to present in this volume a systematic study of the neuroses. Neurotic symptoms are mentioned here only to illustrate some operational modes of the mind. I wish now to explain the dynamic implications of repression, which can be demonstrated best through the phenomena of hysterical conversion symptoms and phobias. In our urban culture severe hysterical conversion symptoms and particularly hysterical spells have become increasingly less frequent, although every experienced psychiatrist still meets them occasionally. Phobias, however, are at least as frequent as at the time when Freud published his first studies on this subject. Yet, the character and the kinds of phobias are also subject to continuous changes, and some kinds of phobias are more frequent in one country, others in another.

For a better understanding of conversion symptoms let us consider for a moment the typical expressions of affects and emotions. As stated previously, feelings, affects, and emotions ensue from processes of discharging nervous tension (cathexis) into vasomotor, vasosecretory and visceral phenomena. Their end-effects are perceived by the ego in various combinations of heartbeat, changes in the respiratory function, in skin sensations produced by blushing, paling, sweating, in trembling, in visceral phenomena, etc. The combination of such phenomena is typical for each kind of emotion, for joy, sorrow, fear, terror, elation, anger, and so on. The ego is unable to control these processes at will, while it can control voluntary muscular actions. No "autonomy" of the ego exists in respect to affects and emotions. More visible and audible expressions of emotions are laughing, crying, screaming, and certain muscular actions which, as expressions of emotions, are not aimed at altering the conditions of the external world. But emotions such as fear, anger, love, etc., can lead as powerful incentives to actions toward objects of the external world. The emotional expressions are typical for each kind of emotion in every individual, so that everyone recognizes —"perceives"—the emotional states of his fellow beings from their visible and audible expressions. Charles Darwin published his *Expression of the Emotions* in 1872, but the psychological meaning of the various emotional expressions is even now not fully understood.

As mentioned previously, Freud tried to explain the concomitant physical phenomena of fear and anxiety through the "repetition compulsion" of the traumatic experience of birth and compared them with hysterical conversion symptoms. If we accept Freud's derivation of these manifestations, we may consider them as a kind of language—as a somatic language, however. Their translation in words would be: "I find myself again in a situation analogous to that of my birth: I am overwhelmed by stimuli beyond my mastery capacity." Birth was the first situation of the kind. As a matter of fact, laughter also can be conceived as a somatic language and translated: "I am joyfully or pleasurably discharging (or getting rid of) a state of tension. Something suddenly brought me relief of a tension." Freud did not formulate the expression of laughter exactly in these terms, but in his classic work, *Wit and its Relation to the Unconscious*,[1] he arrived at this economic concept of laughter in the analysis of the hilarious state of mind. When, for example, a joke unexpectingly evokes in the listener some otherwise repressed emotional content or some effect of the primary mental process before the listener's countercathexis has time to check it, this cathexis becomes then superfluous and together with the cathexis of the previously repressed content is pleasurably discharged, as a relief, in the phenomenon of laughter. But we do not yet understand the features which are characteristic of laughter or other emotional expressions. In common language one calls hysterical any loud, uncontrolled, or excessive emotional manifestation of any kind, particularly of grief or anxiety. But in psychiatric terminology conversion symptoms are those hysterical manifestations which are physical expressions of mental contents; they are unique in every single patient, perhaps with the exception of certain hysterical spells which will be mentioned soon. The meaning of hysterical conversion symptoms cannot be readily understood. These symptoms may not impress other people as expressions of mental phenomena at all but as mere physical symptoms. Only through the analysis of every single case can the psychological meaning of conversion manifestations be understood.

No organic pathology can be found in conversion symptoms, which are usually designated as functional disturbances. Yet the patient himself feels them as manifestations of an organic disease.

They may consist in a paralysis of a limb, or of both legs, of vomiting, the swelling of an organ, or of pains in various parts of the body, of blindness or deafness, the loss of tactile and/or pain sensations, in brief, every kind of physical impairment. In some cases somatic manifestations of such symptoms are of a kind which could not be produced by voluntary actions, such as reddening or swelling of a limb, or even bleeding. Hysterical spells, which are now rather rare among inhabitants of urban areas, may also appear in a great variety of forms. Usually they are pantomimic expressions unintelligible to the onlookers, seemingly senseless and bizarre, as for instance jerking or clonic muscular contractions. But sometimes they appear as meaningful performances, such as coitus movements or, in a woman, the act of giving birth to a child. These spells appear mostly with diminution or complete absence of consciousness. Typical for some hysterical seizures is the *arc de cercle:* The patient, lying supine and supporting his body on his heels and head, lifts himself in a spasmodic convulsion in the shape of an elevated bridge. This position is called in neurologic terminology "epistotonus." At times the seizures are preceded by restlessness or other premonitory sensations. The patient very seldom injures himself during the spell, and upon return to consciousness he feels relieved.

All these hysterical phenomena are called conversion symptoms because they represent repressed instinctive pressures and unconscious conflicts, mostly related to specific memories, which have become "converted" from mental into organic manifestations. But the patient ignores the meaning of his somatic language. In disguised form unconscious dynamic contents have broken through into bodily expressions. The disguise is due to the primary mental process, as we shall illustrate soon. This kind of discharge of pent-up libidinous and aggressive tensions does not interfere, however, with the ego's integrative function. Its thinking, sense of reality, etc., are not impaired, and the patient does not feel at all that his symptoms are related to his mind; thus he denies the existence of the instincts and conflicts which are expressed in his bodily language. The discharge of id tensions, together with defensive efforts through conversion symptoms, makes the employment of the repressing countercathexes superfluous, and so the patient is usually spared anxiety. The dynamic drainage of increased tensions forestalls the sensation of an impending inner danger which would cause anxiety. This emotional calmness of patients who suffer from conversion symptoms was called by Charcot *"la belle indifference des hysteriques,"* as Freud mentioned. Yet in some cases the dynamic tension inherent in the neurotic conflicts cannot be fully discharged by conversion symptoms. Then the residual still-excessive cathexis is felt by the patient as a danger. This is the reason a conversion symptom *may* provoke anxiety; in other words, there are cases in which conversion symptoms are combined with phobic mechanisms.

Often a conversion symptom is precipitated by an emotional event. A thirteen-year-old girl developed an hysterical paralysis of both legs following an ear operation. When she was taken into the operating room she rebelled strongly against the surgical intervention and began to kick the nurses who approached her. Eventually she was overpowered and put under anesthesia. After the successful operation she could no longer move her legs; it was as though she had to persist in the helpless position into which she had been forced. After several months a marked muscular atrophy of the legs developed as a result of complete inactivity. One may see in this hysterical paralysis an expression of spite or retaliation for the subjugation the patient had suffered as well as a reproach to her parents who were responsible for it and had failed to prepare her in advance for the operation. Since they had caused her to be reduced to impotence, she remained that way, forcing them to take care of her. This is certainly a masochistic form of revenge. But she knew nothing of the motivations of her affliction; she only felt physically incapacitated.

This writer was consulted about the case at this stage. Data obtained in the first three sessions revealed the unconscious conflicts which had found expression in the paralysis of her legs. She was the only daughter of very restrictive and religious parents; she had two older brothers who enjoyed greater privileges and freedom than she. As a small child she had reacted with feelings of rebellion against this "injustice." On the other hand, she felt that her father was emotionally more attached to her than to her brothers. Her urge for masculine competition conflicted with her tender feminine feelings toward him. Unable to face this conflict, she was afraid to grow up, and in addition her feminine claims on her father involved her in an unbearable oedipal conflict. Through an infantile attachment to her parents, by remaining or becoming again a helpless child, she could avoid the unsolvable emotional situation.

This regression to an earlier age was due to her longing for the affective gratification which she had actually enjoyed as a beloved child free from sense of responsibility. But her unconscious wish to be a baby who could not walk was only one of the determining causes for her paralysis. Prior to this regression (which in itself was a defensive measure) she desired to go out as freely as her brothers did. In fact, in her conscious daydreams she imagined experiencing all sorts of romantic adventures. And so, her inability to walk was also a guilt reaction to her love fantasies. Thus the "masochistic revenge" was determined also by a self-punitive attitude. Behind the heroes of her fantasy appeared the rejuvenated (as effect of ego passage) image of her father. The patient, of course, had no suspicion of this.

The shocking experience of being forced to undergo the operation intimidated her severely and was felt unconsciously as a punishment; it also made her recognize how powerful parental figures could be. On the occasion of the operation she could resort only to kicking both as a defense (against external danger) and as a rebellion against impositions and frustrations imposed on her by authoritative figures. Her legs, used as an aggressive organ, were finally immobilized by the nurses; thus, her conversion symptom also expressed this extremely traumatic experience.

We see that many expressions appeared condensed in one symptom, the paralysis of the legs. It expressed the patient's inhibition in use of her freedom of movement for forbidden purposes related to the oedipus complex. We observe that this inhibition does not represent an id impulse but a controlling attitude of the ego. This inhibition, as well as the renunciation of masculine competition with her brothers, is a manifestation of that repressed ego state which had to cope with these two tendencies. Accordingly, conversion symptoms express not only id impulses but also attitudes of repressed ego states. Although this has not been formulated in these terms before, the expression of both id and ego participation in the symptom was implicit in Freud's interpretation of conversion symtoms. Furthermore, the patient's paralysis expressed her acceptance of the passive role forced upon her—together, however, with spiteful revenge against her parents (passive resistance). It also showed the unconscious wish to regress to early infancy, to a stage in which, unable to walk, she was free from responsibility. And dynamically it also denoted the fixation to a traumatic situation which, however, would not have materialized if it had not been enhanced by the tendencies mentioned.

The patient was very pleased to tell the analyst about herself and her problems and was happy that someone—a man, a father-figure—spent much time and patience listening to her with sympathy and understanding. In her transference feelings she involved the person of the analyst in her revived fantasies of the kind described above. Hysterical patients react very promptly to transference feelings and may lose their symptoms transitorily, long before they are really cured through an opportune structural change. And so after three sessions this patient who had been paralyzed for six months suddenly could move her legs. She jumped from the couch unaware that her legs could not support her because of the muscle atrophy which had developed meanwhile. Her feeling of having regained complete physical efficiency was in disagreement with her actual physical condition. Although no longer paralyzed, she required support to walk until through exercise she had regained her full muscular strength.

In order to understand the meaning of most conversion symptoms we must consider the primary mental process presented in Chapter X. The id (ucs.) cathexis, unchecked by ego (pcs.) cathexis, finds itself in a free-floating state. The cathexis of one representation runs along associative connections to other representations, which thus become cathected. Moreover, more than one representation, pertaining to different drives, can be aroused simultaneously, giving rise to a combined representation. Or, the cathexes of two or more representations can be condensed into one single representation which is then aroused to great intensity. Accordingly, a conflictual or traumatic situation may appear as a conversion symptom in the reproduction of a past physical condition which the patient had experienced incidentally at the earlier time when he had originally to deal with that situation. A girl patient, for example, who became sick with whooping cough at a time when she

had engaged in sexual play with a boy, later had hysterical cough-
ing attacks when her repressed sexual wishes became aroused.
Self-punitive tendencies, imposed by the superego or due to resonance identification, are likewise sometimes expressed in conversion
symptoms. Identification with another person often expresses the
wish to enjoy some experience of that person. A girl who suffered
from severe backache identified herself with her mother who had
a painful back injury due to an accident sometime in the past.
The meaning of this hysterical identification was related to an oedipal situation and could be expressed in these words: "If you wish
to replace your mother, then replace her completely and take her
suffering also." Unconscious wishes for pregnancy are often expressed by vomiting spells, sometimes by cessation of menstruation
and even by swelling of the abdomen. Most cases of pseudo-
pregnancy are conversion symptoms. Infantile misconceptions of
sexuality and of the act of birth, frequently on a pregenital level,
also appear expressed in conversion symptoms. Even though the
adult patient knows consciously how the sexual act is actually performed and how children are born, the repressed fantasy in the id
has not been modified by the later-acquired knowledge. A girl in
her teens suffered from excessive salivation, and the analysis revealed that this symptom was related to her infantile concept of the
act of impregnation. She imagined that her father had to urinate in
her mother's mouth in order to impregnate her. Her hypersalivation
reproduced the father's urine. Through displacement the genitalia
can be substituted by any other organ of the body: the penis by a
limb, nose, head and even the heart; the vagina by the mouth, ear
or other orifices. Sexual excitement, as well as sexual inhibitions,
can find expression in functional diseases of any part of the body.

Hysterical spells are explosive discharging processes of sexual or
other related tensions. In Freud's opinion the loss of consciousness
during these spells reproduces the state of unconsciousness which
occurs at the height of sexual orgasm. In my opinion it may represent also a defense against recognizing the breaking through of repressed contents, in form of an uncontrollable crisis, no matter how
disguised they may be. As mentioned, an hysterical spell may express both the id impulse and the opposing ego reaction. During

an hysterical spell one of Freud's patients tried to disrobe with one hand and keep her clothes on with the other hand. In this way she identified herself with a man who tried to rape her, and at the same time she tried to defend herself from the sexual attack. Freud explained the *arc de cercle,* which is a typical hysterical spell, as a combination of the feminine supine position during intercourse and her resistance against submitting to it. This writer also found another interpretation of this spell.[2] A female patient of mine dreamed that she had such an attack. In the course of it she pressed out from her clitoris a full-sized penis. The whole convex part of her supine body was felt by her as a concomitant effort to protrude this penis. Thus the *arc de cercle* expressed her desire to possess a masculine organ.

We have seen that in conversion symptoms pent-up tensions force their outlet into physical phenomena. In a certain way these phenomena can be compared with discharging processes which, in their end-effects, are sensed as affects and emotions which are automatic ego functions. Conversion phenomena, and hysterical seizures in particular, bring relief to the individual as the discharge of cathexis into affects and emotions does. One affect or emotion, however, has a special position in mental economy; this is anxiety. It has often been stated that anxiety is a reaction of the ego to a threat of a traumatic condition, i.e., to the threat of an afflux of excitation greater than the ego can handle. The "anxiety signal" enhances the ego's defensive efforts; but in a state of panic or terror too much ego cathexis is employed for binding and isolating the excess of excitation, with the result that the ego remains paralyzed and thus overwhelmed by unrestrainable destructive stimulation. As mentioned, conversion symptoms usually provide a sufficient outlet of inner tension, so that the sensation of threat from a traumatic condition is avoided and thus no anxiety is experienced. Thus Charcot's phrase *"la belle indifférence des hysteriques"* referred to the absence of anxiety and preoccupation on the part of the patient and not to other kinds of affects and emotions which may be concomitant of conversion symptoms. But, we repeat, when conversion symptoms cannot take care of surplus tensions completely, then anxiety develops and is usually related to the conversion symptoms themselves. The failure of repression is then manifested not only in the somatic functional impairment of the individual but also in the arousal of anxiety.

NOTES

(1) Freud, Sigmund. Wit and its Relation to the Unconscious (1905). New York, Moffat Yard, 1917.

(2) Weiss, Edoardo. A contribution to the psychological explanation of the *arc de cercle*. Int. J. Psychoanal., 6:323, 1925.

XXXVIII

Defense Failure in Phobias

PRESSURE from repressed instincts and ego states which does not find outlet (or only insufficient outlet) in conversion symptoms is felt by the ego as a danger. Against such danger the ego first tries to avoid situations which could arouse or enhance the repressed urges. For example, a patient who has repressed strong exhibitionistic tendencies will avoid people whose presence might arouse in him the temptation to indulge in exhibitionistic acts. In this way the defense against an id impulse becomes combined with a defensive measure against certain external situations. The patient behaves as if the source of anxiety were a specific external situation alone and not an inner repressed urge, although he cannot give a rational explanation for his fear. An analogous defensive mechanism was found by Freud and many of his followers in the "street phobia" of some women. These women have repressed strong prostitution fantasies. They fear the street because walking there would stimulate their unconscious temptation to approach men or be approached by them. This writer found that such a repressed tendency plays only a secondary role in some cases of street phobia or agoraphobia. As will be pointed out soon, we find in psychoanalytic literature very inadequate psychological interpretations of this very important and rather frequent phobia both in men and women of our urban population. But before embarking on the dynamic formulation of this phobia, which appears in many varieties, let us consider briefly phobic fear of external objects as another result of failure of repression.

In his classic analysis of the phobia of a five-year-old boy (the famous case of "Little Hans") Freud found that the patient's fear of horses was related to his repressed fear of his father to whom he was strongly attached in love and fear.[1] Unconsciously he feared "castration" by his father for his incestuous oedipal wishes, and also he developed hostile aggressive tendencies against his father. All these tendencies were repressed, so that his overt conscious feelings toward his father did not show abnormal features. But the repressed drive representatives underwent the primary mental process, and through archaic inherited paths the representation of the father was substituted by that of an animal, in this case of a horse. The feared horse represented not only his father but also the boy's own aggressive impulses against him. This substitutive representation was far enough from the repressed drive representatives, so that it could not be recognized by the boy's ego as having anything to do with his father. His strong ambivalent tendencies toward him remained repressed, and instead, the representation of a horse as an object of great interest and fear became conscious to him. This is the way "the repressed returned." In our terminology we would say that the substitutive representation became egotized so that the pressure of the repressed drives could find an emotional outlet, in the horse phobia. The patient did not locate the actual source of danger correctly, i.e., in the pressure of pent-up libidinous and aggressive cathexes, but he felt threatened from an object of the external world. He became very much interested in horses (and in their penises) yet he feared and tried to avoid them. We could say that fear of an id danger was "converted" into fear of an external danger, but the term "conversion" is reserved in psychoanalysis for the somatic symptoms previously presented. Through this projection of an inner (id) danger into an external danger the ego tries to defend itself from a threat. The situation thus established seems to offer the patient an adequate defense against anxiety. But he has to pay a price for it in some restriction of his freedom; he feels safe only as long as he can avoid horses. And this secondary defense is efficient only to a certain extent. The patient experiences anxiety when he sees a horse, but the internal drive pressure cannot be eliminated by avoiding horses. Anxiety increases not only when he contacts the object of fear, but also when the repressed instinctive demands become activated from biological sources. Therefore, the initial attempt to avoid the object becomes more and more inadequate, and the patient becomes increasingly more cautious in his avoidance. In other words, the patient's freedom of movement and action is continually more restricted.

We have seen in this example of the phobic phenomenon another vicissitude of repression which fails. The countercathexis employed in the repressive efforts induced the boy to avoid horses. This is a dynamic operation of that countercathexis which is used to maintain the repression. The resistance against repressed contents appears now in the conscious phobia, aimed at conscious avoidance of the phobically feared object.

The metapsychological difference between conversion hysteria and anxiety hysteria (phobia) is evident. To the extent to which a conversion symptom provides an outlet for the pressure of repressed id contents, no further employment of countercathexis is necessary and no anxiety develops. From my own observation this is particularly true in those cases in which the conversion symptom gives satisfaction to the id impulse and little expression to the ego's reluctance against it.

In all cases of phobia the anxiety is related to an internal danger arising from unconscious conflicts. But in the type of phobias described above the drive danger appears projected onto an external object or situation. The feared object is related not only to specific repressed drives but also to possible painful consequences of their satisfaction. Furthermore, the phobically feared object is so "chosen" as to lend itself to a rationalization of the fear. A phobic child fears dogs, because dogs can actually bite. In this phobia oral-aggressive tendencies of the child are revealed. A phobic patient may be afraid to ride in a train because there could be a wreck. In this case a sadistic concept of intercourse is expressed, as it is in the phobia of being run over by a car. Certainly self-destructive tendencies play an important role in such cases, as in a patient's phobic fear of lightning which can actually strike. In the latter case analysis detects in the patient a severe fear and expectation of punishment for forbidden wishes. This type of phobia, in which a patient has exaggerated fear of an actual and possible external danger, I have called "projection phobia."

There is another type of phobia, in my opinion clearly distinguished from projection phobia, in which the danger is felt consciously as internal, mental, although the patient is unaware of the actual nature of the danger. In some cases of this second type the internal danger, sensed as such, is provoked by specific external conditions. For example, a patient who suffers from "acrophobia" (fear of high places) fears his own sensations of dizziness, at times accompanied by a panic-arousing obsessional impulse to throw himself into the abyss. In "erythrophobia" (fear of blushing) he fears other people only indirectly. He is not afraid of being harmed by them. His own internal automatic reaction is the danger of which he is conscious, i.e., that shocklike attack of blushing which occurs when he meets certain situations in the presence of other people. But it is not our purpose to embark here upon interpretation of these two phobias. They are mentioned only to illustrate the distinction between two types of phobias, the projection phobias and those related to frightening ego states.[2] The failure of repression manifested in this second group is metapsychologically different from that of the projection phobias. This will be made clear in the following discussion of "street phobia," commonly designated by the inclusive term "agoraphobia," which this writer has studied in some detail.[3]

First let us repeat briefly the different consequences, in conversion hysteria and in projection phobia, of excessive pressure derived from unsuccessfully repressed contents. We understand that the internal ego boundary of weak and dreaming egos cannot resist the impact of such pressure, which comes to the ego's awareness in form of hallucinations and delusions, since the sense of reality is not functioning in these egos. But in the two psychoneuroses mentioned the internal ego boundary does resist this pressure. In conversion hysteria the pent-up cathexes find outlet in functional somatic symptoms. In projection phobia these cathexes flow along associative paths in the id (primary mental process) to substitutive representations which the ego cannot recognize in their true nature and so can egotize. This process leads to projection phobia just presented.[4] Often the first anxiety attack is not yet bound to an object but constitutes simply a warning signal that the ego could be overwhelmed by an unmasterable tension. The development of the phobia is already an *organized defense measure*.

Likewise, in the group called "agoraphobia"[5] the first anxiety attack is not always, though frequently, immediately related to leaving a secure place of protection. This anxiety is the ego's reaction both to strongly cathected but repressed sexual drives, which

seek immediate emotional relief, and also to the invincible obstruction to their outlet. As mentioned, the obstructing countercathexis,
which is ego cathexis, operates automatically in the process of repression. The ego is unaware of the repressed contents, but in this
clinical picture it suddenly feels that a proper discharge of an inner
tension of unknown nature is blocked. In other words, not only
the impact of repressed contents but also the repression itself is
sensed as a source of danger. The ego feels functionally or dynamically mutilated. We come thus to the realization that the automatically operating repression can be felt by the ego as a mentally mutilating phenomenon.

For a better understanding of the behavior of agoraphobic patients let us compare it with that of persons who require help from
others because of some actual handicap, physical or mental, transitory or lasting. Such persons avoid the possibility of being cut off
from immediate assistance in case of emergency. People who suffer
from memory disturbances, fainting spells, states of weakness of any
kind, exhaustion, deep depressions, disorientation, etc., behave in
a way similar to that of the agoraphobic patients. The former seem
well-justified in fearing situations in which they might have to
move and act alone without immediate assistance, but to outsiders
there is no such justification in cases of agoraphobia. Yet their inner
experience places them in the same category as those more-appar-
ently handicapped. An ego must feel efficient in its mental functioning, without need of assistance whenever it has to go some distance
alone. The agoraphobic patient has lost this feeling. Too much
countercathexis is employed in repressive processes, so that too
little is left for the maintenance of a reliable ego feeling; besides,
the ego is deprived also of drive cathexis which cannot be egotized
and thus cannot be emotionally utilized. Whenever a drive is excited in the id the ego is automatically alerted to it, and when it cannot "capture" that drive it has a sensation of emotional incomplete-
ness. The economic impairment of the ego feeling, due both to the
excessive employment of repressing countercathexis and to resulting
impoverishment of egotized drive cathexis, causes not only anxiety
but often various kinds of ego disturbances also which in themselves are frightening.

The patient cannot define his frightening ego experiences prop-

344 STRUCTURE AND DYNAMICS OF THE HUMAN MIND

erly, as a rule, and many share the feeling of derealization of the external world and depersonalization. One patient may say that he feels he is going to faint, another that he is losing his memory or orientation or even losing his mind, a third that he is dizzy. Disturbances in bodily feeling may also cause severe anxiety. One patient said that when he proceeded beyond a certain distance his ego faded away progressively. Others describe the ego disturbance as the sensation of an invisible barrier before them which prevents them from proceeding further. Still others have a disagreeable feeling when walking, as though they were on the edge of a precipice. Some indicate that they cannot tell where they themselves end and the external world begins; the blurring of the ego boundaries cannot be expressed more exactly. Such patients feel lost in space and powerless to master the outer world or to control themselves. Everything has lost its shape, and orientation is gone. The picture is sometimes complicated by the appearance of most unpleasant obsessional impulses.

Psychoanalysis of individual agoraphobic patients has revealed that each different kind of disturbance of ego feeling expresses different repressed instinctive drives which seek an outlet. The ego disturbances described may be present in a variety of clinical pictures, besides those of agoraphobia or street phobia. Patients may experience these disturbances when they are at home, even at night in bed. They are, however, typical for neurotic anxiety connected with being alone and/or leaving a fixed point of security. The patient feels that he is venturing into strange unreliable regions.

We are not interested here in the manifold repressed libidinous and aggressive drives of agoraphobic patients which exert a strong pressure toward emotional discharge. This clinical picture is presented here in some detail only to illustrate other complicated consequences of failure of repression, different from those described in conversion hysteria and projection phobia.

Clear understanding of the metapsychological conditions of agoraphobia requires the consideration of five basic points:

(1) The onset situation of this psychoneurosis and the ego disturbances which usually accompany or arouse anxiety. These disturbances are also encountered in other psychoneurotic af-

flictions and even in schizophrenia.

(2) A strong conscious emotional need, be it a strong sexual desire or merely a strong "platonic love" with exclusion of sexuality, but a need coupled with an unbearable internal obstruction to its emotional outlet.

(3) Regression to infantile dependency needs as the consequence of this obstruction which is often felt as a dynamic or emotional mutilation.

(4) The patient's tremendous struggle to rid himself of the obstructing countercathexis which is manifested in various kinds of substitutive urges.

(5) Immediate disappearance of anxiety and the re-establishment of the sensation of emotional entireness as soon as "the gates to emotional discharge" become unblocked. The latter condition is most apparent in the patient's acquired ability to reach full physical and emotional conflictless orgasm.

Seldom is the discharge of aggressive drives blocked in agoraphobia. The irresistible need of the patient to free himself from the clogging and stifling countercathexis is the most interesting phenomenon in the process. We are accustomed to consider the ego's repressing and resisting "activity" only in respect to disturbing objectionable id drives. We learn now that the ego may feel very uneasy about and intolerant of an automatically occurring occlusion of emotional outlet for id drives. This automatic obstruction is itself, as often mentioned, an ego function and is maintained by (ego-)countercathexis. But the ego's reluctance to accept this obstruction—repression—does not remove it. How paradoxical this dynamic situation is can be understood when we realize that the ego would react with a tremendous conflict and integrative anxiety-arousing difficulties if this repression were lifted. To remove the obstruction would be to go from frying pan to fire. The repressed contents are always related to the oedipus complex, even when they have been elaborated into various forms of sexual deviations. We know, in fact, that repression has the function of protecting the ego from these difficulties. Untimely interpretation to the patient of his anxiety-producing repressed contents increases his anxiety. He ignores the nature of the repressed contents; they are not egotized.

Yet, the obstruction itself, and only the obstruction to their access to the ego, is very strongly sensed. This condition helps us to understand more clearly the phenomenon of repression in its actual nature and seems to confirm Federn's view that only the repressed content and not the resistance itself is unconscious, although the latter occurs automatically.

Let us examine now more closely the five basic points to be considered in the metapsychology of agoraphobia.

(1.) If agoraphobia begins suddenly with an unexpected anxiety attack (which is the most frequent onset) analysis will always reveal that a strong repressed drive, usually sexual, was stimulated in that situation. A robust, twenty-three-year-old man had his first severe anxiety attack while attending the opera *Tristan und Isolde,* during the love scene in the second act. From that time on he was afraid to leave his home. When he came into treatment, fortunately only six months after the onset, he revealed to the analyst that he had always been afraid to approach a girl sexually. He had the feeling that intercourse would be followed by death. Analysis revealed that he connected his father's death, when the patient was six years old, with his father's intimate relation with his mother. He must have witnessed the primal scene. When he was five years old he used to play circus (theatre) with other children, and on one occasion he became interested in the genitalia of a girl of his age. Hiding together in a basement they stimulated each other genitally until their strong sexual tension was relieved by uncontrolled urination. Eventually they were discovered and punished, and he was not allowed to see this girl again. The love scene of the opera had reawakened in the mature young man a strong sexual urge together with imagined evil consequences of its satisfaction. It was not only the strongly cathected drive which aroused his anxiety but also the automatic, reflex-like blockage (repression) of any possible emotional outlet of this drive. On the one hand, removal of the automatically operating inhibiting countercathexis—if it could have been possible—would have exposed him to the imagined danger caused by the drive satisfaction, i.e., punishment, death, castration, etc.; on the other hand, maintaining this countercathexis exposed him to the danger of the ever-increasing drive tension itself. He was really trapped. His dynamic maladjustment had robbed him of the feeling of ego efficiency. Such economic impairment induces an ego to take compensatory measures, among which the fear of expanding its extension (boundaries) and the instinctive urge to narrow its extension plays the most important role. Such an ego withdraws "into a corner," as it were; it shuns leaving home. Besides, to walk in the streets, where he might meet attractive women, would enhance his unbearable conflict.

This illustrative case had an exceptional, almost-unique, outcome. Six months after treatment began the patient did dare to become close to a girl, and he was able to engage in sexual intercourse with an extremely successful orgastic experience—the first in his life. Immediately thereafter he felt completely free from anxiety and took great pleasure in walking in crowds on the street. Most agoraphobic patients, however, have such complex and deeply repressed drives that many years of treatment are required before they can improve, and some inveterate cases defy all psychotherapeutic efforts.

An agoraphobic woman had her first anxiety attack while she was looking forward with intense desire to her honeymoon. She and her husband were planning to take the same trip which her parents had taken on their honeymoon. She loved her father very much. This first anxiety attack, in this situation of anticipation of sexual experience with her husband, became organized in agoraphobia. In her marital life she was completely frigid, unable to conceive any outlet for her strong desire.

But not in all cases of agoraphobia can the first anxiety attack be immediately recognized as having such nature. An acute onset may occur during a trip, during a social entertainment, at night after a dream, and in many other situations. After a relatively short psychoanalytic exploration, however, one can always find that the decisive factor for the anxiety attack was the arousal of a strong but repressed sexual striving. When the first anxiety attack has occurred at a time when the patient was trying to emancipate himself from parental restrictions, one detects that the most important motivation for such an emancipation was his wish to engage in an intense love relationship, either a sexual relationship or non-sexual platonic one.

(2.) We may ask why all impotent men and frigid women do not become agoraphobic, and on the other hand, why some agoraphobic patients do experience sexual orgasm. One observation may give a partial answer. Not all impotent men and frigid women have a strong need for love, but all agoraphobic patients do have a strong conscious longing for love, though of various kinds. Some may feel a strong sexual striving, always goal-inhibited; others may crave only an ideal, "pure," platonic love, but equally intense. When, without the slightest sexual desire, a woman falls deeply in love with a man and then becomes agoraphobic, we may say that sublimation of her sexuality, which is another "defense mechanism," did not succeed in absorbing all the sexual tension aroused. And in all cases in which the patient does experience sexual orgasm we make two observations: (a) That these patients feel freer, or without any anxiety, during the time when they can have physical and emotional orgastic outlet for their sexual needs; and (b) that they experience more severe anxiety when the orgastic outlet is blocked. Their anxiety does not result from external circumstances depriving them of sexual satisfaction but from the internal blockage caused by repression.

(3.) Often agoraphobia seems to be merely fear of separation from the mother. But on close examination one finds that the patient's dependent attachment to a mother-figure is itself a defense, namely, a regression from a more mature but blocked drive to an earlier libidinous position. Such a regression is an automatic attempt to channel the blocked drive tension back to more acceptable emotional outlets. The dependent attachment to a loving and protecting parental figure can, in fact, absorb some of the pent-up drive cathexis.

An eighteen-year-old girl who felt very emancipated fell deeply in love with a young man. Her love was of highly platonic nature; the mere thought of sexual contact with him would contaminate her "pure" idealistic feelings for him. When she learned that he did not reciprocate her passion she reacted with deep depression and could hardly endure the realization that she had been rejected by him.

A short time thereafter she had to take a final examination for her teaching diploma. On the morning of the examination her mother said that she wished to walk with her to the school building. The patient reacted with mixed feelings: On the one hand she wanted to feel free and emancipated; on the other hand she was gratified by her mother's expression of love and sympathy. They walked together until they were a short distance from the school; then her mother said goodbye because she wanted to go to a nearby church. At this moment the girl experienced her first anxiety attack. It was terrifying; she had the sensation that something would burst in her system if the anxiety went out of control. She turned toward her mother and called to her, but the mother was already out of hearing. She begged a woman who was passing by to accompany her to the school building, saying that she felt unwell. From that day on she was afraid to walk out alone, sometimes even when accompanied by another person.

We understand that her strong sexual drive could not have remained sublimated, especially after she had been rejected by the man she loved. A longing for motherly affection tended to provide an emotional outlet for the pent-up drive pressure. But when she felt that this means of draining instinctual tension was failing her also, an anxiety attack broke out. Even both defenses together, on top of repression—sublimation of the sexual drive and regression of the libido to an earlier stage—did not provide an adequate relief of drive tension. Many agoraphobic patients resort to such a regression and then feel abandoned.

In psychoanalytic literature the fear of leaving home is often interpreted as separation anxiety from the mother. And we realize now how complex the dependency need of such patients is. In this clinical picture one must consider not only the regression to dependency on the mother but also the patient's need for assistance, since the dynamic ego impairment mentioned has robbed the patient of the feeling of self-reliance. Because of this impairment agoraphobic patients become very dependent on close relatives and friends and feel that they must be available whenever the phobic situation requires it. These assisting people are certainly representatives of parental figures; in order to serve the purpose of being reliable helpers in case of need, they must feel close to the patient and be informed of his difficulty. They have to function, as it were, as alloplastic substitutes for the patient's own ego in case of its complete breakdown.

(4.) It is characteristic for this clinical picture that the patient cannot endure any restriction of freedom of movement. We understood that this is an expression of the patient's intolerance for the drive-stifling countercathexis. The patient cannot stay long in any situation in which he does not feel free to come and go as he pleases. Sitting in a barber chair or at the dentist, attending parties, going to movies or to the theatre, without freedom to leave whenever he feels the need, all arouse in him great anxiety. He cannot keep precise appointments because he has to feel free. Traveling by train makes him more anxious than riding in a car, because he has to submit to the restrictions of schedule on a train, but in a car he can change direction or stop at will. The patient's intolerance for restrictions reflects his feeling of the oppressive effect of the countercathexis. His fear of not being able to maintain this obstructive barrier is also expressed in his anxious feeling that he may lose control and begin to scream or abandon himself to destructive acts. The latter fear, however, expresses the opposite tendency also, namely, the impulse to break down the dynamic inhibition which prevents the id tension from finding relief. It may seem paradoxical, furthermore, that some agoraphobic patients also suffer from claustrophobia. But this should not surprise us, since being closed in a room is actually a restriction of free movement. Agoraphobic patients often fear suffocation and feel that they must keep doors and windows open. Agoraphobia and claustrophobia have in common the fear of not receiving immediate assistance in case of sudden physical or mental emergency.

The urge to rid one's self from oppressing countercathexis is expressed in various ways. One male patient had to remove his belt whenever he had an anxiety attack. Another, who had an anxiety attack during a party on a private lawn, had the impulse (which he did not carry out) to break down the fence surrounding the lawn. An agoraphobic woman, during an attack at home, feared that she might not be able to keep herself from throwing all the objects in the room against the glass windows, as if she had a need to create unlimited openings. A male patient felt relieved from anxiety when he could give himself an enema.

The "structural significance" of such impulses, that is, the urge to remove an internal stifling obstacle, is quite clear in all these cases. We realize, however, that "choice" of the kind of rebellion used against obstructing and restricting forces must have a psychological significance. Upon closer analysis of these dynamic manifestations we find, in fact, that the intolerance for a structural impediment is combined with the urge inherent in the concrete repressed contents. This is particularly evident in those not-infrequent cases in which the repressed content of a female patient includes the desire or fantasy to give birth to a child (usually conceived by the father!). In these cases the urge to get rid of the suffocating countercathexis is combined with the fantasy of delivering a baby. The patient wants to free herself from something within herself. Often this combination is expressed in an hysterical seizure, and thus the patient is immediately afraid of having such a seizure in public or in the presence of other people.

The urge to free one's self from restrictions, combined with other tendencies, can be illustrated by the following case. The eighteen-year-old girl previously described, who had her first anxiety attack when her mother left her in the street, developed in the course of her phobia the feeling that in the event of a very severe attack she had to disrobe immediately and completely in order to survive. Therefore she wore only self-made garments closed in the front with zippers, so that when the anxiety came she could be rid of her clothes with a sudden pull. This patient also wore shoes which she could step out of at will. And as if this were not sufficient precaution, she carried in her purse a pair of scissors in order to cut her clothes from her. This undressing, as it happened, never occurred.

Without further investigation the interpretation of this impulse might seem very simple. It would appear to express an exhibitionistic sexual urge which threatens to break through into consciousness. This patient would not accept this interpretation, of course, because the urge is repressed, but it is possible that this may be a partial interpretation of the impulse. It would be a mistake, however, to neglect the patient's actual conscious feeling of the impulse, namely, that it is an urge to liberate herself from something oppressive and almost "killing." In our interpretation it is the urge to get rid of the clogging countercathexis. But we do not ignore the fact that all neurotic manifestations may be over-determined; the analyst must search for additional, unconscious meanings. And so in this case also the patient furnished important information to explain her impulse to rid herself of her clothes in case of emergency.

She had two younger sisters, and she recalled that all three girls were accustomed to wearing clothes which were buttoned in the back. She reached an age when she was able to button and unbutton her dresses by herself, while the two younger sisters still required their mother's help. The patient was very proud to have emancipated herself, but her mother used to tease her about her feeling of independence, and this angered the patient very much. Her striving for independence had a double purpose, for it served also to control her hostile feelings of jealousy toward her sisters. She wished to deny that she cared for her mother's love and attention.

Often a careful study of the many manifestations of a psychoneurosis (which may seem to be unconnected) can bring together great "circumstantial evidence" for a suspected neurotic conflict. This patient revealed that later on, as a school teacher, she was sometimes tormented by the obsessional impulse to kill her pupils, who were all girls. But the displacement of her initial hostile impulses from her younger sisters to the young girls of her class could not be recognized by the patient. Whenever a patient is confronted with "circumstantial evidence" resulting from various information and dreams, he behaves in a way similar to that of a defendant who minimizes and denies the evidence of guilt brought to his attention, while he emphasizes all the factors in favor of his innocence. But while a defendant may be acting in bad faith the patient's denials are made in good faith. Not only are the meaningful connections unegotized, but also their correct understanding is warded off by resistance. Besides, the patient is, of course, not accused of a crime. His ego must become differently structuralized in order to integrate without conflict the repressed contents which then undergo modifications also.

The emotional situation of our patient at the time of her first anxiety attack illustrates her uncontrollable longing for attention and love from her mother. As soon as she realized that her mother's motive in accompanying her to the school was not so much love for the patient as a wish to go to church, she felt deceived in her hope for consideration from her mother. This regression re-awakened both her original pride in seeking emancipation and her jealousy toward her sisters. The anxiety attack expressed her fear that she might be unable to feel independent. Her ability as a child to dress and undress by herself assumed the significance of being independent in movements and actions, because it expressed at the same time the urge to free herself from obstructing bonds. This impulse was due to a fusion of many tendencies. Thus, she felt the uncontrollable need to provide herself with all possible means for renouncing her mother's help. The zippers in the front of her dresses and the scissors represented necessary insurance for being able to master the situation.

In all cases the intolerance for restrictions develops from an oppressive sensation of mutilating dynamic ego boundaries, and the various forms of its manifestation are determined by a fusion of many psychological contents.

This feeling of intolerance for repression may remind us of another psychological phenomenon, namely, that which Fenichel described and called "counterphobic attitude." Such an attitude is not related to repression itself, however, nor to the repressing ego cathexis as repression-intolerance is, but rather to the experience of anxiety itself. We would say that a patient who faces situations sensed by him as dangerous, defying his anxiety, assumes a "counterphobic attitude." This attitude may be conceived as a reaction formation to a still-effective anxiety. Thus a person who fears dogs may deny his anxiety and/or ignore any danger and approach dogs, even pet them. Likewise, an agoraphobic patient may force himself to leave home alone in defiance of his phobic fear, and on a deeper level in defiance of the condemnation of the superego and believed external consequences of the drive satisfaction. It is clear, however, that counterphobic attitudes, which often fail in their defying purpose, cannot be mistaken for the described intolerance of a stifling countercathexis.

(5.) When the strong pent-up sexual tension becomes unblocked, anxiety disappears. But only in rare cases is there immediate evidence of this connection. Usually the unblocking process is slow or difficult to achieve; often some disarranged forms of libidinal tension are so tenaciously repressed, and recognition of the repressed contents would be so disturbing to the patient, that the therapist must proceed with great caution, and treatment may extend over many years.

In the case of the twenty-three-year-old man the complete disappearance of phobic anxiety immediately after the first, strong and conflictless orgastic experience is clear evidence of the existing connection mentioned. The patient himself felt that it was this never-before imagined emotional event that freed him of his phobia. In Chapter XVII the intense vivification of the feeling tone of all perceptions, immediately after a first orgastic experience, was reported in the case of a young man and in the case of a young woman. The great intensity of the physical and emotional experience of these agoraphobic patients certainly indicates that the pent-up sexual tension must have been very strong. Not only did the orgastic outlet of their sexual tension become unblocked, but the orgastic experience itself in turn unblocked the feeling tone of their visual, acoustic, tactile, and all other perceptions. As mentioned in the earlier chapter, everything around them, all objects, voices and sounds, and particularly music, were perceived more vividly than before and with a pleasantly increased feeling tone. This rich and efficient ego state was sensed as being incompatible with anxiety.

The young woman's explanation of the increased feeling tone of all her perceptions expresses graphically the clogging sensation produced by the stifling countercathexis. When water clogs the auditory canal, she said, all sounds seem muffled; but later when the water comes out one hears again all the sounds vividly, with great relief and pleasure. And analogously all her visual, acoustic, tactile perceptions, etc., even her bodily sensations, the weight of her body, obtained a much more vivid and pleasant feeling tone. From these observations we learn that repression of strong sexual drives may lead to an obnubilation of feelings in general.

Unblocking of sexual tension is important not only because the critical orgastic outlet, of short duration, becomes possible, but also because a great amount of libido is freed and discharged in pleasurable feelings in general, including also those of non-sexual nature. This latter fact confirms Freud's libido theory. In the cases mentioned the orgastic experience breaks down the obstacle to the outlet of great quantities of libido into joy of life. But when, as sometimes happens, an orgastic experience is followed by repressing feelings of guilt or reaction formations, no increase of perceptive feeling tone occurs. Some agoraphobic patients may obtain an orgastic experience to which they react with feelings of guilt and disgust, thus blocking the more important outlet of continuous flow of libido into a pleasurable feeling tone. This second opening-up phenomenon leads to sublimation. In some individuals sublimation can be maintained short of orgastic experiences, when the sexual drive is not repressed but its satisfaction consciously renounced for different reasons. Most artists and scientists, however, must have some unsublimated satisfaction in order to become able to sublimate the remaining flow of libido.

Increased anxiety or the appearance of an anxiety attack can always be traced back to an internally or externally stimulated but internally blocked (repressed) tension. An agoraphobic man experienced a frightening anxiety attack after he had spent a night with a woman toward whom he felt strongly sexually attracted but with whom he could not reach an emotional orgasm for internal inhibiting reasons. In such cases we think also of a possible combination of phobic anxiety with an acute anxiety neurosis which is an actual neurosis.[6]

In some cases the orgastic experience is inseparably bound to a specific objectionable and very conflictual drive object or goal. A young woman who experienced orgasm for the first time in her life, with her husband, immediately connected this experience with the image of her father as he had appeared to her in childhood. When a young man patient, whose oedipus complex was lifted during psychoanalytic treatment, succeeded in experiencing for the first time a very strong orgasm during intercourse, he was reminded—he could not imagine for what reason—of a sexual excitement of early childhood. He described the orgastic emission as an immensely pleasurable urge to urinate which could not be controlled. Initially, instinctively he tried to withhold the ejaculation, he said, and when it occurred in spite of his efforts he immediately connected this experience with the idea of urinating on his mother in night dress as he remembered her in childhood. When the orgastic experience is inseparably bound to specific objectionable and repressed objects or goals, the psychoanalyst encounters the greatest therapeutic difficulties. A young married male patient with a very masculine ego ideal, for example, could seldom reach an emotional orgasm, although he always succeeded in emission. In the course of his analysis it became evident that a full emotional orgasm could be achieved only through homosexual aims, but these were tenaciously repressed. Each time the analyst tried to interpret his homosexuality he reacted with increase of anxiety. Homosexual transference on the analyst could not be prevented; and it created fear of treatment. Once the patient dreamed that the analyst's office looked like a bedroom. Though the analyst cautiously did not interpret this dream, nevertheless after leaving the session the patient almost fainted on the street and then discontinued treatment.

Various sexual deviations can be responsible for the obstruction of an orgastic outlet and must in turn be analyzed. The chief manifestations of repressed urges considered in psychoanalytic literature regarding agoraphobia are exhibitionistic tendencies, prostitution fantasies in women and homosexuality in men. Aggressive urges and birth fantasies are mentioned also, but the metapsychological mechanism of agoraphobia discussed here is ignored.

When sublimation or regression to infantile dependency (often to the oral phase) can absorb enough of the pent-up libido, the patient feels less anxiety. Often patients feel more secure if they carry some food item or sedatives, as though energy supply from without could compensate for the blocked libido supply within. In some cases carrying a specific object, the meaning of which can be revealed through psychoanalytic exploration, gives the patient a feeling of security. Such objects function as compensations for something missing within the patient's own ego. The sensation of emotional or dynamic mutilation is always present in these clinical pictures. This sensation is not verbalized as such by the patient, but upon proper explanation he usually recognizes it.

NOTES

(1) Freud, Sigmund. Analysis of a phobia in a five-year-old boy (1909). Standard Edition, 10:5-149. London, Hogarth, 1955.

(2) Many issues related to anxiety states cannot be presented in this volume. Suffice it to say that Freud distinguished psychoneuroses from actual neu-

roses. The psychoneuroses have a psychological meaning, while the actual neuroses are toxic effects of irregular hormonal secretion which, in turn, is the result of a patient's irregular sexual life. Freud distinguished three forms of actual neuroses: neurasthenia, anxiety neurosis, and hypochondria. The phobias are classed with anxiety hysteria which is a psychoneurosis. The actual neuroses also include acute forms of derealization and depersonalization which, as Federn demonstrated, are due to excessive sexual activity.

(3) Weiss, Edoardo. Agoraphobia and its relation to hysterical attacks and to traumas. Int. J. Psychoanal., 16:59-83, 1935; Agorafobia, isterismo d'angoscia. Rome, Cremonese, 1936; Federn's ego psychology and its application to agoraphobia. J. Am. Psychoanal Assoc., 1:614-628, 1953; Ichstörungen bei der Agoraphobie und verwandten Erscheinungen im Lichte der Federn'schen Ichpsychologie. Psyche (Heidelberg), 11:286-307, 1957.

(4) The different types of repressive failure are due to differences in ego structure and degree of ego development.

(5) We include in this group all patients who experience anxiety when leaving home or any point of security regardless of whether the patient fears open places or narrow streets, tunnels, etc. Often such a patient can venture but a well defined distance from his place of shelter; when he crosses what he senses to be a certain line of demarcation he becomes overwhelmed by anxiety.

(6) See Note 2, above.

XXXIX

Denial

IN the phenomenon of repression, id contents remain unegotized in spite of their strong cathexis. The resistance of the internal ego boundary against the impact of the tension inherent in repressed contents is an expression of ego strength. But the ego perceives also external realities, and it cannot easily withdraw from perceived contents, sensed as external realities. Yet there are pathological cases in which an ego apparently does not perceive an external object, however strongly it stimulates the ego's intact perceptive organs. One calls this event a "negative hallucination." So, reality may be falsified in two ways: (1) a mental content can be perceived as external reality—a (positive) hallucination; (2) a real external object or phenomenon may not be perceived at all in spite of its great "perceptibility"—a negative hallucination. Negative hallucinations are also dynamically determined, and we shall now examine their metapsychological mechanism.

In Chapters XIV and XV we distinguished the internal from the external ego boundary. We understood that the internal ego boundary is windowless, namely without embedded sense organs for the perception of id contents. In normal waking life every id content must be egotized in order to be perceived by the ego as a mental phenomenon; then it is sensed as a part of an ego state. The external ego boundary has embedded windows, the sense organs, and the ego perceives external stimuli without egotizing them; to be more exact, after the ego has abandoned in earliest infancy the ego-cosmic stage, it does not perceive them as parts of ego states. The stronger the external ego boundary which encompasses the sense organs, the more does the ego sense external stimuli as real, without resorting to any reality testing. The more weakly the external ego boundary is cathected, the less does the ego sense external stimuli as real. This state of affairs explains the phenomenon of derealization which may be due to dynamic economic impairment and also may constitute an ego defense, as was presented in the earlier chapters. We repeat: The sense organs, included within the dynamic external ego boundary, remain permeable for external stimuli; in healthy conditions of waking life no dynamic obstacle prevents these stimuli from reaching the ego's awareness. In the ego-cosmic stage these stimuli are sensed as medial experiences, that is, as part of an ego state, but with the development of the interposed external ego boundary, these originally medial ego experiences are turned into perceptions of non-ego phenomena. In other words, the contents of these perceptions are sensed as real external objects and phenomena. At the ego-cosmic stage the sensation of external reality does not exist. "Realization" of contents, i.e., feeling as real, presupposes the existence of a sufficiently strong external ego boundary, and the more this boundary weakens the more the perceived contents become derealized.

In the preceding chapters the dynamics of repression of id contents was presented. No sense organs for the perception of id contents as non-ego phenomena is possible. Id contents can never be perceived as non-ego data, while stimuli of the external world can.[1] When in dreams and psychoses id contents are perceived as realities, they are sensed not as id contents but as external realities —as false realities, to be sure. And when id contents are perceived in their internal, psychological nature, they are perceived only as ego contents. In this way repression of id contents is the ego's automatic refraining from egotization of these contents.

Is repression of perception of external data through sense organs actually possible? Since these perceptive data are normally unegotized anyway, their repression must occur through a mechanism different from that of repression of id contents. Bear in mind that perception through sense organs cannot be blocked in the same manner as can egotization of id contents. If someone does not want to see or hear something, he may close his eyes, turn away, stop up his ears, even though he knows that that object still exists. When some realization is too painful, an ego may fade away, i.e., it may faint. By suppressing itself temporarily, in an act of automatic defense, the ego withdraws not only from a given real object or realized fact but also from the whole external world. Such a withdrawal also occurs in sleep, though sleep may be disturbed or interrupted by too intense stimulations. Some persons can take refuge in sleep as temporary relief from unpleasant realities. Defense through sleep will be more extensively examined in the next section when the psychology of dreams is presented. As indicated in Chapter XIII in discussion of the pleasure and reality principles, an individual may even commit suicide when he cannot endure a painful reality; the thought of suppressing one's self seems preferable to experiencing a too painful existence. In all these cases the ego does not repress the perception of some reality, but it ceases functioning altogether in order to withdraw from or escape external reality. These kinds of defense cannot be called denial of some external reality but are rather refusal to stay, temporarily or permanently, in that reality.

We wish now to examine the ways in which an ego can ward off external realities without withdrawing itself from existence. The ego's direct perception of reality through sense organs must be distinguished from its acknowledgment of real facts through reality testing. In our discussion of conversion hysteria we mentioned hysterical blindness, deafness, and loss of other perceptual sensations. These conversion symptoms consist in direct blocking of sensory perceptions, whereby it would seem that not only circumscribed fields of perception are blocked but that all external data are unseen, unheard, etc. Closer examination reveals, however, that this is often not the case. A woman suffering from hysterical blindness was led out for a short walk, and the following night she dreamed of a beautiful horse-chestnut tree in full bloom. She had actually passed such a tree on her walk, but she had not "seen" it. Persons suffering from hysterical blindness usually do not injure themselves when moving around unaided; they manage to avoid striking against objects in their way even though they do not "see" them. When they do injure themselves, it is frequently the result of self-destructive tendencies. In the presence of patients suffering from hysterical deafness one must be careful not to speak about things they should not hear. While that part of the ego which enters into contact with us feels blind or deaf, another part may unknowingly register some perceptive stimuli.

Hysterical blindness or deafness cannot be considered "negative hallucinations" in the sense mentioned. A blind or deaf hysterical ego—or that part of the ego which is blind or deaf—has "blanked out," so to speak, not only on given objects or given sounds but on any visual or auditory stimuli. Hysterical blindness and deafness have a psychological meaning, as all conversion symptoms have. They express conflicts between repressed drives and opposing tendencies. Freud [2] interpreted the hysterical patient's inability to see ("I cannot see") as his not wanting to see ("I do not want to see") because of resistance against voyeuristic wishes. It also expresses punishment with blindness for having seen or wanting to see forbidden objects or scenes. But patients who can see and hear promptly everything else in reach of their sense organs cannot be actually blind or deaf for single objects or sounds. Denial of certain perceptual data occurs, then, according to a mechanism different from functional blindness or deafness.

Perception of external stimuli is a complex psychological phenomenon in which not only the sense organs and the external ego boundary which encompasses them participate, but also the ego's activity called "attention," its function of "capturing" and "retaining" perceptive data, and its function of automatically connecting these data with previously acquired knowledge. This last function is called "apperception." When an ego fails to catch and retain visual or auditory sensations or disregards them, then it behaves as if it had a "negative hallucination." Often, however, when one directs the patient's attention toward the "not seen" or "not heard" object, event or sound, one can induce him in spite of resistance to perceive the data the existence of which he tried to deny. Such an ego may resort then to other defense mechanisms; it may misinterpret the data or ignore their significance and importance. We shall soon examine other clinically well-known modes of denial.

One form of defense against an unpleasant fact of the external world, that is, denying the external reality altogether, was mentioned in Chapter XIV in our discussion of the phenomenon of "derealization" as a defense mechanism. When the external ego boundary withdraws from or weakens at the sense organs for economic reasons—because of insufficient supply of ego cathexis—the external stimuli which enter the sense organs are sensed as unreal, like dream images as they are recognized upon awakening. This phenomenon, it was said, is called feeling of estrangement or derealization. We learned also that such a withdrawal of ego cathexis from the sense organs may serve a defensive purpose against the acceptance of an unpleasant reality, even when enough ego cathexis is available to the ego. A person who is shocked by a horrifying sight or terrifying news may be unable to accept such a perceived reality; he expresses himself by saying, "I cannot believe it," or "This does not seem real to me." This reaction may be more than the expression of a mere wish; such an ego may actually feel that the world around him has become unreal. This is an evident form of denial of a painful reality, denial performed by the mentioned withdrawal of ego-boundary cathexis. Also in this case the existence of the whole external world is denied and not merely a circumscribed event. This defense mechanism may seem similar to the fainting reaction to a too painful realization. But in defense through fainting the ego removes itself from the external world; in the defense through derealization the ego does not remove itself from existence but makes the external world unreal, in a way which reminds us of the ego-cosmic stage. Often the feeling of derealization itself is frightening and may lead in turn to a fainting reaction. In this case the withdrawal of ego cathexis at the sense organs is followed by withdrawal of ego cathexis altogether; the ego itself fades away, not only its sense of reality.

We understand that an ego which maintains intact its sensory perceptions and its sense of reality cannot easily deny, i.e., refuse to recognize, the existence of actually perceived external data. But it is less difficult for it to ward off a knowledge acquired through reality testing. It may avoid taking cognizance of some painful reality; it may omit drawing conclusions from perceived data, however impelling they may be. We understood that the thinking function is the most important tool in the service of reality testing, a function which can easily be inhibited or deranged when the ego can no longer adhere to the reality principle. Giving up the reality principle in favor of the pleasure-pain principle is a very common defense. Denial by failing to test reality or by testing it in a defective or incomplete way is a frequent occurrence among people who feel lost when they have to accept a too painful reality, or when they are faced with giving up some scientific conviction or religious belief, or abandoning preconceived ideas in their social orientation. A patient revealed in a striking way his obsessional reaction to a commonly encountered denial. Visiting a cemetery he caught the following inscription on a tombstone: "Rest in Peace." In his analytic session he energetically refuted the correctness of this inscription with the exclamation: "But he does not rest, *he is dead!*" The patient knew, of course, the emotional motivation of the survivors for denying the phenomenon of death.

In Chapter XIII cases were mentioned in which some reality was beyond the ego's endurance capacity. In such a situation an individual may break his rapport with reality altogether and fall into an hallucinatory psychosis. Meynert called this form of psychosis "amentia." The "cessation of existence" of an indispensable love object, or the absence of an external condition necessary for the satisfaction of an unbearable need, can be denied by hallucination or belief in the existence of that object or condition. Thus a (positive) hallucination may serve the purpose of denying the existence of an unbearable condition. Such hallucinations are not due to a primary ego-economic deficiency but to a secondary ego impoverishment caused by an unbearable reality. In such cases the hallucinated world is a substitution for an indispensable reality which is actually lost or missed. It is not a restitution at a reality from which the patient has withdrawn in narcissistic regression. It is a dynamic breakdown of the ego due to its need for warding off or enduring pain and frustration. Ernst Federn[3] (son of Paul Federn) uses the phrase "pain defense" for the complete loss of self-control of an ego when "the whole body and the entire ego are concentrated upon the endurance of, and the escape from pain." When such a need absorbs an excessive amount of cathexis, too little is left for maintenance of the sense of reality. Thus some "psychoses" develop from over-demanding external situations. In Freud's opinion[4] neurosis is the result of a conflict between the ego and its id, and psychosis is the analogous result of such a disturbance in relations between ego and the external world. But we wish to emphasize that in such cases the disturbance in relations between ego and the external world results only from unbearable external situations. In Federn's opinion the breakdown in these cases is due also to a dynamic ego-deficiency, as in true schizophrenia.

Some psychoanalysts consider hallucinatory wish fulfillments as

the counterpart of denial proper. But strictly speaking such hallucinations do actually deny the non-existence of something. So one
can deny being deprived of something by wishful thinking or
pleasant daydreams. But usually the dreamer knows that he is only
thinking of the desired situations and that they do not really exist.
Nevertheless he resorts to his mental creations as a meager substitution for what he does not have in reality. We may consider
such a compromise as the result of a split in the ego: One part of
the ego knows that the products of its fantasies are not true, but
another part ignores this in order to be able to enjoy such products.
Such a split of the ego was discussed in the description of hysterical
blindness and deafness. But in these cases the part of the ego which
does register perceptual stimuli is unconscious, while the daydreaming ego knows consciously that the contents of its fantasies are not
real.

In some clinical manifestations such a split of the ego is essential
for a drive satisfaction. That part of the ego which refuses to recognize an experienced reality remains unconscious, and the content
of the denial can be detected only through deep analysis, although
the derived satisfaction is consciously enjoyed by the whole ego.
In analysis of the sexual deviation of "fetishism" Freud discovered
such a split. The fetish—a limb, the ear, nose or a piece of female
garment—toward which the fetishist feels erotically attracted, is
always a substitutive representation for the imagined penis of a
woman, and precisely for the penis which the child ascribed to the
mother. This sexual deviation originates from the child's anatomical
misconception of the female genitalia. Prior to discovery of the
female genitalia the boy expects his mother, and females in general,
to possess a penis. As stated in Chapter XXIV, according to Freud
the boy's discovery of the real anatomical aspect of female genitalia
always shocks him; it impresses him as a ghastly mutilation and
constitutes for him the proof that he himself could suffer the same
fate, i.e., be deprived of his penis. In my opinion the sight of the
female genitalia does not create the same reaction in all boys; it
is not always shocking. Depending on the degree of his externalization of feminine tendencies, it can also excite him sexually. Sexual excitement does not necessarily exclude the shock reaction,

although it may have the effect of neutralizing it. In any case, fetishistic tendencies can develop only in individuals who, for their erotic needs, cannot dispense with masculine features of the mother. In fact, they themselves manifest feminine, sometimes masochistic, attitudes in their relations to women. Their erotic need induces them to deny the actual anatomical truth regarding the sex organs of females, because they are unable to accept emotionally the fact that females do not possess penises. The rational, reality-adapted, conscious part of the ego knows the truth, but, for the purpose of the ego's erotic need, a non-reality-adapted part of the ego maintains the representation of a penis-possessing mother. The ego's denying efforts are analogous to those of a person who enjoys unrealistic daydreams, well-knowing that their contents exist only in his mind. The fetishist displaces his erotic longing for a non-existent female penis onto a fetish which does exist in reality and with which he can enter into physical contact.

We have understood so far that denying attitudes are directed against unacceptable facts which are acknowledgeable by sensory perception and by logical conclusions from perceptions. They are mental acts which are subservient to the function of reality testing. We realize that painful and unwelcomed realities can have a corrupting influence on reality testing; in other words, emotional factors may interfere with a proper functioning of reality testing. The mnemonic function also can be affected by denying attitudes of the ego. The ego's resistance against unpleasant or shocking memories reminds us of the defense mechanism of repression presented in the preceding chapters. It was mentioned that not only instinctive drives but also traumatic memories can undergo repression. And now an important question deserves our full consideration: Is not repression also a form of denial?

So far, it is true, the phenomenon of denial has been presented only in its expression against external realities, accessible to sensory perception and to reality testing. But we shall soon see that internal mental contents, drives and memories also can be denied. In what, then, does the difference between repression and denial of drives and memories consist? The phenomenon of repression can by no means be conceived as a form of denial. Repressed contents lie beyond the internal windowless wall; they are excluded from the ego's perceptive field. Therefore, in repression the ego has no content to deny. Similarly, an external fact which is not perceived by the ego does not exist as a content which could be accepted or rejected. Only contents, internal or external, which enter the ego's field of awareness can be denied.

Let us now return for a moment to Freud's distinction between neurosis and psychosis, mentioned above. In his concept the neurotic mechanism consists in a (unsuccessful) repression of id contents and the psychotic mechanism in a "repression," as it were, of the acknowledgment of external realities. In other words, in psychosis the perception and/or acknowledgment of objects, events and situations of the external world would undergo a process analogous to the exclusion of dynamic id contents from the ego, which is characteristic of the neurosis. As we have mentioned often, this metapsychological interpretation of the psychotic process is at variance with Federn's concept of the dynamic "ego-deficiency" responsible for the psychotic breakdown. In any case, the distinction between "ego-id" and "ego-external world" relations does not explain the difference between repression and denial. The ego can deny only those internal or external contents which it does acknowledge. Therefore, denial presupposes a split of the ego into that part which does acknowledge the existence of the repudiated internal or external contents and that part which behaves as if such contents did not exist. Applying Federn's distinction of different ego states, we would say that in the phenomenon of denial one ego state enters into opposition with another ego state. The denying ego state may or may not remain preconscious. Some psychoanalysts who do not accept Federn's ego psychology or are not familiar with it, see in the phenomenon of denial a rejection by the ego of preconscious contents, but they do not speak of ego states.

The simplest examples of denial of internal experiences are seen in cases of slowly arising physical pains or feelings of discomfort. So, Freud mentioned that the statement, "I am glad that I have not had a headache for such a long time," made just before a headache is consciously experienced, should be interpreted as "I feel the headache coming, but for the time being I can still deny it." Also instinctive drives which encounter the ego's resistance *and escape repression* can be denied. Thus, for example, a male patient may force himself to enter into intimate relationships with women in his efforts to deny homosexual tendencies. And likewise, an ego may deny that it is experiencing various desires or emotional states by its behavior or utterances to the contrary. How often we hear a person say, "I am not envious of him or jealous; I am not angry," etc. And everyone listening realizes that he is actually envious, jealous or angry. Sometimes, it is true, the verbal denial is intended only to "save face" in front of others, but often such a person denies the inner truth to himself as well. While repression is doubtless an ego-defense mechanism, one may hesitate to consider denial a "defense" proper. Indeed, Anna Freud [5] has called the ego's refusal to acknowledge an experienced pain or a feeling of discomfort a "pre-state of defense." On the other hand, however, we must recognize that denial of a memory, a desire, or an ego state may alternate with repression of such contents.

In psychoanalytic literature the phenomenon of "screen memories" is often mentioned in connection with the ego's denying attitudes. This phenomenon should be considered, rather, a form of "return of the repressed." Freud called a "screen memory" a well-preserved memory of an actually experienced situation of childhood which has not impressed the ego very strongly. This phenomenon aroused his interest because, while memories of much greater emotional, even shocking, nature underwent repression, an isolated and apparently quite insignificant content remained well-preserved in the individual's memory. Analysis of such a memory revealed to Freud that its content is a substitution, of little or no emotional importance, for an earlier situation which had been experienced with strong affect. One of my female patients, for example, who did not preserve many memories of early childhood, could remember clearly how her grandmother made her a doll from a handkerchief when she was five years old. And she remembered then how she herself liked to pull at a free corner of the handkerchief, thus undoing the grandmother's production. This event was of no great emotional significance for the patient, and she wondered why she had kept this episode in her memory while many more important events of her childhood were repressed. From the available information of her early life history the meaning of this screen memory became evident. When she was three years old her sister was born; the patient became very much interested in childbirth and at the same time felt jealous of the new intruder with whom she had to share parental love. Although her hostile and death wishes toward her sister were repressed, the cathexis inherent in the repressed memories and hostile wishes still persisted and remained blocked from any emotional expression. This tension gave rise to a need for an acceptable revival of the repressed memory, together, however, with the tendency to avoid the inherent traumatization and conflict. These two conditions could be fulfilled only through replacement of the original strongly affect-laden memory by a less traumatizing one. The handkerchief-doll made by her grandmother two years later and the ease with which this "baby" could be undone were indeed very fit mental substitutions for the birth of her sister and the wish to do away with her.

All persistent memories of childhood which do not seem important are "screening" earlier emotionally more important memories. And when a screen memory itself is somewhat affect-laden we can be sure that the latent one was even more strongly charged. Often memories of parental quarrels or fights screen the memory of the child's more shocking experience related to the "primal scene."

Some psychoanalysts consider screen memories a form of denial because the screening substitution "denies," as it were, the existence of a deeper, more-shocking experience. But, as stated above, screen memories are rather a "return of the repressed."

NOTES

(1) This is one reason why pre-Freudian psychologists were unable to conceive of unconscious mental phenomena.

(2) Freud, Sigmund. The psycho-analytic view of psychogenic disturbance of vision (1910). Standard Edition, 11:209-218. London, Hogarth, 1957.

(3) Federn, Ernst. Essai sur la psychologie de la terreur. Synthèses, 1:no.7: 80-95, and 1:no.8:99-108, 1946; The terror as a system: The concentration camp. Psychiat. Quart. Suppl., 22:52-86, 1948; and The endurance of torture. Complex, no.4:34-41 (Winter) 1951. In these three articles the author (who spent seven years as a prisoner in Dachau and Buchenwald concentration

camps) elaborated from a dynamic psychological point of view on the cruelties inflicted on concentration camp prisoners.

(4) Freud, Sigmund. Neurosis and psychosis (1924). Collected Papers, 2:250-254. London, Hogarth, 1924.

(5) Freud, Anna, op. cit.

XL

Reaction Formations, Undoing, and Isolation

IN the preceding chapter we mentioned the efforts of a male patient to deny his homosexual tendencies by forcing himself to enter into intimate relationships with women. We are reminded of the phenomenon of "reaction formation," presented in Chapter XXX and described by Freud as an impulse which has the purpose of warding off an opposite impulse. The following are some very common examples of reaction formations: a person's exaggerated urge for cleanliness in an effort to deny or to keep repressed his desire for dirt, which is a derivative of anal-erotic, coprophilic tendencies; a person's strong concern to avoid harming or causing suffering to others, in opposition to his unconscious cruel tendencies; an individual's excessively modest attitude, his response with shame and embarrassment to exposing himself, thus counteracting his unacceptable exhibitionistic wishes. As pointed out earlier, reaction formations are powered by countercathexes, that is, by forces which maintain dynamically the repression of instinctive drives.

We may ask now whether reaction formations to denied impulses can be distinguished from reaction formations to repressed impulses. Accurate observation of concrete cases has revealed that reaction formations to repressed drives are not only much more tenacious and consistent than those to denied drives, but also that they involve the entire ego. In other words, they have a structuralizing effect on the character of the personality, which is characteristically obsessional-neurotic. Reaction formations to denied drives do not involve the whole ego and can be much more easily unmasked as such. Furthermore, they sometimes concern a conflictual tendency, such as a hostile attitude, toward only a single individual and not toward other persons in general. For example, a mother may show an exaggerated love for her child and be overconcerned about his welfare in an effort to deny her hostile feelings toward him, while at the same time she may express openly her hostile and cruel wishes toward other persons. It is easier to unmask this mother's ambivalent feelings toward her child, thus making her consciously aware of them, than it is to lift from repression the sadistic and cruel tendencies of an obsessional patient. Reaction formations against emotional attitudes toward single individuals are more frequently encountered in hysterical patients than in obsessional neurotics. In the last phases of psychoanalytic treatment of some obsessional patients I was able to observe clearly the difference between these two types of reaction formation. After the repression of their hostile tendencies has been somewhat lifted, and thus their character distortion slowly straightened out, I noticed that for a certain time repression of repudiated drives alternated with their denial. When such patients began to recognize their hostile tendencies and loose their character defenses, they still wished to exclude single individuals as targets for their hostile feelings. But this exclusion occurred then through denial and no longer through repression.

The emotions inherent in obsessional reaction formations are, we repeat, expressions of countercathexis and are, of course, very conscious to the ego, although it is completely unaware of the warded-off tendencies acting behind the internal windowless wall. For a better understanding of the metapsychological conditions of the reactive character distortion resulting from the repressive mechanism characteristic of obsessional neurosis, let us compare briefly the employment of repressive (counter-)cathexis as it is manifested in obsessional neurosis with that of conversion hysteria, projection phobia and in the group of non-projective phobias already presented. We shall see also that the "choice of the neurosis" is due not only to specific instinctive drives which have undergone repression but also to the ego's particular constitution and degree of development.

In conversion hysteria both the cathexis which powers the repressed libidinous drives and that which is inherent in the resistance against them—the countercathexis—find an outlet in somatic symptoms. To the extent to which this discharge of energetic tension forestalls a "danger situation," the patient avoids being emotionally upset; he remains anxiety free. But we have also seen that the discharge of tension is sometimes inadequate, and anxiety is not averted. In my opinion this is most often the case when conversion symptoms express resisting tendencies, i.e., the countercathexis, more strongly than the satisfaction of the repressed drives. Then they may lead to a phobic mechanism, usually of the nonprojective type. Sometimes agoraphobia is combined with conversion symptoms.

In projection phobia the cathexis inherent in the repressed drives and in thought of the feared consequences of their satisfaction is displaced on unrecognizable substitutive representations, which become the conscious object of fear. The patient behaves as if danger threatened him from the external world. The countercathexis is then revealed in the patient's anxious efforts to avoid the "external danger," the phobically feared objects.

In non-projective phobias the blocking effect of the countercathexis is sensed as a "dynamic mutilation" of the ego, which makes it feel inefficient in functioning without dependence on another individual. Sometimes, too, the patient's ego feeling is disturbed; feelings of derealization and/or depersonalization heighten the anxiety. Two important features characterize this group of phobias: the described rebellion against the blocking countercathexis and the regression to infantile dependency due to the sensation of one's dynamic inefficiency. The rebellion against the drive-stifling countercathexis reveals an opposition between two ego states, since the countercathexis itself is provided from ego cathexis and repression is an automatic ego performance.

In obsessional neurosis, in which ambivalent feelings toward the object play the most important role, the positive object-protective tendencies and desire for cleanliness, as opposed to anal-erotic coprophilic tendencies, become overcathected. This reactive increase in intensity of the positive portion is provided mainly by that amount of ego cathexis which was withdrawn from the objectionable portion of the ambivalent relation to the object. This "ego-withdrawal" from the hostile drive component is precisely the ego's repression of it. The countercathexis is thus consciously manifested in the development of an over-conscientious character of the ego. Federn[1] has given us a clear description of the obsessional ego: Its reaction formations are rigid; no split of the ego occurs in its defensive measures, and every obsessional act must be performed by the ego with full undivided attention, or else it will feel compelled to perform its "ceremonials" anew. These ceremonials are not only expressions of reaction formations to repressed drives but also expressions of the defense mechanisms called "undoing" and "isolation" which will be presented soon. Briefly, in obsessional neurosis the countercathexis is employed in the formation of the indicated character trait of the ego; the ego itself bends itself in an attitude opposite to the repressed drives. As long as the conscientious and meticulous behavior of the obsessional ego is not too exaggerated, it does not necessarily impress one as a pathological manifestation. But when this character trait becomes excessive in the ego's efforts to counteract the impact of the repressed and too strongly cathected drives, then the ego can no longer function in an efficient way in its everyday activities. Too much time and energy is spent in compliance with its obsessional needs. Such a patient cannot possibly act against the impositions of his reaction formations, and it is apparent not only to outsiders but also to the patient himself that he is emotionally disturbed.

When an obsessional neurotic succeeds in finding some disguised satisfaction of his anal-sadistic tendencies or their derivatives, the tension of the repressed drives may be somewhat relieved, thus forestalling a continual increase of reaction formations. An obsessionally overclean and overorderly housewife, for instance, may feel compelled to look meticulously in every corner of her home for the smallest speck of dirt, cigarette ashes, etc., in order to remove them, of course. She is unaware of the fact that she has actually an interest in finding dirt, and that she gets satisfaction every time she detects some. Her urge to remove it immediately is a reaction formation, which permits her to ignore her pleasure in having found it. Obsessional patients often dream, to their great dismay, of dirty objects, of feces and cruel scenes. In these dreams repressed urges break through the inner ego boundary, which is weakened in the state of sleep, and their hallucinatory satisfaction is perceived by the dreaming ego as unegotized and unpleasant events. A mother who is reactively overconcerned about the safety and welfare of her ambivalently loved child, gets unconscious gratification of her sadism in controlling him and depriving him of many pleasures and free movement. We realize, thus, that reaction formation may be combined with devious acts and behavior patterns by which repressed drives are satisfied, while the patient himself senses these acts and his behavior as measures necessary for maintaining order and cleanliness or for protecting love objects from harm and danger. Without any or insufficiently disguised outlet for repressed coprophilic and/or sadistic impulses the reactive system can reach such a high degree of intensity and extension as to cripple the ego in its most elementary everyday activities.

The defense called "undoing" is closely related to reaction formations. It consists in an act or merely a gesture by which an action, a thought or a spoken word or sentence is annulled, i.e., undone, either in reality or in the patient's imagination. In the latter case the act of undoing is sensed by the ego as having a "magic" effect. A simple example of undoing is a schoolboy's urge to write an obscene word on a piece of paper and then immediately erase it. The necessity for this "undoing" is not due to the boy's fear of being detected. He would not be satisfied to tear up the paper and throw it away. He feels the need to preserve that piece of paper so that the situation as it existed before he wrote the word is re-established. Undoing is often preceded by an action, as in this case, the result of which must then be undone, either in reality or only in the patient's imagination. An obsessional pianist sat down at his piano determined to play a sonata as well as he possibly could, thinking that at his next concert he would play this sonata exactly as he played it now. But unfortunately after a few minutes he made a mistake, and therefore this performance had to be annulled; the way he had begun to play was no longer valid for his purpose. In order to undo what he had played he had to close the piano, leave the house for a minute or two, and then return to play the sonata over again. In his imagination his first unsuccessful performance was in this way undone. Analysis revealed that his obsession to be perfectly correct and "clean" in his musical performances was a derivative of a character trait in reaction to anal-coprophilic tendencies. Order, perfection, and cleanliness were inexorable demands of his reactive character. Sometimes such a patient is not sufficiently satisfied by one mode of undoing and has to repeat the undoing actions several times.

Undoing performances do not always act in the direction of reactive tendencies; sometimes they may be intended to undo a reactive act itself, thus conceding some satisfaction to the repressed urge. A woman began a letter to her mother with the words, "My dearest mother." Immediately she tore up the paper, took another sheet and another pen and wrote "Mother." She had withdrawn, undone, her too affectionate appellative, which had been a reactive act to her ambivalent feelings toward her mother. But she was not satisfied with this modification either. It seemed too rude to address her mother in this way, and so she had to write on a third sheet of paper, and with still another pen, simply "Dear Mother." Her defense was directed against her own ambivalent feelings toward her mother and not so much against their overt manifestation. The first acts which had given expression to her ambivalence became "undone." In other words, tearing up the first sheets of paper and using another pen had magic effect in her imagination, namely, that she had never harbored either hostile or excessively affectionate feelings toward her mother. Not only actions but also the pronouncing or mere thinking of certain contents may undergo the undoing process by "magic" gestures, utterances, or thoughts.

The defense called "isolation" consists in disconnecting single acts or thought contents from each other. An ideational content may also be disconnected, isolated, from its pertinent affect, thus losing its emotional significance. This disconnecting or isolating activity is a performance of countercathexis. Obsessional patients usually remember clearly traumatic episodes of their childhood, but these memories are void of the pertinent emotional tone. For example, an obsessional neurotic remembered clearly in every detail the time when his sibling was born, when he was two-and-one-half-years old. He remembered every corner of the apartment in which his family lived at that time, how the news of the birth was brought to him. He could remember his mother's taking care of his sibling and even nursing him; he remembered the face and the name of the nurse. But all these memories were completely detached, isolated, from the emotions which he had actually experienced. His symptoms and dreams revealed clearly that he must have felt very jealous of his sibling and that he must have developed death wishes against him. And when this was communicated to him by the analyst, the patient readily admitted that it might actually have been so. The interpretation did not bring about any change in the patient's reaction formations, however, because it did not repeal the isolation of the ideational content from the pertinent emotion. Obsessional neurotics may even gain a full intellectual understanding of the psychological mechanism of their neuroses, but without feeling relief from their neurotic suffering. While hysterical patients repress the ideational contents of pathogenic memories together with the inherent affect,[2] obsessional patients "repress" only the affect of such memories, and thus they cannot recognize any emotional connection between the well-remembered pathogenic event and their symptoms. This amounts to a repression of the connection between two conscious mental contents. For this reason, the general guiding principle in psychoanalytic treatment of obsessional patients is to focus treatment on freeing their blocked emotions rather than on giving them psychological interpretations of their symptoms. But, I wish to add, explaining to such patients the phenomenon itself of isolation of ideational contents from their pertinent emotions, as a defense mechanism which has to be overcome in the treatment, should not be considered a "psychological interpretation." This is rather a "dynamic explanation," which may in some cases expedite the psychoanalytic process.

Another type of isolation consists in the insertion of an interval of time or space, also an act or thought, between two actions or thought contents, by which the ego endeavors to keep them apart, to "isolate them from each other." A religious patient had a great resistance to touching the Bible immediately after having evacuated, however thoroughly he washed his hands. At least ten minutes was required before he could touch the Bible. Another patient refused to talk about his mother immediately after having spoken of sexual matters. Usually he felt more at ease to talk about her after he had entered another room. An obsessional woman was horrified to think about her children, or about anyone she loved, immediately after having read reports of cruelties in the news-

REACTION FORMATIONS, UNDOING, AND ISOLATION

paper. First she had to put the paper in another room and then, for a short time at least, engage in some activity, such as putting her wardrobe in order, sewing or cooking, before she could feel free to turn her thoughts toward those whom she loved. Interposing these actions between two thought contents constituted for her an "isolating layer," as it were, placed between them. In some cases "isolating" activities can become so complicated, and employ so much time and energy, that they interfere with the patient's most elementary functions. Complicated actions which must be performed precisely in a given order by obsessional patients, in their struggle to comply with the dictates of their reactive character and/or with the requirements of undoing and isolating performances, are called obsessional rituals or ceremonials.

Among the most characteristic features of an obsessional ego are its obsessive doubts arising from uncontrollable ambivalent urges. Often such an ego can never obtain a feeling of certainty that it has really accomplished those acts or taken those precautions "necessary" for forestalling a disaster. One of my patients, having left his apartment after drinking a glass of water in the kitchen, became doubtful whether he had turned off the water faucet. He had to return home to convince himself, not only by seeing that the water was not running but also by turning the faucet more firmly. He went out again and was waiting for a bus when the idea came to his mind that he might have turned the faucet in the wrong direction by mistake and thus have opened it completely. A previous experience supported this possibility: Once the water pipes in his house had been shut off for a short time for repairs. If this should be the case now also, the patient thought, and if the faucet were completely open, then the kitchen and his whole apartment, and even the floor below, would be inundated when the water pipes were reopened in his absence. To prevent such a disaster he had to return home again to assure himself that the faucet was really closed.

When excessive defensive efforts of the kinds described employ too much ego cathexis they may lead to a psychotic breakdown. Undoing and isolating mental attitudes reminded this writer of two schizophrenic, but opposite, symptoms which were described in Chapter XVIII. One of these symptoms consisted in a depletion or "mutilation" of an integrative field (in French's conception); I have called it (integrative) "span mutilation." The other was manifested in a fusion of two unrelated integrative fields. In the first case, mental data essential for integrative behavior fell out from the integrative field, and the patient behaved accordingly in an irrational, puzzling manner. This was the behavior of the young man who climbed the mast of a boat naked in the presence of a crowd. His ego cathexis did not extend over all the mental data appropriate for dealing with the actual situation. A lack of cohesive cathexis was responsible for the absence in this patient's ego of the necessary considerations for adequate behavior. In the second case the patient could not separate the idea of the Russian sputnik from revolutionary events in Algeria. He had learned of these second events shortly after hearing on the radio about the launching of the sputnik. This patient's ego did not have enough "isolating" cathexis available to keep the two unrelated ideas separate. It is interesting to note now that in the obsessional neurosis too much cohesive cathexis is employed in maintaining a consistent reactive character; no mental data fall out from the reactive integrative field. On the contrary, in the obsessional ego too much isolating mental activity takes place, so that there can be no danger of a fusion of unrelated thoughts. Could not the exhaustion of excessively employed cohesive and isolating cathexis be responsible for the fact that severe obsessionals are in danger of becoming schizophrenic?

NOTES

(1) Federn, Paul. The determination of hysteria versus obsessional neurosis. Psychoanal. Rev., 27:265-276, 1940.

(2) Actually, repression of the content prevents the inherent cathexis from finding an emotional outlet.

XLI

Subject-Object Shift

IN 1915 Freud noted two vicissitudes which instincts can undergo as modes of defense.[1] One he called "reversal into its opposite" and the second, "turning round upon the subject's own self."

Let us consider first the reversal into its opposite. An instinct can be reversed either in respect to its aim or in respect to its content. Sadism can be reversed into masochism, scoptophilia into exhibitionism. The urge to torture other beings and to look at exposed bodies of other persons is replaced by the desire to be tortured and to be looked at, respectively. Regarding the content of an emotional attitude toward another person, Freud indicated a single instance, namely, the transformation of love into hatred.[2] At that time Freud had not yet conceived the death instinct, and he assumed that sadism preceded masochism. In this paper he considered also the reflexive aim of an instinct, namely, the subject's desire to hurt himself or to look at himself.

This mode of defense, the turning of an active aim into a reflexive or passive one, can be best understood, from a metapsychological point of view, through Federn's ego-psychological concept. In a number of cases of normal as well as pathological developments, we conceived the processes involved as investment and devestment, respectively, of contents by ego cathexis. We spoke of internalization and externalization rather than of "introjection" and "projection," though the latter terms are more often used in psychoanalytic literature. In the processes of the ego's identification with objects, in the normal structuralization of the ego, as well as in pathological manifestations, object representations become egotized. And when a part of an ego state becomes de-egotized, without undergoing repression, it is turned into an object representation. We have also understood that in normal heterosexual development the countersexual tendencies, contained in the bisexual disposition, are externalized into representations of love objects of the opposite sex. Primary and secondary identification, as well as the superego formation itself, ensue from egotization of object representations. In melancholic afflictions we encounter a reflexive aim of hostile striving, which is most adequately described as one ego state turning its aggression against another ego state. And in general, in feelings of guilt leading to self-punitive attitudes, reflexive masochism is manifested, often in form of 'moral masochism," most frequently in obsessional neurotic patients. The sadistic ego state is the superego. Conversely, in paranoia the sadistic ego state is externalized, and in its psychotic manifestations it is projected onto persons of the external world.

In the paper mentioned Freud discusses the aim reversal of an instinct as a mode of defense. Such an aim reversal, he tells us, is induced by the resistance against an active urge, which enters into a conflict with threatening external situations or with one's own conscience; and through its reversal the ego is not deprived of gratification of the drive. As Freud stated, "the masochist shares in the enjoyment of the assault upon himself, the exhibitionist in the enjoyment of (the sight of) his exposure." We considered this kind of gratification as an effect of resonance identification.

Freud mentioned an important detail concerning the development of the sadistic content in the processes of reversal of sadism into masochism and of re-reversal, so to speak, of masochism into sadism. Originally in his sadistic striving the child does not take account of whether he produces pain and suffering to the object; he feels only the urge to overcome and master the object actively. But upon reversal of his sadistic striving into masochism he experiences on himself the fact that being the target of someone else's sadism causes pain. And when his masochism is turned back to sadism, then he becomes interested in producing pain in the object. Through his masochistic experience the sadistic aim obtained an additional scope: to cause pain and suffering to the object. This development, presented by Freud in 1915, seems to me a clear illustration of the effect of "ego passage" as I described it many years later.[3]

According to Freud's theory at that time, the stages of sadistic and scoptophilic aim reversals differed from each other: While sadism was considered the first phase of the sado-masochistic drive, scoptophilia was thought to be preceded by an auto-erotic phase in which the child finds pleasure in looking at his own body. Only five years later Freud conceived the primary masochism, an expression of the death instinct, as the first phase of "maso-sadism." The medial, intransitive, expression of libido and destructive cathexis, a mode which was described by Federn a few years later, is not mentioned in Freud's writings. Reversal of love into hatred can be conceived as a reaction formation in the service of either a denied or a repressed conflictual attraction to an object.

Freud's description of the second mode of defense mentioned, the "turning round upon one's own self," is not clearly distinguishable from reversal of an active drive goal into a reflexive one. But in psychoanalytic literature when the known defense mechanisms are enumerated, "reversal into its opposite," and "turning round upon one's own self" are usually mentioned separately.

In summary Freud mentions the three great polarities which dominate mental life as follows: ". . . the essential feature in the vicissitudes undergone by instincts lies in the subjection of the instinctual impulses to the influences of the three great polarities that dominate mental life. Of these three polarities we might describe that of activity-passivity as the biological, that of ego-external world as the real, and finally that of pleasure-unpleasure as the economic polarity."

The shift of roles in the subject-object relationships is important also in other defense mechanisms.

It is generally assumed that the ego can be threatened from three directions: from the id, the external world and from the superego. But conflictual situations can arise from various circumstances, as pointed out in the previous section. In discriminating among different defense mechanisms some psychoanalysts stress the importance of the direction from which a danger is threatening the ego. Thus, for example, they describe denial as a defense measure which is taken only against unacceptable external conditions, in antithesis to repression, a defense against unmasterable id contents. But (as pointed out in Chapter XXXVI) drives and memories also can be denied, though only, of course, when they are not repressed.

A frequent defense mechanism against external conditions is

that called by Anna Freud [4] "restriction of ego activities." This defense consists in the ego's withdrawal from or renouncing some activity in which it cannot compete with others who perform better. In order to avoid narcissistic injury the ego loses interest in and renounces such activity, and it may, instead, turn its interest toward another activity in which it can distinguish itself. A person may also give up an activity in which he performs better than others, for fear of arousing their envy and vindictive tendencies toward him. Analyses of such cases, mostly of children and adolescents, revealed to Anna Freud that such an activity, which becomes threatening to the patient for the reasons indicated, revived in him an earlier traumatic experience related to genital inferiority: to the boy's experience of having a smaller penis than his father, and to the girl's dismay at not possessing a penis like the boy. This restriction of ego activity follows a dangerous external situation which was reminiscent of an earlier unacceptable situation, in antithesis to a neurotic inhibition of some activity due to repression of an internal instinctive impulse. Federn[5] comments about this defense mechanism as follows: "Anna Freud has described as a defense mechanism the restriction of ego activities. We may remark that it is not an isolated reaction; whenever a frustration is dealt with by one of the normal reactions, part of the ego activity is put out of action to a certain extent; thus, when there are a great number of frustrations normally reacted to, marked restriction of ego activity ensues."

Another important defense mechanism, defense by means of identification with an external object, now deserves our attention. This is the defense mechanism which Anna Freud [6] calls "identification with the aggressor."

A child who is afraid of another person may behave like that person, the "aggressor," in act or gesture, or may assume only the aggressive expression of the threatening person or being. For example, a school boy scolded by his teacher duplicates his angry facial expression, and a girl who is afraid of a ghost when she walks in the dark imitates the imagined movements of the ghost and thereby feels less anxiety. Often, in fact, we may see a boy who is afraid of dogs trying to overcome his fear by imitating a dog's barking and biting.

Often a child assumes an aggressive attitude which he only expects another person to have against him, and thus he avoids meeting the other's aggression. For example, a child who fears reproach or punishment for misbehavior may start to complain about the way he is treated, thus "identifying" with the aggression he expects from the other person. Sometimes one can understand the deeper meaning of the child's fear from the way he himself expresses aggressive attitudes or by the means he uses to manifest them. For instance, a boy who manipulated knives in his aggressive performances must have been afraid that some part of him could be cut off, and we know that castration fear plays an important role in children's anxiety. It is also interesting to note that children, in their "identification with an expected aggressor," often accuse another person, the aggressor, of misbehaving in the way they themselves have behaved.

Anna Freud sees in the identification of children with the threatening punishment of adults a developmental stage toward superego formation. They internalize the criticism, made by an external authority, about the way they themselves have behaved. This progressive internalization of the qualities and opinions of the educators furnishes the material for superego formation. But at this stage, that is, the stage of applying a critical and punitive attitude toward other persons, no superego can yet be considered. Only when the internalized critical attitude of the educators is applied to one's own behavior can we speak of superego.

Observation has shown that a child may try to master his oedipal conflicts by projecting his own strivings onto a parent and complaining about it. Similarly a husband may accuse his wife of infidelity when he himself has such tendencies. Such complaints about tendencies projected onto a parent figure are sometimes encountered also in analytic transference situations. Thus the defense mechanism of "identification with the aggressor" is strengthened by the projection of one's own guilt onto the other person. Such an ego becomes intolerant toward other persons before it becomes stern toward itself. Anna Freud considers the raging of an ego against the "guilty" persons of the external world as being a precursor of and substitute for feelings of guilt, and an intermediary step to morality. In her opinion actual morals ensue when the internalized critics, as superego exigencies, coincide with the perception of one's own wrongs. Then the superego becomes intolerant toward one's own person rather than toward persons of the external world. Some individuals, however, may stop at the earlier state of development and thus remain intolerant and aggressive against outsiders.

The present writer was very much interested in Anna Freud's statement that in such a case the superego becomes as pitiless toward outsiders as the superego in melancholia is pitiless toward its own ego. And her supposition that "the identification with the aggressor" may be also an intermediary step in the development of paranoid states reminded me of the pathogenic mechanisms which I described ten years earlier[7] in conceiving a "persecuting" and a "persecuted" introject. I described their manifestations, in a structural split of the ego, as they appear in the clinical pictures of melancholia, a form of mania, and in paranoid afflictions. These ideas were presented here in Chapter XXXIV.

We wish now to understand why an ego feels less afraid when it "identifies itself with the aggressor." For the purpose of this investigation let us distinguish two elements in this defense mechanism: the fact of becoming aggressive and the process of identification. One can develop aggressive attitudes independent of identification, and, on the other hand, one may identify one's self with another person without becoming aggressive. Each of these two elements has its specific function. The aggressive reaction lowers the level of anxiety for dynamic reasons, namely, by providing an outlet for the inner tension which the ego has to master. Identification, on the other hand, furnishes a guiding device for one's behavior, in our concept of the extraverted destructive cathexis. Through identification the ego learns "how" to act.

It is well known that when cornered an animal becomes aggressive against its aggressor. In such a situation aggression is the only possible defense. We may wonder whether a cornered animal feels less anxiety when it becomes aggressive. We learned that panic and terror, in antithesis to a fear reaction which only signalizes danger, paralyze the ego and thus reduce it to complete helplessness. The economic explanation of this condition is that too much ego cathexis is employed in binding the excess of aroused stimulation. If we assume that the aggressive cathexis develops as an outlet for the threatening stimulation aroused and that the resulting behavior can still be "goal-directed" (according to an integrative plan, in French's concept), then we can understand that aggressive impulses relieve the inner tension and thus also relieve anxiety. The goal-direction of the single co-ordinated aggressive acts can be only instinctively determined, like walking, eating, etc. And when aggressive impulses cannot be properly goal-directed, unco-ordinated actions ensue which do not relieve anxiety and may impress one as concomitant expressions of panic. Aggression must be goal-directed in order to relieve anxiety. In the case of identification with the aggressor the "plan of action" is taken from the threatening individual.

As far as superego formation is concerned, "identification with the aggressor" is only one of several factors in superego development, as well as being a step in that development. Love for the persons who become internalized in the superego plays a role which must not be underestimated. We recognize, furthermore, that among the precursors of superego formation the phenomenon of "psychic presence," as described by this writer, should not be overlooked.

NOTES

(1) Freud, Sigmund. Instincts and their vicissitudes (1915). Standard Edition, 14:109-140. London, Hogarth, 1957.

(2) Freud did not consider love and hatred as "instincts" but rather as general attitudes toward other persons.

(3) Weiss, Edoardo. Über eine noch nicht beschriebene Phase der Entwicklung zur heterosexuellen Liebe. Int. Z. Psychoanal., 11:429-443, 1925; The phenomenon of "ego passage." J. Am. Psychoanal. Assn., 5:267-281, 1957.

(4) Freud, Anna, op. cit.

(5) Federn, Paul. Ego Psychology and the Psychoses. New York, Basic Books, 1952, p. 265.

(6) Freud, Anna, op. cit.

(7) Weiss, Edoardo. Der Vergiftungswahn im Lichte der Introjektions- und Projektionsvorgänge. Int. Z. Psychoanal., 12:466-477, 1926. See also Note 1 to Chapter XXX.

Section VI

The Dream Phenomenon
and the Dreaming Ego

XLII

Psychological Approach to the Dream Phenomenon

MEANINGFUL implications of dreams have been transmitted to us since the earliest records of civilization. As Freud [1] mentions in his detailed review of the scientific literature dealing with the problem of dreams, people in classical antiquity "took it as axiomatic that dreams were connected with the world of superhuman beings in whom they believed and that they were revelations from gods and demons." Aristotle had a more psychological concept of dreams, but in his opinion too they were of "demonic" rather than divine nature. Although we cannot embark here on a discussion of all the rich contents of the first chapter of Freud's classic and revolutionary book on dreams, mention of a few points will give us a clear conception of the dream phenomenon itself.

During the period of the Enlightenment dreams were depreciated as phenomena unworthy of scientific interest. Only superstitious persons and soothsayers resorted to "dream interpretation." In more recent times physiologists and psychologists considered the dream experience as merely the effect of fortuitous and aimless excitations of brain cells during sleep, little suspecting that dreams had a psychological meaning detectable by specific psychological techniques. As mentioned in Chapter XII, Freud reports also on descriptions of the absurdities of some dream contents and one's deficient critical and mnemonic capacities during dreaming, as published by 19th-century psychologists such as Burdach, Fechner, Strümpell, and Spitta. Freud's recognition that every dream has a psychological significance was a monumental scientific achievement. It required not only an ingenious investigating mind but also rigorous and exhaustive exploration of countless concrete dreams of various kinds, both dreams of healthy persons and those of the emotionally disturbed. His revelation of the psychological character of the dream phenomenon was a natural and understandable consequence of his previous discovery of the existence of an unconscious mental activity. It has already been made clear in this volume that the "unconscious" which Freud unveiled and investigated is a mental activity in the individual which is excluded from the ego as the conscious mental activity of one person is excluded from the direct experience of another person. This is precisely what Freud said in his metapsychological presentation of the unconscious. It is little wonder that in ancient times the manifestations of such a mental activity were thought to be communications from other beings.

The ego perceives its dreams as in waking life it perceives the physical events of the external world. This realm of mental phenomena from which dreams arise could not have been more adequately expressed than by the term "id," the pronoun of the third person. To use our own terminology, we shall say that behind the internal windowless wall not only somatic physiological phenomena take place but also mental phenomena. These mental phenomena are inaccessible as such to the ego, as long as they are not egotized. When they do come to the ego's awareness without being egotized, as in dreams and hallucinations in general, the ego perceives them with the character of external physical phenomena which are perceived by the sense organs, through the "windows embedded in the external ego boundary." The full importance of the discovery that behind or inherent in some perceived physical qualities something psychological takes place—such as wishes, memories, representations, emotions—cannot yet be properly evaluated. Freud's disclosures are greater, perhaps, than he himself could have imagined.

Let us examine for a moment our perception of physical qualities through our sense organs. Visual, acoustic, tactile qualities, etc., are qualities which we ascribe to the various stimuli which reach our sense organs. The "real" nature of the external "reality" is inconceivable to the human mind. Our knowledge of this reality is based on our individual sensory perception of it, not on the particular properties of the reality itself. We cannot even know that another individual perceives exactly as we do. Can we prove that another person sees "red" or hears a given sound in exactly the same way that we do? Whatever physical stimulus excites a specific section of our brain, we perceive either visual qualities, acoustic, thermal, etc.; and our sense organs are so constructed and so connected with specific brain centers that under normal conditions each center is stimulated by a specific kind of physical stimulation. But the physicist teaches us that these different kinds of stimuli, which we sense in these different areas, are not "in reality" of the perceived nature but consist in certain vibrations, waves, or rapid movements of extremely small particles. The physicist's conceptions of physical phenomena are in a continuous state of further development and modification, and their validity is proved by our progress in influencing physical events and so constructing better-perfected tools for mastering nature, for rapid and accurate communication to distant places, etc. In recent years we have come to realize that not only what we call "electricity" and "force of gravity" but even space and time are beyond our sensory conception. In place of our sensory concepts mathematics is constantly gaining value for the exploration and mastery of the external physical world.

In psychology we speak of "external reality" in terms of our adequate perceptions of external events without distinguishing an unrecognizable "actual" external reality from the external reality as we perceive it. It is only the latter which we call external reality. Perceptions of physical qualities which are not induced by adequate external stimuli but which arise from internal stimulations, such as dreams and pathological hallucinations, are called "false realities." Memories and representations of external qualities arise from partial and combined elements of previous perceptions.

Experience shows us that physical events do not occur haphazardly but that there are rules of succession, one given event following another. In other words, we acquire the concepts of "cause" and "effect." If this were not so, world events would be chaotic and there would be no possibility for us to orient ourselves and to act on external reality; we would not survive. In waking life an experience of a chaotic condition of external events, of however short duration, would be the most traumatic experience we could imagine. But in dreams this may occur without such disturbing effect. The chaotic succession of events adheres only to the manifest dream content and has a latent psychological meaning.

We are intellectually accustomed to differentiate the physical causes and effects from the motivating reasons which determine our thinking and acting. We conceive the falling of a stone as the causal effect of the force of gravity and not as an "aim" inherent in the stone to reach the ground. But if someone goes to a place to take food, we conceive that he is motivated to do so. In our orientation aim-directed or goal-directed striving is inherent not only in all mental phenomena but also in all life processes in general. As mentioned in the first section of this book, W. B. Cannon gave clear expression to this point of view in the title he chose for his book in physiology, *The Wisdom of the Body*. One may ask whether there must be inherent in every life process something psychological which determines its goal-direction. This question is unanswerable and therefore pointless. Yet, we do conceive the goal-directed id processes as psychological phenomena.

Close examination of the conceptual difference between physical determinism, based on rigid physical laws, and goal-directed behavior will help us to understand better the psychological nature of dreams. In order to illustrate this difference let us compare two concrete examples: If we accidentally spill ink on a paper, we do not see any "motivating" force which would determine the shape of the spot of ink. If in the spot we see the form of an animal or a human, for example, we know that it is only in our imagination, and that such a similarity is merely a chance coincidence. From the point of view of figurative art the shape of such a spot is "chaotic," aimless. But not so from the point of view of physical determinism. In fact, we understand that in every case in which the same quantity and the same kind of ink was spilled from the same height, on the same kind of paper, etc., an ink spot of exactly the same shape would result. We cannot, of course, determine the exact conditions which were present when the ink was spilled, but we accept the fact that given exactly the same conditions exactly the same spot would occur again. This fact is called "physical determinism." So from the point of view of physical laws the ink spot was not formed "chaotically."

Let us now consider an artist's painting. In this case too all forms and contours, every single shade of color in the exact place where it appears, every single element of the painting, came into existence in obedience to precise physical and chemical laws. But this object of art has in addition a psychological meaning; it represents something which the painter wanted to produce and in the way he wanted to produce it. Such a production is chaotic neither in a physical nor in a psychological sense. These two examples illustrate the difference between physical events which occur only according to strict physical laws of succession and those physical events which occur with the addition of human or other biological intervention, as all alloplastic productions do. Houses, trains, airplanes, weapons, etc., are not chaotic from the point of view of a goal-directed meaning. They are the results of selected direction given to physical and chemical processes. We can also express this by saying that the human mind and all life processes "utilize" what we call physical laws in their goal-directing intervention. This is true not only for alloplastic productions but for autoplastic ones as well: The development and evolution of living matter are based on goal-directed interventions in physical and chemical processes.

At this point we may be diverted briefly by an interesting question: If every physical event is strictly determined by laws of succession, how can living matter intervene selectively in the physical world? Wherefrom can a "choice" of physical processes derive? There are only two answers to this problem: Either all physical processes, including those which involve no life process, are goal-directed in the same manner as life processes are, or life processes as specific phenomena have the capacity to suspend strict physical determinism, somehow and somewhere, if only for the shortest time. But in the first case life processes would not be of a different nature from physical and chemical ones; they would be only very complicated interconnected physical processes, and this is, indeed, very difficult to assume.

Returning now to the dream phenomenon, let us formulate the pertinent question in the following terms: Do dreams come into being by fortuitous planless stimulations of our nervous system, through the capillary blood stream or other minute intracranial chemical or physical processes? Then the dream accident would be analogous to the mentioned spot of spilled ink. Or do dreams arise in a way analogous to the artist's production of a painting, which has a psychological meaning? The study of dreams gives us a precise answer: Applying certain methods of procedure, we find that every dream is meaningful, and every dream is a reaction to our needs which seek satisfaction. Dreams deal always with problems to be solved. This is Freud's conclusion from his method of dream interpretation. It is in no way weakened by the fact that various physical stimulations, e.g., the administration of various drugs, influence the contents of dreams. True, these excitations and intoxications create specific problems and also affect various mental functions chemically, either by stimulating them or by weakening and paralyzing them. But even in these cases dreams are meaningful psychological reactions to needs. The goal-directed nature of the conscious and unconscious mental life, which confers a psychological meaning to all of its manifestations, is already implied in our concept of "cathexis," as emphasized throughout this volume.

We understand that the contents resulting from unconscious mental activity, which have undergone distorting processes, are perceived by the dreaming ego as phenomena of the external world. The hallucinated dream world substitutes for the actual external world from which the sleeping ego has withdrawn. Following Federn's studies of the ego we can now distinguish two factors in the dream phenomenon: the perceived dream contents and the changing states of the dreaming ego itself which experiences and reacts to the dream contents. Freud's achievements in the understanding of dreams concern the latent meaning of dreams and the way in which it can be revealed. And let us not forget that psychoanalysis was originally only psychology of the unconscious. Freud's statements regarding the role of the ego in dream formation can be summarized as follows: In the state of sleep the ego withdraws narcissistically from the external world; its interest is turned inward in compliance with its need for rest. It is precisely this selfish withdrawal from the external world, he tells us, its need to protect itself from external stimulations, that makes it accessible to internal stimulations from the unconscious. And, consistent with the ego's interest in itself, the protagonist of every dream represents a portion of the dreamer's own ego. We would say that this dream person is an externalized part of an ego state.

It was Federn who, in the twenties, publishing his first findings on ego psychology, described many characteristics of the dreaming ego. He characterized it as a weakly cathected ego. And this is evident from the circumstance that non-ego mental phenomena reach the ego's awareness as dream hallucinations, that is, that the internal ego boundary does not resist the impact of the id pressures which thus come to the ego's awareness as unegotized contents. Besides, the ego is not completely awakened by the dream; many of its functions remain dormant, particularly its motility (except in the case of somnambulism which calls for a special explanation). Nor are the ego's critical and mnemonic capacities fully awakened, as many authors, mentioned by Freud, have already observed. Federn teaches us that in many dreams, in his opinion in the majority of dreams, only the mental ego is partially awakened while the body ego remains dormant, but in those dreams which involve emotional and volitional processes the body ego feeling is always present. In waking life the experience of existing only mentally without body would be very bewildering. But the feeling of ego continuity is based on the mental ego, since upon awakening one senses that it was one's own self who had been dreaming, no matter how much the ego feeling was changed during the dream. As mentioned in Chapters XII and XIX, in a dream an ego may be awakened at different age levels.

Should the ego states during dreaming not be considered as parts of the dream? An adult may say that he dreamt of being a boy again. This person considers the regression of his ego to a former state as a part of the dream. Another may consider as a part of his dream his deficiency in discriminating during the dream. Again, in some dreams the ego may react to a manifest dream scene as it would in waking life to the latent scene which underwent a distortion in the dream. For instance, a patient dreamt of a lion without being at all afraid of it. Analysis revealed that the lion in the dream stood for an acquaintance whose name was Leo and not, as might have been supposed, for an aggressive dangerous impulse. So it seems that the dreaming ego may sometimes be nearer to understanding the latent meaning of some dream image or event than the rational ego of waking life can be. In summary we conclude that the relation between the hallucinated dream content and the dreaming ego can be of a very complicated nature. In fact, as Federn has demonstrated, some subjective experiences of the dreaming ego itself lend themselves to specific interpretations of the waking ego's attitude toward external events.

Study of the dreaming ego has added importance also in the fact that, as will be discussed, it shows some features in common with the schizophrenic ego.

NOTES

(1) Freud, Sigmund. The Interpretation of Dreams (1900). Standard Edition, 4 & 5. London, Hogarth, 1953.

XLIII

The Manifest and the Latent Dream Content

FREUD called "manifest dream content" the content of a dream as the dreamer actually experiences it, and he termed "latent dream content" the psychological meaning of the dream which one can recognize after interpretation of the manifest dream.[1] In order to decipher latent dream thoughts it is necessary not only to be acquainted with the dreamer's life situation but also to have the dreamer's "free associations" to the single elements of the dream. One observes then that the dreamer offers resistance to the interpretation of the dream. This is the same resistance described in our discussion of the phenomenon of repression and other defense mechanisms. This resistance is responsible for the dreamer's forgetting his dreams or parts of them upon awakening and also later for his difficulty in furnishing associations to the single dream elements. Accordingly, in order to unearth the latent dream thoughts from the manifest dream the analyst must overcome the patient's resistance against acknowledging the latent dream thoughts.

The following example, a young man's dream, may illustrate how one proceeds in the interpretation:

"I was riding in a car driven by a very young fellow. My wife and a friend of mine were with me, and it seemed as if we were just returning from somewhere after having inspected a home. Then I found myself alone in a garage, in which the car was being repaired, and the garage man said, 'We have to get the key.' "

The dreamer's life situation was as follows: He was unhappily married to a woman who gave him justifiable reasons to be jealous. He had spent the evening before the dream with the friend of whom he dreamed, and had spoken with him about his marital situation. His friend's opinion was that the marriage could be saved if the patient left the city and lived with his wife in a home in the country, near Chicago. The patient remarked that he did not share his

396

friend's opinion; he realized that he had chosen the wrong woman. When the analyst asked him to associate to the driver of the car, the dreamer could only say that the driver must have been too young and too inexperienced to be able to drive a car with safety. He added, "I was quite inexperienced when I married my wife." So, the driver in the dream was an externalized ego state of the dreamer himself. During his analytic treatment he had come to the realization that he had handled the problems which had presented themselves to him in an immature manner. "Driving a car" stood for "dealing with reality problems." The analyst urged him to associate more to the trip. He had then the retrospective sensation that the inspection of the home must have been unsuccessful, and only when the analyst insisted did the patient produce a "vague idea" that in the dream they were returning from Oak Park. Since no associations to Oak Park were forthcoming, it became evident that the patient had a resistance against some thoughts connected with that place. Of the garage too he could give only general associations, such as that it was nice and spacious and reminded him of other garages he knew. Suddenly he remarked that the garage man had a slight resemblance to the analyst. It seems evident indeed that the repair shop for his car was substituted for his treatment where a proper solution—the key—to the patient's problems had to be found.

Summarizing and verbalizing the latent content of this dream so far, we realize that it does not contain anything which had been unconscious to the dreamer before the dream. It may have expressed the following thought: "My friend is wrong in believing that I would solve my marital problem by buying a home outside the city. I can show him that this would be unsuccessful. (The friend was taken along in the dream.) I recognize, however, that I was too immature and inexperienced to handle properly (drive the car) the arising difficulties. The ultimate way to solve my difficulties is through analytic treatment, whereby the analyst will help me to find the right solution." But the analyst was not satisfied with such an interpretation, since this train of thought was not repressed at all, and we wondered why it had to be so much disguised in the form of the manifest dream. One reason could be that thoughts as such cannot be represented in visual pictures; thus for the sake of representability in dream images the thoughts had to be substituted by visual scenes. This is, according to Freud, one among other processes in what he calls the "dream work." But this interpretation contains also an inexact statement. In the dream the dreamer did not show his friend that he had been wrong: Since the home was not bought, he did not demonstrate that his relation to his wife would not improve if the advice were followed. In dream interpretations we must be exact.

In the following analytic session the patient brought a new memory concerning Oak Park, to which he had been unable to associate in the preceding hour. When he was still a child his father had wanted to buy a beautiful home there but for some reason had changed his mind. The analyst remarked that also in the dream the deal was or seemed to be unsuccessful. In later years the patient had once heard his mother complain that his father had failed to make her happy in not purchasing that home for her.

It is evident that the patient's inability to furnish the necessary associations for understanding the latent dream content was due to his resistance against oedipal wishes which aroused a strong conflict. From his analysis it had become clear that the patient as a child felt competitive with his father in regard to making his mother happy. But he would have been afraid to do better than his father and thus provoke his revenge. The processes which had led to this dream are the following: His friend's advice to buy a home for his wife in order to straighten out his relationship with her, an advice given the evening before the dream, entered into associative connection with the forgotten episode of his father's failure and his mother's complaint. This memory was still charged (in the id) with a strong but blocked cathexis. And it was this cathexis that invigorated the thought of the present unhappy marital situation. The advice given him by his friend, who could not understand the real difficulty of the patient, could not have solved his marital difficulties. So, to complete and rectify the interpretation of the dream given so far, we would say: "The advice which my friend has given me reminds me how much I would have liked to make my mother happy, in which my father failed. But I do not dare to outdo my father, especially in competition for my mother's favor. Therefore I do not do better than he. And, as a consequence of my fear of being estranged from him, I do not dare to become a grown man; I have remained immature and have not handled certain situations properly. The reason why I have chosen the wrong woman is that I have remained tied to my mother." Although this interpretation is not yet complete it represents already a condensation of thoughts. The dream likewise reveals a favorable attitude toward the analyst. The patient hopes to settle in the analytic transference relationship the difficulties he had in his relationship with his father. The "key" which has to be found signifies not only the "solution" to his emotional problems but is also a masculine "symbol." Psychoanalytic symbolism will be discussed later. Here we wish only to mention that the "key" which has to be found is related to the patient's redeemable masculinity—and maturity.

From this example we have learned already many factors concerning dream interpretation: In every dream we find that an event from the day prior to the dream has stimulated a train of unconscious thoughts. The cathexis inherent in the repressed wishes flows into the preconscious material through the associative paths which connected the "day residues" (as Freud calls the experiences which immediately preceded the dream) with the repressed wishes. The dreamer has a resistance to recognizing the latent dream thoughts. Therefore the latent content has to be disguised into an unrecognizable manifest content in order to reach the dreamer's awareness, even though only in form of hallucinations. Later Freud equated this resistance with the superego. It is this resistance which Freud called the "dream censor," thus personifying the phenomenon of resistance. In order to elude the awareness of this censor the latent content has to be disguised. We wish now to understand what the function of the dream is according to Freud.

In Freud's opinion the dream has the function of protecting sleep against disturbing stimuli. Dreamless sleep is certainly more restful and refreshing than sleep with dreams. Sometimes dreams may arouse emotions, especially anxiety, as in nightmares which awaken the sleeper. But under certain conditions of excitation one would not sleep at all if he did not dream. So, sleep with dreams, though less restful than dreamless sleep, is preferable to not sleeping at all. According to Freud dreams are mental attempts to appease internal stimuli by producing the illusion (through the hallucinatory experience of fulfilled wishes) that the disturbing stimulations have been taken care of. If a hungry sleeper dreams that he is eating, which is a fulfilled wish, he feels less disturbed by his hunger. The dream says to him, as it were, "Do not worry about your hunger; you are eating right now." Whether a dream is successful in its sleep-protecting function depends on the intensity of the stimulus, on the one hand (in this case the hunger sensation) and the need for sleep on the other hand. But this is an undisguised dream.

When the disturbing stimuli are repressed one has first to decipher the latent dream thoughts before one can detect the sleep-disturbing wishes. Freud's wish-fulfillment theory of dreams is related to the latent dream content when, as in the great majority of dreams of adults, the latent thoughts underwent a disguising process. Let us now return for a moment to the dream reported above. The sleep-disturbing stimuli of the patient were not only his conscious worries about his unhappy marriage but also the arousal of his unconscious unresolved oedipal wishes which heightened his worries about the difficulties with his wife. The latter were blocked by his fear of his father. Following Freud's theory that the dream produces in a disguised form the fulfillment of unsatisfied wishes, one may now ask why the latent content did not express that the dreamer succeeded in making his wife and his mother happy, that his marital difficulties were straightened out and that no conflict or rivalry with his father ensued? Such a latent content would have been analogous to the hungry sleeper's undisguised dream that he was eating. But we realize that the patient had conflicting wishes. To ignore completely all the complicated difficulties of waking life, and to admit to himself that he still cared more for his mother's than for his wife's affection, and that in addition he had sexual desires of infantile origin toward his mother, would amount to a mental performance far beyond the dreamer's capacity. His oedipal wishes interfered with his father's attitude toward them, and he loved and feared his father. Furthermore he was still emotionally unprepared to challenge his father's anger and renounce his own passive submissive attitude toward him. In other words, he had also the wish to be submissive to his father. Later, following his experiences of dreams resulting from unmastered traumatic experiences, Freud more clearly stated his views regarding the wish-fulfillment character of dreams. In the first of his *New Introductory Lectures*[2] he says: "We assert that the dream is a wish fulfillment; in order to take these last objections [namely, concerning traumatic dreams] into account, you may say that the dream is an *attempted* wish fulfillment. But for those who have an understanding of the dynamics of the mind you will not be saying anything different. Under certain conditions the dream can only achieve its end in a very incomplete way, or has to abandon it entirely; an unconscious fixation to the trauma seems to head the list of these obstacles to the dream-function. The sleeper has to dream because the nightly relaxation of repression allows the upward thrust of the traumatic fixation to become active; but sometimes his dream-work, which endeavors to change the memory traces of the traumatic event into a wish fulfillment, fails to operate . . ." Freud concludes with the statement: ". . . so one need not be surprised if lesser disturbances of the function of the dream occur in other circumstances."

To return to the dream under discussion, we notice also that the dreamer did resort to a hope for wish fulfillment, namely, to solve his conflicts and to improve his life situation through treatment.

When a person harbors conflicting wishes, the aim of one wish may be at variance with the aim of another, and this may lead to anxiety dreams. But difficulties arising from conflicting wishes are not the only factors which obscure the wish-fulfillment character of many dreams. We may wonder to what extent the "dream work" can ignore unpleasant reality situations. According to Freud, all mental phenomena in the id (which is ruled by the primary mental process) are guided by the pleasure principle alone and not by the reality principle. In the id there are no contradictions, and ensuing conflicting tendencies lead to a compromise formation. Do the latent dream contents in fact confirm this view of Freud's? Does the ego's integrative function ever influence the latent dream thoughts? All these questions will be discussed, and we shall also examine more thoroughly dreams due to traumatic experiences, which, according to Freud, are exceptions to the wish-fulfillment character of dreams.

Since the dream activity is closely connected with the state of sleep, let us for a moment consider the physiopsychological implications of sleep itself. The ego experience of waking life is due to the continuous afflux of energy from physiological sources into the coherent ego unity, whereby the energy consumed in the ego experience itself, and in the ego functions, exceeds the energy produced. The organism cannot transform physiological energy into ego cathexis as rapidly as it is used up by the waking ego. Therefore, during waking life the amount of available ego cathexis progressively decreases until a certain degree of exhaustion is reached and the need for sleep ensues. It should be noted at this point that functionally different types of ego cathexis arise from different hormonal and other physiological sources which are still unknown to us. Discovery of these hormones would lead to great progress in the organic therapy of various ego deficiencies as described in various clinical manifestations of schizophrenia. But not all ego deficiencies are felt by the ego as a state of exhaustion. Many kinds of deficiencies are manifested in ego disturbances and psychotic symptoms. Only a general exhaustion of ego feeling and its functional capacity is felt as such, namely, as exhaustion and need for sleep. This need is also determined by the habitual periodicity of succession of the waking and sleeping states. The need for withdrawal of ego cathexis (and thus for sleep) is regulated by specific cerebral centers which are supplied by the autonomic nervous system, mainly by the parasympathicus. These centers can be excited or paralyzed by specific drugs. From the purely dynamic point of view, however, it seems evident that the degree of exhaustion of ego cathexis must be a determining factor for the depth of sleep. The ego can postpone the desire for sleep and can by conscious effort utilize the still available (though diminished) ego-cathexis for a great length of time. And daily experience verifies the fact that intense interests forestall the desire to sleep. For weak or psychotic egos, however, this should be avoided.

In the state of dreamless sleep no consumption of ego-cathexis can take place; during this time the "reservoir" of ego-cathexis is being filled. (In my opinion such a reservoir must be postulated.) After sufficient restful sleep the ego acquires a new and abundant supply of ego-cathexis, which is experienced as a vivid alert ego feeling. Even when sleep is disturbed by dreams the ego cathexis is resupplied. The dreaming ego is always weakly cathected, and its consumption of cathexis is slight in comparison to the abundance of the biological regeneration. Federn has shown that sleep is incompatible with a strongly cathected ego. The ego remains cathected, or becomes so, whenever stimuli become too strong. One comes to the obvious conclusion that the stronger the disturbing stimuli, the more must the ego be dynamically exhausted in order to fall asleep. We shall return to this consideration in discussion of dreams caused by traumatic experiences.

French distinguishes between the wish to sleep and the capacity to sleep, and he calls "sleep-preserving function" the integrative mechanism on which the maintenance of sleep depends. To him the "wish to sleep" is the incentive that activates the sleep-preserving mechanism. Internal pressure can be absorbed, he explains, by wish-fulfilling hallucinations and by the physiological state of sleep itself. "The absorption of pressure by wish-fulfilling illusions makes it possible for dreams to prolong sleep; the absorption of pressure by sleep makes the dreamer more easily satisfied by wish-fulfilling dreams than he could be if he were awake." [3] As stated in Chapter XII French conceives the ego from a behavioristic point of view as the integrative function of the mind. He holds that dreams are unnecessary when the "depth of sleep" provides enough physiological absorption of pressure, and the degree of absorption is directly proportionate to the depth of the physiological state of sleep.

Freud, on the other hand, stated that every mental system which is uncathected loses its property of responding to stimulation. When the ego is unconscious (as in sleep) it does not sense any bodily pain or discomfort. As I have shown,[4] sensations of bodily pain which awaken the ego to a dreaming state are often experienced in the dream not as a bodily pain but as mental pain or discomfort. I also noted this occurrence in schizophrenic patients, as I shall discuss later. When the body ego is in a state of sleep, that is, uncathected, the inner Reizschutz (protection against stimuli) is absent. Consequently, when the mental ego is awakened by mental stimuli, it dreams. One may wonder why, when the Reizschutz is absent, the sleeper does not experience nightmares more frequently, as is customary after traumatic events. The explanation for this is precisely (we repeat) that the mind and the body are less accessible to stimulation because they are not cathected.

Federn considered the body ego and the mental ego separately, and found that the body ego may be in deep sleep while the mental ego is awakened to a great intensity. According to Federn the depth of sleep of the body ego can be inferred from the intensity of the stimulus which can be endured without awakening, regardless of its character, whether pleasant or unpleasant. Under general [but not too deep] [5] anesthesia, for instance, in which the dreamer remains asleep, very intense and vivid dreams can occur. They may be extremely pleasurable or very frightening, and the dreaming ego has a strong feeling of the reality of what it is dreaming; indeed, the dream content is often felt as more real than the experience of life during the waking state. (We shall discuss examples of dreams under anesthesia in a later chapter.) In Federn's opinion the strong feeling of reality of the dream content is the effect of an intense mental ego cathexis; and he points out that under such circumstances the mental ego can be very strongly awakened because the sleeper's body ego cannot awaken. According to my observation, however, not all mental functions of such a dream ego are awakened, in spite of the great intensity of the ego feeling and its vivid sensation of the reality of the dream scenes. The decisive factors in such dreams are the intensity of the disturbing stimuli on the one hand and the depth of anesthesia on the other.

In normal physiological sleep, which is incompatible with a strongly cathected mental ego, the threshold is much lower, and, indeed, anxiety dreams and nightmares awaken the sleeper. While French holds that these dreams are due to a lighter sleep, other observers believe that nightmares can occur in deep sleep as well, since a deep sleep also can be brought to an end by strong stimuli.

People are kept awake by painful worries and unsatisfied needs or desires, and it is a common experience that any hope of relief from these unpleasant situations favors sleep. As a rule such hopes derive from reality testing; it seems, however, that wishful thinking may also have an appeasing effect on mental stimuli. There are people who have difficulty falling asleep because of some emotional tension from their daily work and resort to the following device: They imagine they own a magic wand or some similar device with which they could fulfill all their wishes. And while they are enjoying this pleasant fantasy they may fall asleep, long before they reach the end of their wishes. The calming effect of such a device, however, is not always due to wishful thinking but often to the fact that it constitutes a means for diverting one's thoughts from tension-producing contents. Such wishes are usually quite unrelated to the disturbing mental stimuli. Undisguised dreams of children substantiate the wish fulfillment theory. But children are less reality-adapted than adults. It is much more difficult for an adult to appease justified worries or some grief by wishful thinking when the odds are against a solution of his problems. Then sleep ensues only when a certain degree of exhaustion is reached.

According to Freud, the functions and orientations of the waking ego are not completely abolished by sleep. Thus we pointed out in Chapter XI that in his opinion, "the ego's censorship is never quite asleep" and that the "secondary revision" is a performance of the dream work in adaptation to the rational ego, though this secondary revision does not always take place. In accordance with his view that the ego's integrative activity is one of the factors responsible for the dream content, French found that when sleep is not deep, wish fulfillment appears in dreams only if the dreamer in waking life had some hope for a solution to his problem. This hope is not necessarily based on objective conclusions; it may rest either on actual experiences of a successful outcome of similar situations in the past or on an anticipation of a favorable solution derived from available data.

NOTES

(1) This portion of the book will be illustrated by case material drawn from some of my earlier publications as well as by dreams which have not yet been published.

(2) Freud, Sigmund. New Introductory Lectures on Psychoanalysis (1933). New York, Norton, 1933, pp. 45-46.

(3) French, op. cit., Vol. 1, pp. 198-199.

(4) Weiss, Edoardo. Bodily pain and mental pain. Int. J. Psychoanal., 15:1-13, 1934.

(5) I have added the words "but not too deep."

XLIV

Dream Work and Aspects of Wish Fulfillment

WE understand the biological need for sleep, for a state in which the ego is uncathected, as an economic necessity. Since internal and external stimuli excite ego investment, the sleep-needing ego avoids these stimuli in order to lose its cathexis, in other words, to fall asleep. It withdraws from light, sound, or excessive heat or cold. Hunger, thirst, and other physical needs delay or prevent withdrawal of ego cathexis into the biological organism. The infant falls asleep, into a supposed prenatal state, immediately upon being satisfactorily nursed. To Freud sleep is an ego regression to the prenatal stage. All interests other than the selfish desire to sleep keep the ego cathected. Therefore, in order to sleep the ego gives up all its object interests. For this reason Freud considered sleep as a "narcissistic withdrawal." But the connotation of "narcissistic" does not have a structural implication here. Federn himself on one occasion used the term "biological narcissism" complying with Freud's concept of sleep as a narcissistic withdrawal. In Chapter XII we pointed out also that only in Hartmann's expanded concept of narcissism (which we do not accept) can this withdrawal be called "narcissistic."

As far as mental stimuli are concerned the ego can fall asleep when it succeeds in freeing itself from all preconscious, i.e., ego-cathected, contents. Only then does it obtain "freedom from stimulations" within its own domain. But mental stimuli outside its domain, in the non-ego area of the id, can remain cathected in spite of the ego's uncathected state. Moreover certain preconscious data, which have already lost their cathexis, may be re-aroused by repressed contents cathected in this non-ego area. These preconscious data are those which Freud called the "day residues" as well as problems of waking life related to these day residues. A connection has become established between these preconscious data and the repressed contents, and it is the repressed contents which determine the dream content. The dream, in turn, re-awakens the ego, but only partially and incompletely, and only toward the internal stimuli which through the weakened internal ego boundary reach its awareness. The dreaming ego remains isolated from the external world which is substituted by the dream world. The latter is sensed as real. When, however, the dream content arouses excessively strong affects, the ego awakens completely. But even when not completely awake, the ego in a dreaming state regains some of its cathexis (however weak and selected it may be) and reacts to the dream experiences. Thus the ultimate dream formation is due to a combination of id and ego exertions. Freud called "dream work" the processes which transform the latent dream thoughts into the manifest dream.

Let us recapitulate briefly what these processes are:

1) As pointed out in Chapter X, the cathexes in the id do not yet adhere firmly to single representations but are in a "free-floating" state. One representation can be replaced by another; two or more representations can be aroused simultaneously, producing a fusion of these representations into one representation. For example, a dream person may have characteristics of more than one person known to the dreamer. A room may resemble one known place in some respects and another known place in other respects. Furthermore, the cathexes of two or more representations may flow into one representation which thus becomes aroused to great vividness. In the last dream reported the representation of the analyst was substituted by a garage man, and a masculine prerogative (the penis) by a "key" which had to be recovered. Many other factors which rule unegotized id contents were mentioned in Chapter X. In the id there is no discrimination between real and unreal, no contradiction between incompatible contents or wishes, no negation, no concepts of time or causality, in other words, no regard for the reality principle. The mental processes in the id occur according to the pleasure principle alone. These features of the id processes are manifestations of what Freud called the "primary mental process." Only the in-

vestment of id contents by the preconscious ego cathexis puts an end to the primary mental process, thus establishing the rational "secondary mental process."

2) Ideas can be represented in dreams only by visual images. For example, a patient dreamed of going to visit a friend, climbing many flights of stairs to reach his apartment only to find it empty. In reality this friend lived in a single-family house, not in a multistory building, but the dreamer thought of him as being not very intelligent, a thought which was represented in the dream by "nobody is upstairs." In the same dream "driving a car" represented "driving through reality problems."

3) It is a task of the dream work to create a situation of a fulfilled wish, in an attempt to appease disturbing stimuli.

4) The partially awakened ego offers resistance to unwelcome contents. A "dream censor" is at work. Through intervention of the censor some parts of the dream are simply blotted out or forgotten, and a selection of substitutive representations is made, so that the latent dream thoughts become unintelligible. Furthermore, to avoid too much chaos and manifest incoherence arising from the primary mental process a secondary revision (described in Chapter X) sometimes sets in to confer a fictitious "sense," upon the manifest content for the dreaming ego.

Some psychoanalysts do not believe in a complete irrationality of the primary mental process and find every substitution and representation of thoughts that occur in dreams meaningful. We are now prepared to consider the analyses of other concrete dreams.

For practical reasons only short dreams are usually chosen for an exposition of the different problems in dream interpretation. Each dream should illustrate a precise point which the writer wishes to elucidate. This I will do subsequently. But first I wish to present an example of a complicated and difficult-to-interpret dream. Since the analysis of a long dream reveals intimate facts of the dreamer's life, I have chosen a dream which was related to me by a patient in Italy twenty-five years ago. She was a forty-five-year-old married

woman with two adolescent sons. Except for a change in the names
the following report is an exact translation of the dream which I
wrote down, just as it was told to me. Attention may be given not
only to the manifest incoherence of the manifest dream, but also
to the dreaming ego state, to its lack of discriminating capacity and
to its reactions, which would have been more appropriate to the
latent dream thoughts than to the manifest dream scenes themselves. I do not intend to present a deep and "complete" interpretation of this dream, but wish only to give the reader a glimpse of its
latent meaning. A more thorough analysis of this dream would require many chapters and unfold the psychological formulation of
the patient's entire neurosis. The dream follows:

"My son Mario had killed his father. Although it did not occur
in the dream, I knew that he had crushed him to death with a large
stone. Mario was ten years old instead of his actual age. He is now
eighteen years old and has the height of a grown man. We were in
his room or apartment which was very messy and cluttered. It was
not a place familiar to me in reality.

"Mario had his dead father wrapped in a cloth and tied into a
small bundle, about the size of a newborn baby. He was trying to
carry or move it. Someone indistinguishable pretended to try to
help him but was laughing and joking, and taking it too lightly.

"After a short time I saw that Mario, being childlike and irrespon-
sible, had taken pieces of the skull and pasted them on paper. There
were two pieces of the skull, small and flat, not really like a skull
but more like a dried, mummified head and face, about the size of
a newborn baby's.

"I felt adult and responsible, frightened and guilty for Mario. I
took the pieces of skull away, hurriedly tried to hide all the evidence so that the *carabinieri* (the police) would not know he had
killed his father. My husband (Mario's actual father) was there
helping me clean up. He was even more conscientious than I about
picking up every bit and piece of evidence. (Clearly, in the dream
he was *not* the one who had been killed.) When he and I were satisfied that everything was clean, he went outdoors to 'play' with
Mario and our older son.

"I went to our older son's room where everything was neat, with bright-colored books and painted masks on the wall. I said to Mario, 'Why can't you keep your things orderly as your brother does?'

"In a short while the *carabinieri* came for Mario. They knew, in spite of my efforts to cover up. I was not much surprised, but felt that it was inevitable that they would find out. It could not be hidden that Mario had killed his father."

Not only is the manifest content of this dream uncanny (the "secondary revision" was defective), but also the dreaming ego's affective reaction and its lack of understanding of all the incoherences of the dream events is very weird. But before we obtain the meaning of the latent content we cannot exclude the fact that the latent dream content represents somehow the fulfillment of a wish. As mentioned, Freud emphasized that only through our understanding of the latent dream thoughts are we able to detect, somehow and somewhere, a successful or unsuccessful attempt to reach a fulfillment of a conscious or unconscious repressed wish. So let us precede with the interpretation technique.

This was the patient's life situation at the time she had this dream: She felt very dissatisfied and frustrated in her relationship with her husband who neglected her almost completely. He provided only material comfort for his family and cared for his sons. Her great desire for love could be satisfied only through daydreams, and she even had the impression that her husband would not mind if she had a lover.

From her analysis it was learned that her parents had wished her to be a boy. In some ways they treated her like a boy. Her name was Giovanna, but they called her by a shortened, masculine name, Gianni. She remembered in her analysis that her parents often remarked: "Gianni Corsi is a bad girl." (Corsi was her family name.) Her father suffered from a heart condition and died when the patient was ten years old. The analyst remarked that this was Mario's age in the dream.

As mentioned earlier, the protagonist of every dream is an externalized ego state of the dreamer. But this was not communicated to the patient. Usually analysts interpret such a dream person as representing the dreamer himself. Following Federn's concept, however, of many ego states each having its own boundary, we would express ourselves by saying, rather, "This dream figure stands for an ego state of the dreamer, not for the whole dreamer himself." The dreaming ego which reacts to the externalized ego state is not identical with that ego state. And in the same dream many other states and ego stages may appear as dream persons. The following associations substantiate our surmise that the ten-year-old Mario in the dream stood for a specific ego stage of the patient. When she was eight or nine years old she had a sexual experience with a boy of her age. She went through the motions of intercourse with him, and he told her that this is how babies are made. The analyst remarked that in the dream Mario had wrapped his dead father in a cloth and tied it into a small bundle, about the size of a newborn baby, and that later he made something the size of a baby from the skull of the dead father. But the analyst did not reveal to her that a head or a skull is a frequent "symbol" of the penis. She continued: She felt guilty after her experience with the boy (perhaps "messy") and was secretive about the experience because she knew that her parents would disapprove sternly, but she was also proud to have taken part in the adult activity of "making a baby."

When her father learned of this experience he was so shocked that he would not speak to her for several days. Her mother acted as intermediary and tried to explain his attitude. (The analyst remarked that in the dream also the police, the *carabinieri,* had found out.) Her mother explained that her father held girls in high esteem, that he could not bear to think of them being other than wholly "good," and that he was sorrowing very much because she had done such a dreadful thing. Immediately after the dream she remembered her mother saying, "It nearly killed your father to learn about that . . ." Such remarks were very common in her childhood. Her mother often said, "I would die if this or that happened." Also her mother used to say in anger, "I could kill you."

At the time of this experience her father was already very sick, and he died a year or two later. For several years before his death, the patient reported, he was an invalid and "jealously protected from the children (especially me) by my mother." Later the patient had the pervasive feeling that she must have killed her father. The analyst remarked, "So, you thought that you had killed him when you were ten years old, the same age as Mario in the dream."

Associating to the way in which Mario had killed his father in the dream, namely, by crushing him with a large stone, the patient reported that a few days before, while she was working in the garden, her aged cat had presented her with a half-dead mouse. The mouse was still moving, and to spare it suffering she quickly picked up a stone and crushed it dead. Immediately afterwards this seemed horrible to her, and she wondered how she could have done it.

In successive sessions the patient brought increasingly more associations to this dream, and through the understanding of many latent trains of thought which were condensed in the manifest dream and closely related to one another, the neurotic problems of this patient were unfolded. Suffice it here to make only a few important points:

The emotional situation of the patient at the time she killed the mouse (the day residues) was one of extreme frustration for being neglected by her husband in love and sexuality. Illegal sexual activity remained associated in the id with "killing the father," and she wished to indulge in an extramarital affair. But, for her ten-year-old ego state, to do this meant "killing the father." Different ego states may have different wishes, as we shall see also in the analysis of this dream. At the age of ten she was supposed to be Gianni, a boy, but she wanted to assert her femininity by making a baby. The first part of the dream represents an evident wish fulfillment. The equation of "indulging in forbidden sexual activities" with "killing the father" lent itself beautifully to a disguise of her forbidden sexual wishes.

"Killing the father by crushing him with a stone" meant, "While I was crushing the mouse with a stone I was reminded that in my imagination I had killed my father." Relations of time and causality or conditionality are expressed in language by such words as "while," "as long as," "if," "because," etc. But dream images do not have words. Therefore such relations find expression in the dream simply by the hallucinatory production and/or fusion of the related events or images. An example of a conditional relation between two thoughts may be seen in a dream scene of another female patient who dreamt that her mother had an affair. The latent dream thought was: "If my mother had an affair, my father would love me more than my mother." This thought derived from a case of infidelity which had come to the patient's knowledge. And in the dream under discussion the thought, "While I was crushing the mouse I remembered my belief that I had killed my father" was expressed by the fusion of these two parts into the image "my father was crushed by a stone." The "emotional climate" for this first part of the dream was due to the patient's present sexual wishes and her past experience of childhood which was bound to a repressed ego state. These two factors belonged to two different ego states.

Deeper analysis revealed many more components of this dream. In our presentation of psychoanalytic symbols we shall learn that small animals, such as a mouse, rabbit, or cat are associated to babies in the unconscious. And our patient felt horrified at having killed the mouse. As evident in her treatment, she had the fantasy of having a baby from her father as part of her oedipal strivings. We understand now why this externalized ego state of hers was busy constructing a baby from the remains of the destroyed baby, the mouse. In the dream the crushed mouse became inseparably fused with the killed father. Thus the reconstruction (or manufacture) of the baby is related not only to the father's skull (the penis) but also to the mouse. And we should remember that the patient said that she had felt very proud of having learned in her childhood sexual experience how babies are made.

Every single detail of the manifest dream has a meaning or a condensation of meanings. It is easy to understand that thorough analysis of all dream scenes would lead to an almost immeasurable quantity of information about the patient's mental structure and emotional development. Only a few more details from the analysis of this dream may be mentioned before we draw a conclusion from it.

How incorrect and confusing it would be to interpret the ten-year-old Mario simply as the dreamer herself, instead of as only a past ego state of hers! This becomes evident when we consider the non-externalized dreaming ego of the patient. She herself felt adult and responsible in the dream, and together with her husband she wished to protect her son. It is implied that she condemned his deed. We understand now that the father who was killed was really not her husband, as Mario was not actually her son but a former ego state of her own. We see also that the patient's adult dreaming ego was not the punitive superego. The latter was projected onto the police. Her husband who was protective of his sons might also have been protective of her infantile ego state, and (as mentioned above) the patient had the feeling that he would not have minded if she had a lover. Concerning Mario's messy room and the clean, orderly room of her older son in the dream, it was learned that the older son actually did keep himself and his room much cleaner than his younger brother. Therefore the younger son lent himself better to representation of the "messy" and "dirty" infantile ego stage under discussion. In its morally discriminating attitude the adult dreaming ego of the patient compared the two sons, reproaching Mario for not being as "neat" as his older brother. The patient's superego obtained satisfaction also: The police discovered and arrested Mario, as her own father had condemned her for the sexual experience of childhood by refusing to talk with her. In accordance with Paul Federn's concept of the superego as an ego state, we see it externalized in this dream, just as I believe it is to be found in waking life in paranoid conditions.

From the analysis of this dream we learn that the latent dream content may contain several wish fulfillments, and that these may remain in the dream even though in contradiction to one another. But such wish fulfillments are distributed among different ego states, some of which may appear as externalized figures in dream persons, and some of which may not appear at all. And the fulfillment of a wish dealing with an absent ego state may be represented merely by a dream event. A fulfilled wish of the punitive superego may appear as a disturbing stimulus for the dreaming ego, and as such it may awaken the sleeper. This is the character of some anxiety dreams.

Sometimes one analyst may pick up in a dream some detail which escapes another. As a rule such additional details corroborate the first analyst's interpretation or cast some light upon the emotional color of the problems involved. For example, I showed the account of this dream to Dr. Thomas M. French, and while he agreed completely with my interpretation, he was able to add to it. He noted the sentence, "Someone indistinguishable pretended to try to help him but was laughing and joking, and taking it too lightly." It is evident, of course, that this "someone indistinguishable" can be only an ego attitude of the dreamer herself, expressing her effort not to take seriously her mother's judgment that her childhood sexual experience could have killed her father (Mario's crime). Referring to the way the father was killed in the dream, crushed by a stone, in which killing the mouse and killing the father were fused, French stated his view that condensations of representations in a dream do not occur haphazardly but occur only when the two condensed elements are part of the same train of thought. He pointed out that the mouse was already half-dead and that the father was already sick. Killing the mouse to save it further suffering was only half-killing, and her supposed responsibility for killing the father was lessened by the fact that he was already sick. This was a problem-solving device of the preconscious ego to appease its conscience, in line with the dreamer's not taking seriously "Mario's crime."

XLV

Sleep-Disturbing Dreams

WHILE the dream work may succeed in expressing the satisfaction of a given wish, thus pacifying one sleep-disturbing stimulus, the effect of such a wish fulfillment may constitute a new stimulus which will awaken the dreamer if it becomes strong enough. In its postulated protective function the dream work appears to be focused on one immediate goal—a single wish fulfillment—and to be blind to its implications. Since the dream work does not have a great capacity for integrating contradictory wishes, unpleasant dreams or anxiety dreams may ensue. Sometimes a wish unacceptable to the ego is insufficiently disguised and is recognized as such by the ego. This may also be a cause of anxiety dreams. Dreams of unpleasant, sad, or frightening character, we repeat, do not necessarily contradict Freud's theory concerning the general function of the dreams, since the fulfillment of one wish may interfere with another co-existing counter-wish. Someone may dream that a person very close to him, a sibling, his spouse, father, mother, etc., has died. In such a dream the dreamer may be tortured by the most intense grief reaction and may feel happily relieved when, upon awakening, he realizes that it was only a dream. Analysis of such dreams reveals that the dreamer had a repressed death wish against that ambivalently loved person. The grief reaction in the dream serves the purpose of disguising the death wish. This disguising device, which reminds us of reaction formation, becomes itself a sleep-disturbing emotion. According to Freud the intense grief reaction is due to the intervention of the "dream censor," the superego. True, such a person would grieve in reality also if that ambivalently loved person should actually die. But it is precisely this normal emotional reaction of the dreaming ego which keeps it from even suspecting that it harbors such a wish in its unconscious.

The tension resulting from such or similar wishes is often revealed

416

as guilty conscience. This is not felt as such, however, but finds expression in self-punitive dream contents. The dreamer does not know for what reasons some dream makes him suffer. So, atonement-contents may awaken the ego as a guilty conscience would keep it from sleep. Franz Alexander[1] has described "dreams in pairs" as typical of arising conscience-tension: The first dream contains the fulfillment of an objectionable wish which provokes feelings of guilt (which as a new stimulus may awaken the sleeper); the second dream then has the task of silencing the voice of guilty conscience through self-punishment. And the suffering for the punishment undergone in the dream may awaken the dreamer again. A very poor integration indeed! It may be difficult to realize that the need for punishment, claimed by the superego for the ego, may also engender wishes for self-castigation in the attempt to appease a guilty conscience.

Often the dream censor allows the fulfillment of a wish only by inference. For example, a person dreamed of going insane, but without experiencing anxiety. His association to this was that in waking life he thought he would be crazy if he married a certain girl. So his wish was an unconscious desire to marry her. Dreams in which the spouse is unfaithful, to the great concern of the jealous dreamer, were often interpreted by Freud as wish fulfillments "by implication." His formulation can be expressed as follows: "If he is unfaithful to me, then I do not have to feel guilty for being unfaithful to him." The dreamer, wanting to be unfaithful to the marital partner, wishes the other to be unfaithful also, in order to appease his own conscience.

In summary we may say that anxiety dreams and nightmares are due to strong conflicts derived from the breakdown of the repression of forbidden wishes. These wishes become frightening either in themselves or by various implications. Similarly, many neurotic symptoms are the result of such unsuccessful repression, as we noted in the preceding section.

In Chapter XXVIII it was pointed out that the repetition compulsion, in Freud's opinion the fundamental property of living matter, manifests itself independent of the pleasure principle. The power of the repetition compulsion is also revealed in dreams occurring after unmastered traumatic events. Freud first discussed such dreams in 1920 in *Beyond the Pleasure Principle,* the publication where he formulated his concept of the death instinct. After a traumatic train wreck, a shattering war experience, or the unbearable sight of some disaster, the individual dreams over and over again of the traumatic event and awakens in fright and terror. The stimuli which could not be bound (and thus not controlled) undergo the phenomenon of repetition compulsion irrespective of whether they provoke pleasure or unpleasure and terror for the ego. Using French's expanded concept of trauma, we could say: A traumatic condition subsists as long as the individual does not learn how to reach the proper goal and thus free himself from the traumatizing stimulation.

Freud's statement that dreams induced by traumatic experiences are an exception to the wish-fulfillment theory does not imply that there is no attempt to master such experiences by a suitable wish fulfillment. The implication is, rather, that such dreams express an economic condition, namely, the failure of such an attempt to compete successfully with the power of the repetition compulsion.

I wish to emphasize, however, that the actual life situation of the dreamer at the time he dreams is very important for the resulting dream content, whether it represents a wish or only the mental repetition of the trauma. The following short examples should clarify this point:

A patient had been sailing in his cutter with friends and been surprised by a storm at sea. While maneuvering the sail, he was thrown overboard and was barely saved by his companions. He and his friends fought the wind and waves until finally they reached the mainland in the evening. That night he dreamt continuously, with excitement and anxiety, that he was still sailing and fighting the storm. In the dream he often felt completely submerged, while seeing through a greenish medium (the water) his white cutter at a distance, at times drawing near and at times receding from him. This was precisely the tiresome repetition of the traumatic experience which he went through during the actual sailing trip.

Let us now compare this dream with another: A soldier who had to sleep within range of enemy artillery could not fall asleep because of his fear and tension. Although he could hear explosions at irregular intervals, the likelihood of his being struck by a missile was slight. Eventually his fatigue increased until he relaxed and fell asleep, only to dream that he was in his home town in the United States on a Sunday morning, walking with friends. This was a complete denial of the disturbing stimulus.

I have heard many times from Army physicians that soldiers exposed to traumatic war events often have dreams in which they re-experience the traumatic situations only when they feel safe, as for instance when they find themselves sheltered in a hospital far behind the front, and usually not as long as the dangerous situation still exists. Comparing our two examples above, we find that the two dreamers were in different external situations. The first dreamer was safe and out of danger when he had the traumatic dream. But let us suppose that this man had fallen asleep while still in the cutter, riding through the storm. Would he have had the same traumatic dream? And let us suppose that the soldier in the second case had gone to sleep in a safe place, far away from the battle. Would he then have denied the fearful situation? Or would he not have kept dreaming, at least in the beginning, of being exposed to the enemy guns, since this repetition in dreams is apt to occur after long, tiring, or exciting experiences, as well as after severe traumatic events? This question reminded me of dreams reported by companions of the Italian arctic explorer Umberto Nobile. While returning from the North Pole on the dirigible *Italia* in May 1928, Nobile crash-landed on the ice. The airship's gondola and main cabin were smashed and Nobile and several of his crew were thrown out on the ice. Seven others in the party were carried away with the balloon never to be heard from again. Nobile and his companions spent nearly a month on an ice floe in hunger and despair, suffering from the severest privations. Finally, he was rescued by a Swedish plane, and the other survivors were taken aboard a Russian icebreaker several days later. This latter group reported that whenever they could catch some sleep during their stay on the ice floe they always dreamed of green fields and sumptuous meals. But after being rescued and safe aboard the icebreaker they dreamed only and continuously that they were still on the ice floe, anxiously awaiting help, in a hopeless, panic-stricken state. These latter dreams indicated that they were still under the influence of a traumatic emotional condition. Their exciting and shocking experiences returned, in dream form, over and over again—stimuli without resolution, without wish fulfillment—as soon as they withdrew into sleep from the diverting surroundings of the favorably changed external conditions. This does not mean, however, that there was no attempt at all to appease the stimuli but only that such an attempt could no longer compete with the impact of the traumatic state. And the report said that all members of the group had the same dream experiences.

Why did such traumatic dreams occur only after the rescue? Why did the men not dream in the same way while they were still in the hopeless external situation? As we shall see from other examples, every waking experience prior to a dream, which could justify some hope for a wish fulfillment, facilitates a wish-fulfillment content of the dream. French emphasizes the importance of "hope" for the solution of a pending problem in the dream. But in the cases under discussion quite the opposite occurred: During the hopeless external situation their dreams had a wish-fulfillment character, and after the unexpected rescue the dreams acquired a traumatic character, repeating the previously hopeless situation. Is the different depth of sleep perhaps responsible for the different contents of these two types of dreams? On the ice floe Nobile's men could not ignore their actual precarious condition as long as they remained awake, that is, in contact with reality. On the other hand, their need for rest, together with the need to deny unpleasant reality, must have gained progressively in intensity and won the upper hand whenever the limit of endurance was reached. The resulting emotional attitude could be described as follows: "Rescue or no rescue, living or dying, it does not matter to me any more; I am exhausted and I want only to forget and to sleep, no matter what happens to me." [2] After their rescue, however, the men did not need to continue denying a truly dangerous reality, since such a reality no longer existed; the external conditions had been changed in their favor. Instead of having to endure an external traumatic condition, they became then the victims of an internal mental state which had not yet subsided. We call such a mental state caused by unmastered stimulations, a traumatic state. We are reminded of French's theory of "physiological absorption of pressure" which is proportional to the depth of sleep. On the ice floe these men could fall asleep only after a high degree of exhaustion was reached which led to a deep sleep. After their rescue, however, they could fall asleep long before they felt very exhausted; thus their sleep must have been lighter.

We may conceive from another perspective the dynamic condition of individuals who fall asleep under stress. If they should awaken with fright and terror whenever they fall asleep, these individuals would not survive. They would perish from exhaustion before the external situation could put an end to their lives. Under stress or in life-threatening situations increased cathexis may be mobilized or all available cathexis may be concentrated toward the task necessary for immediate survival. As mentioned, Freud explains the nature of "traumatic dreams" from an economic point of view: The capacity for establishing a wish-fulfillment situation in the dream cannot compete successfully with the power of the repetition compulsion. We could now surmise that an immediate vital need for such a wish fulfillment could mobilize additional cathexis, drawn from other systems, for a successful competition either with the repetition compulsion or with the recognition of a hopeless situation. This is an attempt to postpone a seemingly inevitable death. And this attempt to postpone destruction may have been the effective factor in producing wish-fulfillment dreams in the situations under discussion.

In these cases a defensive cathexis is mobilized to strengthen the resistance against mental factors which interfere with life-saving devices. Such a mobilization of cathexis under stress reminded me of dynamic conditions of a different kind, which also elicit a mobilization of a kind of previously deficient cathexis. Some years after the First World War, I was struck by an amazing observation: Some severely schizophrenic patients suddenly recovered from their psychotic state one or two days before they died of a fatal disease. These were mostly chronic catatonic patients with paranoid and hebephrenic features. I remember a young schizophrenic male patient who had been picked up somewhere after the war. He was a severe catatonic who had to be fed through a gastric tube for many years. His name and place of origin were unknown, because he did not talk and hardly moved. Being infected with tuberculosis of the lungs he was put in a separate ward and eventually was reduced to mere skin and bones, expected to die in a day or two. Suddenly, one morning he began to speak to the nurse in a quite coherent manner without displaying the slightest psychotic feature. He indicated his name and place of origin, a small town near the hospital. His family was summoned and rushed to his bed, recognizing him immediately. They could converse with him in a normal way, and he gave all desired information in a feeble and breathless voice but in an intelligent and coherent manner. He died the next day. In a few other cases also I have observed that in the condition of approaching death all available cathexes became directed toward the ego, thus removing symptoms caused by deficiency of ego cathexis.

Wish-fulfillment dreams in hopeless situations have the purpose of postponing probable or unavoidably approaching death. And in dying schizophrenic patients the equivalent of such a postponement seems to be the "awakening of the ego." We come thus to the conclusion that schizophrenic patients do sense their ego weakness and precisely as a "dying process of their ego." And when a physical dying process sets in, in some cases the sensation of such a destruction may revive the ego in a compensatory effort. Years after my observations insulin and other kinds of shock treatment were introduced as a result of observation by clinicians that the experience of some severe shock or traumatic event dissolved (at least temporarily) the psychotic ego state in some schizophrenic patients. We do not wish to probe deeper into this issue at this point, but only to note that the outcome of traumatic experiences may be different in different individuals. If a "mental apparatus" has a limited capacity to mobilize cathexis, a traumatic experience may exhaust the operating ego cathexis, thus provoking a breakdown of the ego or worsening its psychotic state.

From the reported observations we may conclude that many factors determine dream contents. It is not enough to detect the concrete pressures exerted upon the ego by conscious or unconscious, internal or external, problems. In order to evaluate properly a dream content we must examine the dynamic equipment of the ego and become acquainted with the way it is affected by different situations, be they hopeful or hopeless and traumatizing.

NOTES

(1) Alexander, Franz. Dreams in pairs and series. Int. J. Psychoanal., 6:446-452, 1925.

(2) Freud taught that such an attitude leads to hallucinatory wish psychoses. Such psychoses would express the economic condition of resistance which obtains the upper hand over reality recognition. In other words, they would cause the individual to detach himself from reality.

XLVI

Clarifying Dream Examples

A FEW short examples of dreams will show that fulfillment in dreams of conscious wishes may be enhanced by some factors and frustrated by others. Conscious wishes of adult persons, wishes unconnected with repressed contents of infantile origin, usually do not come true in a dream if the dreamer knows that they cannot possibly be fulfilled in reality. For example, a mother deeply grieved over the loss of a child and longing to see him once more in a dream, never did dream of him. As pointed out, an ego falls asleep when it succeeds in freeing itself (in its domain of the preconscious) from excessive stimulation, but preconscious memories and wishes which have already lost their cathexis in the process of falling asleep can become recathected through channels which connect them with repressed (id) contents. The following examples, seemingly related only to conscious wishes, will illustrate this point:

A young man, desperately in love with a girl, had asked her to marry him. But she was in love with another man, with whom he could not compete. When he insisted on her answer, she told him that she would let him know her choice within a few days. He was deeply depressed and tortured by jealousy. Before he learned her decision he dreamt that he entered her living room, where she was sitting on a couch. She got up to greet him and with great embarrassment told him that she had decided to marry the other man. Although her decision was not entirely unexpected, its communication hurt him so much that he awoke with a start and was unable to sleep the rest of the night. This dream, instead of protecting sleep, was itself a strong awakening stimulus.

It is evident that the dreamer clearly sensed the hopelessness of his wish; and indeed, the girl actually did choose his rival. It would be a mistake, however, to draw final conclusions regarding this or any other dream without analysis of the life situation.

The dreamer was too young to assume the responsibilities of a married man and would have been quite unable to support a wife. Well aware of these difficulties, he resorted to the defense of denial. Since renunciation of the young lady's love was unbearable to him, he tried to ignore his difficulties; yet the hopelessness of his love problem amounted to a traumatic situation. In fact, his dream had actually a traumatic character. His denial was easily broken down. Eventually he admitted to the therapist that he had realistic reasons for not wanting to marry the girl. Thus, the dream did contain the fulfillment of one wish, but not of the acute sleep-disturbing wish. Fulfilled was the wish to be restrained from marrying the girl, but, at the same time, his frustrated love goal acted as a trauma which prevented him from sleeping. It was not difficult to detect another, deeper, and more important factor which interfered with the fulfillment of the young man's conscious torturing wish. The competitor was an older, more efficient and more desirable man, and the dreamer himself had feelings of sympathy for him. From the patient's early life situation it became evident that the triangular situation duplicated his infantile oedipal envolvement. Accordingly, the conscious situation at the time of this dream became connected to a repressed oedipal situation, and his hopelessness in competing with his father, plus his guilt in trying to replace him, were the strongest contributing factors for this shocking dream.

Much happier is the following dream: A young, inexperienced, shy patient employed in a government office became infatuated with a pretty, unassuming typist. He was convinced that she did not care for him, and because of his fear of being rejected he made no attempt to approach her. One night he dreamt that she entered the record room while he was looking for a file. He was so delighted to see her that he could not refrain from embracing and kissing her, telling her how much he loved her, whereupon she kissed him back, saying, "I love you too, darling." He became so excited that he woke up, and realized that it had been only a dream. To be sure, it was a wish fulfillment, but, as in the first case, the dream did not succeed in protecting sleep.

The patient's association to the record room was that the employees entered it only when they had to look up some file, and that the girl was often sent there to copy data. He repeated that this girl could not possibly care for him. To increase the patient's self-confidence I expressed the opinion that the girl's rejection had not really been ascertained and encouraged him to be less timid with her. To my amazement the patient misinterpreted my encouragement, believing that he had to try to act in reality exactly as he had done in the dream. This analytic session took place early in the morning before he went to work. When he arrived at his job he went forthwith to the record room and found the girl there. He approached her in a determined manner and embraced her passionately; when she offered no resistance he kissed her, repeating the words he had said in the dream. The effect was magical! She returned his kiss and repeated in turn, though timidly, what she had said in the dream. A prophetic dream, indeed! The only difference between dream and reality was that in the dream he was waiting in the record room for her, while in the succeeding reality situation she was there before he entered the room. Why did the wish come true in the dream in this case?

In spite of his protest to the contrary, the patient must have sensed her feelings for him. If this had not been so he would perhaps not have misinterpreted my encouragement—and it was most fortunate that he was not indignantly rejected, as might have been expected. From his childhood history it was learned that he had developed very early an intuitive capacity for recognizing each affective change toward him for the better or for the worse in his mother and in a governess who took care of him. But for all his great intuition he often complained that he did not understand what these two women demanded from him. We may surmise that his dream was enhanced by an unconscious connection of his current wish with analogous experiences in his childhood in relation to the two "mothers." In any case, the dreamer's hope for success, in this case justified, must have been responsible for the wish fulfillment in the dream.

Hopes may be psychologically well-determined and still be unjustified. In such cases they also seem to enhance a fulfillment in a dream of a conscious wish. A young married woman had indulged in an extramarital affair, not because she was in love with the man but because of a whim, like a spoiled child. As a matter of fact she was attached to her honest, ingenuous husband. One day her affair was discovered, and as a consequence her husband divorced her. She reacted with despair, and for the first time felt aware of her deficient sense of responsibility. Realizing her immaturity and other character difficulties, she sought psychotherapy. Her history revealed that as a child she "got away with murder." To be sure, her father had occasionally scolded her, but she could always count on his casually overlooking her misbehavior.

After a few months of analysis she asked the analyst whether, in his opinion, her husband might possibly take her back. He answered noncommittally that it depended upon her husband, whom he did not know, and upon her own change. After that hour she dreamed that her husband came to her and asked her to return to him—an undeniable dream of wish fulfillment. In this case also we recognize that the patient's hope for a reconciliation with her husband must have played a dynamic role in establishing such a dream content. But we must also recognize that this patient's hope rested on childhood experiences related to her father's forgiving attitude. Her hope, though quite understandable, was not justified. When in reality she approached her husband, she was rejected harshly.

A woman patient awoke from a nightmare. She had dreamed that she had called for her husband in the evening at the shop where he worked and caught him in intimate embrace with a semi-nude salesgirl. Analysis of this dream and the life situation of the patient did not lead to a discovery of a conscious or unconscious wish fulfillment. But, as we shall see, the dream itself fulfilled actually, and not in its content, a wish of the patient. In this case we did not have any reason to interpret the dream in terms of Freud's formulation of a type of dreams of jealousy, mentioned in the preceding chapter: "If he is unfaithful to me, then I do not have to feel guilty for being unfaithful to him." Some weeks later, while the patient was caressing her husband, she smelled cologne on him and realized that it was not any of her perfumes. Remembering her dream, the next day she went to his shop at an unusual hour and surprised him in the embrace of another woman. It seems evident that she had unconsciously, somehow, become aware of her husband's infidelity at some time before the dream took place. Did the unconscious awareness traumatize her? If so, her realization must

428 STRUCTURE AND DYNAMICS OF THE HUMAN MIND

have been preconscious and then denied by her. And if we want to see a wish fulfillment in this dream, this wish could be only: "I wish to know the truth whatever it is, reassuring or shocking." The dream fulfilled her wish in reality. She learned the truth.

Sometimes dreams may be means to fulfilling some wishes in reality. The following example may illustrate this point: A student psychoanalyst, having difficulties with one of his private patients, consulted me for advice, particularly in the understanding of a dream of this patient. This was the dream: "I was riding in a car driven by my father-in-law. I was sitting with my analyst [the student who consulted me] on the back seat, the analyst being just behind my father-in-law, so that his view was obstructed. This situation was very uncomfortable to me, and I had the feeling that my analyst did not know where we were riding, because my father-in-law robbed him of any possibility of getting oriented."

The patient, a young man, was a tenacious case of sexual impotence. He had been married over a year and had been entirely unable to have intercourse with his wife. Annulment of the marriage seemed unavoidable. As a last attempt to save his marriage the patient decided to undergo psychoanalytic treatment. His impotence was one symptom of a general neurotic state manifested in anxiety and over-sensitivity. He was unable to enter into an emotional relationship with a woman. He was self-centered, felt inferior as a man, and tried to compensate for this feeling by displaying strong masculine attitudes. His inability to assert his masculinity toward his wife in the sexual field humiliated him all the more. She was the first woman with whom he had to integrate sexuality and personal relationship on a tender basis. Prior to his marriage he had had only occasional intercourse with a promiscuous girl. He was already very much intimidated by his wife's strong contempt for him. Eventually she would not tolerate any sexual approach by him through forepleasure practices. Her attitude implied: "If you cannot succeed, then do not touch me at all." This intimidated him even more. For him she did not offer enough feminine tenderness to encourage his masculine aggression.

The patient's father-in-law wanted to save the marriage. With the patient's consent he had had an interview with the analyst and begged him to do everything in his power to cure his son-in-law.

His daughter would certainly not find another husband like the patient, he said, such a nice person with such an excellent position. The analyst had rejected offer of reward. He was already paid by his patient, he said, and in any case he could not promise results, though he believed it was very probable that the patient would become potent.

It was pointed out to the young analyst that he had overlooked his analytic task. The patient had come to analysis because he was entangled in an unpleasant situation from which he could not extricate himself without feeling greatly humiliated. This situation seemed to be due only to the patient's impotence, but actually he had been emotionally disturbed long before his marriage. The task of analysis was to cure his neurosis, regardless of whether his adjustment led to saving his marriage or to its annulment.

But the attitude and wish of the patient's father-in-law, who cared only for saving the marriage in the interest of his daughter and himself, had become too important to the analyst, so that the latter was handicapped in correctly visualizing the entire analytic situation. We can already understand clearly the meaning of the dream. A cartoonist could not have expressed it better. The dream says: "The course of the analysis (the moving car) is determined by the desire and attitude of my father-in-law; he drives the car and in a position which obstructs the analyst's view."

Of course we can see wish fulfillments in this dream. For one thing it expressed the patient's wish to reproach the analyst for having relinquished to his father-in-law his guidance and vision in the analytic treatment. "Don't you see," the patient would like to say to his analyst, "that my father-in-law sits at the steering wheel and obstructs your view?"

The analyst was instructed to change the whole management of the treatment, and after a period the case was successfully terminated, though not with the result which the patient's father-in-law had wished. The patient was potent and happy with another wife. The analyst was advised to investigate more thoroughly the patient's relationship with his father, and this led to a deeper understanding of the dream. The patient did not have in his own father a proper identification pattern. His father was a weak character and, to the dismay of the patient, he often yielded his convictions to other people. So as a boy the patient could not develop a sufficiently strong character and self-confidence. Thus, the dream also contained a reproach against his own father, whose attitude became duplicated in the analyst's behavior. The patient's reproach against the analyst was preconscious, but it was enhanced to form such a dream because of the connection of the preconscious thought with the repressed resentment which the patient harbored against his own father. This illustrates again how day residues become recathected from the id during sleep.

The dream examples presented here lend themselves to further examination from various perspectives. In recent years French has undertaken an accurate analysis of the dream activity.[1] Here we can present only some highlights of his conclusions, drawn from his interesting studies. For better understanding of the dream structure French believes the following considerations are essential:

He examines the ways in which different meanings of a dream are related to one another, and calls this the reconstruction of the cognitive structure. In dream analysis one has to understand how the dreamer's present situation, with which he is unconsciously (we would say "preconsciously") preoccupied at the time of the dream, is related to past events in his life. He calls the present situation, from which all dream wishes radiate, the focal problem or focal conflict. In our earlier dream of the young husband riding in a car driven by a younger inexperienced man, the focal problem was how to straighten out his relationship with his wife. This wish entered into relation with the unconscious memory of his father's failure to buy for his mother the home she had desired. The focal conflict of the woman who crushed the mouse was her temptation to have an extramarital affair, and this wish became related to her unconscious memory of the sexual episode of her childhood. In all reported dreams we find a connection between the focal problem and past events in the dreamer's life. French calls the nuclear conflict (or problem) the general conflict pattern resulting from the life situations of childhood, a manifestation or implication which appears in the focal problem. In the last dream the focal problem concerned the unsuccessful analytic situation, and the nuclear problem resulted from his father's ineffectual personality. French also investigates the ways in which the motivating wishes are related to one another and how the dreamer's interest is distributed quantitatively between several meanings of a dream. He designates as a "negative goal" the individual's trying to get away from something, and as a "positive goal" the individual's seeking something. In his concept negative goals are "needs," and positive goals arise from "hopes," from "knowing how." Dreams as well as waking-life behavior are polarized between "needs" and "hopes." Hopes arise from past reassuring memories and from the acknowledgment of present opportunities. The process by which "the dreamer's picture of his conflict situation" is transformed into the manifest dream content is called by French the pattern of dream organization. One reconstructs the steps in this process by interpolating between the focal problem and the manifest content of the dream. In the dream of the young man who kissed the typist in the record room the hope derived from his correct intuition of the reality situation, i.e., of the girl's feelings toward him. The unjustified hopes of the divorced woman who dreamt that her husband returned to her derived from her reassuring memories from childhood about her father's easy forgiveness.

A complete discussion of French's accurate and elaborate conception of dream activity and dream organization would require a much longer exposition than can be given in this volume.

NOTES

(1) French, op. cit.; see especially Vol. 2: The Integrative Process in Dreams.

XLVII

Bodily and Mental Pain in Dreams

AS I have pointed out elsewhere,[1] bodily and mental pain cannot be fully explained through physiology; their understanding also requires metapsychological considerations. The anatomy and physiology of the nervous system teach us that the feeling of pain is a specific sensory feeling, associated with special nerve endings, conducting paths and brain centers, like the sensations of sight, hearing, taste, touch, etc. On the other hand, the pharmacology of the nervous system teaches us that opiates, for example, deaden not only bodily pain but also mental pain and feelings of unpleasure in general. Furthermore, many observations have shown that anatomical and physiological considerations alone do not solve many problems related to pain and pleasure. Only a few of such problems can be mentioned here. We understand that the dose of opium necessary for the alleviation of a specific degree of bodily pain is in proportion to the degree of pain. But physiology cannot explain why the calming effect on the mind (i.e., the production of euphoria) is generally absent in non-addicted people who take it for bodily pain of non-neurotic nature, that is to say, people who are able to abstain from the drug again at once. In the great majority of cases in which opium is used solely for the relief of bodily pain, not neurotically conditioned, the dose need either not be increased at all or only gradually. On the other hand, those cases in which it is necessary to increase the dose rapidly remind us of the precautionary measures adopted by persons suffering from phobias or obsessional neuroses: Such measures have to be multiplied constantly, with the result that the subject's personal freedom becomes more and more restricted. As we have seen, the defense mechanism in projection phobias is manifested in the ego's flight from an external object or situation, while the actual danger threatens from within. And since the ego's withdrawal from external objects does

432

not protect it from internal dangers, its defensive measures, falsely directed against external objects, must steadily increase, thus restricting its freedom of movement more and more. Similarly, neurotic pain, being an expression of drive conflict, cannot be permanently assuaged by the same dose of sedatives.

We have noted that hysterical pains arise from a "conversion" of mental distress into unpleasant bodily sensations. In the analysis of some dreams this writer observed that in the dream state of healthy individuals mental distress can also be converted into bodily pain and, furthermore, that in the dreaming state physical pain due to a bodily affliction can be converted into mental distress. This observation allowed me also to verify my hypothesis that this phenomenon may also occur in the waking state of certain severe schizophrenic patients. As in the dream state of normal egos, an ego in an advanced state of schizophrenia may become insensitive to bodily pains caused by bodily lesions and may experience mental distress instead. This observation confirms Federn's statement that the dreaming ego has some traits in common with the schizophrenic ego. In Chapter X a dream was reported in which a menstruating girl felt mentally distressed instead of experiencing physical pain caused by contraction of the uterus. Not only mental stimuli but sometimes physical stimuli also may disturb sleep, and it is interesting to note how the dream deals with such stimuli. A patient suffering from severe bronchitis dreamt that he had to rack his brains to solve a mathematical problem. It tormented him so much that he woke up, and he then found that he was suffering with dyspnea, because he had assumed an uncomfortable position. A student dreamt that she had to prepare for an examination and was finding it very hard work. However much she tried, she could retain nothing of what she studied. The situation was so unbearable that she awoke—with a violent gastrointestinal disturbance which caused vomiting and diarrhea. What she could not *retain* was in reality the contents of the stomach and intestines, not the results of her studies. In our presentation of the oral and retentive instincts in Chapter XXIII, it was made clear that in the id "taking intellectual possession of something" and "incorporating something orally and retaining it" are equivalent representations which can be substituted one for the other. The phrase "He has not digested what he has learned" is a very common one. It is well known that various bodily sensations of unpleasant nature (such as, fullness of the stomach or congestion) can be converted in dreams into mental feelings with unpleasant tone. Herbert Silberer analyzed many such cases of somatic phenomena. Patients suffering from heart condition have nightmares when during sleep their heart becomes decompensated.

As mentioned above, schizophrenic patients may experience such a conversion in waking state. A schizophrenic who suffered from a severe pleurisy was asked whether he felt pains. He denied it but added, "When will you stop giving me so many puzzles to solve; why don't you leave me in peace?" He did not mean that he was bothered by being asked if he felt pain—normally his condition would be very painful—but he referred to his continuous mental discomfort.

Once I was sewing up a wound on the forehead of a patient who suffered from a severe form of schizophrenia and whose speech was quite unintelligible. He allowed everything to be done to him without any sort of resistance and gave no sign of bodily pain. Instead, throughout the procedure he uttered confused and incoherent lamentations which revealed that he was experiencing mental discomfort. He kept murmuring, "Poor me! What troubles I have; how wretched I am; I cannot bear these worries!"

Since this conversion of bodily pain into mental pain also appears in some schizophrenic patients during waking life, it cannot be a performance of the dream work. Only a metapsychological consideration of the ego can help us to understand this phenomenon. Bodily pain is bound to the body ego. Federn described the continuous variations of mental and body ego feelings. Whether bodily pain is localized, affecting a clearly defined area, or more generally diffused, its appearance presupposes the existence of a body ego feeling relating to the part affected. In the state of sleep as well as in schizophrenic conditions the ego feeling is partially or wholly withdrawn from the body, so that only the mental ego can react to bodily stimulations which in normal waking life would produce bodily pain. In fact, as Federn says, ". . . we do not—in the great majority of all dreams—feel that we are corporally present.

We do not feel our body with its weight and its form. We have no bodily ego feeling with its ego boundaries, as in normal waking life. However, we are not at all aware of this deficiency of the body ego, while we would feel it dreadfully during waking life." [2]

Withdrawal of the flexible ego cathexis from portions of the ego leads also to externalization of parts of ego states into object representations, as we have seen in many examples. We interpret many dream persons as such externalized ego states or stages of the dreamer. For example, when in a woman's dream masculine features contained in her constitutional bisexuality are externalized, the ensuing dream person is a male. And when in a man's dream feminine features are externalized the ensuing dream person is a female. Through externalization, a physical pain may appear as such in a dream, but it appears projected onto the externalized ego state and is not experienced subjectively by the dreaming ego. In such cases, the dreaming ego is always sorry for the suffering of the dream person, and here again physical pain is converted into mental pain.

A highly depressed female patient who suffered from severe headaches had the following dream: "My brother and a friend of his were being punished by having slices of lemon placed on their heads. This caused them frightful pain, and I was very sorry and distressed about their suffering." Upon waking up, she found that she herself had a violent headache. Her headache was connected with her egotization of her masculine urges, and she suffered from penis envy toward her brother. Unconsciously she felt mutilated for not having a penis (the slice of lemon indicated the cutting off of something) as a punishment for infantile sexual desires. In a woman's dream externalized masculine traits are often represented by two men, representing the man and his penis. This meaning of two masculine figures in dreams of women became evident to me from the analysis of many such dreams. A woman patient dreamt that a man, in whom she had become sexually interested, was sitting at a table in front of her. She added, "But in the dream he had a twin brother, and both were facing me. As a matter of fact, I had the feeling that they were Siamese twins, connected to one another under the table." In dreams and conversion hysteria the head symbolizes the penis. The headaches which the first patient suffered in waking life expressed her disappointment for not having a penis, or, in her imagination, for having had it cut off.

Thus, her own headache belonged to one of her masculine ego states which appeared externalized in the dream as male figures. And while her ego feeling was withdrawn during sleep from that ego state, the ensuing headache became converted into mental sorrow for the suffering of that dream person, the castrated man. In this dream the body ego feeling persisted in relation to the head. The body scheme functioned correctly. But, as Federn says, the body ego feeling corresponds to the body scheme only if the body scheme is completely ego-cathected.

In some cases bodily pain is not only projected onto some dream person in a dream but is also displaced onto a different part of that person's body. The following dream of a male patient who suffered from migraine illustrates this process clearly:

"A man whom I know, an army captain, was talking to my father who is in reality a senior officer. As the captain stood at attention, talking of military matters, his trousers opened and there came out a long penis, almost a yard in length, shaped like a medieval sabre with upward curve. My father pretended not to notice it and continued to listen to the report which the captain was making. Suddenly I observed that the projecting penis had turned into an immense bag hanging down from the region of the groin. It was, in fact, a bad hernia, which was causing the captain great pain. My father noticed it but averted his gaze to the window, so as to be able to go on hearing the report without having to call the regimental doctor. The captain suffered agonies and whispered to the other people present to get medical help at once or he would die. But my father looked annoyed as soon as he observed the other people's attention, so that, in spite of his terrible pain and the huge hernia, which grew larger and longer, the captain had to feign an interest in the orders being given by his superior officer. I felt very uncomfortable and greatly at a loss, for I wanted somehow to help the captain. My emotional situation became so painful that I awoke and found that I had a severe attack of migraine, accompanied by a sensation of numbness and paresthesia at the back of my scalp which had 'gone to sleep.' For a long time I kept thinking of this dream which had stirred up memory of my complicated relation-ship with my father. As you know, I had been intimidated by my father to an unusual extent."

We do not wish to embark here on every detail of this dream, the meaning of which became clear from the knowledge of the patient's present and past life situation and from his associations. Here we are interested in the metapsychology of the "pain conversion." The protagonist of this dream, the captain, was, as usual, an ego state of the dreamer himself. It was not the captain's father but the dreamer's father who showed no consideration for the "captain's" plight. It was the persistent headache during the dream, though of psychogenic origin, that prevented the dream work from producing a wish fulfillment. During his analysis, this patient had revealed that his father had intimidated him very much, thus preventing him from asserting his masculinity. In dreams the intensity of a need or an emotion is often represented either by a great vividness of the corresponding images or by a huge size of the objects or body parts involved. In this case also, as in that of the female patient previously mentioned, the headache accompanied by sensations of numbness expressed an intense but repressed phallic need. The headache developed while the patient was sleeping, and, as a mat-ter of fact, the ensuing physical pain did not become reconverted in the dream into mere mental distress but was externalized onto a dream person. Nevertheless, in the process of externalization the bodily pain was correctly localized on the body of the dream per-son, namely, it was re-displaced from the head downward to the penis, where it actually belonged. The pathological effect of the inhibition of such an intense and repressed phallic urge found ex-pression in the transformation of the huge penis into a huge hernia, which expressed a traumatic condition. It is interesting to note that only in the dream was the headache replaced by genital distress, while upon awakening the dreamer realized that he had become victim of one of his attacks of migraine. Yet the pain-fulness of the experience was maintained in the dream state of the ego in form of a mental distress, in the dreamer's pity and distress for the sufferer which led to a wish to help him.

Sometimes, on the other hand, a dreaming ego may experience bodily pains as such, subjectively, and not in projection onto a dream person. This reveals the additional fact that in a dream state some parts of the body or some bodily sensations may be ego cathected. Whether the ego awakens from such stimulations depends on the intensity of the pain and the need for sleep. How often, while dreaming, does one perceive that he has a toothache or a stomach ache. These pain sensations do not belong to the dream, although they may undergo some elaboration in the dream and induce the dreamer to seek a solution of the problem. For example, a dreamer suffering from toothache may dream of going to the dentist, and someone sensing the physical need to empty his bowel or bladder may dream of seeking a bathroom instead of awakening—as long as the need does not put an end to his sleep.

We are interested now in the dynamics of cases in which a person only "dreams" of having a bodily pain which disappears immediately upon awakening. Could such a conversion symptom occur only in the state of sleep, wakening the sleeper into a dream state? Before examining this phenomenon let us consider some concrete examples. A female patient suffering from anxiety hysteria (not from a conversion symptom) often dreamt during a phase of her analysis that her breasts or genitalia were violently pinched or pressed by a man and that this caused her the most intolerable pain. When she awoke the pain vanished immediately. Once she dreamt that a man lifted her up—often a symbol for sexual arousal—pressing his finger into her genitalia so hard that she could not bear the pain. In another dream she met a man and was so completely overwhelmed by sexual desire that she threw herself impatiently into his arms. In this second dream the sexual arousal was experienced as such, not only symbolically as in the previous dream. Then, continuing the second dream, she tore open her blouse, offered him her breast, and he pinched it so violently that the pain woke her up. This dreamer's erotic tension was experienced as pain. And we are not surprised that under such emotional impact the erogenous bodily areas obtained ego cathexis. We can understand also the transformation of erotic tension into pain from a metapsychological point of view.

As pointed out, Freud explains physical pain as the result of a local breakthrough or a lesion of the anatomical *Reizschutz*. From the point of lesion at the periphery, external stimulations stream to the central psychic apparatus. In order to bind, isolate and stop the stream of excitation a countercathexis is mobilized to create a dynamic barrier all around the breach. Because of the huge amount of countercathexis necessary for binding the excessive stimulation, all other psychic systems are impoverished of cathexis, so that widespread paralysis or diminution of other mental activities ensues. According to Freud the local increase of cathexis at the place of the lesion is sensed as pain. In the dreams under discussion it is not the external anatomical *Reizschutz*, but the internal dynamic barrier, the internal ego boundary, strengthened by repressing countercathexes, which is injured. And thus we come to the conclusion that strong erotic stimulations from the id may break through, causing a lesion of the internal dynamic barrier. They cause a lesion because they are not egotized and therefore not emotionally discharged. Representations and memories which come to the ego's awareness without being egotized are perceived as hallucinations, as all dream images are. We should like to add that once erotic tension reaches the ego's awareness without being egotized it is experienced as pain at the erogenous zones, or at that region onto which the erotic tension was symbolically displaced. Such pain is produced in a manner similar to physical pain following a lesion of the external anatomical and dynamic barrier. The pain experienced by this female patient in the dream is not due to the dream work but to an unsuccessful repression of erotic tension, as is the case in conversion hysteria. We also learn from this example that an ego may become susceptible to conversion symptoms in dreams even if it does not suffer from conversion symptoms in waking life.

The next example is designed to illustrate the displacement of pain from the erogenetic zone to another part of the body. The displacement (but not the pain experience itself) is due to the primary mental process, one of the factors operative in the dream work. And we see once more that the part of the body upon which the pain appears displaced obtains ego cathexis in the dream. A male patient dreamt that one of his front teeth began to grow very long, causing him acute pain. The tooth went on growing and growing until it was a yard long. The dreamer then noticed to his horror that a substance like bone marrow was coming from it. He tried to press back both the marrow and the tooth with his finger and finally succeeded in restoring things to their normal state. The dream continued, and its latent content dealt then with problems arising from his successful suppression of erotic urges, but we are interested here only in the earlier part of the dream as reported. In his associations he remembered from his childhood various attempts by his father to frighten him in sexual matters. His father's threatening attitude had inhibited him sexually till after puberty. He was always frightened and embarrassed when he had an erection, fearing that others might notice it. When he had his first "wet dream" he imagined that the discharge of semen was extremely harmful. He wanted to get rid of all traces of it, and always tried to suppress ejaculation.

Furthermore, in this case we see that the erotic stimulation made a breach in the internal ego boundary as established in that dream state, and a symbolic displacement from below upwards occurred. And here, as in all emotional and volitional processes during dreaming, body ego feeling was present.

Not only can repressed erotic stimuli break through an established internal ego boundary without becoming egotized, but any cathexis which leads to emotions or volitions may injure the internal ego boundary. The following example will clarify this point:

A patient while dreaming experienced a violent toothache and dreamt that he went to a dentist. On waking up he found that the toothache was not only "dreamt" but that he actually had a toothache. He went then to a dentist who extracted his tooth. Some days passed, and the pain had long since left him, when one night while dreaming he again had a severe ache in the same "tooth." The pain was so severe that he woke up, only to find that he had no toothache at all. This time it was a conversion symptom which developed during dreaming. But as soon as he woke up he suffered acutely from grief for having been abandoned by a woman he loved very much, a grief which had been torturing him ever since she had left him some weeks previously. It is not difficult to understand the metapsychology of such a physical pain sensation in a dream state. Its explanation requires the consideration of Federn's concept of different ego states, each having its own dynamic boundary, and also of his finding that ego states can be repressed. Simple though its explanation may be, its verbalization may seem involved because it is necessary to indicate relations between different ego states and the way one ego state may affect another.

Let us begin with the phenomenon of grief. Grief presupposes an ego state, and repressed grief belongs to a repressed ego state. Everyone recognizes the "pain character" of grief, which we call "mental pain." Thus grief must have something in common with the effect of an injury—a break in continuity, so to speak, of the internal or external ego boundary. The common factor between grief and the effect of *Reizschutz* lesion must lie in the circumstance that through the loss of a love object quantities of libido invested in that object are torn away from the thought of it. Why does the tearing away of libido from the thought of an object cause a lesion of the ego boundary? The answer to this question can only be that a breach in the ego boundary caused by an object loss can occur only when the love object had been included within the ego boundary. We call such inclusion of a love object in the ego "identification" of the ego with the object.[3] We should note, however, that the term identification is not restricted to meaning the extension of ego cathexis over an actual object but applies equally to the extension of such cathexis over the autoplastic duplication of the object. (Thus, for example, a mother feels her baby a part of herself: Her ego boundary extends over the baby.) This latter form of identification, i.e., extension of ego cathexis over autoplastic duplicates, is essentially a replacement of the actual object. The first form of identification, on the other hand, occurs in varying degrees in every true relationship. We are reminded of the equation, so frequently made, between the ego's love object and parts of its own body. Karl Abraham[4] has made this particularly clear in his cogent observations on the subject. In poetry, proverbs, popular expressions, in every language, we very often encounter such phrases as "the apple of my eye" or, to describe the painful loss of a love object, "the heart of my heart had been torn from me." The libido which was invested in the love object is deprived of the outlet which had been established through the love relationship and then invades the ego through the breach caused in it. As physical wounds tend to heal, so the mental wound ("grief") also tends to heal, and this healing process is called, as we know, "mourning work." It is interesting to learn now that in the mourning work, that is, in the healing process, the first form of identification, the extension of ego cathexis over the actual object, becomes replaced by the second form of identification, namely, by an autoplastic duplication of the lost object, and this duplication absorbs the libido previously invested in the love object. We have already mentioned that the mourner acquires features of the lost object, and when these features are egotized, the injury is cicatrized. We understand clearly that grief presupposes the existence of a dynamic ego boundary which can be injured.

Let us now return to the dream under discussion. In waking life the patient suffered from intense grief: The mental pain was related to his waking ego state. When he fell asleep, however, the ego cathexis withdrew from the ego, and when the ego was reawakened to a dreaming state, this state did not yet extend over the grief. In other words, the dreaming ego did not contain the thought of his abandonment by the girl he loved. The fact that his grief, mental pain, was converted into bodily pain while he was dreaming, leads to the conclusion that the grieving, temporarily repressed ego state could gain in strength without becoming conscious. It may have gained in strength because of some possible connection of the present grief with some repressed grief-reactions of childhood. Furthermore, we conclude that an ego state, which remains repressed while the individual is dreaming, can impinge on the ego boundary of the dreaming ego. Through the lesion thus formed the grief stimuli, unegotized, invade the dreaming ego, causing the latter to experience physical pain. The actual toothache previously experienced must have indicated the location on the body for the conversion pain.

I observed very clearly the repression of painful ego states during dreaming in some severe melancholic patients. A severely depressed female patient, for example, enjoyed the most pleasurable dreams when she could fall asleep. She dreamt of happy family situations, enjoying love relationships with her husband and children, as a compensation, as it were, for her suffering in waking life. But as soon as she started to awaken she returned immediately to the torturing realization of her severe depressive state, even before she awoke completely. She considered her depression as "reality," the dreaming ego state as illusion. Her punitive superego became cathected only in waking state.

NOTES

(1) Weiss, op. cit.

(2) Federn, Paul. Ego feeling in dreams. In Ego Psychology and the Psychoses, p. 77.

(3) Strictly speaking, the term identification should be reserved for ego-invested autoplastic duplicates and not used for ego extension over external objects. In this book, however (as can be seen from the text), I have not restricted my use of identification to meaning investment of internalized objects, but speak of two distinct kinds of identification: (1) ego extension over external objects and (2) ego extension over autoplastic duplicates.

(4) Abraham, Karl. A short study of the development of the libido (1924). In his Selected Papers. London, Hogarth, 1927, p. 418-501.

XLVIII

Dreaming Egos and Schizophrenic Egos

WE have seen that the ego in a dreaming state often feels, functions and reacts to the dream events in a manner quite different from the way it reacts in waking life. We have learned that this is due in part to the fact that the ego is only partially awakened by the dream and often only to an earlier stage. Many essential, old and most recent memories are not awakened while the ego is dreaming, and its thinking function is sometimes extremely deficient. And what impresses one as very uncanny is the dreaming ego's attitude toward the most absurd manifest dream events. In the dream state an ego may be quite casual toward dream situations to which it would react with horror and despair in waking life. In the dream state not only motility and often bodily feelings remain dormant, but the mental ego also is deficient in its reactions, sometimes quite weird. These features and reactions of the dreaming ego are due not only to its incomplete awakening but also to its closer relatedness to the id. In the woman's reported dream, in which her son Mario had crushed his father to death, the dreamer did not feel horrified as she would have been in reality. She did not understand that it would have been impossible for a ten-year-old boy to kill his father in such a manner. She did not remember that her son was actually eighteen years old instead of ten and she failed to realize that her husband, who was alive in the dream, was Mario's father. In her dreaming state she remained quite unaware of all the many absurdities of her dream. But when we consider the latent dream thoughts we are less astonished about the dreaming ego's behavior. Her son in the dream was not actually himself but her own ego stage at the age of ten, and "killing the father," as we have seen, meant "indulging in forbidding sexual activities." So, the dreaming ego's reactions were much more appropriate to the latent dream content than to the manifest one. "Crushing the father with a stone"

444

meant "When I crushed the mouse all these thoughts were aroused in me." The fusion of two thought contents were *sensed*, though not verbalized, as such by the dreaming ego. It seems, indeed, that the dreaming ego could *feel* the latent meaning of the manifest content to a certain extent. Yet, if we ask the waking ego to tell us the meaning of its dreams it could not give us any answer. And when the experienced analyst reaches an understanding of the latent dream content and communicates it to the patient, the latter's resistance often prevents him from accepting the interpretation, however correct it may be. In many cases communication of the meaning of his dreams would be shocking to a patient.

We conclude that the dreaming ego is much closer to the latent meaning of its dreams than the waking ego could ever be. The dreaming ego's feeling of the latent content is evident, we repeat, from its reactions to the dream events while it is still dreaming. In some cases, however, the dreaming ego is awakened to a degree too rational to be sensitive to the latent id processes. It is in such cases that the "secondary revision" intervenes to adapt the manifest dream content to the more rational dreaming ego. But one of the dreaming ego's most characteristic features, among others, is its greater closeness to id processes than a healthy ego can have in waking state. It is interesting to learn that the dreaming ego has this characteristic in common with the schizophrenic ego, and this knowledge is of greatest importance for the psychotherapeutic approach to schizophrenic egos. To illustrate let us consider the attitudes of these egos toward symbolic representations.

Since psychoanalytic symbolism has not yet been presented in this volume (although some symbols have been mentioned) we must take time here to clarify some general issues on this subject. There are hundreds of different definitions of the word "symbol," on which we shall not embark. Freud introduced this term to signify a representation, an image or an act which in the id of every person can be substituted for another representation, image or function. Such substitutions are found in the analyses of dreams, in neurotic symptoms, in the folkloristic expressions and mythology of all nations and of all times. Symbolic substitutions seem to be an archaic trait of the mind. The characteristic feature of symbolization is the mental disposition of everyone to exchange or replace the representations of sexual organs, of biological functions, and of persons, with other objects and acts of his personal experience. In the Freudian sense, this exchange or substitution is called "symbolization." The following can be symbolized: sexual organs without distinguishing between sexes, the male genitalia in their entirety, the penis, the female genitalia, the womb, the female breasts, the erection of the penis, sexual intercourse, masturbation, birth, pregnancy, life and death, persons without distinguishing sex, and also man, woman, child, father, mother. These few representations can be replaced or substituted "symbolically" by a wide variety of objects. But the choice of each concrete symbol has a special connotation. For instance, the necktie, as a penis symbol, has an exhibitionistic connotation, while the knife or gun symbolizes the penis as an aggressive masculine organ. A pet animal can symbolize a child as a love object which the dreamer likes to fondle, while frogs or insects represent unwanted children in a disparaging sense. Fruits, and especially oranges and apples, symbolize the mother's breasts, in a love-giving and oral-dependent sense. To illustrate the general root of psychoanalytic symbolism, manifested in colloquialisms, in many popular expressions, proverbs, and in etymology, in folklore, etc., let us consider but one symbol: the number 3, for the complete masculine genitalia. We call Arabic figures our graphic signs for numbers. The graphic sign for the number 3 derives from the Egyptian hieroglyph of this form: ⛎ . Of this hieroglyph only the sign ﻭ has remained in ancient Sinaitic writings, and from this sign derives the Hebrew letter שׁ called *shin*. The graphic sign of this letter derives from this Egyptian hieroglyph. The word *shin* reproduces phonetically the noise of a stream of urine, and means "the rod for urinating"; *shen* means tooth, a point, a peak, or any organ of the body resembling a tooth. From the same Egyptian hieroglyph is derived the Arabic figure 3 which is written, in Arabic, ٣ . Number two is represented by the sign ٢ and number one by ١ . From these Arabic graphic signs we took our signs 1, 2 and 3. To follow all proofs from mythology, folklore, fairy tales, popular expressions, etc., of all ascertained symbols would require much more space than can be given here. Some dreams reveal clearly the meaning of symbols, and sometimes serve to illustrate the dreaming ego's closeness to id processes. A female patient who liked

very much the physician who cared for her during a short hospitalization had the following erotic dream: "I was lying in bed in the
hospital. Dr. N. (the physician) came to visit me. But there were
three physicians; the other two seemed to be his assistants. I do not
know why I felt sexually aroused. As a matter of fact, only Dr. N.
entered my room; the other two remained outside." The interpretation of this dream with all its condensations—Dr. N. stood also for
his penis, etc.—is self-evident.

A male patient felt very vexed in childhood by his strong and
unsatisfied sexual curiosity. He longed to inspect the hidden genitalia of a woman. His favorite play was to crawl on the floor, mostly
under a chair or table, in hope of catching a glimpse under his
maid's skirts. But all his attempts were futile. The content of this
boy's first "wet dream" at the beginning of puberty was that he
approached his former maid trying to get under her skirts. But
while trying to do so he found himself handling a chair and in-
specting it underneath between its legs. During this "inspection" he
had his first ejaculation. Upon awakening he did not understand
how he could possibly have become sexually aroused in the dream
by a chair. This dream demonstrates that the response of the dreaming ego, incomprehensible to the waking ego, occurs in adaptation
to the latent content of dream scenes. But this dream reveals much
more than this. The substitution of a chair for a woman is not
merely a symbolic substitution. The choice of such a "symbol"
shows that this boy could not integrate a human relationship with
sexual desires for a woman. His sexual curiosity was a mere anatomical one. Besides, his analysis revealed that he was afraid to discover
the female genitalia. He had never succeeded in catching sight of
them in order to avoid the shocking experience of discovering a
mutilation. He must have repressed his earlier knowledge of the
anatomical aspect of female genitalia. And this specific symbol, a
chair, also served the purpose of deflecting his voyeuristic success
from a woman to an inanimate object. The woman became thus de-
humanized or, rather, de-animated. Nevertheless the patient's sexual orgasm was elicited, in the dream state, by a symbolic image,
however overdetermined it might have been.

Clinical experience shows that the schizophrenic ego has in common with the dreaming ego the mode of reaction to symbolic im-

ages: It often reacts to them in accordance with their unconscious meaning. Many psychoanalysts have observed that some schizophrenic patients use a "symbolic language." To give a simple example, a schizophrenic patient stuck his finger in the mud and said to me: "I hope I did not impregnate her," and he did not intend to make a joke. Knowledge of psychoanalytic symbolism permits us to understand the apparently confused talk of some schizophrenics. Marguerite Sèchehaye[1] was successful in her therapeutic approach to schizophrenic patients through what she calls the "symbolic realization of schizophrenic needs." I do not intend to embark here on details of Sèchehaye's therapeutic approach but only to mention the point which interests us in connection with our present discussion.

Her schizophrenic patient, Renée, had been severely traumatized in infancy. The author describes the traumatizing situations as follows: "At the age of three months, because of faulty medical diagnosis, the baby was placed on a diet for gastritis. Much later, when she cried and refused the bottle, it was recognized that the mother had been putting too much water in the milk; the diet was hardly one to satisfy her hunger. Malnourished and anemic, she was progressing toward an alarming state of cachexia when her grandmother realized the infant's crying was due to unsatisfied hunger and not to gastric pain. She took the child in hand and fed it, thus establishing in Renée a strong fixation on herself. So it happened that when the grandmother suddenly left during Renée's twelfth month, the baby felt sorely abandoned and reacted with intense anxiety and self-destructive behavior, striking her head against the wall and clawing her face when her desperate cries failed to produce her grandmother. Her parents displayed complete incomprehension of the child's distress and greediness for food." The child's traumatic conditions were increased by the unfeeling and teasing, oral-aggressive behavior of her father.

Later in her severe schizophrenic state, when she was nineteen years old, Renée felt guilty in eating, and the only nourishment she allowed herself was apples—the mentioned symbol for milk and love-giving mother's breasts. Once when the therapist brought her some magnificent apples, the patient refused them, but still she insisted on "apples." The patient had fallen into a state of severe agitation and confusion following an unfortunate remark by a neighboring farm woman on whose land Renée had been gathering green apples without permission. The patient said that "she would die, for they had taken her most precious belonging, her apples." And when the therapist observed that she need only eat the beautiful apples which she, the therapist, gave her, Renée stopped her abruptly and pointed to the therapist's bosom, saying, "Renée doesn't want the apples of grown-ups, she wants real apples, mama's apples."

The schizophrenic ego's sensitiveness for and response to the symbolic meaning of various objects, acts and gestures, is due to its dynamic weakness. We understand, thus, that one of the most important functions of the ego cathexis is to establish an efficient "secondary mental process" which diminishes or abolishes the ego's sensitiveness for unegotized id processes. Yet, a healthy and intuitive ego can develop a sensitivity for id processes without impairment of its own secondary mental process. It can function in its own life in a perfectly integrated, healthy manner, and yet have developed a new "sense," as it were, a sense for the understanding of id processes. This sense is essential for psychoanalytically oriented psychotherapists.

Strengthening of a schizophrenic ego (i.e., freeing it from its psychotic state) can be considered, in some respects, a process analogous to the arousal of a dreaming ego to a healthy waking state. A schizophrenic patient listening to the talk of another patient who expressed his delusions and revealed the contents of his hallucinations once told me: "Why can't he wake up? He is still dreaming." Recovered schizophrenics often understand other schizophrenic patients better than many psychiatrists do. But it must be borne in mind that the dreaming and schizophrenic egos also differ from each other in other respects.

NOTES

(1) Sèchehaye, Marguerite. A New Psychotherapy in Schizophrenia: Relief of Frustrations by Symbolic Realization. New York, Grune & Stratton, 1956. See also Renée's own Autobiography of a Schizophrenic Girl, with analytic interpretation by Marguerite Sèchehaye. New York, Grune & Stratton, 1951.

XLIX

Dreams in General Anesthesia

AN ego can be awakened to a dreaming state during general anesthesia, during a fainting spell, during a post-epileptic coma, shock
treatment and the like. One would expect that dreams occurring
under such conditions would be always indistinct and faint, but
this is not supported by observation. In some cases such dreams are
very vivid, and the dreaming ego has a strong feeling of reality for
the dream events. Often such dream experiences are much more
vivid and seem to the ego much more real than its experiences in
waking state. We cannot ascribe this vividness always to the effect
of the anesthetic used, because sometimes this vividness also occurs in dreams during fainting spells. Some drugs, it is true, may
produce vivid dreams by their specific action on the central nervous
system. These are not drugs used in medicine for anesthetic purposes
but used by some people, particularly Orientals, for the very purpose of inducing pleasurable dreams. But we shall not consider
such dreams here.

Freud's thesis that dreams protect sleep—that they are its guardians—cannot be easily applied to dreams experienced during
general anesthesia. Could strong enough stimuli awaken the
dreamer from general anesthesia while he is still receiving the anesthetic? If so, would his dreams also constitute an attempt to protect
the "sleep" induced by the anesthetic? In any case, the occurrence of such dreams indicates that the state of unconsciousness is not complete. Persons who awaken from a state of complete
unconsciousness do not have any retrospective feeling of the time
elapsed, but have the impression that they have been unconscious
only for a moment. A patient awakening from deep anesthesia
after an operation which had lasted over an hour asked the nurse
when the doctors would start to operate.

Federn explains the great vividness of dreams under general

anesthesia through the circumstance that the dreamer cannot awaken as long as he is under the effect of the anesthetic. Such vivid perceptions and, I would add, such strong emotions would be incompatible with normal physiological sleep. The state produced by the action of the anesthetic, from which the dreamer cannot be awakened by stimuli, or only with great difficulty, is responsible for the vividness of these dreams accompanied by a strong feeling of reality for the dream experiences. As far as the "wish-fulfillment character" of dreams is concerned, we understand that attempts to find solutions for pending problems—to reach the fulfillment of wishes—is inherent in every mental activity of waking life as well as of dreaming life. We shall not be surprised that the contents of dreams experienced under general anesthesia deal with problems of life and death. The general condition for dreaming, in normal sleep as well as in that produced by anesthetics, is the ego's detachment from the external world. Its perceptive disappearance becomes compensated by a dream world which arises from internal stimuli.

Federn[1] reported a dream which he himself experienced when under general anesthesia in the course of a complicated dental operation, for which nitrous oxide was used. Never, even in waking life, had he experienced anything so vividly or with such intense feeling of reality as in this dream. He reports that suddenly before "going to sleep" there came into his mind, but without any fear, the thought that anesthesia could "kill old fellows like me," that he should use his last moments to think intensely and philosophically about the end of his life, and that he should make some important decision to accomplish something in case he should continue to live. Then he felt the strange but rather sweet taste of the gas, a slight dizziness—and he vanished away as a personality. His dream did not begin immediately after his last conscious thought; there was, he reported, an interval during which his ego had lost all its mental cathexis. When his mental life returned in a dreaming state he did not know that he was dreaming. For the most part his earlier life was not forgotten; he had a new career, but he knew who he had been before. There was no double personality. He had his own character and his own name, but he was in completely changed surroundings. He possessed a strength of will power, a quickness and certainty of decision, an intensity of action, the like of which he had never experienced before, either awake or asleep. As the chief military commander and chief statesman of his new country, he put into order one province after another. In the dream he knew just which Far Eastern country it was, but in recalling he could not decide whether it was China or Greece. The provinces had straight-line frontiers, like some of the states in this country, but it was not America. (Even in his boldest dreams, says Federn, he did not meddle in American problems!)

His dream covered a long period of time, apparently about half a year, and all the while he was reforming many countries, under continual strain and tension. He decided things in a hurry and carried through his decisions quickly. He was severe with himself, but at the same time he was completely and continually contented with his performance. Never before in his life, awake or dreaming, had he felt such happiness or such satisfaction with his personality and with his work. It was the strongest "feeling of one's self" and the greatest enjoyment by one's own self that could be imagined. The singular events followed each other with enormous speed; yet all actions were quickly carried out to perfection and in complete order, one after the other. It was a glorious fight, without any conceit or show, and through it all he felt that he never failed to follow the motto: Do what you have to do.

Alas! Suddenly the miraculous glory ceased—one of the surgeons was speaking to him. Immediately he tried to recall all the details, but he was aware of only the skeleton of the dream. He thanked the doctor for having been the means of giving him one of his happiest experiences.

Federn analyzed this dream very accurately. I cannot embark here upon the details, but this is roughly his analysis:

Before he was given the anesthetic he saw on the wall the rectangular x-ray pictures of his teeth. The provinces which he had to put into order had the same form as these negatives. The dreamer identified himself with the surgeon. His superman attitude was a reaction to the passive attitude into which he was put in reality, sitting back in the dentist's chair. In his interpretation Federn also went back to his childhood. He remembered that at the age of ten he had read with enthusiasm a book for boys, called *Liu-Pa-Yu*, a story of China. He had wanted to go to China and become emperor, and for a long time he was teased with the name *Liu-Pa-Yu*. At the age of thirteen or fourteen he had resented the defeat of Demosthenes and the victory of the Macedonians. Many other details show clearly a connection between his present preoccupation and desires from his boyhood.

Let us not concern ourselves here with the wish-fulfillment character of this dream. Wish fulfillments in dreams and hallucinations, we repeat, constitute a psychological phenomenon which must be studied per se, independent of the sleep-protecting function.

This dream did not awaken the sleeper. He woke up only when the anesthetic wore off and would have liked to continue to sleep. But any dreamer in normal sleep would have been awakened by such a powerful dream, even though it was so enjoyable. In Federn's opinion the dream was so intensely experienced because the dreamer could not wake up. This is true also in nightmares experienced under general anesthesia, as we shall see in the following example, the dream of a patient who was undergoing an abortion:

"I was attached to a kind of planet which was rotating at high speed around some central thing, like a sun. This central thing was away off to my left. Between it and me were millions of other planets with people attached to them, just like me, but I could not communicate with them. I was attached by the right half of my mouth, so that I could not open my mouth altogether and thus had trouble in speaking. I wanted to call to the people on my right, where the 'earth' was, that they should not step off the earth or they too would be fixed on a planet and would have to rotate for eternity. I had a horrible feeling of frustration and doom—that this revolving was to be my fate forever. It was a very real feeling and I actually believed it. My real life took on a dream quality, and this was reality to me. I felt that this was the be-all and the end-all of why people had been put on earth, that everything was really chaos, that the earth and its inhabitants were only an accident and that therefore the efforts of communists and other political philosophers were utterly futile. As I went around (it was terribly uncomfortable) I tried to call to the others, but they could not hear me. I seemed to be in water rather than in air-filled space."

This dream experience was due to various factors. Our distinction between the dream itself, the hallucinated events, and the dreaming ego which reacts to the dream leads us to the proper approach to the mental occurrences while an ego is dreaming. Thus, the dreamer's thoughts while dreaming do not belong to the dream, although they may be related to the latent content. We also realize that physical sensations can be perceived while one is dreaming, as we have seen in some examples. They may be misinterpreted and may be involved in the dream content, often in adaptation to the latent dream content. In this case the patient while dreaming maintained the sensation of the ether or chloroform mask which was firmly held over her mouth and nose. This sensation was then elaborated in the dream into her attachment at the mouth to something. Also in this dream physical pains and discomfort were converted into mental pain: despair, hopelessness, etc. Furthermore, feelings of dizziness produced by the anesthetic often appear in a dream as the sensation of flying around in a circle or of moving at a great speed. In my opinion the great speed of action of the previous dreamer (Federn) expressed a feeling of dizziness. A nine-year-old girl who had a tonsillectomy under not-very-deep general anesthesia dreamt that she was flying at a great speed in a circle, around and around, under a blood-red sky. She had a constant sensation as though there were artificial wings bound under her arms by a girdle which would slide down and had to be pulled up into position again. In reality it was the nurse who held her under her arms.

Let us return to the dream of the female patient who underwent an abortion. Her pregnancy was a premarital "accident." In her dream-thought "the earth and its inhabitants were only an accident." This thought expressed also her "philosophical" thinking about the birth phenomenon, about new individuals coming into being and populating the earth. Besides, she identified herself with the baby of whom she was being deprived. It was the fetus which was attached to her. The earth is a common symbol for mother and maternity; in every language one speaks of "mother earth." It was unjust that only married women were allowed to bear children. The communists stood for the claim that the same rights should be granted to all. The embryo finds itself in water as the dreamer found herself in the dream. Her strong wish to warn "other people" not to "step off" the earth or they would be fixed on a planet as she was, as the embryo is fixed on the uterus, is a warning to herself not to "step off" again from precautionary measures in her love life. This part of the dream is due in part to the mentioned regard for representability of thoughts through perceptive images, and in part to some secondary revision. Mother and uterus are multiplied in the symbols of earth and the millions of planets. Freud taught us that "many" stands often in the dream for "several times." Her perception of having the ether mask over her mouth was utilized for the representation of being attached to the uterus (planet) in her identification with the embryo: She was attached by her mouth. The meaning of "rotating around a center" became clear to me from the observations of other dreams experienced in general anesthesia.[2] Feelings of dizziness which precede the state of unconsciousness develop into a feeling of losing one's own identity and then losing consciousness. A male patient who underwent several operations under ether anesthesia always had the same dream, that someone was holding him by the heels and was swinging him around and around in ever wider circles. He moved faster and faster, describing a huge spiral, farther and farther from the center, until he was finally let loose and thrown by the centrifugal force into infinity. This moment coincided with complete loss of consciousness—and then it was nothingness for him until he began to awaken from the anesthesia. Indeed, a beautiful functional symbolization of loss of consciousness, loss of "I-ness." Flying into infinity signified flying into nothingness, abandoning the self, conceived as a "center," passing out into a timeless, spaceless state. This dream was not unpleasant to him, however. Also in many other dreams "moving away from a center, or moving around a center" derives from the sensation of losing one's own ego. Thus, the sun around which our patient moved, attached to a planet, represented the patient's own ego of which only a partial state, the dreaming ego—at some distance from the waking ego, the sun—was re-awakened.

In the dream during abortion the feeling of the ego that it would persist in that frustrating, uncomfortable position for all eternity deserves our interest. This feeling is a feeling of hopelessness. Hope results from our understanding or our feeling of the possibility for a change, for a solution of an undesirable situation. When an ego is completely immobilized it also feels that it has lost its capacity to change its position, its condition. The position in which it finds itself is felt as "hopelessly permanent." The ego of our patient was awakened to a state in which the motor apparatus still remained paralyzed, while some bodily feelings must have regained some cathexis. Bodily feeling with the sensation of complete motoric paresis is sensed as a hopeless situation; no prospect of a change can be conceived. In summary we recognize the effects of various factors in the formation of this nightmare: the patient's distress at losing a prospective child, her mental attitude toward socially accepted rules, and the very incomplete anesthetic state during which she could perceive disagreeable bodily sensations and dizziness, accompanied by a feeling of total incapacity to cathect her muscular apparatus.

Federn's dream and the dream of this patient were more vivid and accompanied by a more keen sensation of reality than dream scenes are ever experienced in physiological sleep. It is useful to repeat Federn's explanation of this character of dreams under general anesthesia: During normal physiological sleep the body ego, including its sense organs, is not cathected—it "sleeps," except in some special cases which will be mentioned. The dream awakens only the mental ego, and that not too strongly. If the mental ego is too strongly awakened by internal or external stimuli, and especially if they awaken the body ego, the state of physiological sleep cannot be maintained, and the sleeper must awaken. But in the sleep produced by anesthesia, and in states of fainting and other states of incomplete unconsciousness, a stimuli cannot awaken the body ego. Therefore the dreaming ego can obtain a strong cathexis; it can be very strongly awakened, while the body with its sense organs resists complete awakening. Such dreams reveal the efforts to master unbearable dynamic conditions, whether they succeed or fail in their attempts.

In the nightmare of the patient who underwent abortion her dreaming ego felt unable to change its position; the dreamer could not move because she was attached to that planet. This kind of impediment of movement in a dream, namely, the feeling that one can not move because of external obstacles, is due, according to Federn, to an organic neurologic affliction of the motor apparatus. A patient of his in a dream felt handicapped in his movements because a crowd of people stood in his way. This patient suffered from a transitory muscular paresis. Our female patient also was paralyzed by the anesthetic; and it is not clear whether in Federn's own dream the dreaming ego's "putting in order one province after the other" at a great speed implied muscular action or only orders given which were carried out by other people. It must be borne in mind, however, that active ego cathexis is not necessarily motoric capacity. As Federn says: "The will is the turning of the whole active ego cathexis to particular activities, whether they be mere thinking or action."

Dreams in which the dreaming ego wants to move but is prevented from doing so by external factors have a different meaning from dreams in which the dreamer is unable to carry out an intended movement because he feels paralyzed. The latter dreams, called "inhibition dreams," express an internal conflict and are not due to a physiological impairment of the muscular apparatus. A very ambitious patient, for example, who had often been criticized by his parents in childhood for his unrealistic grandiose fantasies, dreamt that he was introduced to the Queen of England during her visit to the United States. And when she extended her hand to him he could not raise his hand; his arm was paralyzed. This dream expressed a victory of his superego which did not permit him to indulge in unrealistic ambitious fantasies. Anxiety dreams in which the ego wants to escape from a threatening danger, but feels paralyzed, are self-punitive dreams: The dreamer's conscience does not allow him to withdraw from punishment.

Federn's contributions to ego psychology bring nearer to our understanding the meaning of the ego experience in dreams. Freud's dream interpretation concerns the unconscious and disregards the part which consciousness and the ego play in dreams. Federn amplified our knowledge of dreams, "particularly by showing that willing, too, can be recognized in dreams." Body ego feelings in dreams indicate the dreamer's will, his "wanting" to do something. When a dreamer carries out a movement which is not accompanied by a corresponding body ego feeling, this means that he would like to be able to do something, but he actually does not want to. So, the concept of "I can, I am able to" and that of "I want to" find clear expression in dreams through specific ego feelings. Also in cases of

458 STRUCTURE AND DYNAMICS OF THE HUMAN MIND

exhibitionistic wishes the body ego feeling is present in a dream. Very interesting is Federn's observation that in somnambulistic dreams the body ego feeling is particularly vivid. The actions which are carried out in somnambulistic actions are commanded by the superego. The dreaming ego's will (wanting to) arises in obedience to the superego. Federn reports, for example, a somnambulic patient who felt it very difficult to get up. He had a sense of anxiety or oppression connected with the fact that he must get up. "He sensed the weight of his body which had to be lifted; that is, it would remain within the dreamer's ego as a burden and an impediment to getting up and subsequently walking. During the act of walking, the bodily ego feeling was exceptionally intense."

Federn contrasts somnambulistic dreams with the inhibition dreams. In the inhibition dreams the ego expresses that it is *not allowed* (by the superego) to do something; in the somnambulistic dreams the ego expresses that it is requested (by the superego) to do something.

NOTES

(1) Federn, Paul. A dream under general anaesthesia: Studies in ego cathexis. Psychiat. Quart., 18:422-438, 1944. Also in his Ego Psychology and the Psychoses, p. 97-114.

(2) Weiss, Edoardo. Some dynamic aspects of dreams. Samiska, 2:209-226, 1948.

Name Index

Abraham, Karl, 174, 441; *cited*, 443 (note 4)

Adler, Alfred, xvi, xvii, 60-61, 62, 168, 183, 199, 200-201

Aichhorn, August, xiv; *cited*, xviii (note 4)

Alexander, Franz, 161-162, 166-167, 217-218, 248, 249, 417; *cited*, 224 (note 4), 423 (note 1)

Aristotle, 388

Benedek, Therese, 169; *cited*, 171 (note 5)

Bergson, Henri, 162

Bernard, Claude, 156

Bernfeld, Siegfried, 100

Bibring, Edward, 270 (note 2)

Bleuler, Eugen, 77, 112

Breuer, Josef, 46; *cited*, 49

Burdach, K. F., 388

Cannon, Walter B., 8, 156; *cited*, 10

Charcot, J.-M., 333, 337

Darwin, Charles, 330

Descartes, René, 67

Driesch, Hans, 247

Ellis, Havelock, 196

Evans, William, 194 (note 3)

Fechner, G. T., 155, 156, 388

Federn, Ernst, xviii, 363; *cited*, xix (note 8), 317 (note 6), 368 (note 3)

Federn, Paul, 66-69, 114, 126, 127, 134, 168, 263, 307, 320, 410; historical and biographical data, xi-xix; loyalty to Freud, xvi; divergence

from Freud, xvii; on abstraction, 112-113; on altruistic surrender, 270 (note 2); on bisexuality, 191; on creativity, 12; on death instinct, 104, 157, 160, 170, 239-240, 248; on defense mechanisms, 257; on denial, 366; on derealization, 89-90, 94 (note); on dreams, 52, 142-143, 393-394, 434-435, 450-453 (in anesthesia), 456-458 (in anesthesia), 457-458 (in somnambulism); on ego boundaries, 84, 92-93, 126; ego concept of, 63 (contrasted with A. Freud's), 16, 68-69 (definitions), 67, 88-89 (derived from study of psychoses); on ego weakness, 74, 366; egotization concept of, 76; on externalization, 97; on hallucinations, 53, 314, 316; on identification, 97; on internalization, 97; on love, 214; on masochism and sadism, 191; on narcissism, 64, 197-198; on obsessions, 372-373; on paranoia, 53-54, 87 (therapy), 316-317 (therapy); on projection, 97; on psychoses, 53-54, 87, 99, 119-121, 301-303; 316-317, 322; on reality, 6, 76; on repression, 38, 40, 105; on restriction of ego activities, 382; on schizophrenia, 53, 99, 119-121, 301-303; self concept of, 64; on sleep, 403, 406; on superego, 281, 284; on synthetic function of the ego, 50; *cited*, xviii-xix, 4, 13, 18, 70, 144, 249, 250, 292, 378, 385, 443, 458

See also the below-listed entries in the Subject Index: De-egotization; Derealization; Ego atony; Ego boundaries; Ego feeling; Ego-cosmic stage; Egotization; Ego stages; Ego states; Ego strength and weakness; "I" and "I-ness"; Medial concept; Orthriogenesis; Reality, sense of; "We" feeling

Federn, Salomon, xiii

Fenichel, Otto, 90, 167, 353; *cited,* 171 (note 3)

Ferenczi, Sandor, 11, 75, 138-140, 174; *cited,* 144 (note 3)

Frazer, James George, 284

Freeman, Thomas, 106; *cited,* 113

French, Thomas M., 111-112, 114, 122, 248, 378, 393, 420; on dream interpretation, 430-431; equates ego and integrative function, 62; on focal and nuclear conflicts, 430-431; on instincts, 249; on psychic trauma, 237, 418; on sleep, 403; on surplus energy, 217-219, 249; *cited,* 70, 113, 121, 224, 249, 431

Freud, Anna, 62, 67, 97, 210, 262, 270 (note 2), 277, 323, 324, 367, 382-385; *cited,* 70, 214, 281, 327, 369, 385

Freud, Sigmund, historical and biographical data, x-xi, 96; reaction to Federn's ego psychology, xvii-xviii; on anaclitic object love, 21, 203, 205, 207, 213; on anxiety, 220-221, 339-341 (phobias); on autoerotism, 195; on bisexuality, 190; on castration, 34, 183-185, 187, 188; on conscience, 200; on conversion; 330-338; on cathexis, 16; death instinct, concept of, 72, 228-234, 238-249; on derealization, 91-92; on dream as protector of sleep, 399-400; on dreams, 52, 388-458, *passim;* ego concept of, 3, 5, 59-62, 66, 67-68; on ego in dreams, 56-57, 143-144; on Eros, 13, 50; on female castration complex, 187, 188; on fetishism, 364-365; on "free" and "bound" energy, 46; on goals, 288; on grief in dreams, 416-417; on hallucinations, 52; on identification, 295; on instincts, 157-158, 225-234, 227 and 238-239 (definitions); on introversion, 54; on laughter, 331; on libido, 50, 161, 164-171, 224 (note 5), 316-317; on melancholia, 303, 307-308; metapsychology of, 13, 61 (early); on mourning work, 79; on narcissism, 64-65, 167-168, 169, 196-198; on need for punishment, 288; on oedipus complex, 33-34, 186-187; on paranoia, 314-317; on phobias, 339-341; on pleasure, 107, 217, 269; on projection, 268-269; on purified pleasure ego, 107, 269; on reality testing, 75; on repetition compulsion, 226, 238, 331; on repression, 37-38, 148, 323-324; on resistance, 147, 149, 399 (in dreams); on schizophrenia, 99, 301-303; on schizophrenic language, 116-117, 118; on screen memories, 367-368; on sexual ideas of children, 201; on sleep, 406; on superego, 284-287; on traumatic dreams, 406, 421; wish-fulfillment, dream theory of, 400-401, 405, 416; *cited,* xix, 24, 49, 70, 94, 171, 194, 204, 214, 234, 249, 260, 270, 292, 303, 317, 338, 356, 368, 369, 385, 405

Glover, Edward, 15, 110; *cited,* 18, 113, 124

Goldstein, Kurt, 247

Gomperz, Heinrich, 193

Groddek, Georg, 43

Groos, Karl, 217

Hartmann, Heinz, 17, 62-64, 65-66, 127, 142, 168, 198, 248, 320, 324; *cited,* 70

Hendrick, Ives, 247-248, *cited,* 250

Jacobson, Edith, 194 (note 3)
Jodl, F., 57
Jones, Ernest, 18 (note 2), 183
Jung, C. G., xvi, 162, 167

Kant, Immanuel, 113 (note 3)
Klein, Melanie, 174, 195-196, 286
Kris, Ernst, 62

Lilly, John C., 144 (note 1)
Lindner, S., 173
Loewenstein, Rudolph M., 62
Low, Barbara, 157-158, 230, 236

McDougall, William, 155
Meynert, Theodor, 363
Moll, A., 236
Monakow, Constantin von, 247
Musset, Alfred de, 213

Nietzsche, Friedrich, 43, 60, 264
Nothnagel, Hermann, xii
Nunberg, Herman, 16, 50-51, 90, 132,
    141, 242; cited, 18, 58, 133, 249

Oberndorff, C. P., xii, xviii

Plato, 153, 193, 233

Rapaport, David, 63; cited, 70 (note
    2)

Reitler, R., xii
Rolland, Romain, 134

Schilder, Paul, 90, 100-101
Schiller, Friedrich, 217; cited, 224
    (note 3)
Sèchehaye, Marguerite, 449
Silberer, Herbert, 434
Spencer, Herbert, 217
Spitta, H., 388
Spitz, René A., 142; cited, 144 (note
    5)
Stekel, Wilhelm, xvi, xvii, 249 (note
    2)
Strümpell, A. von, 57, 388
Sullivan, Harry Stack, 212

Tausk, Viktor, xvi, 90, 140

Waelder, Robert, 54, cited, 7
Wagner von Jauregg, Julius, xi
Weininger, Otto, 213
Weismann, August, 232
Weiss, Edoardo, on death instinct,
    228-229; on derealization, 91; on
    "identification with the aggressor,"
    384; cited, 94 (note 5), 194, 234,
    249, 260 (note 1), 281, 303-304,
    317, 338, 357, 385, 405, 443, 458
Wittels, Fritz, 90

Zola, Émile, 275-276

Subject Index

Abortion, dreams in, 453, 454-456
Abstraction, 112-113, 115, 120
Acropolis, Freud's experience on, 91
Acting out, 227
Actual neuroses, 356-357 (note 2)
Adaptation, physiological, 10
Adolescence, 210 ff., 287-288. *See also* Puberty
Aggression, 218, 223, 239-240, 246-249, 266, 267
Agoraphobia, 343-357, 372
Alcohol, effects of, 136-137
Alloplasticity, 11-13
Altruistic surrender, 262, 264, 270 (note 2)
Ambition, 183
Ambivalence, 31, 178, 245-246, 373-374
Anaclitic object love. *See* Object love, anaclitic
Anal erotism, 177-180, 185
Anal phase, 173, 179, 373
Anal-sadistic tendencies, 373
Analytic situation, 138-140, 306, 321-323
Anesthesia, dreams in, 450-458
Animals, 274
Animals, small, in dreams, 413
Anorexia, 267
Anti-cathexes. *See* Countercathexis
Anxiety, 220-221; defined, 37
Anxiety hysteria. *See* Phobias
Arc de cercle, 337, 338 (note 2)
Asthma, 297-298
Atony, ego. *See* Ego atony
Autism, 77
Autoerotism, 195, 196, 198. *See also* Masturbation
Autoplasticity, 11-13

Baby = feces, 186
Besetzen, Besetzung, etc., 16, 18 (note)
Bewältigungstrieb. *See* Instinct to master
Biological id. *See* Id, biological
Birth trauma, 226, 331
Bisexuality, 190-193, 379-380
Blindness, 360-361
Body ego, 100-104, 110-111, 143, 404
Body image, 100-101
Body in dreams. *See* Dreams, body in
Body scheme. *See* Body image
Borderline states, 322
Boundary formation. *See* Ego boundaries
Breasts, "good" and "bad," 195-196

Cannibalism, 174
Capacity to sleep, 403
Castration complex, 34, 183-185, 186-187, 210, 285; female, 185, 187, 188
Cathexis, 13-14, 15-18, 215-226, 239; defined, 15, 216, 224 (note 1), 270 (note 1); in conversion, 371-372; preconscious, 45; in primary process, 46-49. *See also* Ego cathexis; Libido
Cathexis, destructive. *See* Aggression; Death Instinct; Sadism
Censor, dream (*Censur*), 56, 399, 405, 408, 416-417
Ceremonials, compulsive, 373
Child development, 5-6, 25-27, 31-35, 69, 74-77, 80-82, 84, 142, 172-181, 182-194, 195-196, 205-214, 256-259, 277-280, 285-286, 289

Child rearing. *See* Parent and child; Mother-child relationship

Childbirth, reactions to, 298

Children, wish for, 23, 186, 351

Claustrophobia, 350

Cognitive structure, 114, 122

Coherent ego feeling. *See* Ego feeling, coherent

Coitus, 185-186, 264

Compassion. *See* Pity

Compulsive behavior. *See* Obsessive compulsive reactions

"Conflict-free sphere," 127, 320

Conscience, 28, 30, 36, 200, 220, 259, 271, 288-289, 299, 306. *See also* Superego

Consciousness, 3, 61, (*system*), 328

Conversion, 226, 330, 331-338, 341-342, 360, 372-373, 433-443

Conversion in dreams. *See* Dreams, body in

Constancy, principle, 156, 216

Countercathexis, 32, 36

Counterphobic attitude, 353

Creativity, 11-12

Crime and criminals, 256, 271, 286, 294-295, 322-323, 327 (note 2). *See also* Murder

Day residues, 406

Daydreams, 54-55, 364

Deafness, 360-361

Death, 31, 279, 416. *See also* Grief; Mourning

Death instinct, 72, 104, 157-158, 170, 221, 222-224, 228-234, 238-249, 270 (note 1), 288

De-egotization, 22, 102, 107, 109-110, 263; defined, 107, 109

Defense against stimuli (*Reizschutz*), 36

Defense mechanisms, 95-104, 257, 320-327, 339-357, 370-378, 379-385. *See also* Denial; Identification with the aggressor; Isolation; Repression, Undoing

De-identification. *See* Ego passage

Delusions, 99, 127, 202, 312-317 *See also* Paranoia

Denial, 352, 358-369; derealization as, 91; repression and, 365-366

Depersonalization, 90, 98, 102, 170, 279, 344, 356-357; defined, 263

Depression, 104, 307. *See also* Melancholia

Derealization, 89-91, 97, 170, 316, 356-357 (note 2), 358-359, 361-362

Destrudo. *See also* Aggression

Determinism and indeterminism, 390-392

Displacement, 52

Dizziness, 138-140, 454-455

Dogs, fear of, 342

Dream content, 396-405, 410

Dream interpretation, 46-48, 396-399, 408-415, 424-431; resistance to, 396. *See also* Dreams

Dream work, 406-415. *See also* Dreams, process and formation

Dreams, 43, 51-52, 359, 388-458; body in, 47-48, 432-443, 456-458; ego in, 45-48, 56-58, 142-144, 278-279, 329, 393-395, 399, 402-403, 405; ego states in, 23, 107, 410-411; external physical stimuli in, 433 ff.; forgetting of, 396; in general anesthesia, 450-458; in mourning period, 175; in pairs, 417, 425; process and formation of, 45-48, 148, 392-393, 406-415, 444-449, 457-458; as protector of sleep, 399-400, 450; psychic presence in, 278-279; secondary revision in, 48-49, 56-58; sense of reality in, 404; sleep-disturbing, 416-423; substitution in, 46, 408; in traumatic neuroses, 225-226. *See also* Dream interpretation; Dream content; Dream work

Drive objects and love objects, distinguished, 213-214

Drives (instincts), 43-45; defined,

236; distinguished from instincts, 154-162, 236; dualism of, 63, 65, 225-234. *See also* Id; Instincts

Drugs, 106-107, 136-137, 312, 450

Ectoderm and endoderm, 61-62

Ego, 2-4, 50-58; defined, 7, 16; autonomy of the, 63, 65-66, 73, 74, 127, 198, 320, 324, 330; body (*see* Body ego); interaction with id, 50-58, 63, 323-327, 328 ff.; interaction with superego, 50-58; in intrauterine state, 65; mental, 103, 111; multiple function of, 54; in obsessional neuroses, 372-373; secondary revision of id contents by, 48-49, 56-58; in sleep, 399, 404-405 (*see also* Dreams, ego in); social (*see* "We" feeling); splitting of, 305-317, 360-361, 364; synthetic funtion of, 16, 50-51, 54, 56. *See also* Integrative function; Reality

Ego atony, 100, 125. *See also* Ego strength and ego weakness

Ego boundaries, 66-67, 69, 84, 95-96, 99, 106-109, 146-148, 253, 287, 358-359, 360, 441; defined, 92-93, 147-148; formation, 126; internal and external, 92-93, 358-359; in psychoses, 312; repression and, 39, 312, 325-326; in resonance identification, 265; in schizophrenia, 53; sense of reality and, 90; in waking state, 52

Ego cathexis, 74, 96-97, 100-101, 114-121, 125, 170; coherence of, 100, 328; deficiency of, 114-121, 123-126 (*see also* Ego strength; and Ego weakness); ego feeling and, 95; withdrawal of (*see* De-egotization)

Ego defenses, 37-41, 320-327. *See also* Defense mechanisms

Ego development. *See* Child development

Ego feeling, 3-4, 29, 170, 328; coherent, 95, 101; development of, 69; first use of term, xvi; id and, 43; increase of, 129, 308, 354; reality and, 6-7; repression and, 38, 127-133 (*see also* Repression, lifting of)

Ego functions, 5-7, 54, 66; binding function, 125. *See also* Ego, synthetic function of; Ego boundaries; Integrative function

Ego ideal, 29, 200, 259-260, 288-290; superego and, 288-290, 311

Ego instincts, 60, 231. *See also* Self-preservative instincts; Eros

Ego mastery, 77-78, 80

"Ego narcissism," 198

Ego passage, 296-304, 305, 306, 310; defined, 296

Ego span. *See* Integrative span

Ego stages, 69, 135-144, 322; defined, 138. *See also* Ego-cosmic stage

Ego states, 23, 66-67, 106-111, 135-144, 281, 283-284, 305-317, 366; superego as an, 34; time continuity in, 68-69

Ego strength and ego weakness, 74, 98-99, 100, 119-121, 125, 299, 301-303, 312-317, 322, 329

Ego weakness. *See* Ego strength and ego weakness

Ego-cosmic stage, 27, 69, 106, 107, 108, 134, 358

Egoistic or narcissistic surrender, 270 (note 2)

Egotization, 18, 26, 44, 63, 76, 105-112, *passim*, 146; defined, 44, 262-263. *See also* De-egotization; Identification

Élan vital, 162

Elation, 129, 308, 354. *See also* Hypomania

Electra complex, 214 (note)

Emotions, 219, 330

Empathy, 19-23, 27, 262-263, 266; death and, 279

End-goals. *See* Goals

Endocrine system, 44-45, 169-170, 176, 222, 357 (note 2), 402. *See also* Id, biological

Energy, 215, 247-249; "free" and "bound," 46; surplus, 161-162, 217-218, 249

Enuresis, 183

Envy of women, by men, 192

Erinyes, 274, 298

Erogenous zones, 177. *See also* Skin; Infantile sexuality; Mouth; Orality; Anal phase

Eros, 16, 229-234. *See also* Self-preservative drives.

Erotic energy. *See* Energy, surplus

Erotomania, 315

Erythrophobia, 342

Estrangement, feelings of. *See* Derealization

Ethics, 253-255, 265, 269-270, 290-291

External reality, 6

Externalization, 105, 195-196, 268, 295-303, 306, 311-312, 379, 435. *See also* Projection

Extrapolation, 129

Extrospection. *See* Perception

Fainting, 362

Family, 243-244. *See also* Parent and child; Mother-child relationship; Child development

Fantasy, 54-55

Fate neurosis, 226-227

Fathers and fatherhood, 32-33, 200, 253, 284-287. *See also* Oedipus complex

Fear, 220

Feces, 177-180, 183, 185-186

Female castration complex. *See* Castration complex, female; Penis envy

Fetishism, 364

Fetus, 173

Fixation, 40

Fluid matrix, 156

Focal conflict, 430

Forepleasure, 177

Free-floating cathexis, 46

Frigidity, 347-348

Frustration, 243, 246-247

"Functional readiness," 248

Ganser syndrome. *See* Prison psychoses

Genital phase, 182-194, 245-246

Giddiness. *See* Dizziness

Goals, 8, 111-112, 114, 189, 215-216, 218-219, 223, 232, 288, 391-392, 393, 418, 431; of psychotherapy, 323

God, 306

Grief, 78-80, 175; in dreams, 416, 441-442

Group psychology, xv, 285. *See also* Ethics

Guilt, 132, 242, 271, 281, 293, 294, 306, 380, 383. *See also* Superego; Psychic presence

Hallucinations, 6, 83-84, 99, 148, 312, 314, 360-361; as a defense mechanism, 363-364; in infancy, 75-77; positive and negative, 358

Headaches in dreams, 435-436

Homeostasis, 156, 160-161, 216, 220, 222

Homosexuality, 188-190, 314-317

Hope, 112, 114, 159, 420, 422, 426, 431

Hormones. *See* Endocrine system

Hunger, 216

Hypochondria, 357, 433

Hypomania, 308-310

Hysteria, 102, 330, 331-338, 341, 342, 357 (note 2); as denial, 360-361. *See also* Phobias; Conversion

"I" and "I-ness," 3, 39-40, 43, 44, 45, 67, 263, 287, 455

Id, 42-49, 50-58, 95, 145-250, 358-359, 401; biological, 151; ego feeling and, 43; interaction with ego,

50-58, 63, 67, 105-106, 325-327, 328 ff., 363; interaction with super-ego, 50-58; ruled by pleasure principle, 401. See also Ectoderm and endoderm; Dreams; Primary process

Identification, 18, 97, 105, 135-136, 195-196, 197, 282-292, 295, 380, 441-442, 443 (note 3); ego in, 299 ff., 441 ff.; imitation and, 26-27, 63; primary, 30, 380; substitutive, 31, 33, 295, 301; superego and, 30 ff. See also Identification, resonance; Identification with the aggressor; Egotization; Superego; Incorporation; Introjection, Introjects; Internalization

Identification, resonance, 27-28, 206, 261-270, 443 (note 3); defined, 261; pity and, 268-269; in schizophrenia, 301-303; superego and, 282-283

Identification with the aggressor, 97, 382-385

Identity, 26-27, 279

Imitation, 26-27, 63

Impotence, 347-348

Incorporation, 30, 174, 186, 200; of feared objects, 37 (see also Identification with the aggressor)

Individual psychology. See Adler, Alfred

Infantile neuroses, 324-325. See also Child development

Infantile sexuality, 172-181. See also Child development

"Inferiority complex." See Adler, Alfred

Inferiority, feelings of, 60, 199-201

Inner mentality, 6

Insomnia, 404

Instinct dichotomy. See Instincts, dualism of

Instinct to master, 247-248, 250 (note 11)

Instincts, 43-45, 145-250, passim,

225-234, 236-249, 379 ff.; defined, 227, 236; defined and distinguished from drives, 154-162, 236; dualism of, 63, 65, 225-234. See also Death instinct; Id; Drives; Ego Instincts

Integrative capacity, 112

Integrative field, 111-112, 125, 378

Integrative function, 8-10, 62, 96, 101, 111-112, 252-259, 280-281, 378; defined, 8

Integrative span, 111-112, 122-133, 252; mutilation of, 125, 378. See also Focal conflict; Trauma, psychic

Integration, biological and ego, distinguished, 9

Integration, ego. See Integrative function

Intercourse, sexual. See Coitus

Internal stimuli, 37. See also Id

Internalization, 97, 105, 195-196, 197, 200, 296, 298, 305; in psychoses, 313-317. See also Egotization; Identification; Introjection; Superego

Interpersonal relationships, 205-215. See also Love; Object love; Object relations; Parent and child

Introjection, 35 (note), 174, 195-196, 260 (note), 295; superego and, 34. See also Superego

Introjects, 35 (note), 257, 260 (note), 301-303, 308

Introspection, 5

Introversion, 54

Isolation (defense mechanism), 375-377

Isolation (physical), 134, 144 (note 1)

Jokes. See laughter

Knowledge, 85, 175

Language, 6, 26, 76; in schizophrenia, 115-120

Latency period, 209-210, 286. *See also* Superego

Laughter, 331

Learning, 237. *See also* Knowledge

Libido, 50, 99, 161, 162, 163-171, 205, 214, 224 (note 5), 236-249, 356; *For* Ego libido, *see* Ego strength and ego weakness

Loneliness, 24, 28, 134, 144 (note 1)

Love, 21, 24, 44, 205-214, 379; anaclitic, 21, 203, 205, 207, 213; drive objects and love objects distinguished, 213-214; narcissistic, 24, 203. *See also* Autoerotism; Narcissim; Mother-child relationship; Parent and child

Magic thinking, gestures, etc., 375. *See also* Ceremonials, compulsive

Manic-depressive psychoses, 137, 308-309. *See also* Melancholia; Depression; Elation

"Masculine protest," 60, 168, 185. *See also* Castration complex

Masculinity and femininity, 188 ff., 222

Masochism, 191, 245, 379

Mastery strength. *See* Ego strength and ego weakness

Masturbation, 173. *See also* Autoerotism

Maturity, 22-24

Medial concept, 17, 21, 101, 106, 114, 197-198, 240, 241, 243, 359, 379

Melancholia, 80, 283-284, 302-303, 307-308, 310-311; dreams in, 442-443

Memory and memories, 135-138, 365, 367-368. *See also* Repression

Menstruation, 47-48

Mental apparatus. *See* Metapsychology; Ego; Id; Superego; Cathexis

Mental development. *See* Child development

Mental substructures. *See* Ego; Id; Superego

Metapsychology, 13, 61, 215-226

Mitleid, Mitfreude, 264

Money, 180

Morality. *See* Ethics

Mortido. *See* Death instinct

Mother, inconsistency in the, 81

Mother-child relationship, 81, 142, 175-176, 185, 212-213, 279, 298, 348-349, 373-374, 441

Motility, 6, 75

Mourning, 31, 78-80, 441-442; ego passage in, 300-301

"Multiple function, principle of," 7 (note 1), 54. *See also* Ego functions

Murder, 275-276

Muscles, 100-101

Names, 26-27, 279

Narcissism, 63, 64-65, 142-143, 152, 167-168, 169, 196-203, 254; primary, 197, 240; secondary, 197, 296, 299

Narcissistic object love. *See* Object love, narcissistic

Narcissus (mythical character), 21, 196-197, 198

Neurasthenia, 357 (note 2)

Neuroses, 183-184, 307, 325 ff., 339-356, 356 (note 2); and psychoses, 363, 366. *See also* Obsessive compulsive reactions; Phobias; Psychoneuroses

Neutralization, 248

Nirvana principle, 157-158, 230, 236

Nuclear conflict, 430

Object, 110

Object choice, 23-24. *See also* Object love

Object loss, 78-80, 279-280, 305. *See also* Mourning

Object love, 21, 23-24, 203, 205, 213; anaclitic, 21, 203, 205, 207, 213; narcissistic, 24, 203. *See also* Love; Object loss

Object relations, 205-214; genesis, 195-196; in infantile sexuality, 172-181; in genital phase, 188-194; psychic presence and, 279; two kinds of, 203. *See also* Object love; Object loss; Love; Mother-child relationship

Obsessive compulsive reactions, 124, 371-378

"Oceanic feeling," 134

Oedipus (myth), 184

Oedipus complex, 32-33, 186-187, 206-209, 210, 285-286, 345, 383; superego and, 34

Omnipotence of thought, 75, 202

Oral phase, 174

"Organ inferiority," 200-201

Orgasm, 128-129, 131, 347, 348, 354-356

Orthriogenesis, 143, 144 (note 7)

Pain, 36, 72-82, 155, 268, 363; in dreams, 47-48, 403 ff., 432-443. *See also* Dreams, sleep-disturbing

"Pain defense," 363

Paranoia, 53-54, 86-87, 93-94, 127, 307-317; hypomania and, 309-311; phobia and, 312

Parent and child, 20-21, 22, 23, 31-35, 142, 205-214, 258-259, 284-289, 383. *See also* Mother-child relationship; Oedipus complex; Superego

Part-drives, 237

Peer groups, 287-288

Penis, loss of, 184-185, 201

Penis-ego state, 189

Penis envy, 185, 206

Penis in fetishism, 365

Perception, 5-7, 19, 61 (*system*), 83, 84, 85, 106-112, 359-362, 389-392. *See also* Person perception; Empathy; Ego boundaries

Persecution, delusions of. *See* Paranoia

Person perception, 262, 264. *See also* Empathy

Perversions, 146

Phallic mother, 365

Phallic phase, 186

Phobias, 52-53, 103, 312, 339-357, 356 (note 2); and obsessional neuroses, 371 ff.

Pity, 27, 262, 264, 266-270; exaggerated, 267-270

Play, 217, 248

Pleasure, 72-82, 155-156, 217, 226, 252

Preconscious, 4, 45, 61 (*system*), 97, 328. *See also* Dreams, secondary revision in; Secondary process

Preconscious cathexis, 97

Pregenital erotic manifestations, 177. *See also* Infantile sexuality

Pride, 183

Primal horde, 284-285

Primary process, 46-49, 52, 61, 407-408. *See also* Id; Unconscious; Dreams

Prison psychoses, 80

Projection, 20, 29, 105, 268, 295-303, 306, 383; defined, 20. *See also* Externalization

Projection against stimuli. *See* Defense against stimuli

Pseudocyesis, 351

Psychasthenia, 101

Psychic presence, 35, 253, 255, 271-281, 299; superego and, 273, 276-277, 282, 293-294, 298

Psychoneuroses, 356-357

Psychosomatic disorders, 267, 270 (note 4)

Psychoses, 51-52, 67, 128-132, 140-141, 202, 299, 329, 359; as a defense mechanism, 363; ego weakness and, 98-99, 119-121, 299-303, 312-317; neuroses and, 363, 366; precipitation of, by unskilled therapists, 321-322; therapy of, 53-54, 93-94. *See also* Melancholia; Manic-depressive psychoses; Schizophrenia; Paranoia

Psychotherapy, technique of, 53-54, 93-94, 306, 321-323. *See also* Dream interpretation

Puberty, 210

Punishment, 254, 256

"Purified pleasure ego," 107, 269

Rationalization, 51

Reaction formation, 32, 151, 257-258, 370-374

"Real" and "unreal," 5-6, 51-52, 75

Realistic or objective anxiety, 220

Reality, denial of. *See* Denial

Reality, sense of, 6, 76, 317; in dreams, 404; reality testing and, distinguished, 83-94

Reality feeling in dreams. *See* Dreams, sense of reality in

Reality in schizophrenia. *See* Schizophrenia, reality in

Reality principle, 72-82, 252-259, 269-270, 281

Reality testing, 6, 75, 83-94, 202, 307, 317, 363; dependent on perception, 84-85; distinguished from sense of reality, 83-94

"Realization," 359

Regression, 22, 115, 132, 202, 356; mourning and, 79-80; in schizophrenia, 99, 132; temporary, 246

Reitzschutz. *See* Defense against stimuli

Relative autonomy (of the ego), 324

Religion, 253-255, 265, 305

Repetition compulsion, 169, 225-233, 238, 331, 418

Repression, 36-41, 42-43, 52-53, 54, 127-128, 132, 138-141, 323-324, 358, 367-368; in agoraphobia, 345-347; compared with hysteria, 108; in counterphobic attitude, 353; denial and, 363-364; of ego stages, 138-141; of ego states, 105, 143, 322, 442; lifting of, 66-67, 127-133, 308, 322, 345-346, 354-355; in obsessional neuroses, 371; in phobias, 339-347; preconscious cathexis and, 97; primal, 40, 324; "proper," 324; unsuccessful, 328-338, 339-357, 357 (note 4)

Resistance, 96, 147-152, 241-242, 321-322

Resistance in dreams. *See* Censor, dream

Resistance to dream interpretation, 396

Resonance duplication, 261

Resonance identification. *See* Identification, resonance

Restitution, 99

Restriction of ego activities, 382

Reversal into its opposite, 379-381

Sadism, 191, 218, 264, 265, 269, 379. *See also* Anal-sadistic phase

Schizophrenia, 116-133, *passim;* abstraction in, 120-121; catatonic, 132, 242; ego in, 53, 93-94, 99, 119-121, 123, 125-126, 444-449; externalization and, 301-303; identification in, 301-303; obsessions and, 124; reality in, 99; speech in, 116-120; therapy of, 93-94. *See also* Psychoses, ego weakness and

Schreber case, 208, 214 (note 4), 313-315, 317 (note 4)

Screen memories, 367-368

Secondary process, 50, 61, 326. *See*

also Preconscious; Dreams, secondary revision in
Secondary revision. *See* Dreams, secondary revision in
Self, 17, 63-65, 198
Self-preservative drives (instincts), 5, 16, 170, 216, 230-234
Sense of reality. *See* Reality, sense of
Sexual ideas of children, 52-53, 183-184, 185, 191, 210-211
Sexuality, 213, 357 (note 2). *See also* Infantile sexuality; Anal erotism; Sexual ideas of children
Shame, 132, 370
Siblings and sibling rivalry, 31-32
Skin, 176-177, 195
Sleep, 360, 401-405, 406; death instinct and, 158, 240-241; ego boundaries in, 84; ego's need for, 98; wish to, 403. *See also* Dreams
Smiling response, 142
Somatopsychic conditions, 270 (note 4)
Somnambulism, 457-458
Span disturbances, 122-133, 378
Spastic ego paresis, 115, 132-133, 308
Speech. *See* Language
"Stability principle," 155-156, 230
Structural conflicts, 306-307
Sublimation, 165-166, 356. *See also* Neutralization
Substitution. *See also* Displacement
"Suffering-non-suffering principle," 160
Suicide, 79, 240, 243, 307, 308, 360
Superego, 28, 30-35, 242, 252-317, *passim;* defined, 30; castration complex and, 34; conscience and, 30; in dreams, 399, 414, 458; in ego feeling, 34; ego ideal distinguished from, 200, 259-260, 288-290; and ego state, 34, 281; externalization of, 306 ff.; identification with the aggressor and, 383-385; interaction with ego and id, 50-58; God and,
306; origins of, anthropological, 284-287; psychic presence and, 253, 273, 276-277, 282, 293-294, 298; psychotherapist's personality and patient's, 305. *See also* Censor (dream)
Superego development, 30-35, 196, 277, 284-287, 288, 289, 383-385
Survival factor. *See* Self-preservative drives
Symbolism, 47, 413, 444-449
Sympathy, 27, 262
"Systems of mental apparatus," 61. *See also* Ego; Id; Superego

Teeth in dreams, 440-441
Tension, 155-161, 219, 236
Thanatos. *See* Death instinct
Theaters, 140
Thought and thinking, 105-113, 114-121
Thumb-sucking, 173, 178, 195
Time, 47, 110
Toilet-training, 178, 183
Totemism, 285
Transference, 225, 227
Trauma, 37, 220, 237
Traumatic dreams. *See* Dreams, sleep-disturbing
Triebe, translation of, 154, 236, 249 (note 1)
Triumph, feeling of, 308
"Turning round upon the subject's own self," 379, 381

Unconscious, 3, 61 (*system*), 147-152, 174 (*system*), 326-327 (*system*), 328-338. *See also* Primary process; Dreams; Id
Undoing, 374-375
"Unreal," *See* "Real" and "unreal"
Urethral erotism, 181, 182-183. *See also* Pride

Values. *See* Ethics; Internalization; Superego
Vasomotor and vasosecretory phenomena, 175
Vertigo. *See* Dizziness
Vagina, 186. *See also* Menstruation

"We" feeling, 29, 67, 212, 287, 305
"Will to power," 60, 168

"Windowless wall." *See* Ego boundaries
Wish fulfillment, 400-401, 416-423, 423-429; traumatic dreams an exception to, 418
Wish to sleep, 403
Word associations in schizophrenia, 116 ff.